CHARLIE CHAPLIN was born in London in 1889 to parents who were both on the stage. Parts of his childhood were spent in extreme poverty, and for a period his mother lived with him and his elder brother, Sydney (later his manager), in the Lambeth workhouse. Eventually he obtained work as a comedian with Fred Karno's company and toured the United States, where he was asked to join the Keystone Comedy Film Company in Los Angeles. Chaplin made a string of "single-reelers" for Keystone in 1914 and was soon in a position to dictate his own terms, so immediate and overwhelming was the success of his "tramp." He made films for Essanay, Mutual, and First National between 1915 and 1923, when United Artists, the company formed principally by himself and the Fairbanks, started to claim all his time. His outstanding full-length successes were *The Kid*, *The Gold Rush*, *City Lights*, *Modern Times*, *The Great Dictator*, and *Limelight*, but his immense reputation was created by the "off-the-cuff" fooling of his first films. He was married to Oona, the daughter of Eugene O'Neill, and had three sons and five daughters, as well as two sons by a previous marriage. Charlie Chaplin, who lived his later years in Switzerland, completed *A Countess From Hong Kong* at Pinewood Studios in 1967 and returned to the United States for a visit in April 1972. He was awarded the K.B.E. (Knight Commander of the British Empire) in January 1975, and died on Christmas Day 1977.

# CHARLES CHAPLIN

# *My Autobiography*

A PLUME BOOK

PLUME
Published by the Penguin Group
Penguin Books USA Inc., 375 Hudson Street, New York, New York 10014, U.S.A.
Penguin Books Ltd, 27 Wrights Lane, London W8 5TZ, England
Penguin Books Australia Ltd, Ringwood, Victoria, Australia
Penguin Books Canada Ltd, 10 Alcorn Avenue, Toronto, Ontario, Canada M4V 3B2
Penguin Books (N.Z.) Ltd, 182–190 Wairau Road, Auckland 10, New Zealand

Penguin Books Ltd, Registered Offices: Harmondsworth, Middlesex, England

Published by Plume, an imprint of New American Library,
a division of Penguin Books USA Inc.
Published by arrangement with Random House UK.

First Plume Printing, December, 1992
10 9 8 7 6 5 4 3 2 1

 REGISTERED TRADEMARK—MARCA REGISTRADA

LIBRARY OF CONGRESS CATALOGING-IN-PUBLICATION DATA
Chaplin, Charlie, 1889–1977.
My autobiography / Charles Chaplin.
p.    cm.
ISBN 0-452-27078-2
1. Chaplin, Charlie, 1889–1977.   2. Motion picture actors and
actresses—United States—Biography.   3. Comedians—United States—
Biography.   I. Title.
PN2287.C5A32   1992
791.43′028′092—dc20
[B]                    92-43080
CIP

Printed in the United States of America

BOOKS ARE AVAILABLE AT QUANTITY DISCOUNTS WHEN USED TO PROMOTE PRODUCTS
OR SERVICES. FOR INFORMATION PLEASE WRITE TO PREMIUM MARKETING DIVISION,
PENGUIN BOOKS USA INC., 375 HUDSON STREET, NEW YORK, NEW YORK 10014.

# ACKNOWLEDGEMENTS

Grateful acknowledgements are due to Alfred A. Knopf, Inc. for permission to reprint an extract from *Government by Assassination* by Hugh Byas; to the authors and William Heinemann Ltd for the passage from *A Writer's Notebook* by W. Somerset Maugham and for lines from 'The Widow in the Bye Street' from *The Collected Poems of John Masefield*; to Liveright Publishing Corporation for 'White Buildings' from *The Collected Poems of Hart Crane*.

The publishers also thank copyright-holders for permission to reproduce the following photographs: the National Film Archive for nos. 4, 12, 13, 16, and 50; The Museum of Modern Art, New York, for no. 14 and the photograph (no. 19) by Edward Steichen; Culver Pictures, Inc. for nos. 15 and 37; the *Radio Times* Hulton Picture Library for nos. 20 and 40; the Associated Press Ltd for nos. 31 and 32; Keystone View Co. for no. 38; John Engstead for no. 53; Favez, Vevey, for no. 58; and Peter Moeschlin for no. 59.

**To Oona**

# prelude

BEFORE Westminster Bridge was open, Kennington Road was only a bridle path. After 1750, a new road was laid down from the Bridge forming a direct link to Brighton. As a consequence Kennington Road, where I spent most of my boyhood, boasted some fine houses of architectural merit, fronted with iron grill balconies from which occupants could once have seen George IV coaching on his way to Brighton.

By the middle of the nineteenth century most of the homes had deteriorated into rooming houses and apartments. Some, however, remained inviolate and were occupied by doctors, successful merchants and vaudeville stars. On Sunday morning, along the Kennington Road one could see a smart pony and trap outside a house, ready to take a vaudevillian for a ten-mile drive as far as Norwood or Merton, stopping on the way back at the various pubs, the White Horse, the Horns and the Tankard in the Kennington Road.

As a boy of twelve, I often stood outside the Tankard watching these illustrious gentlemen alight from their equestrian outfits to enter the lounge bar, where the élite of vaudeville met, as was their custom on a Sunday to take a final 'one' before going home to the midday meal. How glamorous they were, dressed in chequered suits and grey bowlers, flashing their diamond rings and tie-pins! At two o'clock on Sunday afternoon, the pub closed and its occupants filed outside and dallied awhile before bidding each other adieu; and I would gaze fascinated and amused, for some of them swaggered with a ridiculous air.

When the last had gone his way, it was as though the sun had gone under a cloud. And I would return to a row of old derelict houses that sat back off the Kennington Road, to 3 Pownall

Terrace, and mount the rickety stairs that led to our small garret. The house was depressing and the air was foul with stale slops and old clothes. This particular Sunday, Mother was seated gazing out of the window. She turned and smiled weakly. The room was stifling, a little over twelve feet square, and seemed smaller and the slanting ceiling seemed lower. The table against the wall was crowded with dirty plates and tea-cups; and in the corner, snug against the lower wall, was an old iron bed which Mother had painted white. Between the bed and the window was a small fire-grate, and at the foot of the bed an old armchair that unfolded and became a single bed upon which my brother Sydney slept. But now Sydney was away at sea.

The room was more depressing this Sunday because Mother had for some reason neglected to tidy it up. Usually she kept it clean, for she was bright, cheerful and still young, not yet thirty-seven, and could make that miserable garret glow with golden comfort. Especially on a wintry Sunday morning when she would give me my breakfast in bed and I would awaken to a tidy little room with a small fire glowing and see the steaming kettle on the hob and a haddock or a bloater by the fender being kept warm while she made toast. Mother's cheery presence, the cosiness of the room, the soft padded sound of boiling water pouring into our earthenware tea-pot while I read my weekly comic, were the pleasures of a serene Sunday morning.

But this Sunday she sat listlessly looking out of the window. For the past three days she had been sitting at that window, strangely quiet and preoccupied. I knew she was worried. Sydney was at sea and we had not heard from him in two months, and Mother's hired sewing machine with which she struggled to support us had been taken away for owing back instalments (a procedure that was not unusual). And my own contribution of five shillings weekly which I earned giving dancing lessons had suddenly ended.

I was hardly aware of a crisis because we lived in a continual crisis; and, being a boy, I dismissed our troubles with gracious forgetfulness. As usual I would run home to Mother after school and do errands, empty the slops and bring up a pail of fresh water, then hurry on to the McCarthys' and spend the evening there – anything to get away from our depressing garret.

The McCarthys were old friends of Mother's whom she had known in her vaudeville days. They lived in a comfortable flat in the better part of Kennington Road, and were relatively well off by our standards. The McCarthys had a son, Wally, with whom I would play until dusk, and invariably I was invited to stay for tea. By lingering this way I had many a meal there. Occasionally Mrs McCarthy would inquire after Mother, why she had not seen her of late. And I would make some sort of excuse, for since Mother had met with adversity she seldom saw any of her theatrical friends.

Of course there were times when I would stay home, and Mother would make tea and fry bread in beef dripping, which I relished, and for an hour she would read to me, for she was an excellent reader, and I would discover the delight of Mother's company and would realize I had a better time staying home than going to the McCarthys'.

And now as I entered the room, she turned and looked reproachfully at me. I was shocked at her appearance; she was thin and haggard and her eyes had the look of someone in torment. An ineffable sadness came over me, and I was torn between an urge to stay home and keep her company, and a desire to get away from the wretchedness of it all. She looked at me apathetically. 'Why don't you run along to the McCarthys'?' she said.

I was on the verge of tears. 'Because I want to stay with you.'

She turned and looked vacantly out of the window. 'You run along to the McCarthys' and get your dinner – there's nothing here for you.'

I felt a reproach in her tone, but I closed my mind to it. 'I'll go if you want me to,' I said weakly.

She smiled wanly and stroked my head. 'Yes, yes, you run along.' And although I pleaded with her to let me stay, she insisted on my going. So I went with a feeling of guilt, leaving her sitting in that miserable garret alone, little realizing that within the next few days a terrible fate awaited her.

# *one*

I was born on 16 April 1889, at eight o'clock at night, in East Lane, Walworth. Soon after, we moved to West Square, St George's Road, Lambeth. According to Mother my world was a happy one. Our circumstances were moderately comfortable; we lived in three tastefully furnished rooms. One of my early recollections was that each night before Mother went to the theatre Sydney and I were lovingly tucked up in a comfortable bed and left in the care of the housemaid. In my world of three and a half years, all things were possible; if Sydney, who was four years older than I, could perform legerdemain and swallow a coin and make it come out through the back of his head, I could do the same; so I swallowed a halfpenny and Mother was obliged to send for a doctor.

Every night, after she came home from the theatre, it was her custom to leave delicacies on the table for Sydney and me to find in the morning – a slice of Neapolitan cake or candies – with the understanding that we were not to make a noise in the morning, as she usually slept late.

Mother was a soubrette on the variety stage, a *mignonne* in her late twenties, with fair complexion, violet-blue eyes and long light-brown hair that she could sit upon. Sydney and I adored our mother. Though she was not an exceptional beauty, we thought her divine-looking. Those who knew her told me in later years that she was dainty and attractive and had compelling charm. She took pride in dressing us up for Sunday excursions, Sydney in an Eton suit with long trousers and me in a blue velvet one with blue gloves to match. Such occasions were orgies of smugness, as we ambled along the Kennington Road.

London was sedate in those days. The tempo was sedate; even the horse-drawn tram-cars along Westminster Bridge Road went at a sedate pace and turned sedately on a revolving table at the terminal near the bridge. In Mother's prosperous days we also lived in Westminster Bridge Road. Its atmosphere was gay and friendly with attractive shops, restaurants and music halls. The fruit-shop on the corner facing the Bridge was a galaxy of colour, with its neatly arranged pyramids of oranges, apples, pears and bananas outside, in contrast to the solemn grey Houses of Parliament directly across the river.

This was the London of my childhood, of my moods and awakenings: memories of Lambeth in the spring; of trivial incidents and things; of riding with Mother on top of a horse-bus trying to touch passing lilac-trees – of the many coloured bus tickets, orange, blue, pink and green, that bestrewed the pavement where the trams and buses stopped – of rubicund flower-girls at the corner of Westminster Bridge, making gay *boutonnières*, their adroit fingers manipulating tinsel and quivering fern – of the humid odour of freshly watered roses that affected me with a vágue sadness – of melancholy Sundays and pale-faced parents and their children escorting toy windmills and coloured balloons over Westminster Bridge; and the maternal penny steamers that softly lowered their funnels as they glided under it. From such trivia I believe my soul was born.

Then objects in our sitting-room that affected my senses: Mother's life-size painting of Nell Gwyn, which I disliked; the long-necked decanters on our sideboard, which depressed me, and the small round music-box with its enamelled surface depicting angels on clouds, which both pleased and baffled me. But my sixpenny toy chair bought from the gypsies I loved because it gave me an inordinate sense of possession.

Memories of epic moments: a visit to the Royal Aquarium,* viewing its side-shows with Mother, watching 'She', the live head of a lady smiling in flames, the sixpenny lucky dip, Mother lifting me up to a large sawdust barrel to pick a surprise packet which contained a candy whistle which would not blow and a

* A large hall which stood on the corner of Victoria Street opposite Westminster Abbey, where there were spectacular entertainments and side-shows.

toy ruby brooch. Then a visit to the Canterbury Music Hall, sitting in a red plush seat watching my father perform . . .

Now it is night and I am wrapped in a travelling rug on top of a four-in-hand coach, driving with Mother and her theatrical friends, cosseted in their gaiety and laughter as our trumpeter, with clarion braggadocio, heralds us along the Kennington Road to the rhythmic jingle of harness and the beat of horses' hoofs.

*

Then something happened! It could have been a month or a few days later – a sudden realization that all was not well with Mother and the outside world. She had been away all the morning with a lady friend and had returned home in a state of excitement. I was playing on the floor and became conscious of intense agitation going on above me, as though I were listening from the bottom of a well. There were passionate exclamations and tears from Mother, who kept mentioning the name Armstrong – Armstrong said this, Armstrong said that, Armstrong was a brute! Her excitement was strange and intense so that I began to cry, so much so that Mother was obliged to pick me up and console me. A few years later I learned the significance of that afternoon. Mother had returned from the law courts where she had been suing my father for non-support of her children, and the case had not gone too well for her. Armstrong was my father's lawyer.

I was hardly aware of a father, and do not remember him having lived with us. He too was a vaudevillian, a quiet, brooding man with dark eyes. Mother said he looked like Napoleon. He had a light baritone voice and was considered a very fine artist. Even in those days he earned the considerable sum of forty pounds a week. The trouble was that he drank too much, which Mother said was the cause of their separation.

It was difficult for vaudevillians not to drink in those days, for alcohol was sold in all theatres, and after a performer's act he was expected to go to the theatre bar and drink with the customers. Some theatres made more profit from the bar than from the box office, and a number of stars were paid large salaries not alone for their talent but because they spent most of their money at the theatre bar. Thus many an artist was ruined by drink – my father was one of them. He died of alcoholic excess at the age of thirty-seven.

Mother would tell stories about him with humour and sadness. He had a violent temper when drinking, and during one of his tantrums she ran off to Brighton with some friends, and in answer to his frantic telegram: 'What are you up to? Answer at once!' she wired back: 'Balls, parties and picnics, darling!'

Mother was the elder of two daughters. Her father, Charles Hill, an Irish cobbler, came from County Cork, Ireland. He had rosy apple cheeks, a shock of white hair and a beard like Carlyle in Whistler's portrait. He was doubled over with rheumatic gout due, he said, to sleeping in damp fields hiding from the police during the nationalist uprisings. He eventually settled in London, establishing himself in a boot-repairing business in East Lane, Walworth.

Grandma was half gypsy. This fact was the skeleton in our family cupboard. Nevertheless, Grandma bragged that her family always paid ground-rent. Her maiden name was Smith. I remember her as a bright little old lady who always greeted me effusively with baby talk. She died before I was six. She was separated from Grandpa, for what reason neither grandparent would tell. But according to Aunt Kate there was a domestic triangle in which Grandpa surprised Grandma with a lover.

To gauge the morals of our family by commonplace standards would be as erroneous as putting a thermometer in boiling water. With such genetic attributes, two pretty cobbler's daughters quickly left home and gravitated to the stage.

Aunt Kate, Mother's younger sister, was also a soubrette; but we knew little about her, for she wove in and out of our lives sporadically. She was pretty and temperamental and never got along very well with Mother. Her occasional visits usually ended abruptly with acrimony at something Mother had said or done.

At eighteen Mother had eloped with a middle-aged man to Africa. She often spoke of her life there; living in luxury amidst plantations, servants and saddle horses.

In her eighteenth year my brother Sydney was born. I was told he was the son of a lord and that when he reached the age of twenty-one he would inherit a fortune of two thousand pounds, which information both pleased and annoyed me.

16

Mother did not stay long in Africa, but returned to England and married my father. I had no knowledge of what ended the African episode, but in our extreme poverty I would reproach her for giving up such a wonderful life. She would laugh and say that she was too young to be cautious or wise.

What degree of feeling she had for my father I never knew, but whenever she spoke of him it was without bitterness, which makes me suspect she was too objective to have been deeply in love. Sometimes she would give a sympathetic account of him, and at other times talk of his drunkenness and violence. In later years, whenever angry with me she would ruefully say: 'You'll finish up in the gutter like your father.'

She had known Father before she went to Africa. They had been sweethearts, and had played together in the same Irish melodrama called *Shamus O'Brien*. At sixteen she played the leading role. While touring with this company, she met and ran off with the middle-aged lord to Africa. When she returned to England, Father took up the broken threads of their romance and they married. Three years later I was born.

What other facts besides drink were involved I do not know, but a year after my birth my parents separated. Mother did not seek alimony. Being a star in her own right, earning twenty-five pounds a week, she was well able to support herself and her children. Only when ill-fortune befell her did she seek relief; otherwise she would never have taken legal steps.

She had been having trouble with her voice. It was never strong, and the slightest cold brought on laryngitis which lasted for weeks; but she was obliged to keep working, so that her voice grew progressively worse. She could not rely on it. In the middle of singing it would crack or suddenly disappear into a whisper, and the audience would laugh and start booing. The worry of it impaired her health and made her a nervous wreck. As a consequence, her theatrical engagements fell off until they were practically nil.

It was owing to her vocal condition that at the age of five I made my first appearance on the stage. Mother usually brought me to the theatre at night in preference to leaving me alone in rented rooms. She was playing the Canteen at Aldershot at the time, a grubby, mean theatre catering mostly to soldiers. They

17

were a rowdy lot and wanted little excuse to deride and ridicule. To performers, Aldershot was a week of terror.

I remember standing in the wings when Mother's voice cracked and went into a whisper. The audience began to laugh and sing falsetto and to make catcalls. It was all vague and I did not quite understand what was going on. But the noise increased until Mother was obliged to walk off the stage. When she came into the wings she was very upset and argued with the stage manager who, having seen me perform before Mother's friends, said something about letting me go on in her place.

And in the turmoil I remember him leading me by the hand and, after a few explanatory words to the audience, leaving me on the stage alone. And before a glare of footlights and faces in smoke, I started to sing, accompanied by the orchestra, which fiddled about until it found my key. It was a well-known song called *Jack Jones* that went as follows:

> Jack Jones well and known to everybody
> Round about the market, don't yer see,
> I've no fault to find with Jack at all,
> Not when 'e's as 'e used to be.
> But since 'e's had the bullion left him
> 'E has altered for the worst,
> For to see the way he treats all his old pals
> Fills me with nothing but disgust.
> Each Sunday morning he reads the *Telegraph*,
> Once he was contented with the *Star*.
> Since Jack Jones has come into a little bit of cash,
> Well, 'e don't know where 'e are.

Half-way through, a shower of money poured on to the stage. Immediately I stopped and announced that I would pick up the money first and sing afterwards. This caused much laughter. The stage manager came on with a handkerchief and helped me to gather it up. I thought he was going to keep it. This thought was conveyed to the audience and increased their laughter, especially when he walked off with it with me anxiously following him. Not until he handed it to Mother did I return and continue to sing. I was quite at home. I talked to the audience, danced, and did several imitations including one of Mother singing her Irish march song that went as follows:

Riley, Riley, that's the boy to beguile ye,
Riley, Riley, that's the boy for me.
In all the Army great and small,
There's none so trim and neat
As the noble Sergeant Riley
Of the gallant Eighty-eight.

And in repeating the chorus, in all innocence I imitated Mother's voice cracking and was surprised at the impact it had on the audience. There was laughter and cheers, then more money-throwing; and when Mother came on the stage to carry me off, her presence evoked tremendous applause. That night was my first appearance on the stage and Mother's last.

When the fates deal in human destiny, they heed neither pity nor justice. Thus they dealt with Mother. She never regained her voice. As autumn turns to winter, so our circumstances turned from bad to worse. Although Mother was careful and had saved a little money, that very soon vanished, as did her jewellery and other small possessions which she pawned in order to live, hoping all the while that her voice would return.

Meanwhile from three comfortable rooms we moved into two, then into one, our belongings dwindling and the neighbourhoods into which we moved growing progressively drabber.

She turned to religion, in the hope, I suppose, that it would restore her voice. She regularly attended Christ Church in the Westminster Bridge Road, and every Sunday I was made to sit through Bach's organ music and to listen with aching impatience to the Reverend F. B. Meyer's fervent and dramatic voice echoing down the nave like shuffling feet. His orations must have been appealing, for occasionally I would catch Mother quietly wiping away a tear, which slightly embarrassed me.

Well do I remember Holy Communion on one hot summer's day, and the cool silver cup containing delicious grape-juice that passed along the congregation – and Mother's gentle restraining hand when I drank too much of it. And how relieved I was when the Reverend closed the Bible, for it meant that the sermon would soon end and they would start prayers and the final hymn.

Since Mother had joined the church she seldom saw her theatrical friends. That world had evaporated, had become only a memory. It seemed that we had always lived in wretched circumstances. The interim of one year seemed a lifetime of travail. Now we existed in cheerless twilight; jobs were hard to find and Mother, untutored in everything but the stage, was further handicapped. She was small, dainty and sensitive, fighting against terrific odds in a Victorian era in which wealth and poverty were extreme, and poorer-class women had little choice but to do menial work or to be the drudges of sweatshops, Occasionally she obtained work nursing, but such employment was rare and of short duration. Nevertheless, she was resourceful: having made her own theatrical costumes, she was expert with her needle and able to earn a few shillings dressmaking for members of the church. But it was barely enough to support the three of us. Because of Father's drinking, his theatrical engagements became irregular, as did his payments of ten shillings a week.

Mother had now sold most of her belongings. The last thing to go was her trunk of theatrical costumes. These things she clung to in the hope that she might recover her voice and return to the stage. Occasionally, she would delve into the trunk to find something, and we would see a spangled costume or a wig and would ask her to put them on. I remember her donning a judge's cap and gown and singing in her weak voice one of her old song successes that she had written herself. The song had a bouncy two-four tempo and went as follows:

I'm a lady judge,
And a good judge too.
Judging cases fairly –
They are so very rarely –
I mean to teach the lawyers
A thing or two,
And show them just exactly
What the girls can do . . .

With amazing ease she would then break into a graceful dance and forget her dressmaking and regale us with her other song successes and perform the dances that went with them until she was breathless and exhausted. Then she would reminisce and show us some of her old playbills. One read:

ENGAGEMENT EXTRAORDINARY
Of the dainty and talented
Lily Harley,
Serio-comedienne, impersonator and dancer.

She would perform before us, not with only her own vaude-ville material, but with imitations of other actresses she had seen in the so-called legitimate theatre.

When narrating a play, she would act the various parts: for instance, in *The Sign of the Cross*, Mercia with divine light in her eyes going into the arena to be fed to the lions. She would imitate the high pontifical voice of Wilson Barrett proclaiming in five-inch elevated shoes – for he was a little man: 'What this Christianity is I know not. But this I do know, that if it made such women as Mercia, Rome, nay, the whole world would be all the purer for it!' . . . which she acted with a suspicion of humour, but not without an appreciation of Barrett's talent.

Her instinct was unfailing in recognizing those that had genuine talent. Whether it was the actress Ellen Terry, or Joe Elvin of the music hall, she would explain their art. She knew technique instinctively and talked of theatre as only one who loved it could.

She would tell anecdotes and act them out, recounting, for instance, an episode in the life of the Emperor Napoleon: tiptoeing in his library to reach for a book and being intercepted by Marshal Ney (Mother playing both characters, but always with humour): 'Sire, allow me to get it for you. I am higher.' And Napoleon with an indignant scowl saying: 'Higher? Taller!'

She would enact Nell Gwyn, vividly describing her leaning over the palace stairs holding her baby, threatening Charles II: 'Give this child a name, or I'll dash it to the ground!' And King Charles hastily concurring: 'All right! The Duke of St Albans.'

I remember an evening in our one room in the basement at Oakley Street. I lay in bed recovering from a fever. Sydney had gone out to night school and Mother and I were alone. It was late afternoon, and she sat with her back to the window reading, acting and explaining in her inimitable way the New Testament and Christ's love and pity for the poor and for little children. Perhaps her emotion was due to my illness, but she gave the most luminous and appealing interpretation of Christ that I have ever heard or seen. She spoke of his tolerant understanding; of the woman who had sinned and was to be stoned by the mob, and of his words to them: 'He that is without sin among you, let him first cast a stone at her.'

She read into the dusk, stopping only to light the lamp, then told of the faith that Jesus inspired in the sick, that they had only to touch the hem of his garment to be healed.

She told of the hate and jealousy of the High Priests and Pharisees, and described Jesus and his arrest and his calm dignity before Pontius Pilate, who, washing his hands, said (this she acted out histrionically): 'I find no fault with this man.' She told how they stripped and scourged him and, placing a crown of thorns on his head, mocked and spat at him, saying: 'Hail, King of the Jews!'

As she continued tears welled up in her eyes. She told of Simon helping to carry Christ's cross and the appealing look of gratitude Jesus gave him; she told of the repentant thief, dying with him on a cross and asking forgiveness, and of Jesus saying: 'Today shalt thou be with me in Paradise.' And from the cross looking down at his mother, saying: 'Woman, behold thy son.' And in his last dying agony crying out: 'My God, why hast thou forsaken me?' And we both wept.

'Don't you see,' said Mother, 'how human he was; like all of us, he too suffered doubt.'

Mother had so carried me away that I wanted to die that very night and meet Jesus. But Mother was not so enthusiastic. 'Jesus wants you to live first and fulfil your destiny here,' she said. In that dark room in the basement at Oakley Street, Mother illuminated to me the kindliest light this world has ever known, which has endowed literature and the theatre with their greatest and richest themes: love, pity and humanity.

*

Living as we did in the lower strata, it was very easy to fall into the habit of not caring about our diction. But Mother always stood outside her environment and kept an alert ear on the way we talked, correcting our grammar and making us feel that we were distinguished.

As we sank further into poverty I would, in my childish ignorance, reproach her for not going back to the stage. She would smile and say that that life was false and artificial, and that in such a world one could so easily forget God. Yet whenever she talked of the theatre she would forget herself and again get carried away with enthusiasm. Some days, after reminiscing, she would fall into a long silence as she bent over her needlework, and I would grow moody because we were no longer a part of that glamorous life. And Mother would look up and see me forlorn and would cheerfully console me.

Winter was approaching and Sydney ran out of clothes; so Mother made him a coat from her old velvet jacket. It had red and black striped sleeves, pleated at the shoulders, which Mother did her best to get rid of, but with little success. Sydney wept when he was made to wear it: 'What will the boys at school think?'

'Who cares what people think?' she said. 'Besides, it looks very distinguished.' Mother had such a persuasive way that Sydney to this day has never understood why he ever submitted to wearing it. But he did, and the coat and a pair of Mother's cut-down high-heeled shoes got him into many a fight at school. The boys called him 'Joseph and his coat of many colours'. And I, with a pair of Mother's red tights cut down for stockings (which looked as though they were pleated), was called 'Sir Francis Drake'.

At the depth of this dolorous period, Mother began to develop migraine headaches and was forced to give up her needlework, and for days was obliged to lie in a dark room with tea-leaf bandages over her eyes. Picasso had a blue period. We had a grey one, in which we lived on parochial charity, soup tickets and relief parcels. Nevertheless, Sydney sold newspapers between school hours, and though his contribution was less than a drop in the bucket, it did give a modicum of aid. But in every crisis there is always a climax – in our case this crisis was a happy one.

One day while Mother was recovering, with a bandage still over her eyes, Sydney came bursting into the darkened room, throwing his newspapers on the bed and exclaiming: 'I've found a purse!' He handed it to Mother. When she opened it she saw

23

a pile of silver and copper coins. Quickly she closed it, then fell back on the bed from excitement.

Sydney had been mounting buses to sell his newspapers. On top of one bus he saw a purse on an empty seat. Quickly he dropped a newspaper over it as if by accident, then picked it up and the purse with it, and hurried off the bus. Behind a bill-board, on an empty lot, he opened the purse and saw a pile of silver and copper coins. He told us that his heart leapt, and without counting the money he closed the purse and ran home.

When Mother recovered, she emptied its contents on the bed. But the purse was still heavy. There was a middle pocket! Mother opened it and saw seven golden sovereigns. Our joy was hysterical. The purse contained no address, thank God, so Mother's religious scruples were little exercised. Although a pale cast of thought was given to the owner's misfortune, it was, however, quickly dispelled by Mother's belief that God had sent it as a blessing from Heaven.

Whether Mother's illness was physical or psychological I do not know. But she recovered within a week. As soon as she was well, we went to Southend-on-Sea for a holiday, Mother outfitting us completely with new clothes.

My first sight of the sea was hypnotic. As I approached it in bright sunlight from a hilly street, it looked suspended, a live quivering monster about to fall on me. The three of us took off our shoes and paddled. The tepid sea unfurling over my insteps and around my ankles and the soft yielding sand under my feet were a revelation of delight.

What a day that was – the saffron beach, with its pink and blue pails and wooden spades, its coloured tents and umbrellas, and sailing boats hurtling gaily over laughing little waves, and up on the beach other boats resting idly on their sides, smelling of seaweed and tar – the memory of it still lingers with enchantment.

In 1957 I went back to Southend and looked in vain for the narrow, hilly street from which I had seen the sea for the first time, but there were no traces of it. At the end of the town were the remnants of what seemed a familiar fishing village with old-fashioned shop-fronts. This had vague whisperings of the past – perhaps it was the odour of seaweed and tar.

Like sand in an hour-glass our finances ran out, and hard times again pursued us. Mother sought other employment, but there was little to be found. Problems began mounting. Instalment payments were behind; consequently Mother's sewing machine was taken away. And Father's payments of ten shillings a week had completely stopped.

In desperation she sought a new solicitor, who, seeing little remuneration in the case, advised her to throw herself and her children on the support of the Lambeth Borough authorities in order to make Father pay for our support.

There was no alternative: she was burdened with two children, and in poor health; and so she decided that the three of us should enter the Lambeth workhouse.

# *two*

ALTHOUGH we were aware of the shame of going to the work-house, when Mother told us about it both Sydney and I thought it adventurous and a change from living in one stuffy room. But on that doleful day I didn't realize what was happening until we actually entered the workhouse gate. Then the forlorn be-wilderment of it struck me; for there we were made to separate, Mother going in one direction to the women's ward and we in another to the children's.

How well I remember the poignant sadness of that first visiting day: the shock of seeing Mother enter the visiting-room garbed in workhouse clothes. How forlorn and embarrassed she looked! In one week she had aged and grown thin, but her face lit up when she saw us. Sydney and I began to weep which made Mother weep, and large tears began to run down her cheeks. Eventually she regained her composure and we sat to-gether on a rough bench, our hands in her lap while she gently patted them. She smiled at our cropped heads and stroked them consolingly, telling us that we would soon all be together again. From her apron she produced a bag of coconut candy which she had bought at the workhouse store with her earnings from crocheting lace cuffs for one of the nurses. After we parted, Sydney kept dolefully repeating how she had aged.

*

Sydney and I quickly adapted ourselves to workhouse life, but in an overcast sadness. I remember little of incident, but the midday meal at a long table with other children was a warm and expectant affair. It was presided over by an inmate of the work-house, an old gentleman of about seventy-five, with a dignified countenance, a thin beard and sad eyes. He elected me to sit next to him because I was the youngest and, until they cropped my head, had the curliest hair. He called me his 'tiger' and said that when I grew bigger I would wear a top hat with a cockade and would sit at the back of his carriage with my arms folded. This honour made me very fond of him. But a day or so later a younger boy appeared on the scene with curlier hair than I had and took my place beside the old gentleman, because, as he whimsically explained, a younger and curlier-headed boy always took precedence.

After three weeks we were transferred from Lambeth Workhouse to the Hanwell Schools for Orphans and Destitute Children about twelve miles out of London. It was an adventurous drive in a horse-drawn bakery van, and rather a happy one under the circumstances, for the country surrounding Hanwell was beautiful in those days, with lanes of horse-chestnut trees, ripening wheat-fields and heavy-laden orchards, and ever since the rich, aromatic smell after rain in the country has always reminded me of Hanwell.

On arriving we were delivered to the approbation ward and put under medical and mental observation before entering the school proper; the reason was that amongst three to four hundred boys a subnormal child or a sick one would be unhealthy for the school as well as being in an unhappy situation himself.

The first few days I was lost and miserable, for at the workhouse I always felt that Mother was near, which was comforting, but at Hanwell we seemed miles apart. Sydney and I graduated from the approbation ward to the school proper, where we were separated, Sydney going with the big boys and I with the infants. We slept in different ward blocks, so we seldom saw each other. I was a little over six years old and alone, which made me feel quite abject; especially on a summer's evening at bed-time during prayers, when, kneeling with twenty other little boys in the centre of the ward in our night-shirts, I would look out of the oblong windows at the deepening sunset and the undulating hills, and feel alien to it all as we sang in throaty off-key voices:

> Abide with me; fast falls the eventide;
> The darkness deepens: Lord, with me abide;

27

When other helpers fail, and comforts flee,
Help of the helpless, O, abide with me.

It was then that I felt utterly dejected. Although I did not understand the hymn, the tune and the twilight increased my sadness.

But, to our happy surprise, within two months Mother had arranged for our discharge, and we were dispatched again to London and the Lambeth workhouse. Mother was at the gate dressed in her own clothes, waiting for us. She had applied for a discharge only because she wanted to spend the day with her children, intending, after a few hours outside together, to return the same day; Mother being an inmate of the workhouse, this ruse was her only means to be with us.

Before we entered our private clothes had been taken from us and steamed; now they were returned unpressed. Mother, Sydney and I looked a crumpled sight as we ambled out through the workhouse gates. It was early morning and we had nowhere to go, so we walked to Kennington Park, which was about a mile away. Sydney had ninepence tied up in a handkerchief, so we bought half a pound of black cherries and spent the morning in Kennington Park, sitting on a bench eating them. Sydney crumpled a sheet of newspaper and wrapped some string around it and for a while the three of us played catch-ball. At noon we went to a coffee-shop and spent the rest of our money on a twopenny tea-cake, a penny bloater and two halfpenny cups of tea, which we shared between us. Afterwards we returned to the park where Sydney and I played again while Mother sat crocheting.

In the afternoon we made our way back to the workhouse. As Mother said with levity: 'We'll be just in time for tea.' The authorities were most indignant, because it meant going through the same procedure of having our clothes steamed and Sydney and I spending more time at the workhouse before returning to Hanwell, which of course gave us an opportunity of seeing Mother again.

But this time we stayed at Hanwell for almost a year – a most formative year, in which I started schooling and was taught to write my name 'Chaplin'. The word fascinated me and looked like me, I thought.

28

Hanwell School was divided in two, a department for boys and one for girls. On Saturday afternoon the bath-house was reserved for infants, who were bathed by the older girls. This, of course, was before I was seven, and a squeamish modesty attended these occasions; having to submit to the ignominy of a young girl of fourteen manipulating a facecloth all over my person was my first conscious embarrassment.

At the age of seven I was transferred from the infants' to the older boys' department, where ages ranged from seven to fourteen. Now I was eligible to participate in all the grown-up functions, the drills and exercises and the regular walks we took outside the school twice a week.

Although at Hanwell we were well looked after, it was a forlorn existence. Sadness was in the air; it was in those country lanes through which we walked, a hundred of us two abreast. How I disliked those walks, and the villages through which we passed, the locals staring at us! We were known as inmates of the 'booby hatch', a slang term for workhouse.

The boys' playground was approximately an acre, paved with slab-stones. Surrounding it were one-storey brick buildings, used for offices, store-rooms, a doctor's dispensary, a dentist's office and a wardrobe for boys' clothing. In the darkest corner of the yard was an empty room, and recently confined there was a boy of fourteen, a desperate character according to the other boys. He had attempted to escape from the school by climbing out of a second-storey window and up on to the roof, defying the officials by throwing missiles and horse-chestnuts at them as they climbed after him. This happened after we infants were asleep: we were given an awed account of it by the older boys the next morning.

For major offences of this nature, punishment took place every Friday in the large gymnasium, a gloomy hall about sixty feet by forty with a high roof, and, on the side, climbing ropes running up to girders. On Friday morning two to three hundred boys, ranging in age from seven to fourteen years, marched in and lined up in military fashion, forming three sides of a square. The far end was the fourth side, where, behind a long school desk the length of an Army mess-table, stood the miscreants waiting for trial and punishment. On the right and in front of the desk was an easel with wrist-straps dangling, and from the frame a birch hung ominously.

For minor offences, a boy was laid across the long desk, face downwards, feet strapped and held by a sergeant, then another sergeant pulled the boy's shirt out of his trousers and over his head, then pulled his trousers tight.

Captain Hindrum, a retired Navy man weighing about two hundred pounds, with one hand behind him, the other holding a cane as thick as a man's thumb and about four feet long, stood poised, measuring it across the boy's buttocks. Then slowly and dramatically he would lift it high and with a swish bring it down across the boy's bottom. The spectacle was terrifying, and invariably a boy would fall out of rank in a faint.

The minimum number of strokes was three and the maximum six. If a culprit received more than three, his cries were appalling. Sometimes he was ominously silent, or had fainted. The strokes were paralysing, so that the victim had to be carried to one side and laid on a gymnasium mattress, where he was left to writhe and wriggle for at least ten minutes before the pain subsided, leaving three pink welts as wide as a washerwoman's finger across his bottom.

The birch was different. After three strokes, the boy was supported by two sergeants and taken to the surgery for treatment.

Boys would advise you not to deny a charge, even if innocent, because, if proved guilty, you would get the maximum. Usually, boys were not articulate enough to declare their innocence.

I was now seven and in the big boys' section. I remember witnessing my first flogging, standing in silence, my heart thumping as the officials entered. Behind the desk was the desperado who had tried to escape from the school. We could hardly see more than his head and shoulders over the desk, he looked so small. He had a thin, angular face and large eyes.

The headmaster solemnly read the charges and demanded: 'Guilty or not guilty?'

Our desperado would not answer, but stared defiantly in front of him; he was thereupon led to the easel, and being small, he was made to stand on a soap-box so that his wrists could be strapped. He received three strokes with the birch and was led away to the surgery for treatment.

On Thursdays, a bugle sounded in the playground and we would all stop playing, taking a frozen position like statues, while Captain Hindrum, through a megaphone, announced the names of those who were to report for punishment on Friday.

One Thursday, to my astonishment I heard my name called. I could not imagine what I had done. Yet for some unaccountable reason I was thrilled – perhaps because I was the centre of a drama. On the day of the trial, I stepped forward. Said the headmaster: 'You are charged with setting fire to the dykes' (the lavatory).

This was not true. Some boys had lit a few bits of paper on the stone floor and while they were burning I came in to use the lavatory, but I had played no part in that fire.

'Are you guilty or not guilty?' he asked.

Nervous and impelled by a force beyond my control, I blurted out: 'Guilty.' I felt neither resentment nor injustice but a sense of frightening adventure as they led me to the desk and administered three strokes across my bottom. The pain was so excruciating that it took away my breath; but I did not cry out, and, although paralysed with pain and carried to the mattress to recover, I felt valiantly triumphant.

As Sydney was working in the kitchen, he had not known about it until punishment day, when he was marched into the gymnasium with the others and to his shocked amazement saw my head peering over the desk. He told me afterwards that when he saw me receiving three strokes he wept with rage.

A younger brother referred to his older brother as 'my young 'un', which made him feel proud and gave him a little security. So occasionally I saw 'my young 'un', Sydney, as I was leaving the dining-room. As he worked in the kitchen, he would surreptitiously hand me a sliced bread roll with a thick lump of butter pressed between, and I would smuggle it under my jersey and share it with another boy – not that we were hungry, but the generous lump of butter was an exceptional luxury. But these delicacies were not to continue, for Sydney left Hanwell to join the *Exmouth* training ship.

At the age of eleven a workhouse boy had the choice of joining the Army or the Navy. If the Navy, he was sent to the

*Exmouth*. Of course, it was not obligatory, but Sydney wanted to make a career of the sea. So that left me alone at Hanwell.

*

Hair is vitally personal to children. They weep vigorously when it is cut for the first time; no matter how it grows, bushy, straight or curly, they feel they are being shorn of a part of their personality.

There had been an epidemic of ringworm at Hanwell and, as it is most contagious, those infected were dispatched to the isolation ward on the first floor overlooking the playground. Often we would look up at the windows and see those wretched boys looking wistfully down at us, their heads shaved all over and stained brown with iodine. They were a hideous sight and we would look up at them with loathing.

Thus when a nurse stopped abruptly behind me in the diningroom and parted the top of my hair and announced: 'Ringworm!' I was thrown into paroxysms of weeping.

The treatment took weeks and seemed like an eternity. My head was shaved and iodined and I wore a handkerchief tied around it like a cotton-picker. But one thing I would not do was to look out of the window at the boys below, for I knew in what contempt they held us.

During my incarceration Mother visited me. She had in some way managed to leave the workhouse and was making an effort to establish a home for us. Her presence was like a bouquet of flowers; she looked so fresh and lovely that I felt ashamed of my unkempt appearance and my shaved iodined head.

'You must excuse his dirty face,' said the nurse.

Mother laughed, and how well I remember her endearing words as she hugged and kissed me: 'With all thy dirt I love thee still.'

Soon afterwards, Sydney left the *Exmouth* and I left Hanwell and we joined Mother again. She took a room at the back of Kennington Park and for a while she was able to support us. But it was not long before we were back in the workhouse again. The circumstances that led up to our return were something to do with Mother's difficulty in finding employment and Father's slump in his theatrical engagements. In that brief interlude we kept moving from one back-room to another; it was like a game of draughts – the last move was back to the workhouse.

Living in a different parish, we were sent to a different work-house, and from there to Norwood Schools, which was more sombre than Hanwell; leaves darker and trees taller. Perhaps the countryside had more grandeur, but the atmosphere was joyless.

One day, while Sydney was playing football, two nurses called him out of the game and told him that Mother had gone insane and had been sent to Cane Hill lunatic asylum. When Sydney heard the news he showed no reaction but went back and continued playing football. But after the game he stole away by himself and wept.

When he told me I could not believe it. I did not cry, but a baffling despair overcame me. Why had she done this? Mother, so light-hearted and gay, how could she go insane? Vaguely I felt that she had deliberately escaped from her mind and had deserted us. In my despair I had visions of her looking pathetic-ally at me, drifting away into a void.

We heard the news officially a week later; we also heard that the court decreed that Father must take over the custody of Sydney and me. The prospect of living with Father was exciting. I had seen him only twice in my life, on the stage, and once when passing a house in the Kennington Road, as he was coming down the front garden path with a lady. I had paused and watched him, knowing instinctively that he was my father. He beckoned me to him and asked my name. Sensing the drama of the situation, I had feigned innocence and said: 'Charlie Chaplin'. Then he glanced knowingly at the lady, felt in his pocket and gave me half a crown, and without further ado I ran straight home and told Mother that I had met my father.

And now we were going to live with him. Whatever happened, Kennington Road was familiar and not strange and sombre like Norwood.

The officials drove us in the bread van to 287 Kennington Road, the house where I had seen my father walking down the garden path. The door was opened by the lady who had been with him at the time. She was dissipated and morose-looking, yet attractive, tall and shapely, with full lips and sad, doe-like eyes; her age could have been thirty. Her name was Louise. It appeared that Mr Chaplin was not at home, but after the usual formalities and the signing of papers the official left us in charge of Louise, who led us upstairs to the first landing into the front sitting-room. A small boy was playing on the floor as we entered, a most beautiful child of four with large dark eyes and rich brown curly hair: it was Louise's son – my half-brother.

The family lived in two rooms and, although the front room had large windows, the light filtered in as if from under water. Everything looked as sad as Louise; the wallpaper looked sad, the horse-hair furniture looked sad, and the stuffed pike in a glass case that had swallowed another pike as large as itself – the head sticking out of its mouth – looked gruesomely sad.

In the back room she had put an extra bed for Sydney and me to sleep on, but it was too small. Sydney suggested sleeping on the sofa in the sitting-room. 'You'll sleep where you're told to,' said Louise. This caused an embarrassing silence as we walked back into the living-room.

Our reception was not an enthusiastic one, and no wonder. Sydney and I had been suddenly thrust upon her, and moreover we were the offspring of Father's estranged wife.

We both sat mutely watching her preparing the table for something to eat. 'Here,' she said to Sydney, 'you can make yourself useful and fill the coal-scuttle. And you,' she said, turning to me, 'go to the cook-shop next to the White Hart and get a shilling's worth of corned beef.'

I was only too pleased to leave her presence and the whole atmosphere, for a lurking fear was growing within me and I began to wish we were back at Norwood.

Father arrived home later and greeted us kindly. He fascinated me. At meals I watched every move he made, the way he ate and the way he held his knife as though it were a pen when cutting his meat. And for years I copied him.

When Louise told of Sydney's complaining about the small bed, Father suggested that Sydney should sleep on the sitting-room sofa. This victory of Sydney's aroused Louise's antagonism and she never forgave him. She continually complained to Father about him. Although Louise was morose and disagreeable, she never once struck me or even threatened to, but the fact that she disliked Sydney held me in fear and dread of her. She

34

drank a great deal, and this exaggerated my fear. There was something frighteningly irresponsible about her when she was drunk; she would smile with amusement at her little boy with his beautiful angelic face, who would swear at her and use vile language. For some reason, I never had contact with the child. Although he was my half-brother, I don't remember ever having exchanged a word with him – of course I was almost four years older than he. Sometimes when drinking Louise would sit and brood and I would be in a state of dread. But Sydney paid little attention to her; he seldom came home until late at night. I was made to come home directly after school and run errands and do odd jobs.

Louise sent us to the Kennington Road School, which was a bleak divertissement, for the presence of other children made me feel less isolated. Saturday was a half-holiday, but I never looked forward to it because it meant going home and scrubbing floors and cleaning knives, and on that day Louise invariably started drinking. While I was cleaning the knives, she would sit with a lady friend, drinking and growing bitterly morose, complaining quite audibly to her friend of having to look after Sydney and me and of the injustice imposed upon her. I remember her saying: 'This one's all right' (indicating me), 'but the other's a little swine and should be sent to a reformatory – what's more, he's not even Charlie's son.' This reviling of Sydney frightened and depressed me and I would go unhappily to bed and lie fretfully awake. I was not yet eight years old, but those days were the longest and saddest of my life.

Sometimes on a Saturday night, feeling deeply despondent, I would hear the lively music of a concertina passing by the back bedroom window, playing a highland march, accompanied by rowdy youths and giggling coster girls. The vigour and vitality of it seemed ruthlessly indifferent to my unhappiness, yet as the music grew fainter into the distance, I would regret it leaving. Sometimes a street-crier would pass: one in particular came by every night who seemed to be shouting 'Rule Britannia', terminating it with a grunt, but he was actually selling oysters. From the pub, three doors away, I could hear the customers at closing time, singing drunks, bawling out a maudlin, dreary song that was popular in those days:

35

For old times' sake don't let our enmity live,
For old times' sake say you'll forget and forgive.
Life's too short to quarrel,
Hearts are too precious to break.
Shake hands and let us be friends
For old times' sake.

I never appreciated the sentiment, but it seemed an appropriate accompaniment to my unhappy circumstances, and lulled me to sleep.

When Sydney came in late, which seemed always, he raided the larder before going to bed. This infuriated Louise, and one night when she had been drinking she came into the room and ripped the bedclothes off him and told him to get out. But Sydney was prepared for her. Quickly he reached under his pillow and whipped out a stiletto, a long button-hook which he had sharpened to a point.

'Come near me,' he said, 'and I'll stick this in you!'

She reared back, startled. 'Why, the bloody young sod! – he's going to murder me!'

'Yes,' said Sydney, dramatically, 'I'll murder you!'

'You wait till Mr Chaplin comes home!'

But Mr Chaplin seldom came home. However, I remember one Saturday night when Louise and Father had been drinking, and for some reason we were all sitting with the landlady and her husband in their front-room parlour on the ground floor. Under the incandescent light Father looked ghastly pale, and in an ugly mood was mumbling to himself. Suddenly he reached into his pocket, pulled out a handful of money and threw it violently to the floor, scattering gold and silver coins in all directions. The effect was surrealistic. No one moved. The landlady sat glum, but I caught her roving eye following a golden sovereign rolling to a far corner under a chair; my eye also followed it. Still no one moved, so I thought I had better start picking it up; the landlady and the others followed suit, picking up the rest of the money, careful to make their actions overt before Father's menacing eyes.

One Saturday, after school, I came home to find no one there. Sydney, as usual, was away all day playing football and the landlady said Louise and her son had been out since early morning. At first I was relieved, for it meant that I did not have to scrub floors and clean knives. I waited until long after lunchtime, then began to get anxious. Perhaps they had deserted me. As the afternoon wore on, I began to miss them. What had happened? The room looked grim and unyielding and its emptiness frightened me. I also began to get hungry, so I looked in the larder, but no food was there. I could stand the gaping emptiness no longer, so in desolation I went out, spending the afternoon visiting nearby market places. I wandered through Lambeth Walk and the Cat, looking hungrily into cook-shop windows at the tantalizing steaming roast joints of beef and pork, and the golden-brown potatoes soaked in gravy. For hours I watched the quacks selling their wares. The distraction soothed me and for a while I forgot my plight and hunger.

When I returned, it was night; I knocked at the door, but no one answered. Everyone was out. Wearily I walked to the corner of Kennington Cross and sat on the kerb near the house to keep an eye on it in case someone returned. I was tired and miserable, and wondered where Sydney was. It was approaching midnight and Kennington Cross was deserted but for one or two stragglers. All the lights of the shops began going out except those of the chemist and the public houses, then I felt wretched.

Suddenly there was music. Rapturous! It came from the vestibule of the White Hart corner pub, and resounded brilliantly in the empty square. The tune was *The Honeysuckle and the Bee*, played with radiant virtuosity on a harmonium and clarinet. I had never been conscious of melody before, but this one was beautiful and lyrical, so blithe and gay, so warm and reassuring. I forgot my despair and crossed the road to where the musicians were. The harmonium-player was blind, with scarred sockets where the eyes had been; and a besotted, embittered face played the clarinet.

It was all over too soon and their exit left the night even sadder. Weak and tired, I crossed the road towards the house, not caring whether anyone came home or not. All I wanted was to get to bed. Then dimly I saw someone going up the garden path towards the house. It was Louise – and her little son running ahead of her. I was shocked to see that she was limping

37

exaggeratedly and leaning extremely to one side. At first I thought she had been in an accident and had hurt her leg, then I realized she was very drunk. I had never seen a lopsided drunk before. In her condition I thought it best to keep out of her way, so I waited until she had let herself in. A few moments later the landlady came home and I went in with her. As I crept up the darkened stairs, hoping to get to bed unnoticed, Louise staggered out on to the landing.

'Where the hell do you think you're going?' she said. 'This is not your home.'

I stood motionless.

'You're not sleeping here tonight. I've had enough of all of you; get out! You and your brother! Let your father take care of you.'

Without hesitation, I turned and went downstairs and out of the house. I was no longer tired; I had got my second wind. I had heard that Father patronized the Queen's Head pub in the Prince's Road, about half a mile away, so I made my way in that direction, hoping to find him there. But soon I saw his shadowy figure coming towards me, outlined against the street-lamp.

'She won't let me in,' I whimpered, 'and I think she's been drinking.'

As we walked towards the house he also staggered. 'I'm not sober myself,' he said.

I tried to reassure him that he was.

'No, I'm drunk,' he muttered, remorsefully.

He opened the door of the sitting-room and stood there silent and menacing, looking at Louise. She was standing by the fireplace, holding on to the mantelpiece, swaying.

'Why didn't you let him in?' he said.

She looked at him bewildered, then mumbled: 'You too can go to hell – all of you!'

Suddenly he picked up a heavy clothes-brush from the sideboard and like a flash threw it violently, the back of it hitting her flat on the side of her face. Her eyes closed, then she collapsed unconscious with a thud to the floor as though she welcomed oblivion.

I was shocked at Father's action; such violence made me lose respect for him. As to what happened afterwards, my memory is vague. I believe Sydney came in later and Father saw us both to bed, then left the house.

I learned that Father and Louise had quarrelled that morning because he had left her to spend the day with his brother, Spencer Chaplin, who owned several public houses round and about Lambeth. Being sensitive of her position, Louise disliked visiting the Spencer Chaplins, so Father went alone, and as a revenge Louise spent the day elsewhere.

She loved Father. Even though very young I could see it in her glance the night she stood by the fireplace, bewildered and hurt by his neglect. And I am sure he loved her. I saw many occasions of it. There were times when he was charming and tender and would kiss her good-night before leaving for the theatre. And on a Sunday morning, when he had not been drinking, he would breakfast with us and tell Louise about the vaudeville acts that were working with him, and have us all enthralled. I would watch him like a hawk, absorbing every action. In a playful mood, he once wrapped a towel round his head and chased his little son around the table, saying: 'I'm King Turkey Rhubarb.'

About eight o'clock in the evening, before departing for the theatre, he would swallow six raw eggs in port wine, rarely eating solid food. That was all that sustained him day after day. He seldom came home, and, if he did, it was to sleep off his drinking.

One day Louise received a visit from the Society for the Prevention of Cruelty to Children, and she was most indignant about it. They came because the police had reported finding Sydney and me asleep at three o'clock in the morning by a watchman's fire. It was a night that Louise had shut us both out, and the police had made her open the door and let us in.

A few days later, however, while Father was playing in the provinces, Louise received a letter announcing that Mother had left the asylum. A day or two later the landlady came up and announced that there was a lady at the front door to call for Sydney and Charlie. 'There's your mother,' said Louise. There was a momentary confusion. Then Sydney leaped downstairs into her arms, I following. It was the same sweet, smiling Mother who affectionately embraced us.

Louise and Mother were too embarrassed to meet, so Mother waited at the front door while Sydney and I collected our things. There was no umbrage or ill-feeling on either side – in fact, Louise's manner was most agreeable, even to Sydney when she bade him good-bye.

*

Mother had taken a room in one of the back streets behind Kennington Cross near Hayward's pickle factory, and the acid smell would start up every afternoon. But the room was cheap and we were all together again. Mother's health was excellent, and the thought that she had been ill never entered our heads.

How we lived through this period I have not the remotest idea. Nonetheless, I remember no undue hardships or insoluble problems. Father's payments of ten shillings a week were almost regular, and, of course, Mother took up her needlework again and renewed her contact with the church.

An incident stands out at that period. At the end of our street was a slaughter-house, and sheep would pass our house on their way to be butchered. I remember one escaped and ran down the street to the amusement of onlookers. Some tried to grab it and others tripped over themselves. I had giggled with delight at its lambent capering and panic, it seemed so comic. But when it was caught and carried back into the slaughter-house, the reality of the tragedy came over me and I ran indoors, screaming and weeping to Mother: 'They're going to kill it! They're going to kill it!' That stark, spring afternoon and that comedy chase stayed with me for days; and I wonder if that episode did not establish the premise of my future films – the combination of the tragic and the comic.

School was now the beginning of new horizons: history, poetry and science. But some of the subjects were prosaic and dull, especially arithmetic: its addition and subtraction gave an image of a clerk and a cash register, its use, at best, a protection against being short-changed.

History was a record of wickedness and violence, a continual succession of regicides and kings murdering their wives, brothers and nephews; geography merely maps; poetry nothing more than exercising memory. Education bewildered me with knowledge and facts in which I was only mildly interested.

If only someone had used salesmanship, had read a stimulating preface to each study that could have titillated my mind, infused me with fancy instead of facts, amused and intrigued me with the legerdemain of numbers, romanticized maps, given me a point of view about history and taught me the music of poetry, I might have become a scholar.

Since Mother had returned to us she had begun to stimulate my interest in the theatre again. She imbued me with the feeling that I had some sort of talent. But it was not until those weeks before Christmas when the school put on its cantata *Cinderella* that I felt an urge to express all that Mother had taught me. For some reason I was not selected to play in it, and inwardly I was envious and felt that I was better able to play in the cantata than those who had been chosen. I was critical of the dull, unimaginative way the boys played their parts. The Ugly Sisters had no zest or comic spirit. They spoke their lines eruditely with a schoolboy inflection and an embarrassing falsetto emphasis. How I would have loved to play one of the Ugly Sisters, with the tutoring Mother could have given me! I was, however, captivated by the girl who played Cinderella. She was beautiful, refined, aged about fourteen, and I was secretly in love with her. But she was beyond my reach both socially and in years.

When I saw the cantata, I thought it dismal but for the beauty of the girl, which left me a little sad. Little did I realize, however, the glorious triumph I was to enjoy two months later when I was brought before each class and made to recite *Miss Priscilla's Cat*. It was a comedy recitation Mother had seen outside a newspaper shop and thought so funny that she copied it from the window and brought it home. During a recess in class, I recited it to one of the boys. Mr Reid, our school-teacher, looked up from his work and was so amused that when the class assembled he made me recite it to them and they were thrown into gales of laughter. As a result of this my fame spread, and the following day I was brought before every classroom in the school, both boys and girls, and made to recite it.

Although I had performed and deputized for Mother in front of an audience at the age of five, this was actually my first conscious taste of glamour. School became exciting. From having been an obscure and shy little boy I became the centre of interest of both the teachers and the children. It even improved my studies. But my education was to be interrupted when I left to join a troupe of clog dancers, the Eight Lancashire Lads.

# *three*

FATHER knew Mr Jackson, who ran the troupe, and convinced Mother that it would be a good start for me to make a career on the stage and at the same time help her economically: I would get board and lodging and Mother would get half a crown a week. She was dubious at first until she met Mr Jackson and his family, then she accepted.

Mr Jackson was in his middle fifties. He had been a school-teacher in Lancashire and had raised a family of three boys and a girl, who were all a part of the Eight Lancashire Lads. He was a devout Roman Catholic and after his first wife died had consulted his children about marrying again. His second wife was a little older than himself, and he would piously tell us how he came to marry her. He had advertised for a wife in one of the newspapers and had received over three hundred letters. After praying for guidance he had opened only one, and that was from Mrs Jackson. She too had been a school-teacher and, as if in answer to his prayer, was also a Catholic.

Mrs Jackson was not blessed with abundant good looks, nor was she a voluptuary in any sense of the word. As I remember her she had a gaunt, skull-like, pale face with manifold wrinkles – due, perhaps, to having presented Mr Jackson with a baby boy rather late in life. Nevertheless, she was a loyal and dutiful wife and, although still nursing her son at the breast, worked hard at helping with the management of the troupe.

When she told her side of the romance, it varied slightly from that of Mr Jackson. They had exchanged letters, but neither one had seen the other until the day of the wedding. And in their first interview alone in the sitting-room while the family waited in another room, Mr Jackson said: 'You're all

43

that I desire,' and she avowed the same. In concluding the story to us boys, she would primly say: 'But I didn't expect to be the immediate mother of eight children.'

The three sons' ages ranged from twelve to sixteen, and the daughter was nine, with hair cut like a boy in order to pass as one in the troupe.

Each Sunday, everyone attended Catholic church but me. Being the only Protestant, I was lonely, so occasionally I went with them. Had it not been for deference to Mother's religious scruples, I could easily have been won over to Catholicism, for I liked the mysticism of it and the little home-made altars with plaster Virgin Marys adorned with flowers and lighted candles which the boys put up in a corner of the bedroom, and to which they would genuflect every time they passed.

After practising six weeks I was eligible to dance with the troupe. But now that I was past eight years old I had lost my assurance and confronting the audience for the first time gave me stage fright. I could hardly move my legs. It was weeks before I could solo dance as the rest of them did.

I was not particularly enamoured with being just a clog dancer in a troupe of eight lads. Like the rest of them I was ambitious to do a single act, not only because it meant more money but because I instinctively felt it to be more gratifying than just dancing. I would have liked to be a boy comedian – but that would have required nerve, to stand on the stage alone. Nevertheless, my first impulse to do something other than dance was to be funny. My ideal was a double act, two boys dressed as comedy tramps. I told it to one of the other boys and we decided to become partners. It became our cherished dream. We would call ourselves 'Bristol and Chaplin, the Millionaire Tramps', and would wear tramp whiskers and big diamond rings. It embraced every aspect of what we thought would be funny and profitable, but, alas, it never materialized.

Audiences liked the Eight Lancashire Lads because, as Mr Jackson said, we were so unlike theatrical children. It was his boast that we never wore grease-paint and that our rosy cheeks were natural. If some of us looked a little pale before going on, he would tell us to pinch our cheeks. But in London, after working two or three music halls a night, we would occasionally forget and look a little weary and bored as we stood on the stage, until we caught sight of Mr Jackson in the wings, grinning emphatically and pointing to his face, which had an electrifying effect of making us suddenly break into sparkling grins.

When touring the provinces we went to a school for the week in each town, which did little to further my education.

At Christmas time we were engaged to play cats and dogs in a Cinderella pantomime at the London Hippodrome. In those days, it was a new theatre, a combination of vaudeville and circus, elaborately decorated and quite sensational. The floor of the ring sank and flooded with water and elaborate ballets were contrived. Row after row of pretty girls in shining armour would march in and disappear completely under water. As the last line submerged, Marceline, the great French clown, dressed in sloppy evening dress and opera hat, would enter with a fishing rod, sit on a camp stool, open a large jewel-case, bait his hook with a diamond necklace, then cast it into the water. After a while he would 'chum' with smaller jewellery, throwing in a few bracelets, eventually emptying in the whole jewel-case. Suddenly he would get a bite and throw himself into paroxysms of comic gyrations struggling with the rod, and eventually pulling out of the water a small trained poodle dog, who copied everything Marceline did: if he sat down, the dog sat down; if he stood on his head, the dog did likewise.

Marceline's comedy was droll and charming and London went wild over him. In the kitchen scene I was given a little comedy bit to do with Marceline. I was a cat, and Marceline would back away from a dog and fall over my back while I drank milk. He always complained that I did not arch my back enough to break his fall. I wore a cat-mask which had a look of surprise, and during the first matinée for children I went up to the rear end of a dog and began to sniff. When the audience laughed, I turned and looked surprised at them, pulling a string which winked a staring eye. After several sniffs and winks the house-manager came bounding back stage, waving frantically in the wings. But I carried on. After smelling the dog, I smelt the proscenium, then I lifted my leg. The audience roared – possibly because the gesture was uncatlike. Eventually the manager caught my eye and I capered off to great applause. 'Never do that again!' he said,

45

breathlessly. 'You'll have the Lord Chamberlain close down the theatre!'

*Cinderella* was a great success, and although Marceline had little to do with plot or story, he was the star attraction. Years later Marceline went to the New York Hippodrome, where he was also a sensation. But when the Hippodrome abolished the circus ring, Marceline was soon forgotten.

In 1918, or thereabouts, Ringling Brothers' three-ring circus came to Los Angeles, and Marceline was with them. I expected that he would be featured, but I was shocked to find him just one of many clowns that ran around the enormous ring – a great artist lost in the vulgar extravagance of a three-ring circus.

I went to his dressing-room afterwards and made myself known, reminding him that I had played Cat at the London Hippodrome with him. But he reacted apathetically. Even under his clown make-up he looked sullen and seemed in a melancholy torpor.

A year later in New York he committed suicide. A small paragraph in the papers stated that an occupant living in the same house had heard a shot and had found Marceline lying on the floor with a pistol in his hand and a record still turning, playing *Moonlight and Roses*.

Many famous English comedians committed suicide. T. E. Dunville, an excellent funny man, overheard someone say as he entered a saloon bar: 'That fellow's through.' The same day he shot himself by the River Thames.

Mark Sheridan, one of England's foremost comedians, shot himself in a public park in Glasgow because he had not gone over well with the Glasgow audience.

Frank Coyne, with whom we played on the same bill, was a gay, bouncy type of comedian, famous for his breezy song:

> You won't catch me on the gee-gee's back again,
> It's not the kind of horse that I can ride on.
> The only horse I know that I can ride
> Is the one the missus dries the clothes on!

Off stage he was pleasant and always smiling. But one afternoon, after planning to take a drive with his wife in their pony and trap, he forgot something and told her to wait while he went upstairs. After twenty minutes she went up to see what was causing

the delay, and found him in the bathroom on the floor in a
pool of blood, a razor in his hand – he had cut his throat, almost
decapitating himself.

Of the many artists I saw as a child, those who impressed me
the most were not always the successful ones but those with
unique personalities off stage. Zarmo, the comedy tramp juggler,
was a disciplinarian who practised his juggling for hours every
morning as soon as the theatre opened. We could see him back
stage balancing a billiard cue on his chin and throwing a billiard
ball up and catching it on the tip of the cue, then throwing up
another and catching that on top of the first ball – which he often
missed. For four years, he told Mr Jackson, he had been practising that trick and at the end of the week he intended to try it out
for the first time with the audience. That night we all stood in
the wings and watched him. He did it perfectly, and the first time!
– throwing the ball up and catching it on the tip of the billiard
cue, then throwing a second and catching that on top of the first.
But the audience only applauded mildly. Mr Jackson often told
the story of that night. Said he to Zarmo: 'You make the trick
look too easy, you don't sell it. You should miss it several times,
then do it.' Zarmo laughed. 'I am not expert enough to miss it
yet.' Zarmo was also interested in phrenology and would read
our characters. He told me that whatever knowledge I acquired,
I would retain and put to good use.

And there were the Griffiths Brothers, funny and impressive,
who confused my psychology, comedy trapeze clowns who, as
they both swung from the trapeze, would ferociously kick each
other in the face with large padded shoes.

'Ouch!' said the receiver. 'I dare you to do it again!'

'Do yer?' . . . Bang!

And the receiver would look surprised and groggy and say:
'He did it again!'

I thought such crazy violence shocking. But off stage they were
devoted brothers, quiet and serious.

Dan Leno, I suppose, was the greatest English comedian since
the legendary Grimaldi. Although I never saw Leno in his prime,
to me he was more of a character actor than a comedian. His
whimsical character delineations of London's lower classes were
human and endearing, so Mother told me.

The famous Marie Lloyd was reputed to be frivolous, yet when we played with her at the old Tivoli in the Strand never was there a more serious and conscientious artist. I would watch her wide-eyed, this anxious, plump little lady pacing nervously up and down behind the scenes, irritable and apprehensive until the moment came for her to go on. Then she was immediately gay and relaxed.

And Bransby Williams, the Dickens delineator, enthralled me with imitations of Uriah Heep, Bill Sykes and the old man of *The Old Curiosity Shop*. The legerdemain of this handsome, dignified young man making up before a rowdy Glasgow audience and transforming himself into these fascinating characters, opened up another aspect of the theatre. He also ignited my curiosity about literature; I wanted to know what was this immured mystery that lay hidden in books – these sepia Dickens characters that moved in such a strange Cruikshankian world. Although I could hardly read, I eventually bought *Oliver Twist*.

So enthralled was I with Dickens characters that I would imitate Bransby Williams imitating them. It was inevitable that such budding talent could not be concealed for long. Thus it was that one day Mr Jackson saw me entertaining the other boys with an imitation of the old man of *The Old Curiosity Shop*. Then and there I was proclaimed a genius, and Mr Jackson was determined to let the world know it.

The momentous event happened at the theatre in Middlesbrough. After our clog dance Mr Jackson walked on stage with the earnestness of one about to announce the coming of a young Messiah, stating that he had discovered a child genius among his boys, who would give an imitation of Bransby Williams as the old man of *The Old Curiosity Shop* who cannot recognize the death of his little Nell.

The audience were not too receptive, having endured a very boring evening's entertainment already. However, I came on wearing my usual dancing costume of a white linen blouse, a lace collar, plush knickerbocker pants and red dancing shoes, and made up to look like an old man of ninety. Somewhere, somehow, we had come into possession of an old wig – Mr Jackson might have bought it – but it did not fit me. Although I had a large head, the wig was larger; it was a bald-headed wig fringed with long, grey, stringy hair, so that when I appeared on the stage bent as an old man, the effect was like a crawling beetle, and the audience endorsed the fact with their titters.

It was difficult to get them quiet after that. I spoke in subdued whispers: 'Hush, hush, you mustn't make a noise or you'll wake my Nelly.'

'Louder! Louder! Speak up!' shouted the audience.

But I went on feebly whispering, all very intimate; so intimate that the audience began to stamp. It was the end of my career as a delineator of Charles Dickens's characters.

Although we lived frugally, life with the Eight Lancashire Lads was agreeable. Occasionally we had out little dissensions. I remember playing on the same bill with two young acrobats, boy apprentices about my own age, who told us confidentially that their mothers received seven and sixpence a week and they got a shilling pocket money put under their bacon-and-egg plate every Monday morning. 'And,' complained one of our boys, 'we only get twopence and a bread and jam breakfast.'

When Mr Jackson's son, John, heard that we were complaining, he broke down and wept, telling us that at times, playing odd weeks in the suburbs of London, his father only got seven pounds a week for the whole troupe and that they were having a hard time making both ends meet.

It was this opulent living of the two young apprentices that made us ambitious to become acrobats. So for several mornings, as soon as the theatre opened, one or two of us would practise somersaults with a rope tied round our waists, attached to a pulley, while one of us would hold the rope. I did very well turning somersaults in this fashion until I fell and sprained my thumb. That ended my acrobatic career.

Besides dancing we were always trying to add to our other accomplishments. I wanted to be a comedy juggler, so I had saved enough money to buy four rubber balls and four tin plates and for hours I would stand over the bedside, practising.

Mr Jackson was essentially a good man. Three months before I left the troupe we appeared at a benefit for my father, who had been very ill; many vaudeville artists donated their services, including Mr Jackson's Eight Lancashire Lads. The night of the benefit my father appeared on the stage breathing with difficulty, and with painful effort made a speech. I stood at the side of the stage watching him, not realizing that he was a dying man.

When we were in London, I visited Mother every week-end. She thought I looked pale and thin and that dancing was affecting my lungs. It worried her so much that she wrote about it to Mr Jackson, who was so indignant that he finally sent me home, saying that I was not worth the bother of such a worrying mother.

A few weeks later, however, I developed asthma. The attacks grew so severe that Mother was convinced I had tuberculosis and promptly took me to Brompton Hospital, where I was given a thorough examination. Nothing was found wrong with my lungs, but I did have asthma. For months I went through agony, unable to breathe. At times I wanted to jump out of the window. Inhaling herbs with a blanket over my head gave little relief. But, as the doctor said I would, I eventually outgrew it.

My memory of this period goes in and out of focus. The outstanding impression was a quagmire of miserable circumstances. I cannot remember where Sydney was; being four years older, he only occasionally entered my consciousness. He was possibly living with Grandfather to relieve Mother's penury. We seemed to vacillate from one abode to another, eventually ending up in a small garret at 3 Pownall Terrace.

I was well aware of the social stigma of our poverty. Even the poorest of children sat down to a home-cooked Sunday dinner. A roast at home meant respectability, a ritual that distinguished one poor class from another. Those who could not sit down to Sunday dinner at home were of the mendicant class, and we were that. Mother would send me to the nearest coffee-shop to buy a sixpenny dinner (meat and two vegetables). The shame of it – especially on Sunday! I would harry her for not preparing something at home, and she would vainly try to explain that cooking at home would cost twice as much.

However, one lucky Friday, after winning five shillings at horse-racing, Mother, to please me, decided to cook dinner on Sunday. Amongst other delectables she bought a piece of roasting meat that could not make up its mind whether to be beef or a lump of suet. It weighed about five pounds and had a sign stuck in it: 'For Roasting'.

Mother, having no oven, used the landlady's and, being too

shy to keep going in and out of her kitchen, had haphazardly guessed the time needed to roast it. Consequently, to our dismay, our joint had shrunk to the size of a cricket ball. Nevertheless, in spite of Mother's averring that our sixpenny dinners were less trouble and more palatable, I enjoyed it and felt the gratification of having lived up to the Joneses.

*

A sudden change came into our lives. Mother met an old friend who had become very prosperous, a flamboyant, good-looking, Junoesque type of woman who had given up the stage to become the mistress of a wealthy old colonel. She lived in the fashionable district of Stockwell; and in her enthusiasm at meeting Mother again, she invited us to stay with her during the summer. As Sydney was away in the country hop-picking, it took little inducement to persuade Mother, who, with the wizardry of her needle, made herself quite presentable, and I, dressed in my Sunday suit, a relic of the Eight Lancashire Lads, looked quite presentable for the occasion.

Thus overnight we were transported to a very sedate corner house in Lansdowne Square, ensconced in the lap of luxury, with a house full of servants, pink and blue bedrooms, chintz curtains and white bear-rugs; moreover, we lived on the fat of the land. How well I remember those large, blue, hothouse grapes that ornamented the sideboard in the dining-room and my feeling of guilt at their mysterious diminishing, looking more skeleton-like each day.

The household staff consisted of four women: the cook and three maids. In addition to Mother and me, there was another guest, a very tense, good-looking young man with a cropped red moustache. He was most charming and gentlemanly, and seemed a permanent fixture in the house – until the grey-whiskered Colonel appeared. Then the handsome young man would disappear.

The Colonel's visits were sporadic, once or twice a week. While he was there, mystery and omnipresence pervaded the house, and Mother would tell me to keep out of the way and not to be seen. One day I ran into the hall as the Colonel was descending the stairs. He was a tall, stately gentleman in a frock-coat and

51

top hat, a pink face, long grey side-burns and a bald head. He smiled benignly at me and went on his way.

I did not understand what all the hush and fuss was about and why the Colonel's arrival created such an effect. But he never stayed long, and the young man with the cropped moustache would return, and the house would function normally again.

I grew very fond of the young man with the cropped moustache. We would take long walks together over Clapham Common with the lady's two beautiful greyhound dogs. Clapham Common had an elegant atmosphere in those days. Even the chemist's shop, where we occasionally made a purchase, exuded elegance with its familiar admixture of aromatic smells, perfumes, soaps and powders – ever since, the odour of certain chemists' shops has a pleasant nostalgia. He advised Mother to have me take cold baths every morning to cure my asthma, and possibly they helped; they were most invigorating and I grew to like them.

It is remarkable how easily one adapts oneself to the social graces. How genteel and accustomed one becomes to creature comforts! In less than a week I took everything for granted. What a sense of well-being – going through that morning ritual, exercising the dogs, carrying their new brown leather leashes, then returning to a beautiful house with servants, to await lunch served in elegant style on silver platters.

Our back garden connected with another house whose occupants had as many servants as we had. They were a family of three, a young married couple and their son, who was about my own age and who had a nursery stocked with beautiful toys. I was often invited to play with him and to stay for dinner, and we became very good friends. His father held some important position in a City bank, and his mother was young and quite pretty.

One day I overheard our maid confidentially conversing with the boy's maid, who was saying that their boy needed a governess. 'That's what this one needs,' said our maid referring to me. I was thrilled to be looked upon as a child of the rich, but I never quite understood why she had elevated me to this status, unless it was to elevate herself by inferring that the people she worked for were as well off and as respectable as the neighbours next door. After that, whenever I dined with the boy next door I felt somewhat of an impostor.

Although it was a mournful day when we left the fine house to return to 3 Pownall Terrace, yet there was a sense of relief in getting back to our own freedom; after all, as guests we were living under a certain tension, and, as Mother said, guests were like cakes: if kept too long they became stale and unpalatable. Thus the silken threads of a brief and luxurious episode snapped, and we fell again into our accustomed impecunious ways.

# *four*

1899 was an epoch of whiskers: bewhiskered kings, statesmen, soldiers and sailors, Krugers, Salisburys, Kitcheners, Kaisers and cricketers – incredible years of pomp and absurdity, of extreme wealth and poverty, of inane political bigotry of both cartoon and press. But England was to absorb many shocks and indignations. A few Boer farmers in the African Transvaal were warring unfairly, shooting our red-coated soldiers, excellent targets, from behind boulders and rocks. Then the War Office saw the light, and our red coats were quickly changed to khaki. If the Boers wanted it that way, they could have it.

I was vaguely aware of war through patriotic songs, vaudeville sketches and cigarette pictures of the generals. The enemy, of course, were unmitigated villains. One heard dolorous news about the Boers surrounding Ladysmith and England went mad with hysterical joy at the relief of Mafeking. Then at last we won – we muddled through. All this I heard from everyone but Mother. She never mentioned the war. She had her own battle to fight.

Sydney was now fourteen and had left school and got a job at the Strand Post Office as a telegraph boy. With Sydney's wages and Mother's earnings at her sewing machine, our economy was almost feasible – although Mother's contribution was a modest one. She worked for a sweat-shop doing piece-work, sewing blouses for one and sixpence a dozen. Even though the patterns were delivered already cut out, it took twelve hours to make a dozen blouses. Mother's record was fifty-four blouses in a week, which amounted to six shillings and ninepence.

Often at night I would lie awake in our garret watching her bent over her sewing machine, her head haloed against the light of the oil-lamp, her face in soft shadow, her lips faintly parted with strain as she guided the rapidly running seams through her machine, until the drone of it would send me off to sleep again. When she worked late this way, it was usually to meet a monetary deadline. There was always the problem of instalment payments.

And now a crisis had arisen. Sydney needed a new suit of clothes. He had worn his telegraph uniform every day in the week, including Sundays, until his friends began to joke about it. So for a couple of week-ends he stayed home until Mother was able to buy him a blue serge suit. In some way she managed to scrape together eighteen shillings. This created an insolvency in our economy, so that Mother was obliged to pawn the suit every Monday after Sydney went back to work in his telegraph uniform. She got seven shillings for the suit, redeeming it every Saturday for Sydney to wear over the week-end. This weekly custom became an habitual ceremony for over a year until the suit became threadbare. Then came a shock!

Monday morning, as usual, Mother went to the pawnshop. The man hesitated. 'I'm sorry, Mrs Chaplin, but we can't lend you seven shillings any longer.'

Mother was astonished. 'But why?' she asked.

'It's too much of a risk; the trousers are threadbare. Look,' he said, putting his hand in the seat of them, 'you can see right through them.'

'But they'll be redeemed next Saturday,' said Mother.

The pawnbroker shook his head. 'The best I can do is three shillings for the coat and waistcoat.'

Mother rarely wept, but it was such a drastic blow that she came home in tears. She depended on that seven shillings to carry us through the week.

Meanwhile my own vestments were, to say the least, in disrepair. What was left of my Eight Lancashire Lads' outfit was a motley sight. There were patches everywhere, on the elbows, trousers, shoes and stockings. And in this condition I ran smack into my nice little boy friend from Stockwell. What he was doing in Kennington I did not know and was too embarrassed to find out. He greeted me friendlily enough, but I could see him eyeing my deplorable appearance. To offset my embarrassment I assumed a *dégagé* manner and in my best, cultured voice told him that I was wearing my old clothes because I had just come from a beastly carpentry lesson.

But the explanation had little interest for him. He began to look crestfallen and to cast his eyes aside to hide his embarrassment. He inquired after Mother.

I answered briskly that she was away in the country and turned the attention on him: 'Are you living in the same place?'

'Yes,' he answered, surveying me as though I had committed some cardinal sin.

'Well, I'll run along,' I said abruptly.

He faintly smiled. 'Good-bye,' he said, and we parted, he walking off sedately in one direction and I, furious and ashamed, running helter-skelter in the opposite one.

*

Mother had a saying: 'You can always stoop and pick up nothing.' But she herself did not adhere to this adage, and my sense of propriety was often outraged. One day, returning from Brompton Hospital, Mother stopped to upbraid some boys tormenting a derelict woman who was grotesquely ragged and dirty. She had a cropped head, unusual in those days, and the boys were laughing and pushing each other towards her, as if to touch her would contaminate them. The pathetic woman stood like a stag at bay until Mother interfered. Then a look of recognition came over the woman's face. 'Lil,' she said, feebly, referring to Mother's stage name, 'don't you know me – Eva Lestock?'

Mother recognized her at once, an old friend of her vaudeville days.

I was so embarrassed that I moved on and waited for Mother at the corner. The boys walked past me, smirking and giggling. I was furious. I turned to see what was happening to Mother and, lo, the derelict woman had joined her and both were walking towards me.

Said Mother: 'You remember little Charlie?'

'Do I!' said the woman, dolefully. 'I've held him in my arms many a time when he was a baby.'

The thought was repellent, for the woman looked so filthy and loathsome. And as we walked along, it was embarrassing to see people turn and look at the three of us.

56

Mother had known her in vaudeville as 'the Dashing Eva Lestock'; she was pretty and vivacious then, so Mother told me. The woman said that she had been ill in the hospital, and that since leaving it, she had been sleeping under arches and in Salvation Army shelters.

First Mother sent her to the public baths, then to my horror brought her home to our small garret. Whether it was illness alone that was the cause of her present circumstances, I never knew. What was outrageous was that she slept in Sydney's armchair bed. However, Mother gave her what clothes she could spare and loaned her a couple of bob. After three days she departed, and that was the last we ever saw or heard of 'the Dashing Eva Lestock'!

*

Before Father died, Mother moved from Pownall Terrace and rented a room at the house of Mrs Taylor, a friend of Mother's, a church member and devoted Christian. She was a short, square-framed woman in her middle fifties with a square jaw and a sallow, wrinkled face. While watching her in church I discovered she had false teeth. They would drop from her upper gums on to her tongue while she sang – the effect was hypnotic.

She had an emphatic manner and abundant energy. She had taken Mother under her Christian wing, and had rented her a front room, at a very reasonable rent, on the second floor of her large house which was next to a graveyard.

Her husband, a facsimile of Dickens's Mr Pickwick, was a precision ruler maker and had his workshop on the top floor. The roof had a skylight and I thought the place heavenly, it was so peaceful there. I often watched Mr Taylor at work, fascinated as he peered intensely through his thick-lensed spectacles with a large magnifying glass, making a steel ruler that would measure one-fiftieth part of an inch. He worked alone and I often ran errands for him.

Mrs Taylor's one desire was to convert her husband, who, according to her Christian scruples, was a sinner. Her daughter, whose features were of the same cast as the mother's except that she was less sallow and, of course, much younger, would have been attractive but for her hauteur and objectionable manner. Like her father, she never attended church. But Mrs Taylor never gave up hope of converting them both. The daughter was the apple of her mother's eye – but not of my mother's eye.

One afternoon, while on the top floor watching Mr Taylor at work, I heard an altercation below between Mother and Miss Taylor. Mrs Taylor was out. I do not know how it started, but they were both shouting loudly at each other. As I reached our landing, Mother was leaning over the banisters: 'Who do you think you are? Lady Shit?'

'Oh!' shouted the daughter. 'That's nice language coming from a Christian!'

'Don't worry,' said Mother quickly, 'it's in the Bible, my dear: Deuteronomy, twenty-eighth chapter, thirty-seventh verse, only there's another word for it. However, shit will suit you.'

After that, we moved back to Pownall Terrace.

*

The Three Stags in the Kennington Road was not a place my father frequented, yet as I passed it one evening an urge prompted me to peek inside to see if he was there. I opened the saloon door just a few inches, and there he was, sitting in the corner! I was about to leave, but his face lit up and he beckoned me to him. I was surprised at such a welcome, for he was never demonstrative. He looked very ill; his eyes were sunken, and his body had swollen to an enormous size. He rested one hand, Napoleon-like, in his waistcoat as if to ease his difficult breathing. That evening he was most solicitous, inquiring after Mother and Sydney, and before I left took me in his arms and for the first time kissed me. That was the last time I saw him alive.

Three weeks later, he was taken to St Thomas's Hospital. They had to get him drunk to get him there. When he realized where he was, he fought wildly – but he was a dying man. Though still very young, only thirty-seven, he was dying of dropsy. They tapped sixteen quarts of liquid from his knee.

Mother went several times to see him and was always saddened by the visit. She said he spoke of wanting to go back to her and start life anew in Africa. When I brightened at such a prospect, Mother shook her head, for she knew better. 'He was saying that only to be nice,' she said.

One day she came home from the hospital indignant over what

the Reverend John McNeil, Evangelist, had said when he paid Father a visit: 'Well, Charlie, when I look at you, I can only think of the old proverb: "Whatsoever a man soweth, that shall he also reap".'

'Nice words to console a dying man,' said Mother. A few days later Father was dead.

The hospital wanted to know who would bury him. Mother, not having a penny, suggested the Variety Artists' Benevolent Fund, a theatrical charity organization. This caused an uproar with the Chaplin side of the family – the humiliation of being buried by charity was repugnant to them. An Uncle Albert from Africa, my father's youngest brother, was in London at the time and said he would pay for the burial.

The day of the funeral we were to meet at St Thomas's Hospital, where we were to join the rest of the Chaplins and from there drive out to Tooting Cemetery. Sydney could not come, as he was working. Mother and I arrived at the hospital a couple of hours before the allotted time because she wanted to see Father before he was enclosed.

The coffin was enshrouded in white satin and around the edge of it, framing Father's face, were little white daisies. Mother thought they looked so simple and touching and asked who had placed them there. The attendant told her that a lady had called early that morning with a little boy. It was Louise.

In the first carriage were Mother, Uncle Albert and me. The drive to Tooting was a strain, for she had never met Uncle Albert before. He was somewhat of a dandy and spoke with a cultured accent; although polite, his attitude was icy. He was reputed to be rich; he had large horse ranches in the Transvaal and had provided the British Government with horses during the Boer War.

It poured with rain during the service; the grave-diggers threw down clods of earth on the coffin which resounded with a brutal thud. It was macabre and horrifying and I began to weep. Then the relatives threw in their wreaths and flowers. Mother, having nothing to throw in, took my precious black-bordered handkerchief. 'Here, sonny,' she whispered, 'this will do for both of us.' Afterwards the Chaplins stopped off at one of their pubs for lunch, and before leaving asked us politely where we desired to be dropped. So we were driven home.

When we returned there was not a particle of food in the cupboard except a saucer of beef dripping, and Mother had not a penny, for she had given Sydney her last twopence for his lunch money. Since Father's illness she had done little work, and now, near the end of the week, Sydney's wages of seven shillings as a telegraph boy had already run out. After the funeral we were hungry. Luckily the rag-and-bone man was passing outside and we had an old oil stove, so reluctantly she sold it for a halfpenny and bought a halfpenny worth of bread to go with the dripping.

Mother, being the legal widow of my father, was told the next day to call at the hospital for his belongings, which consisted of a black suit spotted with blood, underwear, a shirt, a black tie, an old dressing-gown, and some plaid house slippers with oranges stuffed in the toes. When she took the oranges out, a half sovereign fell out of the slippers on to the bed. This was a godsend!

For weeks I wore crêpe on my arm. These insignia of grief became profitable when I went into business on a Saturday afternoon, selling flowers. I had persuaded Mother to loan me a shilling, and went to the flower market and purchased two bundles of narcissus, and after school busied myself making them into penny bundles. All sold, I could make a hundred per cent profit.

I would go into the saloons, looking wistful, and whisper: 'Narcissus, miss!' 'Narcissus, madame!' The women always responded: 'Who is it, son?' And I would lower my voice to a whisper: 'My father,' and they would give me tips. Mother was amazed when I came home in the evening with more than five shillings for an afternoon's work. One day she bumped into me as I came out of a pub, and that put an end to my flower-selling; that her boy was peddling flowers in bar-rooms offended her Christian scruples. 'Drink killed your father, and money from such a source will only bring us bad luck,' she said. However, she kept the proceeds, though she never allowed me to sell flowers again.

There was a strong element of the merchant in me. I was continuously preoccupied with business schemes. I would look at empty shops, speculating as to what profitable businesses I could make of them, ranging from fish and chips to grocery shops. It had always to do with food. All I needed was capital – but how does one get capital? Eventually I talked Mother into letting me leave school and get a job.

I became a veteran of many occupations. First I was an errand boy in a chandler's shop. Between errands I was delightfully occupied in the cellar, immured in soap, starch, candles, sweets and biscuits, sampling all the sweetmeats till I made myself sick.

Then I was a doctor's boy for Hool and Kinsey-Taylor, insurance doctors in Throgmorton Avenue, a job I inherited from Sydney, who recommended me. It was lucrative, and I was paid twelve shillings a week to act as receptionist with the duties of cleaning out the offices after the doctors had gone. As a receptionist I was a great success and charmed all the waiting patients, but when it came to cleaning up the offices my heart was not in it – Sydney was much better. I did not mind emptying the phials of urine, but cleaning those ten-foot office windows was indeed a gargantuan task; so that the offices grew dimmer and dustier until I was told politely that I was too small for the job.

When I heard the news I broke down and wept. Dr Kinsey-Taylor, married to a very wealthy lady with a large house in Lancaster Gate, took pity on me and said he would fit me in as a page-boy in his house. Immediately my heart lightened. A page-boy in a private house, and a very posh one at that!

It was a happy job, for I was the pet of all the housemaids. They treated me like a child and kissed me good night before I went to bed. But for Fate I might have become a butler. Madame wanted me to clean out a cellar in the area where there were packing cases and debris piled high that had to be sorted, cleaned and arranged. I was diverted from the task by my interest in an iron pipe about eight feet long, through which I blew like a trumpet. Just as I was enjoying myself, Madame appeared – and I was given three days' notice.

I enjoyed working for W. H. Smith and Son, the newsagents and booksellers, but lost the job as soon as they found I was under age. Then for a day I was a glass-blower. I had read about glass-blowing at school and thought it romantic, but the heat overcame me and I was carried out unconscious and laid on a sand pile. That was enough; I never went back even to collect my day's salary. Then I worked at Straker's, the printers and stationers. I

61

tried to bluff them that I could run a Wharfedale printing machine – an enormous thing, over twenty feet long. I had seen it in action, looking into the cellar from the street, and the task looked easy and simple to do. A card read: 'Boy wanted as layer-on for a Wharfedale printing machine.' When the foreman brought me to it, it loomed up monstrously. To operate it, I had to stand upon a platform five feet high. I felt I was at the top of the Eiffel Tower.

'Strike her!' said the foreman.

'Strike her?'

Seeing me hesitate, he laughed. 'You've never worked on a Wharfedale.'

'Just give me the chance, I'll pick it up quite easily,' I said.

'Strike her' meant pull the lever to start the brute. He showed me the lever, then put the beast at half-speed. It started to roll, grind and grunt; I thought it was going to devour me. The sheets were enormous; you could have wrapped me in one. With an ivory scraper I fanned the paper sheets, picking them up by the corners and placing them meticulously against the teeth in time for the monster to clutch them, devour them and regurgitate until they rolled out at the rear end. The first day I was a nervous wreck from the hungry brute wanting to get ahead of me. Nevertheless, I was given the job at twelve shillings per week.

There was romance and adventure about getting out on those cold mornings, before daylight, and going to work, the streets silent and deserted except for one or two shadowy figures making their way to the beacon light of Lockhart's tea-room for breakfast. One had a feeling of well-being with one's fellow men, sipping hot tea in the glow and warmth of that momentary respite before a day's work. And the printing job was not unpleasant; but for the heavy work at the end of the week, having to wash the ink off those tall, heavy, gelatine rollers weighing more than a hundred pounds each, the work was tolerable. However, after three weeks there, I came down with influenza, and Mother insisted that I return to school.

Sydney was now sixteen, and came home excited because he had obtained a job as a bugler on a Donovan and Castle Line passenger boat sailing to Africa. His duties were to blow the calls for lunch etc. He had learnt to play the bugle on the *Exmouth* training ship; now it was paying off. He was to receive two pounds ten a month, and tips from waiting at three tables in the second class. Thirty-five shillings he was to get in advance before sailing, which, of course, he would give to Mother. With such happy prospect, we moved into two rooms over a barber's shop in Chester Street.

Sydney's return from his first trip was the occasion for celebration, for he came back with over three pounds in tips and all in silver. I remember him pouring the money out of his pockets on to the bed. It seemed more money than I had ever seen in my life and I could not keep my hands off it. I scooped it up, dropped it, stacked it and played with it until both Mother and Sydney declared that I was a miser.

What luxury! What indulgence! It was summer and this was our cake and ice-cream period – we had many other luxuries besides. It was also our period of bloaters, kippers, haddocks and toasted tea-cakes for breakfast, and muffins and crumpets on Sunday morning.

Sydney caught cold and languished in bed for several days, and Mother and I waited on him. It was then that we indulged ourselves in ice-cream, a pennyworth in a large tumbler which I presented at the Italian ice-cream shop, much to the irritation of the owner. On my second visit he suggested I bring a bath-tub. A favourite summer drink of ours was sherbet and milk – the sherbet fizzing up through the over-skimmed milk was indeed delectable.

Sydney told us many amusing stories about his voyage. Before sailing he almost lost the job when he blew the first bugle call for lunch. He was out of practice and the soldiers aboard let up a chorus of howls. The chief steward came in a fury. 'What the hell do you call that?' 'Sorry, sir,' said Sydney, 'I haven't got my lip in yet.' 'Well, you'd better get your bloody lip in before the boat sails, otherwise you'll be put ashore.'

During meals there would be a long line of stewards in the kitchen filling their orders. But by the time Sydney's turn came he had forgotten his order, so he would have to go to the end of the line again. Sydney said that for the first few days while everyone was finishing their dessert he was serving soup.

Sydney stayed home until his money was spent. However, he

was booked for a second trip and again they advanced him thirty-five shillings, which he gave to Mother. But this did not last long. After three weeks we were scraping the bottom of the barrel, and there was another three weeks to go before Sydney's return. Although Mother continued working at her sewing machine, what she earned was not enough to keep us going. Consequently we were in another crisis.

But I was resourceful. Mother had a pile of old clothes, and, as it was Saturday morning, I suggested that I should try and sell them in the market place. Mother was a little embarrassed, and said they were quite worthless. Nevertheless, I wrapped them up in an old sheet and wended my way to Newington Butts and there laid my ignoble congeries on the pavement – a drab and sorry sight – then stood in the gutter and shouted: 'Here!' – picking up an old shirt, then a pair of old corsets – 'what will you give me? – a shilling, sixpence, threepence, twopence?' Not even at a penny could I make a sale. People would stop, look astonished, then laugh and go on their way. I began to feel embarrassed, especially when the occupants of a jeweller's shop opposite began looking at me through the shop window. However, nothing deterred me. Eventually a pair of gaiters that did not look so depressing sold for sixpence. But the longer I stayed the uneasier I felt. Later the gentleman from the jeweller's shop came over to me and asked, in a thick Russian accent, how long I had been in business. In spite of his solemn face, I detected humour in his remark and told him I had just started. He walked slowly back to his two grinning partners, who were looking through the shop window at me. That was enough! I thought it time to wrap up my wares and return home. When I told Mother I had sold a pair of gaiters for sixpence, she was indignant. 'They should have brought more,' she said. 'They were a beautiful pair!'

At this juncture we were not too concerned about paying rent; that problem was easily solved by being out for the day when the rent man called, and, as our belongings were of little value, it would cost more than we owed to cart them away. However, we moved back to 3 Pownall Terrace.

At this time I came to know an old man and his son who worked in a mews at the back of Kennington Road. They were travelling toy-makers who came from Glasgow, making toys and selling them as they wandered from town to town. They were free and unencumbered and I envied them. Their profession needed little capital. With as small an investment as a shilling they could start in business. They would collect shoe-boxes, which every shoe-shop was only too pleased to give them, and cork sawdust in which grapes were packed which they also got gratis. Their initial outlay consisted only in the purchase of a penny-worth of glue, a pennyworth of wood, twopence worth of twine, a pennyworth of Christmas coloured paper and three twopenny balls of coloured tinsel. For a shilling they could make seven dozen boats and sell them for a penny apiece. The sides were cut from shoe-boxes and were sewn on to a cardboard base, the smooth surface was covered with glue, then poured over with cork sawdust. The masts were rigged with coloured tinsel, and blue, yellow and red flags were stuck on the topmast and on the end of the booms, fore and aft. A hundred or more of these little toy boats, with their coloured tinsel and flags, was a gay and festive sight that attracted customers, and they were easy to sell.

As a result of our acquaintance I began helping them to make boats, and very soon I was familiar with their craft. When they left our neighbourhood I went into business for myself. With a limited capital of sixpence, and at the cost of blistered hands through cutting up cardboard, I was able to turn out three dozen boats within a week.

But there was not enough space in our garret for Mother's work and my boat-making. Besides, Mother complained of the odour of boiling glue, and that the glue pot was a constant menace to her linen blouses, which, incidentally, crowded most of the space in the room. As my contribution was less than Mother's, her work took precedence and my craft was abandoned.

We had seen little of Grandfather during this time. For the past year he had not been doing too well. His hands were swollen with gout, which made it difficult for him to work at his shoe-repairing. In the past he had helped Mother when he could afford with a couple of bob or so. Sometimes he would cook dinner for us, a wonderful bargoo stew composed of Quaker Oats and onions boiled in milk with salt and pepper. On a wintry night it was our constitutional base to withstand the cold.

As a boy I thought Grandpa a dour, fractious old man who was always correcting me either about my manners or my grammar. Because of these small encounters, I had grown to dislike him. Now he was in the infirmary with rheumatism, and Mother would go every visiting day to see him. These visits were profitable, because she usually returned with a bag full of fresh eggs, quite a luxury in our recessional period. When unable to go herself, she would send me. I was always surprised when I found Grandpa most agreeable and happy to see me. He was quite a favourite with the nurses. He told me in later life that he would joke with them, saying that in spite of his crippling rheumatism not all his machinery was impaired. This sort of rodomontade amused the nurses. When his rheumatism allowed him, he worked in the kitchen, whence came our eggs. On visiting days, he was usually in bed, and from his bedside cabinet would surreptitiously hand me a large bag of them, which I quickly stowed in my sailor's tunic before departing.

For weeks we lived on eggs, dished up in every form, boiled, fried and custardized. In spite of Grandpa's assurance that the nurses were his friends and knew more or less what was going on, I was always apprehensive when leaving the hospital ward with those eggs, terrified of slipping on the beeswax polished floor, or that my tumorous bulk would be apprehended. Curiously enough, when I was ready to leave, the nurses were always conspicuous by their absence. It was a sorry day for us when Grandpa was rid of his rheumatism and left the hospital.

Now six weeks had elapsed and still Sydney had not returned. At first this did not alarm Mother, but after another week's delay she wrote to the offices of the Donovan and Castle Line and received information that he had been put ashore at Cape Town for treatment of rheumatism. This news worried Mother and affected her health. Still she continued working at her sewing machine and I was fortunate in obtaining a little work by giving a few dancing lessons to a family after school for the sum of five shillings a week.

About this time the McCarthys came to live in Kennington Road. Mrs McCarthy had been an Irish comedienne and was a friend of Mother's. She was married to Walter McCarthy, a chartered accountant. But when Mother was obliged to give up

66

the stage we lost sight of Mr and Mrs McCarthy and not until seven years later did we meet them again, when they came to live at Walcott Mansions in the select part of Kennington Road.

Their son, Wally McCarthy, and I were the same age. As little children, we used to play at grown-ups, pretending we were vaudevillians, smoking our imaginary cigars and driving in our imaginary pony and trap, much to the amusement of our parents.

Since the McCarthys had come to live in Walcott Mansions, Mother had rarely seen them, but Wally and I had formed an inseparable friendship. As soon as I was through with school I would race home to Mother to find out if she needed any errands done, then race up to the McCarthys'. We would play theatre at the back of Walcott Mansions. As the director, I always gave myself the villain parts, knowing instinctively they were more colourful than the hero. We would play until Wally's supper-time. Usually I was invited. At mealtimes I had an ingratiating way of making myself available. There were occasions, however, when my manoeuvring did not work and I would reluctantly return home. Mother was always happy to see me and would prepare something for me, fried bread in dripping or one of Grandfather's eggs and a cup of tea. She would read to me or we would sit together at the window and she would amuse me by making remarks about the pedestrians as they passed by. She would invent stories about them. If it were a young man with a breezy, bobbing gait she would say: 'There goes Mr Hopand-scotch. He's on his way to place a bet. If he's lucky today he's going to buy a second-hand tandem for him and his girl.'

Then a man would pass slowly, moping along. 'Hm, he's going home to have stew and parsnips for dinner, which he hates.'

Then someone with an air of superiority would walk by. 'Now there's a refined young man, but at the moment he's worried about the hole in the seat of his pants.'

Then another with a fast gait would streak past. 'That gentle-man has just taken Eno's!' And so she would go on, sending me into gales of laughter.

Another week had gone by and not a word from Sydney. Had I been less a boy and more sensitive to Mother's anxiety I might have realized what was impending. I might have noticed that for several days she had been sitting listlessly at the window, had neglected to tidy up the room, had grown unusually quiet. I might have been concerned when the firm of shirtmakers began finding fault with her work and stopped giving it to her, and when they took away her sewing machine for arrears in payments, and when the five shillings I earned from dancing lessons suddenly ended; through all this I might have noticed that Mother remained indifferent, apathetic.

Mrs McCarthy suddenly died. She had been ailing for some time, and her health rapidly deteriorated until she passed on. Immediately, thoughts invaded my mind: how wonderful if Mr McCarthy married Mother – Wally and I being such good friends. Besides, it would be an ideal solution to all Mother's problems.

Soon after the funeral I spoke to Mother about it: 'You should make it your business to see a lot of Mr McCarthy. I bet he'd like to marry you.

Mother smiled wanly. 'Give the poor man a chance,' she said.

'If you were all dressed up and made yourself attractive, as you used to be, he would. But you don't make any effort; all you do is to sit around this filthy room and look awful.'

Poor Mother. How I regret those words. I never realized that she was weak from malnutrition. Yet the next day, by some super-human effort, she had tidied up the room.

The school's summer holidays were on, so I thought I would go early to the McCarthys' – anything to get away from the wretchedness of our garret. They had invited me to stay for lunch, but I had an intuition that I should return home to Mother. When I reached Pownall Terrace, I was stopped at the gate by some children of the neighbourhood.

'Your mother's gone insane,' said a little girl.

The words were like a slap in the face.

'What do you mean?' I mumbled.

'It's true,' said another. 'She's been knocking at all our doors, giving away pieces of coal, saying they were birthday presents for the children. You can ask my mother.'

Without hearing more, I ran up the pathway, through the open door of the house and leaped up the stairs and opened the door of our room. I stood a moment to catch my breath, intensely scrutinizing her. It was a summer's afternoon and the atmosphere was close and oppressive. Mother was sitting as usual at the window. She turned slowly and looked at me, her face pale and tormented.

'Mother!' I almost shouted.

'What is it?' she said listlessly.

Then I ran and fell on my knees and buried my face in her lap, and burst into uncontrollable weeping.

'There, there,' she said gently, stroking my head. 'What's wrong?'

'You're not well,' I cried between sobs.

She spoke reassuringly: 'Of course I am.'

She seemed so vague, so preoccupied.

'No! No! They say you've been going to all the houses and –' I could not finish, but continued sobbing.

'I was looking for Sydney,' she said weakly; 'they're keeping him away from me.'

Then I knew that what the children had said was true.

'Oh, Mummy, don't talk like that! Don't! Don't!' I sobbed. 'Let me get you a doctor.'

She continued, stroking my head: 'The McCarthys know where he is, and they're keeping him away from me.'

'Mummy, please let me get a doctor,' I cried. I got up and went towards the door.

She looked after me with a pained expression. 'Where are you going?'

'To get a doctor. I won't be long.'

She never answered, but looked anxiously after me. Quickly I rushed downstairs to the landlady. 'I've got to get a doctor at once, Mother's not well!'

'We've already sent for him,' the landlady said.

The parish doctor was old and grumpy and after hearing the landlady's story, which was similar to that of the children, he made a perfunctory examination of Mother. 'Insane. Send her to the infirmary,' he said.

The doctor wrote out a paper; besides other things it said she was suffering from malnutrition, which the doctor explained to me, saying that she was undernourished.

'She'll be better off and get proper food there,' said the landlady by way of comforting me.

She helped to gather up Mother's clothes and to dress her

69

Mother obeyed like a child; she was so weak, her will seemed to have deserted her. As we left the house, the neighbours and children were gathered at the front gate, looking on with awe.

The infirmary was about a mile away. As we ambled along Mother staggered like a drunken woman from weakness, veerign from side to side as I supported her. The stark, afternoon sun seemed to ruthlessly expose our misery. People who passed us must have thought Mother was drunk, but to me they were like phantoms in a dream. She never spoke, but seemed to know where we were going and to be anxious to get there. On the way I tried to reassure her, and she smiled, too weak to talk.

When at last we arrived at the infirmary a young doctor took her in charge. After reading the note, he said kindly: 'All right, Mrs Chaplin, come this way.'

She submitted obediently. But as the nurses started to lead her away she turned suddenly with a painful realization that she was leaving me behind.

'See you tomorrow,' I said, feigning cheerfulness.

They led her away looking anxiously back at me. When she had gone, the doctor turned. 'And what will become of you, young man?'

Having had enough of workhouse schools, I replied politely: 'Oh, I'll be living with my aunt.'

As I walked from the hospital towards home, I could feel only a numbing sadness. Yet I was relieved, for I knew that Mother would be better off in the hospital than sitting alone in that dark room with nothing to eat. But that heart-breaking look as they led her away I shall never forget. I thought of all her endearing ways, her gaiety, her sweetness and affection; of that weary little figure that used to come down the streets looking tired and pre-occupied until she saw me charging towards her; how she would change immediately and become all smiling as I looked eagerly inside the paper bag she carried for those little niceties that she always brought home for Sydney and me. Even that morning she had saved some candy – had offered it to me while I wept in her lap.

I did not go straight home, I could not. I turned in the direction of the Newington Butts market and looked in shop windows until late afternoon. When I returned to the garret it looked reproachfully empty. On a chair was a wash-tub, half-filled with water. Two of my shirts and a chemise were soaking in it. I began to investigate; there was no food in the cupboard except a small half-filled package of tea. On the mantelpiece was her purse, in which I found three halfpence, some keys and several pawn tickets. On the corner of the table was the candy she had offered me. Then I broke down and wept again.

Emotionally exhausted, I slept soundly that night. In the morning I awoke to a haunting emptiness in the room; the sun streaming in on the floor seemed to heighten Mother's absence. Later the landlady came up and said that I could stay on there until she let the room and that if I needed food I had only to ask for it. I thanked her and told her that Sydney would pay all our debts when he returned. But I was too shy to ask for food.

I did not go to see Mother the next day as promised. I could not; it would have been too upsetting. But the landlady saw the doctor, who said that she had already been transferred to Cane Hill asylum. This melancholy news relieved my conscience, for Cane Hill was twenty miles away and I had no means of getting there. Sydney would soon return and then we could see her together. For the first few days I neither saw nor spoke to anyone I knew.

I would steal out in the early morning and stay out all day; I always managed to get food somewhere – besides, missing a meal was no hardship. One morning the landlady caught me creeping downstairs and asked if I had had my breakfast. I shook my head. 'Then come on,' she said in her gruff way.

I kept away from the McCarthys because I did not want them to know about Mother. Like a fugitive, I kept out of everyone's way.

*

It was one week since Mother had gone away, and I had settled into a precarious habit of living which I neither lamented nor enjoyed. My major concern was the landlady, for if Sydney did not return, sooner or later she would have to report me to the parish authorities and I would be sent again to Hanwell Schools. Thus I avoided her presence, even sleeping out occasionally.

I fell in with some wood-choppers who worked in a mews at the back of Kennington Road, derelict-looking men who worked hard in a darkened shed and spoke softly in undertones, sawing and chopping wood all day, making it into halfpenny bundles. I would hang about the open door and watch them. They would take a block of wood a foot square and chop it into inch slices and put these slices together and chop them into sticks. They chopped wood so rapidly that it fascinated me and made the job seem attractive. Very soon I was helping them. They bought their lumber from demolition contractors, and would cart it to their shed, stack it up, which took at least a day, then saw the wood one day and chop the next. On Friday and Saturday they would sell the firewood. But the selling of it did not interest me; it was more clubby working together in the shed.

They were affable, quiet men in their late thirties, but looked and acted much older. The boss (as we called him) had a diabetic red nose and no upper teeth except one fang. Yet there was a gentle sweetness about his face. He had a ridiculous grin that exposed prodigiously his one tooth. When short of an extra tea-cup he would pick up an empty milk-tin, rinse it and, grinning, say: 'How's this for one?' The other man, though agreeable, was quiet, sallow-faced, thick-lipped and talked slowly. Around one o'clock the boss would look up at me: 'Have yer ever tasted Welsh rarebit made of cheese rinds?'

'We've had it many times,' I replied.

Then with a chortle and a grin he would give me twopence, and I would go to Ashe's, the tea grocers on the corner, who liked me and always gave me a lot for my money, and buy a pennyworth of cheese rinds and a pennyworth of bread. After washing and scraping the cheese we would add water and a little salt and pepper. Sometimes the boss would throw in a piece of bacon fat and a sliced onion, which together with a can of hot tea made a very appetizing meal.

Although I never asked for money, at the end of the week the boss gave me sixpence, which was a pleasant surprise.

Joe, the sallow-faced one, suffered from fits and the boss would burn brown paper under his nose to bring him to. Sometimes he would foam at the mouth and bite his tongue, and when he recovered would look pathetic and ashamed.

The wood-choppers worked from seven in the morning until seven at night, sometimes later, and I always felt sad when they locked up the shed and went home. One night the boss decided to treat us to a twopenny gallery seat at the South London Music Hall. Joe and I were already washed and cleaned up, waiting for the boss. I was thrilled because Fred Karno's comedy *Early Birds* (the company I joined years later) was playing there that week. Joe was leaning against the wall of the mews and I was standing opposite him, enthusiastic and excited, when suddenly he let out a roar and slid down sideways against the wall in one of his fits. The anticipation had been too much. The boss wanted to stay and look after him, but Joe insisted that the two of us go without him and that he would be all right in the morning.

The threat of school was an ogre that never left me. Once in a while the wood-choppers would question me about it. They became a little uneasy when the holidays were over, so I would stay away from them until four-thirty, when school was let out. But it was a long, lonely day in the glare of incriminating streets, waiting until four-thirty to get back to my shadow retreat and the wood-choppers.

While I was creeping up to bed one night the landlady called me. She had been sitting up waiting. She was all excited and handed me a telegram. It read: 'Will arrive ten o'clock tomorrow morning at Waterloo Station. Love, Sydney.'

I was not an imposing sight to greet him at the station. My clothes were dirty and torn, my shoes yawned and the lining of my cap showed like a woman's dropping underskirt; and what face-washing I did was at the wood-choppers' tap, because it saved me having to carry a pail of water up three flights of stairs and pass the landlady's kitchen. When I met Sydney the shades of night were in my ears and around my neck.

Looking me over, he said: 'What's happened?'

I did not break the news too gently. 'Mother went insane and we had to send her to the infirmary.'

His face clouded, but he checked himself. 'Where are you living?'

'The same place, Pownall Terrace.'

He turned away to look after his baggage. I notice he looked pale and gaunt. He ordered a brougham and the porters piled his luggage on top of it – amongst other things a crate of bananas!

'Is that ours?' I asked eagerly.

He nodded. 'They're too green; we'll have to wait a day or so before we can eat them.'

On the way home he began asking questions about Mother. I was too excited to give him a coherent account, but he got snatches. Then he told me he had been left behind in a hospital in Cape Town for medical treatment and that on the return trip he had made twenty pounds, money he looked forward to giving Mother. He had made it from the soldiers, organizing sweepstakes and lotteries.

He told me of his plans. He intended giving up the sea and becoming an actor. He figured that the money would keep us for twenty weeks, in which time he would seek work in the theatre.

Our arrival in a cab with a crate of bananas impressed both the neighbours and the landlady. She told Sydney about Mother, but did not go into harrowing details.

The same day Sydney went shopping and outfitted me with new clothes, and that night, all dressed up, we sat in the stalls of the South London Music Hall. During the performance Sydney kept repeating: 'Just think what tonight would have meant to Mother.'

That week we went to Cane Hill to see her. As we sat in the visiting room, the ordeal of waiting became almost unbearable. I remember the keys turning and Mother walking in. She looked pale and her lips were blue, and, although she recognized us, it was without enthusiasm; her old ebullience had gone. She was accompanied by a nurse, an innocuous, glib woman, who stood and wanted to talk. 'It's a pity you came at such a time,' she said, 'for we're not quite ourselves today, are we, dear?'

Mother politely glanced at her and half smiled as though waiting for her to leave.

'You must come again when we're a little more up to the mark,' added the nurse.

Eventually she went, and we were left alone. Although Sydney tried to cheer Mother up, telling her of his good fortune and the money he had made and his reason for having been away so long, she just sat listening and nodding, looking vague and preoccupied. I told her that she would soon get well. 'Of course,' she said dolefully, 'if only you had given me a cup of tea that afternoon, I would have been all right.'

The doctor told Sydney afterwards that her mind was undoubtedly impaired by malnutrition, and that she required proper medical treatment, and that although she had lucid moments, it would be months before she completely recovered. But for days I was haunted by her remark: 'If only you had given me a cup of tea I would have been all right.'

# *five*

JOSEPH CONRAD wrote to a friend to this effect: that life made him feel like a cornered blind rat waiting to be clubbed. This simile could well describe the appalling circumstances of us all; nevertheless, some of us are struck with good luck, and that is what happened to me.

I had been newsvendor, printer, toy-maker, glass-blower, doctor's boy etc., but during these occupational digressions, like Sydney, I never lost sight of my ultimate aim to become an actor. So between jobs I would polish my shoes, brush my clothes, put on a clean collar and make periodical calls at Blackmore's theatrical agency in Bedford Street off the Strand. I did this until the state of my clothes forbade any further visits.

The first time I went there, the office was adorned with immaculately dressed Thespians of both sexes, standing about talking grandiloquently to each other. With trepidation I stood in a far corner near the door, painfully shy, trying to conceal my weather-worn suit and shoes slightly budding at the toes. From the inner office a young clerk sporadically appeared and like a reaper would cut through the Thespian hauteur with the laconic remark: 'Nothing for you – or you – or you' – and the office would clear like the emptying of a church. On one occasion I was left standing alone! When the clerk saw me he stopped abruptly. 'What do you want?'

I felt like Oliver Twist asking for more. 'Have you any boys' parts?' I gulped.

'Have you registered?'

I shook my head.

To my surprise he ushered me into the adjoining office and took my name and address and all particulars, saying that if anything came up he would let me know. I left with a pleasant sense of having performed a duty, but also rather thankful that nothing had come of it.

And now one month after Sydney's return I received a post-card. It read: 'Would you call at Blackmore's agency, Bedford Street, Strand?'

In my new suit I was ushered into the very presence of Mr Blackmore himself, who was all smiles and amiability. Mr Blackmore, whom I had imagined to be all-mighty and scrutinizing, was most kindly and gave me a note to deliver to Mr C. E. Hamilton at the offices of Charles Frohman.

Mr Hamilton read it and was amused and surprised to see how small I was. Of course I lied about my age, telling him I was four-teen – I was twelve and a half. He explained that I was to play Billie, the page-boy in *Sherlock Holmes*, for a tour of forty weeks which was to start in the autumn.

'In the meantime,' said Mr Hamilton, 'there is an exceptionally good boy's part in a new play *Jim, the Romance of a Cockney*, written by Mr H. A. Saintsbury, the gentleman who is to play the title role in *Sherlock Holmes* on the forthcoming tour.' *Jim* would be produced in Kingston for a trial engagement, prior to the tour of *Holmes*. The salary was two pounds ten shillings a week, the same as I would get for *Sherlock Holmes*.

Although the sum was a windfall I never batted an eye. 'I must consult my brother about the terms,' I said solemnly.

Mr Hamilton laughed and seemed highly amused, then brought out the whole office staff to have a look at me. 'This is our Billie! What do you think of him?'

Everyone was delighted and smiled beamingly at me. What had happened? It seemed the world had suddenly changed, had taken me into its fond embrace and adopted me. Then Mr Hamilton gave me a note to Mr Saintsbury, whom he said I would find at the Green Room Club in Leicester Square, and I left, walking on clouds.

The same thing happened at the Green Room Club, Mr Saints-bury calling out other members to have a look at me. Then and there he handed me the part of Sammy, saying that it was one of the important characters in his play. I was a little nervous for fear he might ask me to read it on the spot, which would have been embarrassing as I was almost unable to read; fortunately he told me to take it home and read it at leisure, as they would not be starting rehearsals for another week.

I went home on the bus dazed with happiness and began to get the full realization of what had happened to me. I had suddenly left behind a life of poverty and was entering a long-desired dream – a dream my mother had often spoken about, had revelled in. I was to become an actor! It had all come so suddenly, so unexpectedly. I kept thumbing the pages of my part – it had a new brown paper cover – the most important document I have ever held in my life. During the ride on the bus I realized I had crossed an important threshold. No longer was I a nondescript of the slums; now I was a personage of the theatre, I wanted to weep.

Sydney's eyes were filmy when I told him what had happened. He sat crouched on the bed, thoughtfully looking out of the window, shaking and nodding his head; then said gravely: 'This is the turning point of our lives. If only Mother was here to enjoy it with us.'

'Think of it,' I continued, enthusiastically. 'Forty weeks at two pounds ten. I told Mr Hamilton you attended to all business matters, so,' I added eagerly, 'we might even get more. Anyway, we can save sixty pounds this year!'

After our enthusiasm had simmered down we reasoned that two pounds ten was hardly enough for such a big part. Sydney went to see if he could raise the ante – 'there's no harm in trying,' I said – but Mr Hamilton was adamant. 'Two pounds ten is the maximum,' he said – and we were happy to get it.

Sydney read the part to me and helped me to memorize the lines. It was a big part, about thirty-five sides, but I knew it all by heart in three days.

The rehearsals of *Jim* took place in the upstairs foyer of the Drury Lane Theatre. Sydney had so zealously coached me that I was almost word-perfect. Only one word bothered me. The line was: 'Who do you think you are – Mr Pierpont Morgan?' and I would say: 'Putterpint Morgan'. Mr Saintsbury made me keep it in. Those first rehearsals were a revelation. They opened up a new world of technique. I had no idea that there was such a thing as stage-craft, timing, pausing, a cue to turn, to sit, but it came naturally to me. Only one fault Mr Saintsbury corrected: I moved my head and 'mugged' too much when I talked.

After rehearsing a few scenes he was astonished and wanted to know if I had acted before. What a glow of satisfaction, pleasing Mr Saintsbury and the rest of the cast! However, I accepted their enthusiasm as though it were my natural birthright.

*Jim* was to be a try-out for one week at the Kingston Theatre and for another week at the Fulham. It was a melodrama patterned on Henry Arthur Jones's *Silver King*: the story of an aristocrat suffering from amnesia, who finds himself living in a garret with a young flower-girl and a newspaper boy, Sammy – my part. Morally, it was all on the up and up: the girl slept in the cupboard of the garret, while the Duke, as we called him, enjoyed the couch, and I slept on the floor.

The first act was at No. 7A Devereux Court, the Temple, the chambers of James Seaton Gatlock, a wealthy lawyer. The tattered Duke, having called on his rival of a past love affair, begs for alms to help his sick benefactor, the flower-girl who had supported him during his amnesia.

In an altercation, the villain says to the Duke: 'Get out! Go and starve, you and your coster mistress!'

The Duke, though frail and weak, picks up a paper-knife from the desk as if to strike the villain, but it drops from his hands on to the desk as he is stricken with epilepsy, falling unconscious at the villain's feet. At this juncture, the villain's ex-wife, with whom the tattered Duke was once in love, enters the room. She also pleads for the tattered Duke, saying: 'He failed with me; he failed at the Bar! At least you can help him!'

But the villain refuses. The scene rises to a climax, in which he accuses his ex-wife of infidelity with the derelict and denounces her also. In a frenzy she picks up the paper-knife that fell from the derelict's hand and stabs the villain, who falls dead in his armchair, while the derelict still lies unconscious at his feet. The woman disappears from the scene, and the Duke, regaining consciousness, discovers his rival dead. 'God, what have I done?' says he.

Then business follows. He searches the dead man's pockets, finds a wallet in which he fingers several pounds, a diamond ring and jewellery, all of which he takes, and as he leaves by the win-

dow he turns, saying: 'Goodbye, Gatlock; you did help me, after
all.' Curtain.

The next act was the garret in which the Duke lived. The scene
opened with a lone detective looking into a cupboard. I enter
whistling, then stop, seeing the detective.

NEWSBOY: Oi, you. Do you know that's a lady's bedroom?

DETECTIVE: What! That cupboard? Come here!

BOY: The cool cheek of him!

DETECTIVE: You stow that. Come in and shut the door.

BOY [*walking towards him*]: Polite, ain't you, inviting blokes into
their own drawing-room?

DETECTIVE: I'm a detective.

BOY: What, a cop? I'm off!

DETECTIVE: I'm not going to hurt you. All I want is a little information that will help to do someone a good turn.

BOY: A good turn indeed! If a bit of luck comes to anyone here,
it won't be through the cops!

DETECTIVE: Don't be a fool. Would I have started by telling you
I was in the Force?

BOY: Thanks for nothing. I can see your boots.

DETECTIVE: Who lives here?

BOY: The Duke.

DETECTIVE: Yes, but what's his real name?

BOY: I don't know. The Duke is a 'nom de guerre' as he calls it,
though blow me if I know what it means.

DETECTIVE: And what does he look like?

BOY: As thin as a lath. Grey hair, clean shaven, wears a top hat
and an eye-glass. And blimey, the way he looks at you through
it!

DETECTIVE: And Jim – who's he?

BOY: He? You mean she!

DETECTIVE: Ah, then she's the lady who –

BOY [*interrupting*]: Who sleeps in the cupboard – this here room's
ours, mine and the Duke's, etc. etc.

There was much more to the part, and, believe it or not, it was
highly amusing to the audience, due, I think, to my looking much
younger than I was. Every line I spoke got a laugh. Only mechanics bothered me: the business of making real tea on the stage. I
would get confused about whether to put the tea in the pot first or

the hot water. Paradoxically enough, it was easier for me to talk lines than to carry out stage business.

*Jim* was not a success. The reviewers panned the play unmercifully. Nevertheless, I received favourable notices. One, which Mr Charles Rock, a member of our company, showed me, was exceptionally good. He was an old Adelphi actor of considerable reputation, and I played most of my scenes with him. 'Young man,' said he solemnly, 'don't get a swollen head when you read this.' And after lecturing me about modesty and graciousness he read the review of the *London Topical Times*, which I remember word for word. After writing disparagingly of the play it continued: 'But there is one redeeming feature, the part of Sammy, a newspaper boy, a smart London street Arab, much responsible for the comic part. Although hackneyed and old-fashioned, Sammy was made vastly amusing by Master Charles Chaplin, a bright and vigorous child actor. I have never heard of the boy before, but I hope to hear great things of him in the near future.' Sydney bought a dozen copies.

After completing the two week's run of *Jim*, we started rehearsals for *Sherlock Holmes*. During this time Sydney and I were still living at Pownall Terrace, because economically we were not too sure of our footing.

During rehearsals Sydney and I went to Cane Hill to see Mother. At first the nurses told us that she could not be seen as she was not well that day. They took Sydney aside out of my hearing, but I heard him say: 'No, I don't think he would.' Then turning to me sadly: 'You don't want to see Mother in a padded room?'

'No, no! I couldn't bear it!' I said, recoiling.

But Sidney saw her, and Mother recognized him and became rational. A few minutes later a nurse told me that Mother was well enough, if I wished to see her, and we sat together in her padded room. Before leaving she took me aside and whispered forlornly: 'Don't lose your way, because they might keep you here.' She remained eighteen months at Cane Hill before regaining her health. But Sydney saw her regularly while I was on tour.

\*

Mr H. A. Saintsbury, who played Holmes on tour, was a living replica of the illustrations in the *Strand Magazine*. He had a long, sensitive face and an inspired forehead. Of all those who played Holmes he was considered the best, even better than William Gillette, the original Holmes and author of the play.

On my first tour, the management decided that I should live with Mr and Mrs Green, the carpenter of the company, and his wife, the wardrobe lady. This was not very glamorous. Besides, Mr and Mrs Green drank occasionally. Moreover, I did not always want to eat when they did, or eat what they ate. I am sure my living with the Greens was more irksome to them than to me. So after three weeks we mutually agreed to part, and being too young to live with other members of the cast, I lived alone. I was alone in strange towns, alone in back rooms, rarely meeting anyone until the evening performance, only hearing my own voice when I talked to myself. Occasionally, I would go to the saloons where members of the company gathered, and watch them play billiards; but I always felt that my presence cramped their conversation, and they were quite obvious in making me feel so. I could not smile at their levity without being frowned upon.

I began to grow melancholy. Arriving in northern towns on a Sunday night, hearing the doleful clanging of church bells as I walked the darkened main street, added little comfort to my loneliness. On week-day I would scan the local markets and do my shopping, buying groceries and meat for the landlady to cook. Sometimes I would get board and lodging, and eat in the kitchen with the family. I liked this, for north-country kitchens were clean and wholesome, with polished fire-grates and blue hearths. When the landlady baked bread, it was cheerful to come out of a cold dark day into the red glow of a Lancashire kitchen fire, and see tins of unbaked loaves around the hearth, and sit down to tea with the family – the taste of hot bread just out of the oven with fresh butter was relished with grave solemnity.

I had been in the provinces for six months. Meanwhile Sydney had had little success in getting a job in the theatre, so he was obliged to descend from his Thespian ambition and apply for a job as a bartender at the Coal Hole in the Strand. Out of one hundred and fifty applicants he got the job. But he had fallen ignominiously from his own graces, as it were.

He wrote to me regularly and kept me posted about Mother,

but I seldom answered his letters; for one reason, I could not spell very well. One letter touched me deeply and drew me very close to him; he reproached me for not answering his letters and recalled the misery we had endured together which should unite us even closer. 'Since Mother's illness,' wrote Sydney, 'all we have in the world is each other. So you must write regularly and let me know that I have a brother.' His letter was so moving that I replied immediately. Now I saw Sydney in another light. His letter cemented a brotherly love that has lasted throughout my life.

I got accustomed to living alone. But I got so much out of the habit of talking that when I suddenly met a member of the company I suffered intense embarrassment. I could not collect myself quickly enough to answer questions intelligently and they would leave me, I am sure, with alarm and concern for my reason. Miss Greta Hahn, for instance, our leading lady, was beautiful, charming and most kindly; yet when I saw her crossing the road to-towards me, I would quickly turn and look into a shop window or go down another street in order to avoid her.

I began to neglect myself and became desultory in my habits. When travelling with the company, I was always late at the rail-way station, arriving at the last moment, dishevelled and without a collar, and was continually reprimanded for it.

For company, I bought a rabbit and wherever I stayed I would smuggle it into my room unknown to the landlady. It was an endearing little thing, though not house-broken. Its fur looked so white and clean that it belied its pungent odour. I kept it in a wooden cage hidden under the bed. The landlady would cheerfully enter the room with my breakfast, until she contacted the odour, then she would leave, looking worried and confused. The moment she was gone I would release the rabbit and it would lope about the room.

Before long I had it trained to run to its box every time there was a knock at the door. If the landlady discovered my secret I would have the rabbit perform this trick, which usually won her heart, and she would put up with us for the week.

But in Tonypandy, Wales, after I showed my trick, the land-lady smiled cryptically and made no comment; but when I returned from the theatre that night my pet had gone. When I inquired about it, the landlady merely shook her head. 'It must have run away or someone must have stolen it.' She had in her own way handled the problem efficaciously.

From Tonypandy we went to the mining town of Ebbw Vale, a three-night stand, and I was thankful it was not longer, for Ebbw Vale was a dank, ugly town in those days, with row upon row of hideous, uniform houses, each house consisting of four small rooms lit by oil-lamps. Most of the company put up at a small hotel. Fortunately I found a front room in a miner's house, and, though small, it was comfortable and clean. At night after the play my supper was left in front of the fire to keep warm.

The landlady, a tall, handsome, middle-aged woman, had an aura of tragedy about her. She came in, in the morning, with my breakfast and hardly spoke a word. I noticed that the kitchen door was always shut; whenever I wanted anything I had to knock, and the door opened only a few inches.

The second night, while I was having my supper, her husband came in, a man about the same age as his wife. He had been to the theatre that evening and had enjoyed the play. He stood a while conversing, holding a lighted candle, ready for bed. He came to a pause and seemed to think of what he wanted to say. 'Listen, I've got something that might fit your kind of business. Ever seen a human frog? Here, hold the candle and I'll take the lamp.'

He led the way into the kitchen and rested the lamp on the dresser, which had a curtain strung across the bottom of it in place of cupboard doors. 'Hey, Gilbert, come on out of there!' he said, parting the curtains.

A half a man with no legs, an oversized, blond, flat-shaped head, a sickening white face, a sunken nose, a large mouth and powerful muscular shoulders and arms, crawled from underneath the dresser. He wore flannel underwear with the legs of the garment cut off to the thighs, from which ten thick, stubby toes stuck out. The grisly creature could have been twenty or forty. He looked up and grinned, showing a set of yellow, widely spaced teeth.

'Hey, Gilbert, jump!' said the father and the wretched man lowered himself slowly, then shot up by his arms almost to the height of my head.

'How do you think he'd fit in with a circus? The human frog!'

I was so horrified I could hardly answer. However, I suggested the names of several circuses that he might write to.

He insisted on the wretched creature going through further tricks, hopping, climbing and standing on his hands on the arms of a rocking chair. When at last he had finished I pretended to be most enthusiastic and complimented him on his tricks.

'Good night, Gilbert,' I said before leaving, and in a hollow voice, and tongue-tied, the poor fellow answered: 'Good night.'

Several times during the night I woke up and tried my locked door. The next morning the landlady seemed pleasant and communicative. 'I understand you saw Gilbert last night,' she said. 'Of course, he only sleeps under the dresser when we take in people from the theatre.'

Then the awful thought came to me that I had been sleeping in Gilbert's bed. 'Yes,' I answered, and talked with measured enthusiasm of the possibilities of his joining a circus.

She nodded. 'We have often thought of it.'

My enthusiasm – or whatever it was – seemed to please the landlady, and before leaving I went into the kitchen to say good-bye to Gilbert. With an effort to be casual I shook his large calloused hand, and he gently shook mine.

\*

After forty weeks in the provinces, we returned to play eight weeks around the suburbs of London. *Sherlock Holmes*, being a phenomenal success, was to start a second tour, three weeks after the finish of the first one.

Now Sydney and I decided to give up our quarters in Pownall Terrace and take up more respectable ones in the Kennington Road; like snakes we wanted to slough our skins, shedding every vestige of the past.

I spoke to the management about Sydney for a small part in the next tour of *Holmes*, and he got it – thirty-five shillings a week! Now we were on tour together.

Sydney wrote to Mother every week and towards the end of our second tour we received a letter from Cane Hill asylum stating that she had fully recovered her health. This was indeed good news. Quickly we made arrangements for her discharge, and made preparations for her to join us in Reading. To celebrate the occasion we took a special apartment de luxe, consisting of two bedrooms and a sitting-room with a piano, fixed up her bed-room with flowers, and arranged an elaborate dinner to boot.

Sydney and I waited for her at the railroad station, tense and happy, yet I could not help feeling anxious as to how she would fit into our lives again, knowing that the close ties of other days could never be recaptured.

At last the train arrived. With excitement and uncertainty we scanned the faces of the passengers as they left the carriages. Then at last there she was, smiling and walking sedately toward us. She displayed no great emotion as we went to meet her, but greeted us with affectionate decorum. She evidently was also undergoing an adjustment.

In that short ride in a cab to our rooms, we talked of a hundred different things, relevant and irrelevant.

After the first flush of enthusiasm of showing her the apart-ment and the flowers in the bedroom, we found ourselves in the sitting-room looking breathlessly at each other. It was a sunny day, and our apartment was on a quiet street, but now the silence of it was uncomfortable and in spite of my wanting to be happy I found myself fighting back a depression. Poor Mother, who wanted so little out of life to make her gay and cheerful, reminded me of my unhappy past – the last person in the world who should have affected me this way. But I did my best to hide the fact. She had aged a little and gained weight. I had always been proud of the way Mother looked and dressed and wanted to show her off to the company at her best, but now she appeared rather dowdy. She must have sensed my misgivings, for she turned inquiringly.

Coyly I adjusted a strand of her hair. 'Before you meet the company,' I smiled, 'I want you to be at your best.'

She looked at me, then took out her powder-puff and rubbed it over her face. 'I'm just happy to be alive,' she said cheerfully.

It was not long before we were fully adjusted to one another and my dejection passed. That we had outgrown the intimacy she had known when we were children, she understood better than we did, which made her all the more endearing to us. On tour she did the shopping and catering, bringing home fruits and delicacies and always a few flowers. For no matter how poor we had been in the past, when shopping on Saturday nights she had always been able to buy a pennyworth of wallflowers. Occasionally she was quiet and reserved, and her detachment saddened me. She acted more like a guest than our mother.

After a month she wanted to return to London, because she was anxious to get settled down so that she would have a home for us after our tour; besides, as she said, it would be less costly than travelling over the country and having to pay an extra fare.

She rented the flat over the barber's shop in Chester Street where we had once lived, and with ten pounds bought furniture on the instalment plan. The rooms had not the spaciousness of Versailles, or its elegance; but she did wonders in the bedrooms by covering orange-crates with cretonne to make them look like commodes. Between us Sydney and I were earning four pounds five shillings a week and sending one pound five shillings of it to Mother.

Sydney and I returned home after our second tour and spent a few weeks with her. Although we were happy to be with Mother, we were secretly glad to get away on tour again, for Chester Street had not the requisite comforts that provincial apartments had – those little amenities to which Sydney and I were now accustomed. And Mother no doubt realized this. When she saw us off at the station she seemed cheerful enough, but we both thought she looked wistful as she stood on the platform smiling and waving her handkerchief as the train pulled away.

During our third tour Mother wrote to us that Louise, with whom Sydney and I had lived in the Kennington Road, had died, ironically enough, in the Lambeth workhouse, the same place in which we had been confined. She survived Father only by four years, leaving her little son an orphan, and he also had been sent to the same Hanwell Schools that Sydney and I had been sent to.

Mother wrote that she had visited the boy, explaining who she was, and that Sydney and I had lived with him and his father and mother in the Kennington Road. But he hardly remembered, as he had been only four years old at the time. He also had no recollection of his father. And now he was ten. He was registered under Louise's maiden name, and as far as Mother could find out he had no relatives. She described him as being a handsome boy, very quiet, shy and preoccupied. She brought him a bag of sweets and some oranges and apples and promised to visit him regularly, which I believe she did, until she herself became ill again and was sent back to Cane Hill.

The news of Mother's relapse came like a stab in the heart. We never knew the details. We received only a curt official notice that she had been found wandering and incoherent in the streets. There was nothing we could do but accept poor Mother's fate. She never again recovered her mind completely. For several years she languished in Cane Hill asylum until we could afford to put her into a private one.

Sometimes the gods of adversity tire of their sport and show mercy, as they did with Mother. For the last seven years of her life she was to live in comfort, surrounded by flowers and sunshine, to see her grown sons endowed with fame and fortune beyond anything she had ever imagined.

*

Because of our tour with *Sherlock Holmes* it was many weeks before Sydney and I could again see Mother. The tour with the Frohman company ended permanently. Then Mr Harry York, proprietor of the Theatre Royal, Blackburn, bought the rights of *Holmes* from Frohman to play the smaller towns. Sydney and I were engaged by the new company, but at reduced salaries of thirty-five shillings each.

It was a depressing come-down, playing the small towns of the North with an inferior company. Nevertheless, it enlivened my discrimination, comparing the company with the one we had just left. This comparison I tried to conceal, but at rehearsals in my zeal to help the new director, who would ask me about stage directions, cues and business etc., I would eagerly tell him how it was done in the Frohman company. This, of course, did not make me particularly popular with the cast and I was looked upon as a precocious brat. Later, a new stage manager had it in for me and fined me ten shillings for having a button missing from my uniform, about which he had warned me several times.

William Gillette, author of *Sherlock Holmes*, came to London with Marie Doro in a play called *Clarissa* which he had written. The critics were unkind to the play and to the manner of Gillette's speech, which led him to write a curtain-raiser, *The Painful Predicament of Sherlock Holmes*, in which he himself never spoke a

88

word. There were only three in the cast, a mad-woman, Holmes and his page-boy. It was like tidings from heaven to receive a telegram from Mr Postance, Gillette's manager, asking me if I were available to come to London to play the part of Billie with William Gillette in the curtain-raiser.

I trembled with anxiety, for it was doubtful if our company could replace Billie in the provinces on such short notice, and for several days I was left in agonizing suspense. However, they did find another Billie.

Returning to London to play in a West End theatre I can only describe as my renaissance. My brain was spinning with the thrill of every incident – arriving in the evening at the Duke of York's Theatre and meeting Mr Postance, the stage-manager, who brought me to Mr Gillette's dressing-room, and his words after I was introduced to him: 'Would you like to play in *Sherlock Holmes* with me?' And my burst of nervous enthusiasm: 'Oh very much, Mr Gillette!' And the next morning, waiting on the stage for rehearsals, and seeing Marie Doro for the first time, dressed in the loveliest white summer dress. The sudden shock of seeing someone so beautiful at that hour! She had been riding in a hansom cab and had discovered an ink spot on her dress, and wanted to know if the property man had anything that would take it out, and to his answer of doubt she made the prettiest expression of irritation: 'Oh, isn't that too beastly!'

She was so devastatingly beautiful that I resented her. I resented her delicate, pouting lips, her regular white teeth, her adorable chin, her raven hair and dark brown eyes. I resented her pretence of irritation and the charm she exuded through it. Through all this querying between herself and the property man she was ignorant of my presence, although I stood quite near, staring, transfixed by her beauty. I had just turned sixteen, and the propinquity of this sudden radiance evoked my determination not to be obsessed by it. But, oh God, she was beautiful! It was love at first sight.

In *The Painful Predicament of Sherlock Holmes* Miss Irene Vanbrugh, a remarkably gifted actress, played the madwoman and did all the talking, while Holmes just sat and listened. This was his joke on the critics. I had the opening lines, bursting into Holmes's apartment and holding on to the doors while the mad-woman beats against them outside, and then, while I excitedly try to explain to Holmes the situation, the mad woman bursts in! For twenty minutes she never stops raving incoherently about some case she wants him to solve. Surreptitiously Holmes writes a note, rings a bell and slips it to me. Later two stalwart men lead the lady off, leaving Holmes and me alone, with me saying: 'You were right, sir; it was the right asylum.'

The critics enjoyed the joke, but the play *Clarissa*, which Gillette wrote for Marie Doro, was a failure. Although they raved about Marie's beauty, they said it was not enough to hold a maudlin play together, so he completed the rest of his season with the revival of *Sherlock Holmes*, in which I was retained for the part of Billie.

In my excitement to play with the famous William Gillette, I had forgotten to ask about terms. At the end of the week Mr Postance came apologetically with my pay envelope. 'I'm really ashamed to give you this,' he said, 'but at the Frohman office they said I was to pay you the same as you were getting with us before: two pounds ten.' I was agreeably surprised.

At rehearsals of *Holmes*, I met Marie Doro again – more beautiful than ever! – and in spite of my resolutions not to be overwhelmed by her, I began to sink further into the hopeless mire of silent love. I hated this weakness and was furious with myself for lack of character. It was an ambivalent affair. I both hated and loved her. What's more, she was charming and gracious to boot.

In *Holmes* she played Alice Faulkner, but in the play we never met. I would wait, however, timing the moment when I could pass her on the stairs and gulp 'Good evening', and she would answer cheerfully 'Good evening'. And that was all that ever passed between us.

*Holmes* was an immediate success. During the engagement Queen Alexandra saw the play; sitting with her in the Royal Box were the King of Greece and Prince Christian. The Prince was evidently explaining the play to the King and during the most tense and silent moment, when Holmes and I were alone on the stage, a booming voice with an accent resounded throughout the theatre: 'Don't tell me! Don't tell me!'

Dion Boucicault had his offices in the Duke of York's Theatre, and in passing he would give me an approving little tap on the head; as did Hall Caine, who frequently came back stage to see Gillette. On one occasion I also received a smile from Lord Kitchener.

During the run of *Sherlock Holmes*, Sir Henry Irving died and I attended the funeral at Westminster Abbey. Being a West End actor, I was given a special pass and I felt very proud of the fact. At the funeral, I sat between the solemn Lewis Waller, then the romantic matinée idol of London, and 'Dr' Walford Bodie of bloodless surgery fame, whom I later burlesqued in a vaudeville skit. Waller looked handsomely profiled for the occasion, sitting stiffly, looking neither right nor left. But 'Dr' Bodie, in order to get a better view as they lowered Sir Henry into the crypt, kept stepping on the chest of a supine duke, much to the indignation and contempt of Mr Waller. I gave up trying to see anything and sat down, resigned to viewing the backsides of those in front of me.

Two weeks before the ending of *Sherlock Holmes*, Mr Boucicault gave me a letter of introduction to the illustrious Mr and Mrs Kendal, with the prospects of getting a part in their new play. They were terminating a successful run at the St James's Theatre. The appointment was for ten a.m., to meet the lady in the foyer of the theatre. She was twenty minutes late. Eventually, a silhouette appeared off the street: it was Mrs Kendal, a stalwart imperious lady, who greeted me with: 'Oh, so you're the boy! We are shortly to begin a tour of the provinces in a new play, and I'd like to hear you read for the part. But at the moment we are very busy. So will you be here tomorrow morning at the same time?'

'I'm sorry, madam,' I replied coldly, 'but I cannot accept anything out of town.' And with that I raised my hat, walked out of the foyer, hailed a passing cab – and was out of work for ten months.

The night *Sherlock Holmes* ended its run at the Duke of York's Theatre and Marie Doro was to return to America, I went off alone and got desperately drunk. Two or three years later in Philadelphia, I saw her again. She dedicated the opening of a new theatre in which I was playing in Karno's comedy company. She was still as beautiful as ever. I stood in the wings watching her in my comedy make-up while she made a speech, but I was too shy to make myself known to her.

At the closing of *Holmes* in London the company in the provinces also ended, so both Sydney and I were out of work. But Sydney lost no time in getting another job. As a result of seeing an advertisement in the *Era*, a theatrical paper, he joined Charlie Manon's troupe of knockabout comedians. In those days there were several of these troupes touring the halls: Charlie Baldwin's Bank Clerks, Joe Boganny's Lunatic Bakers, and the Boicette troupe, all of them pantomimists. And although they played slapstick comedy, it was performed to beautiful music *à la ballet* and was most popular. The outstanding company was Fred Karno's, who had a large repertoire of comedies. Each one was called 'Birds'. There were *Jail Birds*, *Early Birds*, *Mumming Birds*, etc. From these three sketches Karno built a theatrical enterprise of more than thirty companies, whose repertoire included Christmas pantomimes and elaborate musical comedies, from which he developed such fine artists and comedians as Fred Kitchen, George Graves, Harry Weldon, Billie Reeves, Charlie Bell and many others.

It was while Sydney was working with the Manon troupe that Fred Karno saw him and signed him up at a salary of four pounds a week. Being four years younger than Sydney, I was neither fish nor fowl for any form of theatrical work, but I had saved a little money from the London engagement and while Sydney was working in the provinces I stayed in London and played around pool-rooms.

# *six*

I HAD arrived at that difficult and unattractive age of adolescence, conforming to the teenage emotional pattern. I was a worshipper of the foolhardy and the melodramatic, a dreamer and a moper, raging at life and loving it, a mind in a chrysalis yet erupting with sudden bursts of maturity. In this labyrinth of distorting mirrors I dallied, my ambition going in spurts. The word 'art' never entered my head or my vocabulary. The theatre meant a livelihood and nothing more.

Through this haze and confusion I lived alone. Whores, sluts and an occasional drinking bout weaved in and out of this period, but neither wine, women nor song held my interest for long. I really wanted romance and adventure.

I can well understand the psychological attitude of the teddy boy with his Edwardian dress; like all of us he wants attention, romance and drama in his life. Why should he not indulge in moments of exhibitionism and horseplay, as does the public-school boy with his gadding and ragging? Is it not natural that when he sees the so-called better classes asserting their foppery he wants to assert his own?

He knows that the machine obeys his will as it does the will of any class; that it requires no special mentality to shift a gear or press a button. In this insensate age is he not as formidable as any Lancelot, aristocrat or scholar, his finger as powerful in destroying a city as any Napoleonic army? Is not the teddy boy a phoenix rising from the ashes of a delinquent ruling class, his attitude perhaps motivated by a subconscious feeling: that man is only a half-tame animal who has for generations governed others by deceit, cruelty and violence? But, as Bernard Shaw said: 'I am digressing as a man with a grievance always does.'

93

I eventually obtained work with a vaudeville sketch, Casey's Circus, doing a burlesque on Dick Turpin, the highwayman, and 'Dr' Walford Bodie. With 'Dr' Bodie I had a modicum of success, for it was more than just low comedy; it was a characterization of a professorial, scholarly man, and I conceived the happy idea of making up to look exactly like him I was the star of the company, and earned three pounds a week. It included a troupe of kids playing at grown-ups in an alley scene; it was an awful show, I thought, but it gave me a chance to develop as a comedian.

When Casey's Circus played in London, six of us boarded in the Kennington Road with Mrs Fields, an old widowed lady of sixty-five, who had three daughters: Frederica, Thelma and Phoebe. Frederica was married to a Russian cabinet-maker, a gentle but an extremely ugly man, with a broad Tartar face, blond hair, blond moustache and a cast in his eye. The six of us ate in the kitchen, and we got to know the family very well. Sydney when working in London also lived there.

When eventually I left Casey's Circus, I returned to Kennington Road and continued to board with the Fields. The old lady was kindly, patient and hard-working and her sole income came from renting rooms. Frederica, the married daughter, was supported by her husband. Thelma and Phoebe helped with the housework. Phoebe was fifteen and beautiful. Her features were long and aquiline, and she had a strong appeal for me both physically and sentimentally; the latter I resisted because I was not quite seventeen and had only the worst of intentions about girls. But she was saintly and nothing ever came of it. She grew fond of me, however, and we became very good friends.

The Fields were an intensely emotional family and would occasionally break out into passionate quarrelling with each other. The basis of contention was usually whose turn it was to do the housework. Thelma, who was about twenty, was the lady of the family and the lazy one, and always claimed that it was Frederica's or Phoebe's turn. This would develop from an argument into a brawl, in which buried grievances and family skeletons were hewed up and cast about for all to view, Mrs Fields revealing the fact that since Thelma had run off and lived with a young Liverpool lawyer she thought she was a lady and that she was too good to do housework, climaxing her tirade by saying: 'Well, if you're such a lady, clear out and go back and live with your Liverpool lawyer – only he won't have you.' And for final emphasis Mrs Field would pick up a teacup and smash it on the floor. During this Thelma would sit at the table, ladylike and unperturbed. Then calmly she would take a cup and do likewise, lightly dropping it on the floor, saying: 'I too, can lose my temper,' dropping another cup, then another, then another and another until the floor was strewn with broken crockery. 'I, too, can make a scene.' And the poor mother and the sisters would look on helplessly. 'Look at her! Look what she's doing!' moaned the mother. 'Here! Here's something else you can smash,' handing Thelma the sugarbowl, and Thelma would take it and calmly drop it.

On these occasions Phoebe was the arbitrator. She was fair and just and had the respect of the family, and she would usually end the argument by offering to do the work herself, which Thelma would not allow her to do.

I had been out of work for almost three months and Sydney had been supporting me, paying Mrs Fields fourteen shillings a week for my board and lodgings. He was now a leading comedian with Fred Karno, and had often spoken to Karno about his talented young brother, but Karno turned a deaf ear, because he thought I was too young.

At the time Jewish comedians were all the rage in London, so I thought I would hide my youth under whiskers. Sydney gave me two pounds, which I invested in musical arrangements for songs and funny dialogue taken from an American joke-book, *Madison's Budget*. For weeks I practised, performing in front of the Fields family. They were attentive and encouraging but nothing more.

I had obtained a trial week without pay at the Forester's Music Hall, which was a small theatre situated off the Mile End Road in the centre of the Jewish quarter. I had played there previously with Casey's Circus and the management thought I was good enough to be given a chance. My future hopes and dreams depended on that trial week. After the Foresters' I would play all the important circuits in England. Who knows? Within a year I might rise to be one of vaudeville's biggest headliners. I had promised the whole Fields family that I would get them tickets towards the end of the week, when I was thoroughly at home with my act.

'I suppose you won't want to live with us after your success,' said Phoebe.

'Of course I will,' I said graciously.

Twelve o'clock Monday morning was band rehearsal for songs and cues etc., which I carried out professionally. But I had not given sufficient thought to my make-up. I was undecided how I should look. For hours before the night show I was in the dressing-room experimenting, but no matter how much crêpe hair I used I could not hide my youth. Although I was innocent of it, my comedy was most anti-Semitic, and my jokes were not only old ones but very poor, like my Jewish accent. Moreover, I was not funny.

After the first couple of jokes the audience started throwing coins and orange-peel and stamping their feet and booing. At first I was not conscious of what was going on. Then the horror of it filtered into my mind. I began to hurry and talk faster as the jeers, the raspberries, and the throwing of coins and orange-peel increased. When I came off the stage, I did not wait to hear the verdict from the management; I went straight to the dressing-room, took off my make-up, left the theatre and never returned, not even to collect my music books.

It was late when I returned home to Kennington Road and the Field family had all gone to bed, and I was thankful they had. In the morning at breakfast Mrs Fields was anxious to know how the show went. I bluffed indifference and said: 'All right, but it needs a few alterations.' She said that Phoebe had gone to see me, but had told them nothing, as she was too tired and wanted to get to bed. When I saw Phoebe later she did not mention it, neither did I; nor did Mrs Fields or any of the family ever mention it again, or show any surprise at my not continuing the week.

Thank God Sydney was in the provinces, so I had not the painful ordeal of telling him what had happened – but he must have guessed, or the Fields might have told him, because he never did inquire about it. I did my best to erase that night's horror from my mind, but it left an indelible mark on my confidence. That ghastly experience taught me to see myself in a truer light; I realized I was not a vaudeville comedian, I had not that intimate, come-hither faculty with an audience; and I consoled myself with being a character comedian. However, I was to have one or two more disappointments before landing on my professional feet.

At seventeen I played a juvenile lead in a sketch called *The Merry Major*, a cheap, depressing affair lasting only a week. The leading lady, my wife, was a woman of fifty. Each night she reeled on to the stage smelling of gin, and I, the enthusiastic loving husband, would have to take her in my arms and kiss her. That experience weaned me away from any ambition to be a leading man.

Then I tried authorship. I wrote a comedy sketch called *Twelve Just Men*, a slapstick affair about a jury arguing a case of breach of promise. One of the jury was a deaf-mute, another a drunk and another a quack doctor. I sold the idea to Charcoate, a vaudeville hypnotist who would hypnotize a stooge and make him drive through the town in a landau, blindfold, while he sat in the back throwing magnetic impulses at him. He gave me three pounds for my script, providing I directed it. We engaged a cast and rehearsed over the Horns public house clubrooms in the Kennington Road. One disgruntled old actor said that the sketch was not only illiterate but silly.

The third day, in the middle of rehearsals, I received a note from Charcoate to say he had decided not to produce it. Not being the valiant type, I put the note in my pocket and went on rehearsing. I had not the courage to tell the cast. Instead, at lunch-time, I took them home to our rooms and told them my brother wished to talk to them. I took Sydney into the bedroom and showed him the note. After reading it he said: 'Well, didn't you tell them?'

'No,' I whispered.

'Well, tell them.'

'I can't,' I said. 'I just can't, after their having rehearsed three days for nothing.'

'But that's not your fault,' said Sydney. 'Go and tell them,' he shouted.

I lost courage and began to weep. 'What can I say?'

'Don't be a fool!' He got up and went into the next room and showed them Charcoate's letter, explaining what had happened,

97

then he took us all to the corner pub for a sandwich and a drink.

Actors are unpredictable. The old chap who had grumbled so much was the most philosophical, and laughed when Sydney told him of the awful state I was in. 'It's not your fault, sonny,' he said, patting me on the back. 'It's that bloody old scoundrel, Charcoate.'

*

After my failure at the Foresters', everything I attempted met with disaster. However, a most formidable element in optimism is youth, for it instinctively feels that adversity is *pro tem* and that a continual run of ill luck is just as implausible as the straight and narrow path of righteousness. Both eventually must deviate.

My luck changed. One day Sydney told me that Mr Karno wanted to see me. It appears he was dissatisfied with one of the comedians playing opposite Mr Harry Weldon in *The Football Match*, one of Karno's most successful sketches. Weldon was a very popular comedian who remained popular up to the time of his death in the thirties.

Mr Karno was a thick-set, bronzed little man, with keen sparkling eyes that were always appraising. He had started as an acrobat on the horizontal bars, then got together three knock-about comedians. This quartette was the nucleus of his comedy pantomime sketches. He himself was an excellent comedian and originated many comedy roles. He continued playing even when he had five other companies on the road.

One of the original members tells the story of his retirement. One night in Manchester, after a performance, the troupe complained that Karno's timing was off and that he had ruined the laughs. Karno, who had then accumulated £50,000 from his five shows, said: 'Well, boys, if that's the way you feel, I'll quit!' then, taking off his wig, he dropped it on the dressing-table and grinned. 'You can accept that as my resignation.'

Mr Karno's home was in Coldharbour Lane, Camberwell; annexed to it was a warehouse in which he stored the scenery for his twenty productions. He also maintained his offices there. When I arrived he received me kindly. 'Sydney's been telling me how good you are,' he said. 'Do you think you could play opposite Harry Weldon in *The Football Match*?'

Harry Weldon was specially engaged at a high salary, getting thirty-four pounds a week.

'All I need is the opportunity,' I said confidently.

He smiled. 'Seventeen's very young, and you look even younger.'

I shrugged off-handedly. 'That's a question of make-up.'

Karno laughed. That shrug, he told Sydney later, got me the job.

'Well, well, we'll see what you can do,' he said.

It was to be a trial engagement of two weeks at three pounds ten a week, and if I proved satisfactory I would get a year's contract.

*

I had a week to study the part before opening at the London Coliseum. Karno told me to go to Shepherd's Bush Empire, where *The Football Match* was playing, and to watch the man whose part I was to play. I must confess he was dull and self-conscious and, without false modesty, I knew that I had him beat. The part needed more burlesque. I made up my mind to play him just that way.

I was given only two rehearsals, as Mr Weldon was not available for more; in fact, he was rather annoyed at having to show up at all because it broke into his game of golf.

At rehearsals I was not impressive. Being a slow reader, I felt that Weldon had reservations about my competence. Sydney, having played the same part, might have helped me had he been in London, but he was playing in the provinces in another sketch.

Although *The Football Match* was a burlesque slapstick affair, there was not a laugh in it until Weldon appeared. Everything led up to his entrance, and of course Weldon, excellent comedian that he was, kept the audience in continuous laughter from the moment he came on.

On the opening night at the Coliseum my nerves were wound tight like a clock. That night meant re-establishing my confidence and wiping out the disgrace of that nightmare at the Foresters'. At the back of the enormous stage I walked up and down, with anxiety superimposed on fear, praying to myself.

There was the music! The curtain rose! On the stage was a chorus of men exercising. Eventually they exited, leaving the stage

99

empty. That was my cue. In an emotional chaos I went on. One either rises to an occasion or succumbs to it. The moment I walked on to the stage I was relieved, everything was clear. I entered with my back to the audience – an idea of my own. From the back I looked immaculate, dressed in a frock-coat, top-hat, cane and spats – a typical Edwardian villain. Then I turned, showing my red nose. There was a laugh. That ingratiated me with the audience. I shrugged melodramatically, then snapped my fingers and veered across the stage, tripping over a dumb-bell. Then my cane became entangled with an upright punching bag, which rebounded and slapped me in the face. I swaggered and swung, hitting myself with my cane on the side of the head. The audience roared.

Now I was relaxed and full of invention. I could have held the stage for five minutes and kept them laughing without uttering a word. In the midst of my villainous strutting my trousers began to fall down. I had lost a button. I began looking for it. I picked up an imaginary something, then indignantly threw it aside; 'Those confounded rabbits!' Another laugh.

Harry Weldon's head came round the wings like a full moon. There had never been a laugh before he came on.

When he made his entrance I dramatically grabbed his wrist and whispered: 'Quick! I'm undone! A pin!' All this was *ad lib* and unrehearsed. I had conditioned the audience well for Harry, he was a tremendous success that evening and together we added many extra laughs. When the curtain came down, I knew I had made good. Several members of the troupe shook hands and congratulated me. On the way to the dressing-room, Weldon looked over his shoulder and said dryly: 'That was all right – fine!'

That night I walked home to get unwound. I paused and leaned over Westminster Bridge and watched the dark, silky waters drifting under it. I wanted to weep for joy, but I couldn't. I kept straining and grimacing, but no tears would come, I was empty. From Westminster Bridge I walked to the Elephant and Castle and stopped at a coffee-stall for a cup of tea. I wanted to talk to someone, but Sydney was in the provinces. If only he were here so that I could tell him about tonight, how much it all meant to me, especially after the Foresters'.

I could not sleep. From the Elephant and Castle I went on to

Kennington Gate and had another cup of tea. On the way I kept talking and laughing to myself. It was five in the morning before I got to bed, exhausted.

Mr Karno was not there the first night, but came the third, on which occasion I received applause when I made my entrance. He came round afterwards, all smiles, and told me to come to his office in the morning and sign the contract.

I had not written to Sydney about the first night, but sent him a succinct wire: 'Have signed contract for one year at four pounds per week. Love, Charlie.' *The Football Match* stayed in London fourteen weeks, then went on tour.

Weldon's comedy character was of the cretinous type, a slow-speaking Lancashire boob. That went very well in the North of England, but in the South he was not too well received. Bristol, Cardiff, Plymouth, Southampton, were slump towns for Weldon; during those weeks he was irritable and performed perfunctorily and took his spleen out on me. In the show he had to slap and knock me about quite a bit. This was called 'taking the nap', that is, he would pretend to hit me in the face, but someone would slap their hands in the wings to give it a realistic effect. Sometimes he really slapped me and unnecessarily hard, provoked, I think, by jealousy.

In Belfast the situation came to a head. The critics had given Weldon a dreadful panning, but had praised my performance. This was intolerable to Weldon, so that night on the stage he let me have a good one which took all the comedy out of me and made my nose bleed. Afterwards I told him that if he did it again I would brain him with one of the dumb-bells on the stage, and added that if he was jealous, not to take it out on me.

'Jealous of you,' said he contemptuously, on our way to the dressing-room. 'Why, I have more talent in my arse than you have in your whole body!'

'That's where your talent lies,' I retorted, and quickly closed the dressing-room door.

\*

When Sydney came to town we decided to get a flat in the Brixton Road and to furnish it to the extent of forty pounds. We went to a second-hand furniture shop in Newington Butts and told the owner how much we could afford to spend, and that we had four rooms to furnish. The owner took a personal interest in our problem and spent many hours helping us pick out bargains. We carpeted the front room and linoleumed the others and bought an upholstered suite – a couch and two armchairs. In one corner of the sitting-room we put a fretwork Moorish screen, lighted from behind by a coloured yellow bulb, and in the opposite corner, on a gilt easel, a pastel in a gilded frame. The picture was of a nude model standing on a pedestal, looking sideways over her shoulder as a bearded artist is about to brush a fly off her bottom. This *objet d'art* and the screen, I thought, made the room. The final décor was a combination of a Moorish cigarette shop and a French whore-house. But we loved it. We even bought an upright piano, and although we spent fifteen pounds over our budget, we certainly had value for it. The flat at 15 Glenshaw Mansions, Brixton Road, was our cherished haven. How we looked forward to it after playing in the provinces! We were now prosperous enough to help Grandfather and give him ten shillings a week and we were able to engage a maid to come twice a week and clean up the flat, but it was hardly necessary, for we rarely disturbed a thing. We lived in it as though it were a holy temple. Sydney and I would sit in our bulky armchairs with smug satisfaction. We had bought a raised brass fender with red leather seating around it and I would go from the armchair to the fender, testing them for comfort.

*

At sixteen my idea of romance had been inspired by a theatrical poster showing a girl standing on a cliff with the wind blowing through her hair. I imagined myself playing golf with her – a game I loathe – walking over the dewy downs, indulging in throbbing sentiment, health and nature. That was romance. But young love is something else. It usually follows a uniform pattern. Because of a glance, a few words at the beginning (usually asinine words), in a matter of minutes the whole aspect of life is changed, all nature is in sympathy with us, and suddenly reveals its hidden joys. And that is what happened to me.

I was almost nineteen and already a successful comedian in the Karno Company, but something was lacking. Spring had come and gone and summer was upon me with an emptiness. My daily routine was stale, my environment dreary. I could see nothing in my future but a commonplaceness among dull, commonplace people. To be occupied with the business of just grubbing for a living was not good enough. Life was menial and lacked enchantment. I grew melancholy and dissatisfied and took lonely walks on Sunday and listened to park bands. I could support neither my own company nor that of anyone else. And of course, the obvious thing happened: I fell in love.

We were playing at the Streatham Empire. In those days we performed at two or three music halls nightly, travelling from one to the other in a private bus. At Streatham we were on early in order to appear later at the Canterbury Music Hall and then the Tivoli. It was daylight when we started work. The heat was oppressive and the Streatham Empire was half empty, which, incidentally, did not detract from my melancholy.

A song-and-dance troupe preceded us called 'Bert Coutts' Yankee-Doodle Girls.' I was hardly aware of them. But the second evening, while I stood in the wings indifferent and apathetic, one of the girls slipped during the dance and the others began to giggle. One looked off and caught my eye to see if I was also enjoying the joke. I was suddenly held by two large brown eyes sparkling mischievously, belonging to a slim gazelle with a shapely oval face, a bewitching full mouth, and beautiful teeth – the effect was electric. When she came off, she asked me to hold a small mirror while she arranged her hair. This gave me a chance to scrutinize her. That was the beginning. By Wednesday I had asked her if I could meet her on Sunday. She laughed. 'I don't even know what you look like without the red nose!' – I was playing the comedy drunk in *Mumming Birds*, dressed in long tails and a white tie.

'My nose is not quite this red, I hope, and I'm not quite as decrepit as I look,' I said, 'and to prove it I'll bring a photo of myself tomorrow night.'

I gave her what I thought was a flattering one of a sad, callow youth, wearing a black stock tie.

'Oh, but you're quite young,' she said. 'I thought you were much older.'

'How old did you think I was?'

'At least thirty.'

I smiled. 'I'm going on for nineteen.'

As we were rehearsing every day, it was impossible to meet her during the week. However, she promised to meet me at Kennington Gate at four o'clock on Sunday afternoon.

Sunday was a perfect summer's day and the sun shone continuously. I wore a dark suit that was cut smartly in at the waist, also a dark stock tie, and sported a black ebony cane. It was ten minutes to four, and I was all nerves, waiting and watching passengers alighting from tram-cars.

As I waited I realized I had not seen her without make-up. I began to lose the vision of what she looked like. Much as I tried, I could not recall her features. A mild fear seized me. Perhaps her beauty was bogus! An illusion! Every ordinary-looking young girl that alighted sent me into throes of despair. Would I be disappointed? Had I been duped by my own imagination or by the artifices of theatrical make-up?

At three minutes to four, someone got off a tram-car and came towards me. My heart sank. Her looks were disappointing. The depressing thought of facing the whole afternoon with her, keeping up a pretence of enthusiasm, was already deplorable. However, I raised my hat and beamed; she stared indignantly and passed on. Thank God it was not she.

Then precisely at one minute past four, a young girl alighted from a tram-car, came forward and stopped before me. She was without make-up and looked more beautiful than ever, wearing a simple sailor hat, a blue reefer coat with brass buttons, with her hands dug deep in her overcoat pockets. 'Here I am,' she said.

Her presence so overwhelmed me that I could hardly talk. I became agitated. I could think of nothing to say or do. 'Let's take a taxi,' I said huskily, looking up and down the road, then turned to her. 'Where would you like to go?'

She shrugged. 'Anywhere.'

'Then let's go over to the West End for dinner.'

'I've had dinner,' she said calmly.

'We'll discuss it in the taxi,' I said.

The intensity of my emotion must have bewildered her, for all during the drive I kept repeating: 'I know I'm going to regret this – you're too beautiful!' I tried vainly to be amusing and impress her. I had drawn three pounds from the bank and had planned to take her to the Trocadero, where, in an atmosphere of music and plush elegance, she could see me under the most romantic auspices. I wanted to sweep her off her feet. But she remained cool-eyed and somewhat perplexed at my utterances, one in particular: that she was my Nemesis, a word I had recently acquired.

How little she understood what it all meant to me. It had little to do with sex; more important was her association. To meet elegance and beauty in my station of life was rare.

That evening at the Trocadero, I tried to persuade her to have dinner, but to no avail. She would have a sandwich to keep me company, she said. As we were occupying a whole table in a very posh restaurant, I felt it incumbent to order an elaborate meal which I really did not want. The dinner was a solemn ordeal: I was uncertain which implement to eat with. I bluffed through the meal with a *dégagé* charm, even to my casualness in using the finger-bowl, but I think we were both happy to leave the restaurant and relax.

After the Trocadero she decided to go home. I suggested a taxi, but she preferred to walk. As she lived in Camberwell nothing suited me better; it meant I could spend more time with her.

Now that my emotions had simmered down she seemed more at ease. That evening we walked along the Thames Embankment, Hetty chattering away about her girl friends, pleasantries and other inconsequential things. But I was hardly aware of what she was saying. I only knew that the night was ecstatic – that I was walking in Paradise with inner blissful excitement.

After I left her I returned to the Embankment, possessed! And illumined with kindly light and a fervent goodwill, I distributed among the derelicts who slept on the Thames Embankment the remainder of my three pounds.

We promised to meet the following morning at seven o'clock because she had rehearsals at eight o'clock somewhere in Shaftesbury Avenue. It was a walk of about a mile and a half from her house to the Underground in the Westminster Bridge Road, and although I worked late, never getting to bed before two o'clock, I was up at dawn to meet her.

Camberwell Road was now touched with magic because Hetty Kelly lived there. Those morning walks with hands clasped all the way to the Underground were bliss mingled with confused longings. Shabby, depressing Camberwell Road, which I used to avoid, now had lure as I walked in its morning mist, thrilled at Hetty's outline in the distance coming towards me. During those walks I never remembered anything she said. I was too enthralled, believing that a mystic force had brought us together and that our union was an affinity predetermined by fate.

Three mornings I had known her; three abbreviated little mornings which made the rest of the day non-existent, until the next morning. But on the fourth morning her manner changed. She met me coldly, without enthusiasm, and would not take my hand. I reproached her for it and jokingly accused her of not being in love with me.

'You expect too much,' she said. 'After all I am only fifteen and you are four years older than I am.'

I would not assimilate the sense of her remark. But I could not ignore the distance she had suddenly placed between us. She was looking straight ahead, walking elegantly with a schoolgirl stride, both hands dug in her overcoat pockets.

'In other words, you really don't love me,' I said.

'I don't know,' she answered.

I was stunned. 'If you don't know, then you don't.' For answer, she walked in silence. 'You see what a prophet I am,' I continued lightly. 'I told you I would regret ever having met you.'

I tried to search her mind and find out to what extent her feeling was for me, and to all my questions she kept replying: 'I don't know.'

'Would you marry me?' I challenged.

'I'm too young.'

'Well, if you were compelled to marry would it be me or some-one else?'

But she was non-committal and kept repeating: 'I don't know . . . I like you . . . but –'

'But you don't love me,' I interposed with a sinking feeling.

She was silent. It was a cloudy morning and the streets looked drab and depressing.

'The trouble is I have let this thing go too far,' I said huskily. We had reached the entrance to the Underground. 'I think we'd better part and never see each other again,' I said, wondering what would be her reaction.

She looked solemn.

I took her hand and patted it tenderly. 'Good-bye, it's better this way. Already you have too much of a power over me.'

'Good-bye,' she answered. 'I'm sorry.'

The apology struck me as deadly. And as she disappeared into the Underground, I felt an unbearable emptiness.

What had I done? Was I too rash? I should not have challenged her. I'd been a pompous idiot and made it impossible to see her again – unless I made myself ridiculous. What was I to do? I could only suffer. If only I could submerge this mental agony in sleep until I meet her again. At all costs I must keep away from her until she wants to see me. Perhaps I was too serious, too intense. The next time we meet I shall be levitous and detached. But will she want to see me again? Surely she must! She cannot dismiss me so easily.

The next morning I could not resist walking up the Camberwell Road. I did not meet her, but met her mother. 'What have you done to Hetty!' she said. 'She came home crying and said you never wanted to see her again.'

I shrugged and smiled ironically. 'What has she done to me?' Then hesitantly I asked if I could see her again.

She shook her head warily. 'No, I don't think you should.'

I invited her to have a drink, so we went to a corner pub to talk it over, and after I entreated her to let me see Hetty again she consented.

When we reached the house, Hetty opened the door. She was surprised and concerned when she saw me. She had just washed her face with Sunlight soap – it smelt so fresh. She remained standing at the front door, her large eyes looking cold and objective. I could see it was hopeless.

'Well,' I said, attempting to be humorous, 'I've come to say good-bye again.'

She didn't answer, but I could see she was anxious to be rid of me.

I extended my hand and smiled. 'So good-bye again,' I said.

'Good-bye,' she answered coldly.

I turned and heard the street door gently closing behind me.

Although I had met her but five times, and scarcely any of our meetings lasted longer than twenty minutes, that brief encounter affected me for a long time.

# *seven*

IN 1909 I went to Paris. Monsieur Burnell of the Folies Bergère had engaged the Karno Company to play for a limited engagement of one month. How excited I was at the thought of going to a foreign country! The week before sailing we played at Woolwich, a dank, miserable week in a miserable town, and I looked forward to the change. We were to leave early Sunday morning. I almost missed the train, running down the platform and catching the last luggage van, in which I rode all the way to Dover. I had a genius for missing trains in those days.

The rain came down in torrents over the Channel, but the first sight of France through the mist was an unforgettable thrill. 'It isn't England,' I had to keep reminding myself, 'it's the Continent! France!' It had always appealed to my imagination. My father was part French, in fact the Chaplin family originally came from France. They landed in England in the time of the Huguenots. Father's uncle would say with pride that a French general established the English branch of the Chaplin family.

It was late autumn and the journey from Calais to Paris was dreary. Nevertheless, as we neared Paris my excitement grew. We had passed through bleak, lonely country. Then gradually out of the darkened sky we saw an illumination. 'That,' said a Frenchman in the carriage with us, 'is the reflection of Paris.'

Paris was everything I expected. The drive from the Gare du Nord to the rue Geoffroy-Marie had me excited and impatient; I wanted to stop at every corner and walk. It was seven in the evening; the golden lights shone invitingly from the cafes and their outside tables spoke of an enjoyment of life. But for the innovation of a few motor-cars, it was still the Paris of Monet, Pissarro and Renoir. It was Sunday and everyone seemed pleasure-bent. Gaiety and vitality were in the air. Even my room in the rue Geoffroy-Marie, with its stone floor, which I called my Bastille, could not dampen my ardour, for one lived sitting at tables outside bistros and cafés.

Sunday night was free, so we could see the show at the Folies Bergère, where we were to open the following Monday. No theatre, I thought, ever exuded such glamour, with its gilt and plush, its mirrors and large chandeliers. In the thick-carpeted foyers and dress circle the world promenaded. Bejewelled Indian princes with pink turbans and French and Turkish officers with plumed helmets sipped cognac at liqueur bars. In the large outer foyer music played as ladies checked their wraps and fur coats, baring their white shoulders. They were the habituées who discreetly solicited and promenaded the foyers and the dress circle. In those days they were beautiful and courtly.

The Folies Bergère also had professional linguists who strolled about the theatre with the word 'Interpreter' on their caps, and I made a friend of the head one, who could speak several languages fluently.

After our performance I would wear my stage evening-dress clothes and mingle with the promenaders. One gracile creature with a swan-like neck and white skin made my heart flutter. She was a tall Gibson Girl type, extremely beautiful, with retroussé nose and long dark eye-lashes, and wore a black velvet dress with long white gloves. As she went up the dress-circle stairs, she dropped a glove. Quickly I picked it up.

'*Merci*,' she said.

'I wish you would drop it again,' I said mischievously.

'*Pardon?*'

Then I realized she did not understand English and I spoke no French. So I went to my friend the interpreter. 'There's a dame that arouses my concupiscence. But she looks very expensive.'

He shrugged. 'Not more than a louis.'

'Good,' I said, although a louis in those days was a lot, I thought – and it was.

I had the interpreter put down a few French *phrases d'amour* on the back of a postcard: '*Je vous adore*', '*Je vous ai aimée la première fois que je vous ai vue*', etc., which I intended to use at the propitious moment. I asked him to make the preliminary arrangements and he acted as courier, going from one to the other. Eventually he came back and said: 'It's all settled, one louis, but you must pay her cab-fare to her apartment and back.'

I temporized a moment. 'Where does she live?' I asked.

'It won't cost more than ten fancs.'

Ten francs was disastrous, as I had not anticipated that extra charge. 'Couldn't she walk?' I said, jokingly.

'Listen, this girl is first-class, you must pay her fare,' he said.

So I acquiesced.

After the arrangements had been settled, I passed her on the dress-circle stairs. She smiled and I glanced back at her. '*Ce soir!*'

'*Enchantée, monsieur!*'

As we were on before the interval I promised to meet her after my performance. Said my friend: 'You hail a cab while I get the girl, then you won't waste time.'

'Waste time?'

As we drove along the Boulevard des Italiens, the lights and shadows passing over her face and long white neck, she looked ravishing. I glanced surreptitiously at my French on the postcard. '*Je vous adore,*' I began.

She laughed, showing her perfect white teeth. 'You speak very well French.'

'*Je vous ai aimée la première fois que je vois ai vue,*' I continued emotionally.

She laughed again and corrected my French, explaining that I should use the familiar '*tu*'. She thought about it and laughed again. She looked at her watch, but it had stopped; she indicated she wanted to know the time, explaining that at twelve o'clock she had a very important appointment.

'Not this evening.' I said coyly.

'*Oui, ce soir.*'

'But you're fully engaged this evening, *toute la nuit!*'

She suddenly looked startled. '*Oh, non, non, non! Pas toute la nuit!*'

Then it became sordid. '*Vingt francs pour le moment?*'

'*C'est ça!*' she replied emphatically.

'I'm sorry,' I said, 'I think I'd better stop the cab.'

And after paying the driver to take her back to the Folies Bergère, I got out, a very sad and disillusioned young man.

We could have stayed at the Folies Bergère ten weeks, as we were a great success, but Mr Karno had other bookings. My salary was six pounds a week, and I spent every penny of it. A cousin of my brother's, related to Sydney's father in some way, made himself known to me. He was rich and belonged to the so-called upper class, and during his stay in Paris he showed me a very good time. He was stage-struck and even went so far as having his moustache shaved off in order to pass as a member of our company, so that he could be allowed back stage. Unfortunately, he had to return to England, where I understand he was hauled over the coals by his august parents and sent to South America.

Before going to Paris, I had heard that Hetty's troupe were playing at the Folies Bergère, so I was all set to meet her again. The night I arrived I went back stage and made inquiries, but I learnt from one of the ballet girls that the troupe had left a week previously for Moscow. While I was talking to the girl a harsh voice came over the stairs:

'Come here at once! How dare you talk to strangers!'

It was the girl's mother. I tried to explain that I merely wanted information about a friend of mine, but the mother ignored me. 'Never mind talking to that man, come up here at once.'

I was annoyed at her crassness. Later, however, I became better acquainted with her. She lived in the same hotel as I did with her two daughters, who were members of the Folies Bergère ballet. The younger, thirteen, was the *première danseuse*, very pretty and talented, but the older one, fifteen, had neither talent nor looks. The mother was French, buxom and about forty, married to a Scotsman who was living in England. After we opened at the Folies Bergère, she came to me and apologized for being so abrupt. That was the beginning of a very friendly relationship. I was continually invited to their rooms for tea, which they made in their bedroom.

When I think back, I was incredibly innocent. One afternoon when the children were out and Mama and I were alone her attitude became strange and she began to tremble as she poured the tea. I had been talking about my hopes and dreams, my loves and disappointments, and she became quite moved. As I got up to put my tea-cup on the table, she came over to me.

'You are sweet,' she said, cupping my face with her hands and looking intensely into my eyes. 'Such a nice boy as you should not be hurt.' Her gaze became inverse, strange and hypnotic, and her voice trembled. 'Do you know, I love you like a son,' she said, still holding my face in her hands. Then slowly her face came to mine, and she kissed me.

'Thank you,' I said, sincerely – and innocently kissed her back. She continued transfixing me with her gaze, her lips trembling and her eyes glazed, then, suddenly checking herself, she went about pouring a fresh cup of tea. Her manner had changed and a certain humour played about her mouth. 'You are very sweet,' she said, 'I like you very much.'

She confided in me about her daughters. 'The young one is a very good girl,' she said, 'but the older must be watched; she is becoming a problem.'

After the show she would invite me to supper in her large bedroom in which she and her younger daughter slept, and before returning to my room I would kiss the mother and her younger daughter good-night; I would then have to go through a small room where the elder daughter slept. One night as I was passing through the room, she beckoned to me and whispered: 'Leave your door open and I will come up when the family is asleep.' Believe it or not, I threw her back on her bed indignantly and stalked out of the room. At the end of their engagement at the Folies Bergère, I heard that the elder daughter, still in her fifteenth year, had run off with a dog-trainer, a heavy-set German of sixty.

But I was not as innocent as I appeared. Members of the troupe and I occasionally spent a night carousing through the bordels and doing all the hoydenish things that youth will do. One night, after drinking several absinthes, I got into a fight with an ex-lightweight prize-fighter named Ernie Stone. It started in a restaurant, and after the waiters and the police had separated us he said: 'I'll see you at the hotel,' where we were both staying. He had the room above me, and at four in the morning I rolled home and knocked at his door.

'Come in,' he said briskly, 'and take off your shoes so we won't make a noise.'

Quietly we stripped to the waist, then faced each other. We hit and ducked for what seemed an interminable length of time. Several times he hit me square on the chin, but to no effect. 'I thought you could punch,' I sneered. He made a lunge, missed and smashed his head against the wall, almost knocking himself out. I tried to finish him off, but my punches were weak. I could hit him with impunity, but I had no strength behind my punch. Suddenly, I received a blow full in the mouth which shook my front teeth, and that sobered me up. 'Enough,' I said. 'I don't want to lose my teeth.' He came over and embraced me, then looked in the mirror: I had cut his face to ribbons. My hands were swollen like boxing gloves, and blood was on the ceiling, on the curtains and on the walls. How it got there, I do not know.

During the night the blood trickled down the side of my mouth and across my neck. The little *première danseuse*, who used to bring me up a cup of tea in the morning, screamed, thinking I had committed suicide. And I have never fought anyone since.

One night the interpreter came to me saying that a celebrated musician wanted to meet me, and would I go to his box? The invitation was mildly interesting, for in the box with him was a most beautiful, exotic lady, a member of the Russian Ballet. The interpreter introduced me. The gentleman said that he had enjoyed my performance and was surprised to see how young I was. At these compliments I bowed politely, occasionally taking a furtive glance at his friend. 'You are instinctively a musician and a dancer,' said he.

Feeling there was no reply to this compliment other than to smile sweetly, I glanced at the interpreter and bowed politely. The musician stood up and extended his hand and I stood up. 'Yes,' he said, shaking my hand, 'you are a true artist.' After we left I turned to the interpreter: 'Who was the lady with him?'

'She is a Russian ballet dancer, Mademoiselle —' It was a very long and difficult name.

'And what was the gentleman's name?' I asked.

'Debussy,' he answered, 'the celebrated composer.'

'Never heard of him,' I remarked.

It was the year of the famous scandal and trial of Madame Steinheil, who was tried and found not guilty of murdering her husband; the year of the sensational 'pom-pom' dance that showed couples indecently rotating together in a libidinous display; the year incredible tax laws were passed of sixpence in the pound on personal income; the year Debussy introduced his *Prélude à l'Après-midi d'un Faune* to England, where it was booed and the audience walked out.

*

With sadness I returned to England and began a tour of the provinces. What a contrast to Paris! Those mournful Sunday evenings in northern towns: everything closed, and the doleful clang of reprimanding bells that accompanied carousing youths and giggling wenches parading the darkened high streets and back alleys. It was their only Sunday evening diversion.

Six months had drifted by in England and I had settled down to my usual routine, when news came from the London office that made life more exciting. Mr Karno informed me that I was to take the place of Harry Weldon in the second season of *The Football Match*. Now I felt that my star was in the ascendant. This was my chance. Although I had made a success in *Mumming Birds* and other sketches in our repertoire, those were minor achievements compared to playing the lead in *The Football Match*. Moreover, we were to open at the Oxford, the most important music hall in London. We were to be the main attraction and I was to have my name featured for the first time at the top of the bill. This was a considerable step up. If I were a success at the Oxford it would establish a kudos that would enable me to demand a large salary and eventually branch out with my own sketches, in fact it would lead to all sorts of wonderful schemes. As practically the same cast was engaged for *The Football Match*, we needed only a week's rehearsal. I had thought a great deal about how to play the part. Harry Weldon had a Lancashire accent. I decided to play it as a cockney.

But at the first rehearsal I had an attack of laryngitis. I did everything to save my voice, speaking in whispers, inhaling vapours and spraying my throat, until anxiety robbed me of all unctuousness and comedy for the part.

On the opening night, every vein and cord in my throat was strained to the utmost with a vengeance. But I could not be heard. Karno came round afterwards with an expression of mingled disappointment and contempt. 'No one could hear you,' he said reprovingly. I assured him that my voice would be better the next night, but it was not. In fact it was worse, for it had been forced to such a degree that I was in danger of losing it completely. The next night my understudy went on. As a consequence the engagement finished after the first week. All my hopes and dreams of that Oxford engagement had collapsed, and the disappointment of it laid me low with influenza.

*

I had not seen Hetty in over a year. In a state of weakness and melancholy after the flu, I thought of her again and wandered late one night towards her home in Camberwell. But the house was empty with a sign: 'To Let'.

I continued wandering the streets with no special objective. Suddenly out of the night a figure appeared, crossing the road and coming towards me.

'Charlie! What are you doing up this way?' It was Hetty. She was dressed in a black sealskin coat with a round sealskin hat.

'I came to meet you,' I said jokingly.

She smiled. 'You're very thin.'

I told her I had just recovered from flu. She was seventeen now, quite pretty and smartly dressed.

'But the thing is, what are you doing up this way?' I asked.

'I've been visiting a friend and now I'm going to my brother's house. Would you like to come along?' she answered.

On the way, she told me that her sister had married an American millionaire, Frank J. Gould, and that they lived in Nice, and that she was leaving London in the morning to join them.

That evening I stood watching her dancing coquettishly with her brother. She was acting silly and siren-like with him, and in spite of myself I could not preclude a feeling that my ardour for her had slightly diminished. Had she become commonplace like any other girl? The thought saddened me, and I found myself looking at her objectively.

Her figure had developed, and I noticed the contours of her breasts and thought their protuberance small and not very alluring. Would I marry her even if I could afford to? No, I did not want to marry anyone.

As I walked home with her on that cold and brilliant night, I must have been sadly objective as I spoke about the possibility of her having a very wonderful and happy life. 'You sound so wistful, I could almost weep,' she said.

That night I went home feeling triumphant, for I had touched her with my sadness and had made my personality felt.

Karno put me back into *Mumming Birds* and, ironically, it was not more than a month before I completely recovered my voice. Great as my disappointment was about *The Football Match*, I tried not to dwell on it. But I was haunted by a thought that perhaps I was not equal to taking Weldon's place. And behind it all was the ghost of my failure at the Foresters'. As I had not fully retrieved my confidence, every new sketch in which I played the leading comedy part was a trial of fear. And now the alarming and a most resolute day came to notify Mr Karno that my contract had run out and that I wanted a raise.

Karno could be cynical and cruel to anyone he disliked. Because he liked me I had never seen that side of him, but he could indeed be most crushing in a vulgar way. During a performance of one of his comedies, if he did not like a comedian, he would stand in the wings and hold his nose and give an audible raspberry. But he did this once too often and the comedian left the stage and lunged at him; that was the last time he resorted to such vulgar measures. And now I stood confronting him about a new contract.

'Well,' he said, smiling cynically, 'you want a raise and the theatre circuits want a cut.' He shrugged. 'Since the fiasco at the Oxford Music Hall, we've had nothing but complaints. They say the company's not up to the mark – a scratch crowd.'*

'Well, they can hardly blame me for that,' I said.

'But they do,' he answered, pinning me with a steady gaze.

'What do they complain about?' I asked.

He cleared his throat and looked at the floor. 'They say you're not competent.'

Although the remark hit me in the pit of the stomach, it also infuriated me, but I replied calmly: 'Well, other people don't think so, and they're willing to give me more than I'm getting here.' This was not true – I had no other offer.

'They say the show is awful and the comedian's no good.

* In the Karno troupe it took at least six months working together before we could perfect a tempo. Until then it was called a 'scratch crowd'.

Here,' he said, picking up the phone, 'I'll call up the Star, Bermondsey, and you can hear for yourself . . . I understand you did poor business last week,' he said over the phone.

'Lousy!' came a voice.

Karno grinned. 'How do you account for it?'

'A dud show!'

'What about Chaplin, the principal comedian? Wasn't he any good?'

'He stinks!' said the voice.

Karno offered me the phone and grinned. 'Listen for yourself.'

I took the phone. 'Maybe he stinks, but not half as much as your stink-pot theatre!' I said.

Karno's attempt to cut me down was not a success. I told him that if he also felt that way there was no need to renew my contract. Karno in many ways was a shrewd man, but he was not a psychologist. Even if I did stink it wasn't good business of Karno to have a man at the other end of the phone tell me so. I was getting five pounds and, although my confidence was low, I demanded six. To my surprise Karno gave it to me, and again I entered his good graces.

\*

Alf Reeves, the manager of Karno's American company, returned to England and rumour had it that he was looking for a principal comedian to take back with him to the States.

Since my major setback at the Oxford Music Hall, I was full of the idea of going to America, not alone for the thrill and adventure of it, but because it would mean renewed hope, a new beginning in a new world. Fortunately *Skating*, one of our new sketches in which I was the leading comedian, was going over with great success in Birmingham and when Mr Reeves joined our company there I pinned on as much charm as I could; with the result that Reeves wired Karno that he had found his comedian for the States. But Karno had other plans for me. This sickening fact left me in doubt for several weeks until he became interested in a sketch called *The Wow-wows*. It was a burlesque on inititating a member into a secret society. Reeves and I thought the show silly, fatuous and without merit. But Karno was obsessed with the idea and insisted that America was full of secret societies and that a burlesque on them would be a great success there, so to my happy relief and excitement, Karno chose me to play the principal part in *The Wow-wows* for America.

This chance to go to the United States was what I needed. In England I felt I had reached the limit of my prospects; besides, my opportunities there were circumscribed. With scant educational background, if I failed as a music-hall comedian I would have little chance but to do menial work. In the States the prospects were brighter.

The night before sailing, I walked about the West End of London, pausing at Leicester Square, Coventry Street, the Mall and Piccadilly, with the wistful feeling that it would be the last time I would see London, for I had made up my mind to settle permanently in America. I walked until two in the morning, wallowing in the poetry of deserted streets and my own sadness.

I loathed saying good-bye. Whatever one feels about parting from relations and friends, to be seen off by them only rubs it in. I was up at six in the morning. Therefore, I did not bother to wake Sydney, but left a note on the table stating: 'Off to America. Will keep you posted. Love, Charlie.'

# *eight*

We were twelve days on the high seas in terrible weather, bound for Quebec. For three days we lay to with a broken rudder. Nevertheless, my heart was light and gay at the thought of going to another land. We travelled via Canada on a cattle boat, and although there were no cattle aboard there were plenty of rats and they perched arrogantly at the foot of my bunk until I threw a shoe at them.

It was the beginning of September and we passed Newfoundland in a fog. At last we sighted the mainland. It was a drizzling day, and the banks of the St Lawrence River looked desolate. Quebec from the boat looked like the ramparts where Hamlet's ghost might have walked, and I began to wonder about the States.

But as we travelled on to Toronto, the country became increasingly beautiful in autumnal colours and I became more hopeful. In Toronto we changed trains and went through the American Immigration. At ten o'clock on a Sunday morning we at last arrived in New York. When we got off the street-car at Times Square, it was somewhat of a let-down. Newspapers were blowing about the road and pavement, and Broadway looked seedy, like a slovenly woman just out of bed. On almost every street corner there were elevated chairs with shoe-lasts sticking up and people sitting comfortably in shirt-sleeves getting their shoes shined. They gave one the impression of finishing their toilet on the street. Many looked like strangers, standing aimlessly about the sidewalks as if they had just left the railroad station and were filling in time between trains.

However, this was New York, adventurous, bewildering, a little frightening. Paris, on the other hand, had been friendlier. Even though I could not speak the language, Paris had welcomed me on every street corner with its bistros and outside cafés. But New York was essentially a place of big business. The tall skyscrapers seemed ruthlessly arrogant and to care little for the convenience of ordinary people; even the saloon bars had no place for the customers to sit, only a long brass rail to rest a foot on, and the popular eating places, though clean and done in white marble, looked cold and clinical.

I took a back room in one of the brownstone houses off Forty-third Street, where the Times building now stands. It was dismal and dirty and made me homesick for London and our little flat. In the basement was a cleaning and pressing establishment and during the week the fetid odour of clothes being pressed and steamed wafted up and added to my discomfort.

That first day I felt quite inadequate. It was an ordeal to go into a restaurant and order something because of my English accent – and the fact that I spoke slowly. So many spoke in a rapid, clipped way that I felt uncomfortable for fear I might stutter and waste their time.

I was alien to this slick tempo. In New York even the owner of the smallest enterprise acts with alacrity. The shoe-black flips his polishing rag with alacrity, the bartender serves a beer with alacrity, sliding it up to you along the polished surface of the bar. The soda clerk, when serving an egg malted milk, performs like a hopped-up juggler. In a fury of speed he snatches up a glass, attacking everything he puts into it, vanilla flavour, blob of ice-cream, two spoonfuls of malt, a raw egg which he deposits with one crack, then adding milk, all of which he shakes in a container and delivers in less than a minute.

On the Avenue that first day many looked as I felt, lone and isolated; others swaggered along as though they owned the place. The behaviour of many people seemed dour and metallic as if to be agreeable or polite would prove a weakness. But in the evening as I walked along Broadway with the crowd dressed in their summer clothes, I became reassured. We had left England in the middle of a bitter cold September and arrived in New York in an Indian summer with a temperature of eighty degrees; and as I walked along Broadway it began to light up with myriads of coloured electric bulbs and sparkled like a brilliant jewel. And in the warm night my attitude changed and the meaning of

120

America came to me: the tall skyscrapers, the brilliant, gay lights, the thrilling display of advertisements stirred me with hope and a sense of adventure. 'That is it!' I said to myself. 'This is where I belong!'

Everyone on Broadway seemed to be in show business; actors, vaudevillians, circus performers and entertainers were everywhere, on the street, in restaurants, hotels and department stores, all talking shop. One heard names of theatre-owners, Lee Shubert, Martin Beck, William Morris, Percy Williams, Klaw and Erlanger, Frohman, Sullivan and Considine, Pantages. Whether charwoman, elevator boy, waiter, street-car conductor, barman, milkman or baker, they all talked like showmen. One heard snatches of conversation in the streets, motherly old women, looking like farmers' wives, saying: 'He's just finished three a day out West for Pantages.* With the right material that boy should make big-time vaudeville.' 'Did you catch Al Jolson at the Winter Garden?' says a janitor. 'He certainly saved the show for Jake.'

Newspapers each day devoted a whole page to theatre, got up like a racing chart, indicating vaudeville acts coming in first, second and third in popularity and applause, like race-horses. We had not entered the race yet and I was anxious to know in what position we would finish on the chart. We were to play the Percy Williams circuit for six weeks only. After that we had no further bookings. On the result of that engagement depended the length of our stay in America. If we failed, we would return to England.

We took a rehearsal room and had a week of rehearsing *The Wow-wows*. In the cast was old Whimsical Walker, the famous Drury-Lane clown. He was over seventy, with a deep, resonant voice, but had no diction, as we discovered at rehearsals, and he had the major part of explaining the plot. Such a line as 'The fun will be furious, ad libitum', he could not say and never did. The first night he spluttered: 'Ablib-blum', and eventually it became 'ablibum', but never the correct word.

In America, Karno had a great reputation. We were, therefore, the headline attraction over a programme of excellent artists. And although I hated the sketch, I naturally tried to make the best of it. I was hopeful that it might be what Karno called 'the very thing for America'.

* Pantages circuit, which gave three shows a day.

I will not describe the nerves, agony and suspense that preceded my entrance the first night, or my embarrassment as the American artists stood in the wings watching us. My first joke was considered a big laugh in England and a barometer for how the rest of the comedy would go over. It was a camping scene. I entered from a tent with a tea-cup.

ARCHIE (me): Good morning, Hudson. Do you mind giving me a little water?

HUDSON: Certainly. What do you want it for?

ARCHIE: I want to take a bath.

(A faint snicker, then cold silence from the audience.)

HUDSON: How did you sleep last night, Archie?

ARCHIE: Oh, terribly. I dreamt I was being chased by a caterpillar.

Still deadly silence. And so we droned on, with the faces of the Americans in the wings growing longer and longer. But they were gone before we had finished our act.

It was a silly, dull sketch and I had advised Karno not to open with it. We had other much funnier sketches in our repertoire, such as *Skating*, *The Dandy Thieves*, *The Post Office* and *Mr Perkins*, *M.P.*, which would have been amusing to an American audience. But Karno was stubborn.

To say the least, failure in a foreign country is distressing. Appearing each night before a cold and silent audience as they listened to our effusive, jovial English comedy was a grim affair. We entered and exited from the theatre like fugitives. For six weeks we endured this ignominy. The other performers quarantined us as if we had the plague. When we gathered in the wings to go on, crushed and humiliated, it was as though we were about to be lined up and shot.

Although I felt lonely and rejected, I was thankful to be living alone. At least I had not to share my humiliation with others. During the day I walked interminably through long avenues that seemed to lead to nowhere, interesting myself in visiting zoos, parks, aquariums and museums. Since our failure, New York now seemed too formidable, its buildings too high, its competitive atmosphere overpowering. Those magnificent houses on Fifth Avenue were not homes but monuments of success. Its opulent towering buildings and fashionable shops seemed a ruthless reminder of how inadequate I was.

I took long walks across the city towards the slum district, passing through the park in Madison Square, where derelict old gargoyles sat on benches in a despairing stupor, staring at their feet. Then I moved on to Third and Second Avenues. Here poverty was callous, bitter and cynical, a sprawling, yelling, laughing, crying poverty piling around doorways, on fire escapes and spewing about the streets. It was all very depressing and made me want to hurry back to Broadway.

The American is an optimist preoccupied with hustling dreams, an indefatigable tryer. He hopes to make a quick 'killing'. Hit the jackpot! Get out from under! Sell out! Make the dough and run! Get into another racket! Yet this immoderate attitude began to brighten my spirit. Paradoxically enough, as a result of our failure I began to feel light and unhampered. There were many other opportunities in America. Why should I stick to show business? I was not dedicated to art. Get into another racket! I began to regain confidence. Whatever happened I was determined to stay in America.

As a distraction from failure I wanted to improve my mind and educate myself; so I began browsing around the second-hand bookshops. I bought several text-books – Kellogg's *Rhetoric*, an English grammar and a Latin-English dictionary – with a determination to study them. But my resolutions went awry. No sooner had I looked at them than I packed them in the bottom of my trunk and forgot them – and not until our second visit to the States did I look at them again.

On the bill the first week in New York was an act called *Gus Edwards's School Days*, composed of children. In this troupe was a rather attractive scallywag who looked small for his sophisticated manner. He had a mania for gambling with cigarette coupons, which could be exchanged at the United Cigar Stores for items from a nickel-plated coffee-pot up to a grand piano; he was ready to shoot dice for them with stage-hands or anyone. He was an extraordinarily fast talker, by the name of Walter Winchell and though he never lost his rapid-fire talk, in later years his accuracy in reporting the truth often misfired.

Although our show was a failure, I personally got very good

notices. Sime Silverman of *Variety* said of me: 'There was at least one funny Englishman in the troupe and he will do for America.'

By now we had resigned ourselves to pack up and return to England after six weeks. But the third week we played at the Fifth Avenue Theatre, to an audience composed largely of English butlers and valets. To my surprise on the opening Monday night we went over with a bang. They laughed at every joke. Everyone in the company was surprised including myself, for I had expected the usual indifferent reception. In giving a perfunctory performance, I suppose I was relaxed. Consequently I could do no wrong.

During the week an agent saw us and booked us for a twenty-week tour out West on the Sullivan and Considine circuit. It was cheap vaudeville and we had to give three shows a day.

Although on that Sullivan and Considine first tour we were not a roaring success, we passed muster by comparison with the other acts. In those days the Middle West had charm. The tempo was slower, and the atmosphere was romantic; every drug-store and saloon had a dice-throwing desk in the entrance where one gambled for whatever products they sold. On Sunday morning Main Street was a continual hollow sound of rattling dice, which was pleasant and friendly; and many a time I won a dollar's worth of goods for ten cents.

Living was cheap. At a small hotel one could get a room and board for seven dollars a week, with three meals a day. Food was remarkably cheap. The saloon free-lunch counter was the mainstay of our troupe. For a nickel one could get a glass of beer and the pick of a whole delicatessen counter. There were pigs' knuckles, sliced ham, potato salad, sardines, macaroni cheese, a variety of sliced sausages, liverwurst, salami and hot dogs. Some of our members took advantage of this and piled up their plates until the barman would intervene: 'Hey! Where the hell are you tracking with that load – to the Klondike?'

There were fifteen or more in our troupe and yet every member saved at least half of his wages, even after paying his own sleeping berth on the train. My salary was seventy-five dollars a week and fifty of it went regularly and resolutely into the Bank of Manhattan.

The tour took us to the Coast. Travelling with us out West on the same vaudeville bill was a handsome young Texan, a trapeze performer who could not make up his mind whether to continue with his partner on the trapeze or become a prize-fighter. Every morning I would put on the gloves with him, and, although he was taller and heavier than I was, I could hit him at will. We became very good friends, and after a boxing bout we would lunch together. His folks, he told me, were simple Texan farmers, and he would talk about life on the farm. Very soon we were talking ourselves into leaving show business and going into partnership, raising hogs.

Between us we had two thousand dollars and a dream of making a fortune; we planned to buy land for fifty cents an acre in Arkansas, two thousand acres to start with, and spend the rest buying hogs and improving the land. If all went well, we had it figured out that with the compound birth of hogs, averaging a litter of five a year, we could in five years make a hundred thousand dollars apiece.

Travelling on the train, we would look out of the window and see hog farms and go into paroxysms of excitement. We ate, slept and dreamed hogs. But for buying a book on scientific hog-raising I might have given up show business and become a hog-farmer, but that book, which graphically described the technique of castrating hogs, cooled my ardour and I soon forgot the enterprise.

On this tour I carried my violin and 'cello. Since the age of sixteen I had practised from four to six hours a day in my bedroom. Each week I took lessons from the theatre conductor or from someone he recommended. As I played left-handed, my violin was strung left-handed with the bass bar and sounding post reversed. I had great ambitions to be a concert artist, or, failing that, to use it in a vaudeville act, but as time went on I realized that I could never achieve excellence, so I gave it up.

In 1910 Chicago was attractive in its ugliness, grim and be-grimed, a city that still had the spirit of frontier days, a thriving, heroic metropolis of 'smoke and steel', as Carl Sandburg says. The vast flat plains approaching it are, I imagine, similar to the Russian steppes. It had a fierce pioneer gaiety that enlivened the senses, yet underlying it throbbed masculine loneliness. Counteracting this somatic ailment was a national distraction known as the burlesque show, consisting of a coterie of rough-and-tumble comedians supported by twenty or more chorus girls. Some were pretty, others shopworn. Some of the comedians were funny, most of the shows were smutty harem comedies – coarse and cynical affairs. The atmosphere was 'he-man', charged with profane sex antagonism which, paradoxically, insulated the audience from any normal sex desire – their reaction was to snivel at it. Chicago was full of these shows; one called *Watson's Beef Trust* had twenty enormously fat, middle-aged women displaying themselves in tights. Their combined weight went into tons, so it was advertised. Their photographs outside the theatre, showing them posing coyly, were sad and depressing.

In Chicago we lived up-town on Wabash Avenue in a small hotel; although grim and seedy, it had a romantic appeal, for most of the burlesque girls lived there. In each town we always made a bee-line for the hotel where the show girls stayed, with a libidinous hope that never materialized. The elevated trains swept by at night and flickered on my bedroom wall like an old-fashioned bioscope. Yet I loved that hotel, though nothing adventurous ever happened there.

One young girl, quiet and pretty, was for some reason always alone and walked with a self-conscious air. Occasionally I would pass her going in and out of the hotel lobby, but I never had the temerity to get acquainted, and I must say she gave me little encouragement.

When we left Chicago for the coast she was on the same train; burlesque companies going west usually toured the same route we were travelling and played in the same towns. Passing through the train, I saw her talking to a member of our company. Later he came and took his seat beside me. 'What sort of a girl is she?' I asked.

'Very sweet. Poor kid, I'm sorry for her.'

'Why?'

He leaned closer. 'Remember the rumour going around that one of the girls in the show had syphilis? Well, that's the one.'

In Seattle she was obliged to leave the company and enter a hospital. We made a collection for her, all the travelling companies contributing. Poor girl, everyone knew what was the matter with her. Nevertheless, she was thankful and later rejoined her company, cured by injections of Salvarsan, a new drug at that time.

In those days the red-light districts were rampant throughout America. Chicago was especially noted for the House of All Nations, run by the Everly sisters, two middle-aged spinsters; it was notorious for having women of every nationality. Rooms were furnished in every style and décor: Turkish, Japanese, Louis XVI, even an Arab tent. It was the most elaborate establishment in the world, and the most expensive. Millionaires, industrial tycoons, cabinet ministers, senators and judges alike were its customers. Members of a convention usually terminated their concord by taking over the whole establishment for the evening. One wealthy sybarite was known to take up his abode there for three weeks without seeing daylight.

The further west we went the better I liked it. Looking out of the train at the vast stretches of wild land, though it was drear and sombre, filled me with promise. Space is good for the soul. It is broadening. My outlook was larger. Such cities as Cleveland, St Louis, Minneapolis, St Paul, Kansas City, Denver, Butte, Billings, throbbed with the dynamism of the future, and I was imbued with it.

We made many friends with the members of other vaudeville companies. In each town we would get together in the red-light district, six or more of us. Sometimes we won the affection of the madam of a bordel and she would close up the 'joint' for the night and we would take over. Occasionally some of the girls fell for the actors and would follow them to the next town.

The red-light district of Butte, Montana, consisted of a long street and several by-streets containing a hundred cribs in which young girls were installed ranging in age from sixteen up for one dollar. Butte boasted of having the prettiest women of any red-light district in the Middle West, and it was true. If one saw a pretty girl smartly dressed, one could rest assured she was from the red-light quarter doing her shopping. Off duty they looked neither right nor left and were most respectable. Years later I argued with Somerset Maugham about his Sadie Thompson character in the play *Rain*. Jeanne Eagels dressed her rather grotesquely, as I remember, with spring-side boots. I told him that no harlot in Butte, Montana, could make money if she dressed like that.

In 1910 Butte, Montana, was still a 'Nick Carter' town, with miners wearing top-boots and two-gallon hats and red neckerchiefs. I actually saw gun-play in the street, a fat old sheriff shooting at the heels of an escaped prisoner, who was eventually cornered in a blind alley without harm, fortunately.

My heart grew lighter as we travelled west: cities looked cleaner. Our route was Winnipeg, Tacoma, Seattle, Vancouver, Portland. In Winnipeg and Vancouver, audiences were essentially English and in spite of my pro-American leanings it was pleasant to play before them.

At last California! – a paradise of sunshine, orange groves, vineyards and palm-trees stretching along the Pacific coast for a thousand miles. San Francisco, the gateway to the Orient, was a city of good food and cheap prices; the first to introduce me to frogs legs *à la provençale*, strawberry shortcake and avocado pears. We arrived in 1910, after the city had risen from the earthquake of 1906, or the fire, as they prefer to call it. There were still one or two cracks in the hilly streets, but little remnant of damage was left. Everything was new and bright, including my small hotel.

We played at the Empress, owned by Sid Grauman and his father, friendly, gregarious people. It was the first time I was featured alone on a poster with no mention of Karno. And the audience, what a delight! In spite of *The Wow-wows* being a dull show, there were packed houses every performance and screams of laughter. Grauman said enthusiastically: 'Any time you're through with the Karno outfit, come back here and we'll put on shows together.' This enthusiasm was new to me. In San Francisco one felt the spirit of optimism and enterprise.

Los Angeles, on the other hand, was an ugly city, hot and oppressive, and the people looked sallow and anaemic. It was a much warmer climate but had not the freshness of San Francisco; nature has endowed the north of California with resources that will endure and flourish when Hollywood has disappeared into the prehistoric tar-pits of Wilshire Boulevard.

We finished our first tour in Salt Lake City, the home of the Mormons, which made me think of Moses leading the children of Israel. It is a gaping wide city, that seems to waver in the heat of the sun like a mirage, with wide streets that only a people who had traversed vast plains would conceive. Like the Mormons, the city is aloof austere – and so was the audience.

After playing *The Wow-wows* on the Sullivan and Considine circuit, we came back to New York with the intention of returning directly to England, but Mr William Morris, who was fighting the other vaudeville trusts, gave us six weeks to play our whole repertoire at his theatre on Forty-second Street, New York City. We opened with *A Night in an English Music Hall*, which was a tremendous success.

During the week a young man and his friend had a late date with a couple of girls, so to kill time they wandered into William Morris's American Music Hall, where they happened to see our show. One remarked: 'If ever I become a big shot, there's a guy I'll sign up.' He was referring to my performance as the drunk in *A Night in an English Music Hall*. At the time he was working for D. W. Griffith as a movie extra in the Biograph Company, getting five dollars a day. He was Mack Sennett, who later formed the Keystone Film Company.

Having played a very successful six weeks' engagement for William Morris in New York, we were again booked for another twenty weeks' tour on the Sullivan and Considine circuit.

I felt sad as we drew near to the end of our second tour. There were three weeks more, San Francisco, San Diego, then Salt Lake City and back to England.

The day before leaving San Francisco, I took a stroll down Market Street and came upon a small shop with a curtained window and a sign reading: 'Your fortune told by hands and cards – one dollar.' I went in, slightly embarrassed, and was confronted by a plump woman of about forty who came from an inner room still chewing an interrupted meal. Perfunctorily she pointed to a small table against the wall facing the door, and without looking at me said: 'Sit down, please,' then she sat opposite. Her manner was abrupt. 'Shuffle these cards and cut them three times towards me, then lay the palms of your hands upwards on the table, please.' She turned the cards over and spread them, studied them, then looked at my hands. 'You're thinking about a long journey, which means you'll be leaving the States. But you return again shortly, and will enter a new business – something different from what you're doing at present.' Here she hesitated and became confused. 'Well, it's almost the same but it's different. I see tremendous success in this new venture; there's an extraordinary career ahead of you, but I don't know what it is.' For the first time she looked up at me, then took my hand. 'Oh yes, there's three marriages: the first two are not successful, but you end your life happily married with three children.' (She was wrong there!) Then she studied my hand again. 'Yes, you will make a tremendous fortune, it's a money-making hand.' Then she studied my face. 'You will die of bronchial pneumonia, at the age of eighty-two. A dollar, please. Is there any question you'd like to ask?'

'No,' I laughed, 'I think I'll leave well enough alone.'

In Salt Lake City, the newspapers were full of hold-ups and bank robberies. Customers in night-clubs and cafés were being lined up against the wall and robbed by masked bandits with stockings over their faces. There were three robberies in one night and they were terrorizing the whole city.

After the show we usually went to a nearby saloon for a drink, occasionally getting acquainted with the customers. One evening a fat, jovial round-faced man came in with two other men. The fat one, the oldest of the three, came over. 'Aren't you fellows playing the Empress in that English act?'

We nodded smilingly.

'I thought I recognized you! Hey, fellows! Come on over.' He hailed his two companions and after introducing them asked us to have a drink.

The fat one was an Englishman, although little trace of the accent was left; a man about fifty, good-natured, with small twinkling eyes and a florid face.

As the night wore on his two friends and members of our company drifted away from us towards the bar, and I found myself alone with 'Fat', as his young friends called him.

He became confidential. 'I was back in the old country three years ago,' he said, 'but it ain't the same – this here's the place. Came here thirty years ago, a sucker, working my arse off in them Montana copperfields – then I got wise to myself. "That's a mug's game," I says. Now I've got chumps working for me.' He pulled out an enormous wad of bills. 'Let's have another drink.'

'Be careful,' I said, jokingly. 'You might get held up!'

He looked at me with a most evil, knowing smile, then winked. 'Not this baby!'

A terrifying feeling came over me after that wink. It had implied a great deal. He continued smiling, without taking his eyes from me. 'Catch on?' he said.

I nodded wisely.

Then he spoke confidentially, bringing his face close to my ear.

'See those two guys?' he whispered, referring to his friends. 'That's my outfit, two dumb clucks – no brains but plenty o' guts.'

I put a finger to my lips cautiously, indicating that he might be overheard.

'We're O.K., brother, we're shipping out tonight.' He continued: 'Listen, we're limeys, ain't we – from the old smoke? I seen you at the Islington Empire many a time, falling in and out of that box.' He grimaced. 'That's a tough racket, brother.'

I laughed.

As he grew more confidential, he wanted to make a lifelong friend of me and to know my address in New York. 'I'll drop you a line just for old times' sake,' he said. Fortunately, I never heard from him again.

# *nine*

I was not too upset at leaving the States, for I had made up my mind to return; how or when I did not know. Nevertheless, I looked forward to returning to London and our comfortable little flat. Since I had toured the States it had become a sort of shrine.

I had not heard from Sydney in a long time. His last letter stated that Grandfather was living in the flat. But on my arrival in London, Sydney met me at the station and told me that he had given up the flat, that he had married and was living in furnished rooms along the Brixton Road. This was a severe blow to me – to think that that cheerful little haven that had given substance to my sense of living, a pride in a home, was no more. . . . I was homeless. I rented a back room in the Brixton Road. It was so dismal that I resolved to return to the United States as soon as possible. That first night, London seemed as indifferent to my return as an empty slot machine when one had put a coin in it.

As Sydney was married and working every evening, I saw little of him; but on Sunday we both went to see Mother. It was a depressing day, for she was not well. She had just got over an obstreperous phase of singing hymns, and had been confined to a padded room. The nurse had warned us of this beforehand. Sydney saw her, but I had not the courage, so I waited. He came back upset, and said that she had been given shock treatment of icy cold showers and that her face was quite blue. This made us decide to put her into a private institution – we could afford it now – so we had her transferred to the same institution in which England's great comedian, the late Dan Leno, had been confined.

Each day I felt more of a nondescript and completely uprooted. I suppose had I returned to our little flat, my feelings might have been different. Naturally, gloom did not completely take over. Familiarity, custom and my kinship with England were deeply moving to me after arriving from the States. It was an ideal English summer and its romantic loveliness was unlike anything I had known elsewhere.

Mr Karno, the boss, invited me down to Tagg's Island for a week-end on his house-boat. It was rather an elaborate affair, with mahogany panelling and state-rooms for guests. At night it was lit up with festoons of coloured lights all round the boat, gay and charming, I thought. It was a beautiful warm evening, and after dinner we sat out on the upper deck under the coloured lights with our coffee and cigarettes. This was the England that could wean me away from any country.

Suddenly, a falsetto, foppish voice began screaming hysterically: 'Oh, look at my lovely boat, everyone! Look at my lovely boat! And the lights! Ha! ha! ha!' The voice went into hysterics of derisive laughter. We looked to see where the effusion came from, and saw a man in a rowing-boat, dressed in white flannels, with a lady reclining in the back seat. The ensemble was like a comic illustration from *Punch*. Karno leaned over the rail and gave him a very loud raspberry, but nothing deterred his hysterical laughter. 'There is only one thing to do,' I said: 'to be as vulgar as he thinks we are.' So I let out a violent flow of Rabelaisian invective, which was so embarrassing for his lady that he quickly rowed away.

The idiot's ridiculous outburst was not a criticism of taste, but a snobbish prejudice against what he considered lower-class ostentatiousness. He would never laugh hysterically at Buckingham Palace and scream: 'Oh, look what a big house I live in!' or laugh at the Coronation coach. This ever-present class tabulating I felt keenly while in England. It seems that this type of Englishman is only too quick to measure the other fellow's social inferiorities.

Our American troupe was put to work and for fourteen weeks we played the halls around London. The show was received well and the audiences were wonderful, but all the time I was wondering if we'd ever get back to the States again. I loved England, but it was impossible for me to live there; because of my background I had a disquieting feeling of sinking back into a depressing commonplaceness. So that when news came that we were booked for another tour in the States I was elated.

On Sunday Sydney and I saw Mother and she seemed in better health, and before Sydney left for the provinces we had supper together. On my last night in London, emotionally confused, sad, and embittered, I again walked about the West End, thinking to myself: 'This is the last time I shall ever see these streets.'

*

This time we arrived via New York on the *Olympic* second-class. The throb of the engines slowed down, signifying that we were approaching our destiny. This time I felt at home in the States – a foreigner among foreigners, allied with the rest.

As much as I like New York I also looked forward to the West, to greeting again those acquaintances whom I now looked upon as warm friends: the Irish bar-tender in Butte, Montana, the cordial and hospitable real estate millionaire of Minneapolis, the beautiful girl in St Paul with whom I had spent a romantic week, MacAbee, the Scottish mine-owner of Salt Lake City, the friendly dentist in Tacoma, and in San Francisco, the Graumans.

Before going to the Pacific Coast we played around the 'smalls' – the small theatres around the outlying suburbs of Chicago and Philadelphia and industrial towns such as Fall River and Duluth, etc.

As usual I lived alone. But it had its advantages, because it gave me an opportunity to improve my mind, a resolution I had held for many months but never fulfilled.

There is a fraternity of those who passionately want to know. I was one of them. But my motives were not so pure; I wanted to know, not for the love of knowledge but as a defence against the world's contempt for the ignorant. So when I had time I browsed around the second-hand bookshops.

In Philadelphia, I inadvertently came upon an edition of Robert Ingersoll's *Essays and Lectures*. That was an exciting discovery; his atheism confirmed my own belief that the horrific cruelty of the Old Testament was degrading to the human spirit. Then I discovered Emerson. After reading his essay on 'Self-Reliance' I felt I had been handed a golden birthright. Schopenhauer followed. I bought three volumes of *The World as Will and*

*Idea*, which I have read on and off, never thoroughly, for over forty years. Walt Whitman's *Leaves of Grass* annoyed me and does to this day. He is too much the bursting heart of love, too much a national mystic. In my dressing-room between shows I had the pleasure of meeting Twain, Poe, Hawthorne, Irving and Hazlitt. On that second tour I may not have absorbed as much classic education as I would have desired, but I did absorb a great deal of tedium in the lower strata of show business.

These cheap vaudeville circuits were bleak and depressing, and hopes about my future in America disappeared in the grind of doing three and sometimes four shows a day, seven days a week. Vaudeville in England was a paradise by comparison. At least we only worked there six days a week and only gave two shows a night. Our consolation was that in America we could save a little more money.

We had been working the 'sticks' continuously for five months and the weariness of it had left me discouraged, so that when we had a week's lay-off in Philadelphia, I welcomed it. I needed a change, another environment – to lose my identity and become someone else. I was fed up with the drab routine of tenth-rate vaudeville and decided that for one week I would indulge in the romance of graceful living. I had saved a considerable sum of money, and in sheer desperation, I decided to go on a spending spree. Why not? I had lived frugally to save it, and when out of work I would continue to live frugally on it; so why not spend a little of it now?

I bought an expensive dressing-gown and a smart over-night suitcase, which cost me seventy-five dollars. The shopkeeper was most courteous: 'Can we deliver them for you, sir?' Just his few words gave me a lift, a little distinction. Now I would go to New York and shed myself of tenth-rate vaudeville and its whole drab existence.

I took a room at the Hotel Astor which was quite grandiose in those days. I wore my smart cut-away coat and derby hat and cane, and of course carried my small suitcase. The splendour of the lobby and the confidence of the people strutting about it made me tremble slightly as I registered at the desk.

The room cost $4.50 a day. Timidly I asked if I should pay

in advance. The clerk was most courteous and reassuring: 'Oh no, sir, it isn't necessary.'

Passing through the lobby with all its gilt and plush did something to me emotionally, so that when I reached my room I felt I wanted to weep. I stayed in it over an hour, inspecting the bathroom with its elaborate plumbing fixtures and testing its generous flush of hot and cold water. How bountiful and reassuring is luxury!

I took a bath and combed my hair and put on my new bathrobe, intending to get every ounce of luxury out of my four dollars fifty worth: . . . If only I had something to read, a newspaper. But I had not the confidence to telephone for one. So I took a chair and sat in the middle of the room surveying everything with a feeling of luxuriant melancholy.

After a while I dressed and went downstairs. I asked for the main dining-room. It was rather early for dinner; the place was almost empty but for one or two diners. The maître d'hôtel led me to a table by the window. 'Would you like to sit here, sir?'

'Anywhere will do,' I said in my best English voice.

Suddenly an industry of waiters whirled about me, delivering ice water, the menu, the butter and bread. I was too emotional to be hungry. However, I went through the gestures and ordered consommé, roast chicken, and vanilla ice-cream for dessert. The waiter offered me a wine-list, and after careful scrutiny I ordered a half-bottle of champagne. I was too preoccupied living the part to enjoy the wine or the meal. After I had finished, I tipped the waiter a dollar, which was an extraordinarily generous tip in those days. But it was worth it for the bowing and attention I received on my way out. For no apparent reason I returned to my room and sat in it for ten minutes, then washed my hands and went out.

It was a soft summer evening in keeping with my mood as I walked sedately in the direction of the Metropolitan Opera House. *Tannhäuser* was playing there. I had never seen grand opera, only excerpts of it in vaudeville – and I loathed it. But now I was in the humour for it. I bought a ticket and sat in the second circle. The opera was in German and I did not understand a word of it, nor did I know the story. But when the dead Queen was carried on to the music of the Pilgrim's Chorus, I wept bitterly. It seemed to sum up all the travail of my life. I could hardly control myself; what people sitting next to me must have thought I don't know, but I came away limp and emotionally shattered.

I took a walk down town, choosing the darkest streets, as I could not cope with the vulgar glare of Broadway, nor could I return to that silly room at the hotel until my mood had worn off. When I recovered I intended going straight to bed. I was emotionally and physically exhausted.

As I entered the hotel I suddenly ran into Arthur Kelly, Hetty's brother, who used to be manager of the troupe that she was in. Because he was her brother I had cultivated him as a friend. I had not seen Arthur in several years.

'Charlie! Where are you going?' he said.

Nonchalantly I nodded in the direction of the Astor. 'I was about to go to bed.'

The effect was not lost on Arthur.

He was with two friends, and after introducing me he suggested that we should go to his apartment on Madison Avenue for a cup of coffee and a chat.

It was quite a comfortable flat and we sat around and made light conversation, Arthur carefully avoiding any reference to our past. Nevertheless, because I was staying at the Astor, he was curious to glean information. But I told him little, only that I had come to New York for two or three days' holiday.

Arthur had come a long way since living in Camberwell. He was now a prosperous business man working for his brother-in-law, Frank J. Gould. As I sat listening to his social chatter, it increased my melancholy. Said Kelly, referring to one of his friends: 'He's a nice chap, comes from a very good family, I understand.' I smiled to myself at his genealogical interest and realized that Arthur and I had little in common.

I stayed only one day in New York. The following morning I decided to return to Philadelphia. Although that one day had been the change I needed, it had been an emotional and a lonely one. Now I wanted company. I looked forward to our Monday morning performance and meeting members of the troupe. No matter how irksome it was returning to the old grind, that one day of graceful living had sufficed me.

When I got back to Philadelphia I dropped by the theatre. There was a telegram addressed to Mr Reeves, and I happened to be there when he opened it. 'I wonder if this means you,' he said. It read: 'Is there a man named Chaffin in your company or something like that stop if so will he communicate with Kessel and Bauman 24 Longacre Building Broadway.'

There was no one by that name in the company, but, as Reeves suggested, the name might mean Chaplin. Then I became excited, for Longacre Building, I discovered, was in the centre of Broadway and was full of lawyers' offices; remembering that I had a rich aunt somewhere in the States, my imagination took flight; she might have died and left me a fortune. So I wired back to Kessel and Bauman that there was a Chaplin in the company whom they perhaps meant. I waited anxiously for a reply. It came the same day. I tore open the telegram. It read: 'Will you have Chaplin call at our office as soon as possible?'

With excitement and anticipation, I caught the early morning train for New York, which was only two and a half hours from Philadelphia. I did not know what to expect – I imagined sitting in a lawyer's office listening to a will being read.

When I arrived, however, I was somewhat disappointed, for Kessel and Bauman were not lawyers but producers of motion pictures. However, the actual facts of the situation were to be thrilling.

Mr Charles Kessel, one of the owners of the Keystone Comedy Film Company, said that Mr Mack Sennett had seen me playing the drunk in the American Music Hall on Forty-second Street and if I were the same man he would like to engage me to take the place of Mr Ford Sterling. I had often played with the idea of working in films, and even offered to go into partnership with Reeves, our manager, to buy the rights of all Karno's sketches and make movies of them. But Reeves had been sceptical and sensibly so, because we knew nothing about making them.

Had I seen a Keystone Comedy? asked Mr Kessel. Of course, I had seen several, but I did not tell him that I thought they were a crude mélange of rough and rumble. However, a pretty, dark-eyed girl named Mabel Normand, who was quite charming, weaved in and out of them and justified their existence. I was not terribly enthusiastic about the Keystone type of comedy, but I realized their publicity value. A year at that racket and I could return to vaudeville an international star. Besides, it would mean a new life and a pleasant environment. Kessel said the contract would call for appearing in three films a week at a salary of one hundred and fifty dollars. This was twice what I was getting with the Karno Company. However, I hemmed and hawed and said I could not accept less than two hundred dollars a week. Mr Kessel said that was up to Mr Sennett; he would notify him in California and let me know.

I did not exist while waiting to hear from Kessel. Perhaps I had asked too much? At last the letter came, stating they were willing to sign a year's contract for one hundred and fifty dollars the first three months and one hundred and seventy-five dollars for the remaining nine, more money than I had ever been offered in my life. It was to start with the termination of our Sullivan and Considine tour.

When we played the Empress in Los Angeles, we were a howling success, thank God. It was a comedy called *A Night at the Club*. I played a decrepit old drunk and looked at least fifty years old. Mr Sennett came round after the performance and congratulated me. In that short interview, I was aware of a heavy-set man with a beetling brow, a heavy, coarse mouth and a strong jaw, all of which impressed me. But I wondered how sympathetic he would be in our future relationship. All through that interview I was extremely nervous and was not sure whether he was pleased with me or not.

He asked casually when I would join them. I told him that I could start the first week in September, which would be the termination of my contract with the Karno Company.

I had qualms about leaving the troupe in Kansas City. The company was returning to England, and I to Los Angeles, where I would be on my own, and the feeling was not too reassuring. Before the last performance I ordered drinks for everyone and felt rather sad at the thought of parting.

A member of our troupe, Arthur Dando, who for some reason disliked me, thought he would play a joke and conveyed by whispered innuendoes that I was to receive a small gift from the company. I must confess I was touched by the thought. However, nothing happened. When everyone had left the dressing-room, Fred Karno Junior confessed that Dando had arranged to make a speech and present me with the gift, but after I had bought drinks for everyone he had not had the courage to go through with it and had left the so-called 'present' behind the dressing-table mirror. It was an empty tobacco-box, wrapped in tinfoil, containing small ends of old pieces of grease-paint.

# ten

EAGER and anxious, I arrived in Los Angeles and took a room at a small hotel, the Great Northern. The first evening I took a busman's holiday and saw the second show at the Empress, where the Karno Company had worked. The attendant recognized me and came a few moments later to tell me that Mr Sennett and Miss Mabel Normand were sitting two rows back and had asked if I would join them. I was thrilled, and after a hurried, whispered introduction we all watched the show together. When it was over, we walked a few paces down Main Street, and went to a rathskeller for a light supper and a drink. Mr Sennett was shocked to see how young I looked. 'I thought you were a much older man,' he said. I could detect a tinge of concern, which made me anxious, remembering that all Sennett's comedians were oldish-looking men. Fred Mace was over fifty and Ford Sterling in his forties. 'I can make up as old as you like,' I answered. Mabel Normand, however, was more reassuring. Whatever her reservations were about me, she did not reveal them. Mr Sennett said that I would not start immediately, but should come to the studio in Edendale and get acquainted with the people. When we left the café, we bundled into Mr Sennett's glamorous racing car and I was driven to my hotel.

The following morning I boarded a street-car for Edendale, a suburb of Los Angeles. It was an anomalous-looking place that could not make up its mind whether to be a humble residential district or a semi-industrial one. It had small lumber-yards and junk-yards, and abandoned-looking small farms on which were built one or two shacky wooden stores that fronted the road. After many inquiries I found myself opposite the Keystone Studio. It was a dilapidated affair with a green fence round it, one hundred and fifty feet square. The entrance to it was up a garden path through an old bungalow – the whole place looked just as anomalous as Edendale itself. I stood gazing at it from the opposite side of the road, debating whether to go in or not.

It was lunch-time and I watched the men and women in their make-up come pouring out of the bungalow, including the Keystone Cops. They crossed the road to a small general store and came out eating sandwiches and hot dogs. Some called after each other in loud, raucous voices: 'Hey, Hank, come on!' 'Tell Slim to hurry!'

Suddenly I was seized with shyness and walked quickly to the corner at a safe distance, looking to see if Mr Sennett or Miss Normand would come out of the bungalow, but they did not appear. For half an hour I stood there, then decided to go back to the hotel. The problem of entering the studio and facing all those people became an insuperable one. For two days I arrived outside the studio, but I had not the courage to go in. The third day Mr Sennett telephoned and wanted to know why I had not shown up. I made some sort of excuse. 'Come down right away, we'll be waiting for you,' he said. So I went down and boldly marched into the bungalow and asked for Mr Sennett.

He was pleased to see me and took me immediately into the studio. I was enthralled. A soft even light pervaded the whole stage. It came from broad streams of white linen that diffused the sun and gave an ethereal quality to everything. This diffusion was for photographing in daylight.

After being introduced to one or two actors I became interested in what was going on. There were three sets side by side, and three comedy companies were at work in them. It was like viewing something at the World's Fair. In one set Mabel Normand was banging on a door shouting: 'Let me in!' Then the camera stopped and that was it – I had no idea films were made piecemeal in this fashion.

On another set was the great Ford Sterling whom I was to replace. Mr Sennett introduced me to him. Ford was leaving Keystone to form his own company with Universal. He was immensely popular with the public and with everyone in the studio. They surrounded his set and were laughing eagerly at him.

Sennett took me aside and explained their method of working. 'We have no scenario – we get an idea then follow the natural sequence of events until it leads up to a chase, which is the essence of our comedy.'

This method was edifying, but personally I hated a chase. It dissipates one's personality; little as I knew about movies, I knew that nothing transcended personality.

That day I went from set to set watching the companies at work. They all seemed to be imitating Ford Sterling. This worried me, because his style did not suit me. He played a harassed Dutchman, ad-libbing through the scene with a Dutch accent, which was funny but was lost in silent pictures. I wondered what Sennett expected of me. He had seen my work and must have known that I was not suitable to play Ford's type of comedy; my style was just the opposite. Yet every story of situation conceived in the studio was consciously or unconsciously made for Sterling; even Roscoe Arbuckle was imitating Sterling.

The studio had evidently been a farm. Mabel Normand's dressing-room was situated in an old bungalow and adjoining it was another room where the ladies of the stock company dressed. Across from the bungalow was what had evidently been a barn, the main dressing-room for minor members of the stock company and the Keystone Cops, the majority of whom were ex-circus clowns and prize-fighters. I was allotted the star dressing-room used by Mack Sennett, Ford Sterling and Roscoe Arbuckle. It was another barn-like structure which might have been the harness-room. Besides Mabel Normand, there were several other beautiful girls. It was a strange and unique atmosphere of beauty and beast.

For days I wandered around the studio, wondering when I would start work. Occasionally I would meet Sennett crossing the stage, but he would look through me, preoccupied. I had an uncomfortable feeling that he thought he had made a mistake in engaging me which did little to ameliorate my nervous tension.

Each day my peace of mind depended on Sennett. If perchance he saw me and smiled, my hopes would rise. The rest of the company had a wait-and-see attitude but some, I felt, considered me a doubtful substitute for Ford Sterling.

When Saturday came Sennett was most amiable. Said he:

'Go to the front office and get your cheque.' I told him I was more anxious to get to work. I wanted to talk about imitating Ford Sterling, but he dismissed me with the remark: 'Don't worry, we'll get round to that.'

Nine days of inactivity had passed and the tension was excruciating. Ford, however, would console me and after work he would occasionally give me a lift down-town, where we would stop in at the Alexandria Bar for a drink and meet several of his friends. One of them, a Mr Elmer Ellsworth, whom I disliked at first and thought rather crass, would jokingly taunt me: 'I understand you're taking Ford's place. Well, are you funny?'

'Modesty forbids,' I said squirmishly. This sort of ribbing was most embarrassing, especially in the presence of Ford. But he graciously took me off the hook with a remark. 'Didn't you catch him at the Empress playing the drunk? Very funny.'

'Well, he hasn't made me laugh yet,' said Ellsworth.

He was a big, cumbersome man, and looked glandular, with a melancholy, hangdog expression, hairless face, sad eyes, a loose mouth and a smile that showed two missing front teeth. Ford whispered impressively that he was a great authority on literature, finance and politics, one of the best-informed men in the country, and that he had a great sense of humour. However, I did not appreciate it and would try to avoid him. But one night at the Alexandria bar, he said: 'Hasn't this limey got started yet?'

'Not yet,' I laughed uncomfortably.

'Well, you'd better be funny.'

Having taken a great deal from the gentleman, I gave him back some of his own medicine: 'Well, if I'm half as funny as you look, I'll do all right.'

'Blimey! A sarcastic wit, eh? I'll buy him a drink after that.'

*

At last the moment came. Sennett was away on location with Mabel Normand as well as the Ford Sterling Company, so there was hardly anyone left in the studio. Mr Henry Lehrman, Keystone's top director after Sennett, was to start a new picture and wanted me to play a newspaper reporter. Lehrman was a vain man and very conscious of the fact that he had made some successful comedies of a mechanical nature; he used to say that he didn't

144

need personalities, that he got all his laughs from mechanical effects and film-cutting.

We had no story. It was to be a documentary about the printing press done with a few comedy touches. I wore a light frock-coat, a top hat and a handlebar moustache. When we started I could see that Lehrman was groping for ideas. And of course being a newcomer at Keystone, I was anxious to make suggestions. This was where I created antagonism with Lehrman. In a scene in which I had an interview with an editor of a newspaper I crammed in every conceivable gag I could think of, even to suggesting business for others in the cast. Although the picture was completed in three days, I thought we contrived some very funny gags. But when I saw the finished film it broke my heart, for the cutter had butchered it beyond recognition, cutting into the middle of all my funny business. I was bewildered and wondered why they had done this. Henry Lehrman confessed years later that he had deliberately done it, because, as he put it, he thought I knew too much.

The day after I finished with Lehrman, Sennett returned from location. Ford Sterling was on one set, Arbuckle on another; the whole stage was crowded with three companies at work. I was in my street clothes and had nothing to do, so I stood where Sennett could see me. He was standing with Mabel, looking into a hotel lobby set, biting the end of a cigar. 'We need some gags here,' he said, then turned to me. 'Put on a comedy make-up. Anything will do.'

I had no idea what make-up to put on. I did not like my get-up as the press reporter. However, on the way to the wardrobe I thought I would dress in baggy pants, big shoes, a cane and a derby hat. I wanted everything a contradiction: the pants baggy, the coat tight, the hat small and the shoes large. I was undecided whether to look old or young, but remembering Sennett had expected me to be a much older man, I added a small moustache, which, I reasoned, would add age without hiding my expression.

I had no idea of the character. But the moment I was dressed, the clothes and the make-up made me feel the person he was. I began to know him, and by the time I walked on to the stage he was fully born. When I confronted Sennett I assumed the character and strutted about, swinging my cane and parading before him. Gags and comedy ideas went racing through my mind.

The secret of Mack Sennett's success was his enthusiasm. He was a great audience and laughed genuinely at what he thought funny. He stood and giggled until his body began to shake. This encouraged me and I began to explain the character: 'You know this fellow is many-sided, a tramp, a gentleman, a poet, a dreamer, a lonely fellow, always hopeful of romance and adventure. He would have you believe he is a scientist, a musician, a duke, a polo-player. However, he is not above picking up cigarette-butts or robbing a baby of its candy. And, of course, if the occasion warrants it, he will kick a lady in the rear–but only in extreme anger!'

I carried on this way for ten minutes or more, keeping Sennett in continuous chuckles. 'All right,' he said, 'get on the set and see what you can do there.' As with the Lehrman film, I knew little of what the story was about, other than that Mabel Normand gets involved with her husband and a lover.

In all comedy business an attitude is most important, but it is not always easy to find an attitude. However, in the hotel lobby I felt I was an imposter posing as one of the guests, but in reality I was a tramp just wanting a little shelter. I entered and stumbled over the foot of a lady. I turned and raised my hat apologetically, then turned and stumbled over a cuspidor, then turned and raised my hat to the cuspidor. Behind the camera they began to laugh.

Quite a crowd had gathered there, not only the players of the other companies who left their sets to watch us, but also the stage-hands, the carpenters and the wardrobe department. That indeed was a compliment. And by the time we had finished rehearsing we had quite a large audience laughing. Very soon I saw Ford Sterling peering over the shoulders of others. When it was over I knew I had made good.

At the end of the day when I went to the dressing-room, Ford Sterling and Roscoe Arbuckle were taking off their make-up. Very little was said, but the atmosphere was charged with cross-currents. Both Ford and Roscoe liked me, but I frankly felt they were undergoing some inner conflict.

It was a long scene that ran seventy-five feet. Later Mr Sennett and Mr Lehrman debated whether to let it run its full length, as the average comedy scene rarely ran over ten. 'If it's funny,' I said, 'does length really matter?' They decided to let the scene run its full seventy-five feet. As the clothes had imbued me with the character, I then and there decided I would keep to this costume whatever happened.

That evening I went home on the street-car with one of the small-bit players. Said he: 'Boy, you've started something; nobody ever got those kind of laughs on the set before, not even Ford Sterling – and you should have seen his face watching you, it was a study!'

'Let's hope they'll laugh the same way in the theatre,' I said, by way of suppressing my elation.

\*

A few days later, at the Alexandria Bar, I overheard Ford giving his description of my character to our mutual friend Elmer Ellsworth: 'The guy has baggy pants, flat feet, the most miserable, bedraggled-looking little bastard you ever saw; makes itchy gestures as though he's got crabs under his arms – but he's funny.'

My character was different and unfamiliar to the American, and even unfamiliar to myself. But with the clothes on I felt he was a reality, a living person. In fact he ignited all sorts of crazy ideas that I would never have dreamt of until I was dressed and made up as the Tramp.

I became quite friendly with a small-bit player, and each night going home on the street-car he would give me a bulletin of the studio's reactions that day and talk of my comedy ideas. 'That was a wonderful gag, dipping your fingers in the finger-bowl, then wiping them on the old man's whiskers – they've never seen that kind of stuff around there.' And so he would carry on, having me stepping on air.

Under Sennett's direction I felt comfortable, because everything was spontaneously worked out on the set. As no one was positive or sure of himself (not even the director), I concluded that I knew as much as the other fellow. This gave me confidence; I began to offer suggestions which Sennett readily accepted. Thus grew a belief in myself that I was creative and could write my own stories. Sennett indeed had inspired this belief. But although I had pleased Sennett I had yet to please the public.

In the next picture I was assigned to Lehrman again. He was leaving Sennett to join Sterling and to oblige Sennett was staying on two weeks longer than his contract called for. I still had abundant suggestions when I started working with him. He would listen and smile but would not accept any of them. 'That may be funny in the theatre,' he would say, 'but in pictures we have no time for it. We must be on the go – comedy is an excuse for a chase.'

I did not agree with this generality. 'Humour is humour,' I argued, 'whether in films or on the stage.' But he insisted on the same rigmarole, doing what the Keystone had always done. All action had to be fast – which meant running and climbing on top of the roofs of houses and street-cars, jumping into rivers and diving off piers. In spite of his comedy theories I happened to get in one or two bits of individual funny business, but, as before, he managed to have them mutilated in the cutting-room.

I do not think Lehrman gave a very promising report to Sennett about me. After Lehrman, I was assigned to another director, Mr Nichols, an oldish man in his late fifties who had been in motion pictures since their inception. I had the same trouble with him. He had but one gag, which was to take the comedian by the neck and bounce him from one scene to another. I tried to suggest subtler business, but he too would not listen. 'We have no time, no time!' he would cry. All he wanted was an imitation of Ford Sterling. Although I only mildly rebelled, it appears that he went to Sennett saying that I was a son of a bitch to work with.

About this time the picture which Sennett had directed, *Mabel's Strange Predicament*, was shown down-town. With fear and trepidation, I saw it with an audience. With Ford Sterling's appearance there was always a stir of enthusiasm and laughter, but I was received in cold silence. All the funny stuff I had done in the hotel lobby hardly got a smile. But as the picture progressed, the audience began to titter, then laugh, and towards the end of the picture there were one or two big laughs. At that showing I discovered that the audience were not partial to a newcomer.

I doubt whether this first effort came up to Sennett's expectations. I believe he was disappointed. He came to me a day or so later: 'Listen, they say you're difficult to work with.' I tried to explain that I was conscientious and was working only for the good of the picture. 'Well,' said Sennett, coldly, 'just do what you're told and we'll be satisfied.' But the following day I had another altercation with Nichols, and I blew up. 'Any three-dollar-a-day extra can do what you want me to do,' I declared. 'I want to do something with merit, not just be bounced around and fall off street-cars. I'm not getting a hundred and fifty dollars a week just for that.'

Poor old 'Pop' Nichols, as we called him, was in a terrible state. 'I've been in this business over ten years,' he said. 'What the hell do you know about it?' I tried to reason with him, but to no avail. I tried to reason with members of the cast, but they also were against me. 'Oh, he knows, he knows, he's been in the business much longer than you have,' said an old actor.

I made about five pictures and in some of them I had managed to put over one or two bits of comedy business of my own, in spite of the butchers in the cutting-room. Familiar with their method of cutting films, I would contrive business and gags just for entering and exiting from a scene, knowing that they would have difficulty in cutting them out. I took every opportunity I could to learn the business. I was in and out of the developing plant and cutting-room, watching the cutter piece the films together.

Now I was anxious to write and direct my own comedies, so I talked to Sennett about it. But he would not hear of it; instead he assigned me to Mabel Normand who had just started directing her own pictures. This nettled me, for, charming as Mabel was, I doubted her competence as a director; so the first day there came the inevitable blow-up. We were on location in the suburbs of Los Angeles and in one scene Mabel wanted me to stand with a hose and water down the road so that the villain's car would skid over it. I suggested standing on the hose so that the water can't come out, and when I look down the nozzle I unconsciously step off the hose and the water squirts in my face. But she shut me up quickly: 'We have no time! We have no time! Do what you're told.'

That was enough, I could not take it – and from such a pretty girl. 'I'm sorry, Miss Normand, I will not do what I'm told. I don't think you are competent to tell me what to do.'

149

The scene was in the centre of the road, and I left it and sat down on the kerb. Sweet Mabel – at that time she was only twenty, pretty and charming, everybody's favourite, everybody loved her. Now she sat by the camera bewildered; nobody had ever spoken to her so directly before. I also was susceptible to her charm and beauty and secretly had a soft spot in my heart for her, but this was my work. Immediately the staff and the cast surrounded Mabel and went into conference. One or two extras, Mabel told me afterwards, wanted to slug me, but she stopped them from doing so. Then she sent the assistant over to find out if I was going to continue working. I crossed the road to where she was sitting. 'I'm sorry,' I said apologetically, 'I just don't think it's funny or amusing. But if you'll allow me to offer a few comedy suggestions – .' She did not argue. 'Very well,' she said. 'If you won't do what you're told, we'll go back to the studio.' Although the situation was desperate I was resigned, so I shrugged. We had not lost much of the day's work, for we had been shooting since nine in the morning. It was now past five in the afternoon and the sun was sinking fast.

At the studio, while I was taking off my grease-paint, Sennett came bursting into the dressing-room. 'What the hell's the idea?' he said.

I tried to explain. 'The story needs gagging up,' I said, 'but Miss Normand will not listen to any suggestions.'

'You'll do what you're told or get out, contract or no contract,' he said.

I was very calm. 'Mr Sennett,' I answered, 'I earned my bread and cheese before I came here, and if I'm fired – well, I'm fired. But I'm conscientious and just as keen to make a good picture as you are.'

Without saying anything further he slammed the door.

That night going home on the street-car with my friend I told him what had happened.

'Too bad. You were going great there for a while,' he said.

'Do you think they'll fire me?' I said cheerfully, in order to hide my anxiety.

'I wouldn't be at all surprised. When I saw him leaving your dressing-room he looked pretty mad.'

'Well, it's O.K. with me. I've got fifteen hundred dollars in my belt and that will more than pay my fare back to England. However, I'll show up tomorrow and if they don't want me – *c'est la vie*.'

There was an eight o'clock call the following morning and I was not sure what to do, so I sat in the dressing-room without making up. About ten minutes to eight Sennett poked his head in the door. 'Charlie, I want to talk to you, let's go into Mabel's dressing-room.' His tone was surprisingly friendly.

'Yes, Mr Sennett,' I said, following him.

Mabel was not there; she was in the projection-room looking at rushes.

'Listen,' said Mack, 'Mabel's very fond of you, we all are fond of you and think you're a fine artist.'

I was surprised at this sudden change and I immediately began to melt. 'I certainly have the greatest respect and admiration for Miss Normand,' I said, 'but I don't think she is competent to direct – after all she's very young.'

'Whatever you think just swallow your pride and help out,' said Sennett, patting me on the shoulder.

'That's precisely what I've been trying to do.'

'Well, do your best to get along with her.'

'Listen, if you'll let me direct myself, you'll have no trouble,' I said.

Mack paused a moment. 'Who's going to pay for the film if we can't release it?'

'I will,' I answered. 'I'll deposit fifteen hundred dollars in any bank and if you can't release the picture you can keep the money.'

Mack thought a moment. 'Have you a story?'

'Of course, as many as you want.'

'All right,' said Mack, 'finish the picture with Mabel, then I'll see.' We shook hands in a most friendly manner. Later I went to Mabel and apologized, and that evening Sennett took us both out to dinner. The next day Mabel could not have been sweeter. She even came to me for suggestions and ideas. Thus, to the bewilderment of the camera crew and the rest of the cast, we happily completed the picture. Sennett's sudden change of attitude baffled me. It was months later, however, that I found out the reason: it appears that Sennett intended firing me at the end of the week, but the morning after I had quarrelled with Mabel,

Mack received a telegram from the New York office telling him to hurry up with more Chaplin pictures as there was a terrific demand for them.

The average number of prints for a Keystone Comedy release was twenty. Thirty was considered quite successful. The last picture, which was the fourth one, reached forty-five copies, and demands for further copies were increasing. Hence Mack's friendliness after the telegram.

The mechanics of directing were simple in those days. I had only to know my left from my right for entrances and exists. If one exited right from a scene, one came in left in the next scene; if one exited towards the camera, one entered with one's back to the camera in the next scene. These, of course, were primary rules.

But with more experience I found that the placing of a camera was not only psychological but articulated a scene; in fact it was the basis of cinematic style. If the camera is a little too near, or too far, it can enhance or spoil an effect. Because economy of movement is important you don't want an actor to walk any unnecessary distance unless there is a special reason, for walking is not dramatic. Therefore placement of camera should effect composition and a graceful entrance for the actor. Placement of camera is cinematic inflection. There is no set rule that a close-up gives more emphasis than a long shot. A close-up is a question of feeling; in some instances a long shot can effect greater emphasis.

An example of this is on one of my early comedies, *Skating*. The tramp enters the rink and skates with one foot up, gliding and twirling, tripping and bumping into people and getting into all sorts of mischief, eventually leaving everyone piled up on their backs in the foreground of the camera while he skates to the rear of the rink, becoming a very small figure in the background, and sits amongst the spectators innocently reviewing the havoc he has just created. Yet the small figure of the tramp in the distance was funnier than he would have been in a close-up.

When I started directing my first picture, I was not as confident as I thought I would be; in fact, I had a slight attack of panic. But after Sennett saw the first day's work I was reassured. The picture was called *Caught in the Rain*. It was not a world-beater, but it was funny and quite a success. When I finished it, I was anxious to know Sennett's reaction. I waited for him as he came out of the projection-room. 'Well, are you ready to start another?' he said. From then on I wrote and directed all my own comedies. As an inducement, Sennett gave me twenty-five dollars' bonus for each picture.

He now practically adopted me, and took me to dinner every night. He would discuss stories for the other companies with me and I would suggest crazy ideas which I felt were too personal to be understood by the public. But Sennett would laugh and accept them.

Now, when I saw my films with an audience, their reaction was different. The stir and excitement at the announcement of a Keystone Comedy, those joyful little screams that my first appearance evoked even before I had done anything, were most gratifying. I was a great favourite with the audience: if I could just continue this way of life I could be satisfied. With my bonus I was making two hundred dollars a week.

Since I was engrossed in work I had little time for the Alexandria Bar or my sarcastic friend, Elmer Ellsworth. I met him, however, weeks later, on the street. 'Say, listen,' said he, 'I've been seeing your pictures lately, and, by God, you're good! You have a quality entirely different from all the rest. And I'm not kidding. You're funny! Why the hell didn't you say so in the first place?' Of course, we became very good friends after that.

There was a lot Keystone taught me and a lot I taught Keystone. In those days they knew little about technique, stage-craft, or movement, which I brought to them from the theatre. They also knew little about natural pantomime. In blocking a scene, a director would have three or four actors blatantly stand in a straight line facing the camera, and, with the broadest gestures, one would pantomime 'I-want-to-marry-your-daughter' by pointing to himself, then to his ring finger, then to the girl. Their miming dealt little with subtlety or effectiveness, so I stood out in contrast. In those early movies, I knew I had many advantages, and that, like a geologist, I was entering a rich unexplored field. I suppose that was the most exciting period of my career, for I was on the threshold of something wonderful.

Success makes one endearing and I became the familiar friend of everyone in the studio. I was 'Charlie' to the extras, to the stage-hands, the wardrobe department, and the camera-men. Although I am not a fraternizer, this pleased me indeed, for I knew that this familiarity meant I was a success.

Now I had confidence in my ideas, and I can thank Sennett for that, for although unlettered like myself, he had belief in his own taste, and such belief he instilled in me. His manner of working had given me confidence; it seemed right. His remark that first day at the studio: 'We have no scenario. We get an idea, then follow the natural sequence of events' had stimulated my imagination.

*

Creating this way made films exciting. In the theatre I had been confined to a rigid, non-deviating routine of repeating the same thing night after night; once stage business had been tried out and set, one rarely attempted to invent new business. The only motivating thing about acting in the theatre was a good performance or a bad one. But films were freer. They gave me a sense of adventure. 'What do you think of this for an idea?' Sennett would say, or: 'There's a flood down town on Main Street.' Such remarks launched a Keystone comedy. It was this charming alfresco spirit that was a delight – a challenge to one's creativeness. It was so free and easy – no literature, no writers, we just had a notion around which we built gags, then made up the story as we went along.

For instance, in *His Prehistoric Past* I started with one gag, which was my first entrance. I appeared dressed as a prehistoric man wearing a bearskin, and, as I scanned the landscape, I began pulling the hair from the bearskin to fill my pipe. This was enough of an idea to stimulate a prehistoric story, introducing love, rivalry, combat and chase. This was the method by which we all worked at Keystone.

I can trace the first prompting of desire to add another dimension to my films besides that of comedy. I was playing in a picture called *The New Janitor*, in a scene in which the manager of the office fires me. In pleading with him to take pity on me and let me retain my job, I started to pantomime appealingly that I had a large family of little children. Although I was enacting mock sentiment, Dorothy Davenport, an old actress, was on the sidelines watching the scene, and during rehearsal I looked up and to my surprise found her in tears. 'I know it's supposed to be funny,' she said, 'but you just make me weep.' She confirmed something I already felt: I had the ability to evoke tears as well as laughter.

The 'he-man' atmosphere of the studio would have been almost intolerable but for the pulchritudinous influence. Mabel Normand's presence, of course, graced the studio with glamour. She was extremely pretty, with large heavy-lidded eyes and full lips that curled delicately at the corners of her mouth, expressing humour and all sorts of indulgence. She was light-hearted and gay, a good fellow, kind and generous; and everyone adored her.

Stories went around of Mabel's generosity to the wardrobe woman's child, of the jokes she played on the camera-man. Mabel liked me in a sisterly fashion, for at that time she was very much enamoured of Mack Sennett. Because of Mack I saw a lot of Mabel; the three of us would dine together and afterwards Mack would fall asleep in the hotel lobby and we would while away an hour at the movies or in a café, then come back and wake him up. Such propinquity one might think would result in a romance, but it did not; we remained, unfortunately, only good friends.

Once, however, when Mabel, Roscoe Arbuckle and I appeared for some charity at one of the theatres in San Francisco, Mabel and I came very near to being emotionally involved. It was a glamorous evening and the three of us had appeared with great success at the theatre. Mabel had left her coat in the dressing-room and asked me to take her there to get it. Arbuckle and the others were waiting below outside in a car. For a moment we were alone. She looked radiantly beautiful and as I placed her wrap over her shoulders I kissed her and she kissed me back. We might have gone further, but people were waiting. Later I tried to follow up the episode, but nothing ever came of it. 'No, Charlie,' she said good-humouredly, 'I'm not your type, neither are you mine.'

About this time Diamond Jim Brady came to Los Angeles – Hollywood was then in embryo. He arrived with the Dolly Sisters and their husbands, and entertained lavishly. At a dinner he gave at the Alexandria Hotel there were the Dolly Twins and their husbands, Carlotta Monterey, Lou Tellegen, leading man of Sarah Bernhardt, Mack Sennett, Mabel Normand, Blanche Sweet, Nat Goodwin and many others. The Dolly Twins were sensationally beautiful. The two of them, their husbands and Diamond Jim Brady were almost inseparable; their association was puzzling.

Diamond Jim was a unique American character, who looked like a benign John Bull. That first night I could not believe my eyes, for he wore diamond cuff-links and studs in his shirtfront, each stone larger than a shilling. A few nights later we dined at Nat Goodwin's Café on the pier, and this time Diamond Jim showed up with his emerald set, each stone the size of a small matchbox. At first I thought he was wearing them as a joke, and innocently asked if they were genuine. He said they were. 'But,' I said, with astonishment, 'they are fabulous.' 'If you want to see beautiful emeralds, here,' he replied. He lifted his dress waistcoat, showing a belt the size of the Marquess of Queensberry's championship belt, completely covered with the largest emeralds I have ever seen. He was quite proud to tell me that he had ten sets of precious stones and wore a different set every night.

It was 1914 and I was twenty-five years old, in the flush of youth and enamoured with my work, not alone for the success of it, but for its enchantment, as it gave me an opportunity of meeting all the film stars – and I was their fan at one time or other. Mary Pickford, Blanche Sweet, Miriam Cooper, Clara Kimball Young, the Gish sisters and others – all of them beautiful, and actually to meet them face to face was Elysian.

Thomas Ince gave barbecues and dances at his studio, which was in the wilds of northern Santa Monica, facing the Pacific Ocean. What wondrous nights – youth and beauty dancing to plaintive music on an open-air stage, with the soft sound of waves pounding on the nearby shore.

Peggy Pierce, an exceptionally beautiful girl with delicately chiselled features, beautiful white neck and a ravishing figure, was my first heart-throb. She did not make her appearance until my third week at the Keystone, having been ill with flu. But the moment we met we ignited; it was mutual, and my heart sang. How romantic were those morning's turning up for work with the anticipation of seeing her each day.

On Sunday I would call for her at her parents' apartment. Each night we met was an avowal of love, each night was a struggle. Yes. Peggy loved me, but it was a lost cause. She resisted and resisted, until I gave up in despair. At that time I had no desire to marry anyone. Freedom was too much of an adventure. No woman could measure up to that vague image I had in my mind.

Each studio was like a family. Films were made in a week, feature-length films never took more than two or three weeks. We worked by sunlight, which was why we worked in California: it was known to have nine months of sunshine each year.

Klieg lights came in about 1915; but Keystone never used them because they wavered, were not as clear as sunlight, and the lamps took up too much time to arrange. A Keystone Comedy rarely took more than a week to make, in fact I had made one in an afternoon, a picture called *Twenty Minutes of Love*, and it was a continuous laugh throughout. *Dough and Dynamite*, a most successful film, took nine days, at a cost of eighteen hundred dollars. And because I went over the budget of one thousand dollars, which was the limit for a Keystone comedy, I lost my bonus of twenty-five dollars. The only way they could retrieve themselves, said Sennett, would be to put it out as a two-reeler, which they did, and it grossed more than one hundred and thirty thousand dollars the first year.

*

Now I had several successful pictures under my belt, including *Twenty Minutes of Love*, *Dough and Dynamite*, *Laughing Gas*, and *The Stage Hand*. During this time Mabel and I starred in a feature picture with Marie Dressler. It was pleasant working with Marie, but I did not think the picture had much merit. I was more than happy to get back to directing myself again.

I recommended Sydney to Sennett; as the name Chaplin was being featured, he was only too pleased to annex another member of our family. Sennett signed him up for a year at a salary of two hundred dollars a week, which was twenty-five dollars more than I was getting. Sydney and his wife, fresh from England, came to the studio as I was leaving for location. Later that evening we dined together. I inquired how my pictures went in England.

Before my name was advertised, he said, many music-hall artists had spoken enthusiastically to him about a new American cinema comedian they had just seen. He also told me that before

157

he had seen any of my comedies he called up the film exchange to find out when they would be released and, when he told them who he was, they invited him to see three of them. He had sat alone in the projection room and laughed like the devil.

'What was your reaction to all this?' I asked him.

Sydney expressed no great wonderment. 'Oh, I knew you'd make good,' he said confidently.

Mack Sennett was a member of the Los Angeles Athletic Club, which entitled him to give a temporary membership card to a friend, and he gave one to me. It was the headquarters of all the bachelors and business men in town, an elaborate club with a large dining-room and lounge rooms on the first floor, which were open to the ladies in the evening, and a cocktail bar.

I had a large corner room on the top floor, with a piano and a small library, next to Mose Hamberger, who owned the May Department Store (the largest in town). The cost of living was remarkably cheap in those days. I paid twelve dollars a week for my room, which gave me the use of all the facilities of the club, including elaborate gymnasiums, swimming pools and excellent service. All told, I lived in a sumptuous style for seventy-five dollars a week, out of which I kept my end up in rounds of drinks and occasional dinners.

There was a camaraderie about the club which even the declaration of the First World War did not disturb. Everyone thought it would be over in six months; that it would last for four years, as Lord Kitchener predicted, people thought preposterous. Many were rather glad that war had been declared, for now we would show the Germans. There was no question of the outcome; the English and the French would lick them in six months. The war had not really got into its stride and California was far away from the scene of action.

About this time Sennett began to talk of renewing my contract, and wanted to know my terms. I knew to some degree the extent of my popularity, but I also knew the ephemera of it, and believed that, at the rate I was going, within a year I would be all dried up, so I had to make hay while the sun shone. 'I want a thousand dollars per week!' I said deliberately.

Sennett was appalled. 'But *I* don't make that,' he said.

'I know it,' I answered, 'but the public doesn't line up outside the box-office when your name appears as they do for mine.'

'Maybe,' said Sennett, 'but without the support of our organization you'd be lost.' He warned: 'Look what's happening to Ford Sterling.'

This was true, for Ford had not fared very well since leaving Keystone. But I told Sennett: 'All I need to make a comedy is a park, a policeman and a pretty girl.' As a matter of fact I had made some of my most successful pictures with just about that assembly.

Sennett, in the meantime, had wired to Kessel and Bauman, his partners, for advice about my contract and my demand. Later Sennett came to me with a proposition: 'Listen, you have four months to go. We'll tear up your contract and give you five hundred dollars now, seven hundred for the next year, and fifteen hundred for the following year. That way you'll get your thousand dollars a week.'

'Mack,' I answered, 'if you'll just reverse the terms, give me fifteen hundred the first year, seven hundred the second year, and five hundred the third, I'll take it.'

'But that's a crazy idea,' said Sennett.

So the question of a new contract was not discussed again.

*

I had a month to go with Keystone, and so far no other company had made me an offer. I was getting nervous and I fancy Sennett knew it and was biding his time. Usually he came to me at the end of a picture and jokingly hustled me up about starting another; now, although I had not worked for two weeks, he kept away from me. He was polite, but aloof.

In spite of the fact, my confidence never left me. If nobody made me an offer I would go into business for myself. Why not? I was confident and self-reliant. I remember the exact moment that feeling was born: I was signing a requisition slip against the studio wall.

After Sydney joined the Keystone Company, he made several successful films. One that broke records throughout the world was *The Submarine Pirate*, in which Sydney contrived all sorts of camera tricks. As he was so successful, I approached him about joining me and starting our own company. 'All we need is a camera and a back lot,' I said. But Sydney was conservative. He thought it was taking too much of a chance. 'Besides,' he added, 'I don't feel like giving up a salary which is more than I have ever earned in my life.' So he continued with Keystone for another year.

One day I received a telephone call from Carl Laemmle of the Universal Company. He was willing to give me twelve cents a foot and finance my pictures, but he would not give me a salary of a thousand dollars a week, so nothing came of it.

A young man named Jess Robbins, who represented the Essanay Company, said he had heard that I wanted a ten-thousand-dollar bonus before signing a contract, and twelve hundred and fifty dollars a week. This was news to me. I had never thought of a ten-thousand-dollar bonus until he mentioned it, but from that happy moment it became a fixation in my mind.

That night I invited Robbins to dinner and let him do all the taking. He said that he had come directly from Mr G. M. Anderson, known as Bronco Billy, of the Essanay Company, who was a partner of Mr George K. Spoor, with an offer of twelve hundred and fifty dollars a week, but he was not sure about the bonus. I shrugged. 'That seems to be a hitch with so many of them,' I said. 'They're all full of big offers, but they don't put up any cash.' Later, he telephoned to Anderson in San Francisco, telling him that the deal was on, but that I wanted ten thousand dollars down as a bonus. He turned to the table all glowing. 'The deal's on,' he said, 'and you get your ten thousand dollars tomorrow.'

I was elated. It seemed too good to be true. Alas, it was, for the next day Robbins handed me a cheque for only six hundred dollars, explaining that Mr Anderson was coming himself to Los Angeles and that the matter of the ten thousand dollars would be taken care of then. Anderson arrived full of enthusiasm and assurance about the deal, but no ten thousand dollars. 'My partner, Mr Spoor, will attend to that when we get to Chicago.'

Although my suspicions were aroused, I preferred to bury them in optimism. I had two more weeks to go with Keystone. Finishing my last picture, *His Prehistoric Past*, was a strain, because it was hard to concentrate with so many business propositions dangling before me. Nevertheless, the picture was eventually completed.

# *eleven*

IT was a wrench leaving Keystone, for I had grown fond of Sennett and everyone there. I never said goodbye to anyone, I couldn't. It all happened in a ruthlessly simple way. I finished cutting my film on Saturday night and left with Mr Anderson the following Monday for San Francisco, where we were met by his new green Mercedes car. We paused only for lunch at the St Francis Hotel, then went on to Niles, where Anderson had his own small studio in which he made his Bronco Billy Westerns for the Essanay Company (Essanay, a corruption, standing for the initials of Spoor and Anderson).

Niles was an hour's drive outside San Francisco, situated along the railroad track. It was a small town with a population of four hundred and its precoccupation was alfalfa and cattle-raising. The studio was situated in the centre of a field, about four miles outside. When I saw it my heart sank, for nothing could have been less inspiring. It had a glassed-in roof, which made it extremely hot when working in the summer. Anderson said that I would find the studios in Chicago more to my liking and better equipped for making comedies. I stayed only an hour in Niles while Anderson transacted some business with his staff. Then we both left for San Franciso again, where we embarked for Chicago.

I liked Anderson; he had a special kind of charm. On the train he tended me like a brother, and at the different stops would buy magazines and candy. He was shy and uncommunicative, a man about forty, and when business was discussed would magnanimously remark: 'Don't worry about that. It'll be O.K.' He had little conversation and was very much preoccupied. Yet I felt underneath he was shrewd.

The journey was interesting. On the train were three men. We first noticed them in the dining-car. Two looked quite prosperous, but the third looked out of place, a common, rough-looking fellow. It was strange to see them dining together. We speculated that the two might be engineers and the derelict-looking one a labourer to do the rough work. When we left the dining-car, one of them came to our compartment and introduced himself. He said he was sheriff of St Louis and had recognized Bronco Billy. They were transferring a criminal from San Quentin prison back to St Louis to be hanged, but, since they could not leave the prisoner alone, would we mind coming to their compartment to meet the district attorney?

'Thought you might like to know the circumstances,' said the sheriff confidentially. 'This fellow had quite a criminal record. When the officer arrested him in St Louis, he asked to be allowed to go to his room and take some clothes from his trunk; and while he was going through his trunk he suddenly whipped round with a gun and shot the officer dead, then escaped to California, where he was caught burglaring and was sentenced to three years. When he came out the district attorney and I were waiting for him. It's a cut-and-dried case – we'll hang him,' he said complacently.

Anderson and I went to their compartment. The sheriff was a jovial, thickset man, with a perpetual smile and a twinkle in his eye. The district attorney was more serious.

'Sit down,' said the sheriff, after introducing us to his friend. Then he turned to the prisoner. 'And this is Hank,' he said. 'We're taking him back to St Louis, where he's in a bit of a jam.'

Hank laughed ironically, but made no comment. He was a man six feet tall, in his late forties. He shook hands with Anderson, saying: 'I seen you many times, Bronco Billy, and by God, the way you handle them guns and them stick-ups is the best I've ever seen.' Hank knew little about me, he said; he had been in San Quentin for three years – 'and a lot goes on on the outside that you don't get to know about.'

Although we were all convivial there was an underlying tension which was difficult to cope with. I was at a loss what to say, so I just grinned at the sheriff's remarks.

'It's a tough world,' said Bronco Billy.

'Well,' said the sheriff, 'we want to make it less tough. Hank knows that.'

'Sure,' said Hank, brusquely.

The sheriff began moralizing: 'That's what I told Hank when he stepped out of San Quentin. I said if he'll play square with us, we'll play square with him. We don't want to use handcuffs or make a fuss; all he's got on is a leg-iron.'

'A leg-iron! What's that?' I asked.

'Haven't you ever seen one?' said the sheriff. 'Lift up your trouser, Hank.'

Hank lifted his trouser-leg and there it was, a nickel-plated cuff about five inches in length and three inches thick, fitting snugly around his ankle, weighing forty pounds. This led to commenting on the latest type of leg-irons. The sheriff explained that this particular one had rubber insulation on the inside so as to make it easier for the prisoner.

'Does he sleep with that thing?' I asked.

'Well, that depends,' said the sheriff, looking coyly at Hank.

Hank's smile was grim and cryptic.

We sat with them till dinner-time and as the day wore on the conversation turned to the manner in which Hank had been re-arrested. From the interchange of prison information, the sheriff explained, they had received photographs and finger-prints and decided that Hank was their man. So they had arrived outside the prison gates of San Quentin the day Hank was to be released.

'Yes,' said the sheriff, his small eyes twinkling and looking at Hank, 'we waited for him on the opposite side of the road. Very soon Hank came out of the side door of the prison gate.' The sheriff slid his index finger along the side of his nose and slyly pointed in the direction of Hank and with a diabolical grin said slowly: 'I – think – that's – our man!'

Anderson and I sat fascinated as he continued. 'So we made a deal,' said the sheriff, 'that if he'd play square with us, we'd treat him right. We took him to breakfast and gave him hot cakes and bacon and eggs. And here he is, travelling first class. That's better than going the hard way in handcuffs and chains.'

Hank smiled and mumbled: 'I could have fought you on extradition if I'd wanted to.'

The sheriff eyed him coldly. 'That wouldn't have done you much good, Hank,' he said slowly. 'It would just have meant a little delay. Isn't it better to go first class in comfort?'

'I guess so,' said Hank, jerkily.

As we neared Hank's destination, he began to talk about the jail in St Louis almost with affection. He rather enjoyed the anticipation of his trial by the other prisoners: 'I'm just thinking what those gorillas will do to me when I get before the Kangaroo Court! Guess they'll take all my tobacco and cigarettes away from me.'

The sheriff's and the attorney's relationship with Hank was like a matador's fondness for the bull he is about to kill. When they left the train, it was the last day of December, and as we parted the sheriff and the attorney wished us a happy New Year. Hank also shook hands, saying grimly that all good things must come to an end. It was difficult to know how to bid him goodbye. His crime had been a ruthless and cowardly one, yet I found myself wishing him good luck as he limped from the train with his heavy leg-iron. Eventually we heard that he was hanged.

＊

When we arrived in Chicago, we were greeted by the studio manager, but no Mr Spoor. Mr Spoor, he said, was away on business and would not return until after the New Year holiday. I did not think Spoor's absence had any significance then, because nothing would happen at the studio until after the first of the year. Meanwhile I spent New Year's Eve with Anderson, his wife and family. On New Year's Day Anderson left for California, assuring me that as soon as Spoor returned he would attend to everything, including the ten-thousand-dollar bonus. The studio was in the industrial district, and, at one time, had evidently been a warehouse. The morning I showed up there, no Spoor had yet arrived, nor were there any instructions left about my business arrangements. Immediately I sensed that something was fishy and that the office knew more than they cared to divulge. But it didn't worry me; I was confident that a good picture would solve all my problems. So I asked the manager if he knew that I was to get the full cooperation of the studio staff and *carte blanche* for all their facilities. 'Of course,' he replied. 'Mr Anderson has left instructions about that.'

'Then I would like to start work immediately,' I said.

'Very well,' he answered. 'On the first floor you will find the head of the scenario department, Miss Louella Parsons, who will give you a script.'

'I don't use other people's scripts, I write my own,' I snapped.

I was belligerent because they seemed so vague about everything and because of Spoor's absence; besides, the studio personnel were stuffy and went around like bank clerks, carrying requisition papers as though they were members of the Guaranty Trust Company – the business end of it was very impressive, but not their films. In the upstairs office the different departments were partitioned like tellers' grilles. It was anything but conducive to creative work. At six o'clock, no matter whether a director was in the middle of a scene or not, the lights were turned off and everybody went home.

The next morning I went to the casting grille. 'I would like a cast of some sort,' I said dryly, 'so will you kindly send me members of your company who are unoccupied?'

They presented people whom they thought might be suitable. There was a chap with cross eyes named Ben Turpin, who seemed to know the ropes and was not doing much with Essanay at the time. Immediately I took a liking to him, so he was chosen. But I had no leading lady. After I had had several interviews, one applicant seemed a possibility, a rather pretty young girl whom the company had just signed up. But oh, God! I could not get a reaction out of her. She was so unsatisfactory that I gave up and dismissed her. Gloria Swanson years later told me that she was the girl and that, having dramatic aspirations and hating slapstick comedy, she had been deliberately uncooperative.

Francis X. Bushman, then a great star with Essanay, sensed my dislike of the place. 'Whatever you think about the studio,' he said, 'it is just the antithesis': but it wasn't; I didn't like the studio and I didn't like the word 'antithesis'. Circumstances went from bad to worse. When I wanted to see my rushes, they ran the original negative to save the expense of a positive print. This horrified me. And when I demanded that they should make a positive print, they reacted as though I wanted to bankrupt them. They were smug and self-satisfied. Having been one of the first to enter the film business, and being protected by patent rights which gave them a monopoly, their last consideration was the making of good pictures. And although other companies were challenging their patent rights and making better films, Essanay still went smugly on, dealing out scenarios like playing cards every Monday morning.

I had almost finished my first picture, which was called *His New Job*, and two weeks had elapsed and still no Mr Spoor had shown up. Having received neither the bonus nor my salary, I was contemptuous. 'Where is this Mr Spoor?' I demanded at the front office. They were embarrassed and could give no satisfactory explanation. I made no effort to hide my contempt and asked if he always conducted his business affairs in this way.

Years later I heard from Spoor himself what had happened. It appears that when Spoor, who had never heard of me at that time, learned that Anderson had signed me up for a year at twelve hundred dollars a week with a ten-thousand-dollar bonus, he sent Anderson a frantic wire, wanting to know if he had done mad. And when Spoor heard that Anderson had signed me purely as a gamble, on the recommendation of Jess Robbins, his anxiety was twofold. He had comics who were getting only seventy-five dollars a week, the best of them, and their comedies barely paid for themselves. Hence Spoor's absence from Chicago.

When he returned, however, he lunched at one of the big Chicago hotels with several friends who, to his surprise, complimented him about my joining his company. Also, more than the usual publicity began piling up in the studio office about Charlie Chaplin. So he thought he would try an experiment. He gave a page-boy a quarter and had me paged throughout the hotel. As the boy went through the lobby shouting: 'Call for Mr Charlie Chaplin,' people began to congregate until it was packed with stir and excitement. This was his first indication of my popularity. The second was what had happened at the film exchange while he was away: he discovered that even before I had started the picture there was an advance sale of sixty-five copies, something unprecedented, and by the time I had finished the film a hundred and thirty prints were sold and orders were still pouring in. Immediately they raised the price from thirteen cents to twenty-five cents a foot.

When Spoor eventually showed up, I confronted him about my salary and bonus. He was profuse with apologies, explaining that he had told the front office to take care of all business arrangements. He had not seen the contract, but assumed that the front office knew all about it. This cock-and-bull story infuriated me. 'What were you scared about?' I said, laconically. 'You can still get out of your contract if you wish – in fact I think you've already broken it.'

Spoor was a tall, portly individual, soft-spoken and almost good-looking but for a pale flabbiness of face and an acquisitive top lip that sat over the lower one.

'I'm sorry you feel this way,' he said, 'but, as you must know, Charlie, we are a reputable firm and always live up to our contract.'

'Well, you haven't lived up to this one,' I interposed.

'We'll take care of that matter right now,' he said.

'I'm in no hurry,' I answered sarcastically.

*

During my short stay in Chicago, Spoor did everything to placate me, but I could never really warm up to him. I told him I was unhappy working in Chicago and that if he wanted results he should arrange for me to work in California. 'We'll do everything we can to make you happy,' he said. 'How would you like to go to Niles?'

I was not too pleased at the prospect, but I liked Anderson better than Spoor; so after completing of *His New Job* I went to Niles.

Bronco Billy made all his Western movies there; they were one-reelers that took him a day to make. He had seven plots which he repeated over and over again, and from which he made several million dollars. He would work sporadically. Sometimes he would turn out seven one-reel Westerns in a week, then go on holiday for six weeks.

Surrounding the studio at Niles were several small Californian bungalows which Bronco Billy had built for members of his company, and a large one which he occupied himself. He told me that if I desired I could live there with him. I was delighted at the prospect. Living with Bronco Billy, the millionaire cowboy who had entertained me in Chicago at his wife's sumptuous apartment, would at least make life tolerable in Niles.

It was dark when we entered his bungalow, and when we switched on the light I was shocked. The place was empty and drab. In his room was an old iron bed with a light-bulb hanging over the head of it. A rickety old table and one chair were the other furnishings. Near the bed was a wooden box upon which was a brass ash-tray filled with cigarette-butts. The room allotted to me was almost the same, only it was minus a grocery box. Nothing worked. The bathroom was unspeakable. One had to take a jug and fill it from the bath tap and empty it down the flush to make the toilet work. This was the home of G. M. Anderson, the multi-millionaire cowboy.

I came to the conclusion that Anderson was an eccentric. Although a millionaire, he cared little for graceful living; his indulgences were flamboyant-coloured cars, promoting prize-fighters, owning a theatre and producing musical shows. When he was not working in Niles, he spent most of his time in San Francisco, where he stayed in small moderate-priced hotels. He was an odd fellow, vague, erratic and restless, who sought a solitary life of pleasure; and although he had a charming wife and daughter in Chicago, he rarely saw them. They lived their lives separately and apart.

It was disturbing moving again from one studio to another. I had to organize another working unit, which meant selecting a satisfactory camera-man, an assistant director and a stock company, the latter being difficult because there was little to choose from in Niles. There was one other company at Niles besides Anderson's cowboy outfit: this was a nondescript comedy company that kept things going and paid expenses when G. M. Anderson was not working. The stock company consisted of twelve people, and these were mostly cowboy actors. Again I had the problem of finding a pretty girl for a leading lady. Now I was anxious to get to work. Although I hadn't a story, I ordered the crew to build an ornate café set. When I was lost for a gag or an idea a café would always supply one. While it was being built I went with G. M. Anderson to San Francisco to look for a leading lady among the chorus girls of his musical comedy, and, although it was nice work, none of them was photogenic. Carl Strauss, a handsome young German-American cowboy working with Anderson, said he knew of a girl who occasionally went to Tate's Café on Hill Street. He did not know her personally, but she was pretty and the proprietor might know her address.

Mr Tate knew her quite well. She lived with her married sister, she was from Lovelock, Nevada, her name was Edna Purviance. Immediately we got in touch with her and made an appointment to meet her at the St Francis Hotel. She was more than pretty, she was beautiful. At the interview she seemed sad and serious. I learned afterwards that she was just getting over a love affair. She had been to college and had taken a business course. She was quiet and reserved, with beautiful large eyes, beautiful teeth and a sensitive mouth. I doubted whether she could act or had any humour, she looked so serious. Nevertheless, with these reservations we engaged her. She would at least be decorative to my comedies.

The next day we returned to Niles, but the café was not ready, and what they had built was crude and awful; the studio was certainly lacking technically. After giving orders for a few alterations, I began to think of an idea. I thought of a title: *His Night Out* – a drunk in pursuit of pleasure – that was enough to start with. I added a fountain to the night-club, feeling I could get some gags out of it, and I had Ben Turpin as a stooge. The day before we started the picture a member of Anderson's company invited me to a supper party. It was a modest affair, with beer and sandwiches. There were about twenty of us, including Miss Purviance. After supper some played cards while others sat around and talked. We got on to the subject of hypnotism and I bragged about my hypnotic powers. I boasted that within sixty seconds I could hypnotize anyone in the room. I was so convincing that most of the company believed me, but Edna did not.

She laughed. 'What nonsense! No one could hypnotize me!'

'You,' I said, 'are just the perfect subject. I bet you ten dollars that I'll put you to sleep in sixty seconds.'

'All right,' said Edna, 'I'll bet.'

'Now, if you're not well afterwards don't blame me for it – of course it will be nothing serious.'

I tried to scare her into backing out, but she was resolute. One woman begged her not to allow it. 'You're very foolish,' she told her.

'The bet still goes,' said Edna, quietly.

'Very well,' I answered. 'I want you to stand with your back firmly against the wall, away from everybody, so that I can get your undivided attention.'

She obeyed, smiling superciliously. By this time everyone in the room was interested.

'Somebody watch the time,' I said.

'Remember,' said Edna, 'you're to put me to sleep in sixty seconds.'

'In sixty seconds you will be completely unconscious,' I answered.

'Go!' said the time-keeper.

Immediately I made two or three dramatic passes, staring intensely into her eyes. Then I came near to her face and whispered so that the other could not hear: 'Fake it!' and made passes, saying: 'You will be unconscious – you are unconscious, unconscious!'

Then I drew back and she began to stagger. Quickly I caught her in my arms. Two of the onlookers screamed. 'Quick!' I said. 'Someone help me put her on the couch.'

When she came to, she feigned bewilderment and said the felt tired. Although she could have won her argument and proved her point to all present, she had generously relinquished her triumph for the sake of a good joke. This won her my esteem and affection and convinced me that she had a sense of humour.

I made four comedies at Niles, but as the studio facilities were not satisfactory, I did not feel settled or contented there, so I suggested to Anderson my going to Los Angeles, where they had better facilities for making comedies. He agreed, but also for another reason: because I was monopolizing the studio, which was not big enough or adequately staffed for three companies. So he negotiated the renting of a small studio at Boyle Heights, which was in the heart of Los Angeles.

While we were there, two young men who were just beginning in the business came and rented studio space, named Hal Roach and Harold Lloyd.

As the value of my comedies increased with every new picture, Essanay began demanding unprecedented terms, charging exhibitors a minimum of fifty dollars a day rental for my two-reel comedies. This meant that they were collecting over fifty thousand dollars in advance for each picture.

One evening, after I had returned to the Stoll Hotel, where I was staying, a middle-rate place but new and comfortable, there was an urgent telephone call from the Los Angeles *Examiner*. They read a telegram they had received from New York stating:

WILL GIVE CHAPLIN $25,000 FOR TWO WEEKS
TO APPEAR FIFTEEN MINUTES EACH EVENING AT
THE NEW YORK HIPPODROME. THIS WILL NOT
INTERFERE WITH HIS WORK.

Immediately I put in a call to G. M. Anderson in San Francisco. It was late and I was not able to reach him until three in the morning. Over the phone I told him of the telegram and asked if he would let me off for two weeks in order to earn that twenty-five thousand dollars. I suggested that I could start a comedy on the train going to New York, and while there finish it. But Anderson did not want me to do it.

My bedroom window opened out on the well of the hotel, so that the voice of anyone talking resounded through the rooms. The telephone connexion was bad – 'I don't intend to pass up twenty-five thousand dollars for two weeks' work!' I had to shout several times.

A window opened above and a voice shouted back: 'Cut out that bull and go to sleep, you big dope!'

Anderson said over the phone that, if I gave Essanay another two-reeler comedy, they would give me the twenty-five thousand. He agreed to come to Los Angeles the following day and give me the cheque and draw up an agreement. After I had finished telephoning I turned off the light and was about to go to sleep, then, remembering the voice, I got out of bed, opened the window and shouted up: 'Go to hell!'

Anderson came to Los Angeles the following day with a cheque for twenty-five thousand dollars, and the New York company that made the original offer went bankrupt two weeks later. Such was my luck.

Now back in Los Angeles I was much happier. Although the studio at Boyle Heights was in a slummy neighbourhood, it enabled me to be near my brother, whom I occasionally saw in the evening. He was still at Keystone and would finish his contract there about a month earlier than the completion of mine with Essanay. My success had taken on such proportions that Sydney now intended devoting his whole time to my business affairs. According to reports, my popularity kept increasing with each succeeding comedy. Although I knew the extent of my success in Los Angeles by the long lines at the box-office, I did not realize to what magnitude it had grown elsewhere. In New York, toys and statuettes of my character were being sold in all the department stores and drugstores. Ziegfeld Follies Girls were doing Chaplin numbers, marring their beauty with moustaches, derby hats, big shoes and baggy trousers, singing a song called *Those Charlie Chaplin Feet*.

We were also inundated with all manner of business propositions involving books, clothes, candles, toys, cigarettes and toothpaste. Also stacks upon stacks of increasing fanmail became a problem. Sydney insisted that it should all be answered, in spite of the expense of having to engage an extra secretary.

Sydney spoke to Anderson about selling my pictures separately from the rest of the routine product. It did not seem fair that the exhibitors should make all the money. Even though Essanay were selling hundreds of copies of my films, they were selling them along old-fashioned lines of distribution. Sydney suggested scaling the larger theatres according to their seating capacity. With this plan each film could increase the receipts to a hundred thousand dollars or more. Anderson thought this was impossible; it would butt up against the policy of the whole Motion Picture Trust, involving sixteen thousand theatres, whose rules and methods of buying pictures were irrevocable; few exhibitors would pay such terms.

Later the *Motion Picture Herald* announced that the Essanay

Company had discarded its old method of selling and, as Sydney had suggested, was scaling its terms according to the seating capacity of a theatre. This, as Sydney said it would, upped the receipts a hundred thousand dollars on each of my comedies. This news made me prick up my ears. Getting only twelve hundred and fifty dollars a week and doing all the work of writing, acting and directing, I began to complain that I was working too hard and that I needed more time to make my pictures. I had a year's contract and had been turning out comedies every two to three weeks. Action soon came from Chicago; Spoor hopped a train to Los Angeles and as an extra inducement made an agreement to give me a ten-thousand-dollar bonus with each picture. With this stimulus my health improved.

About this time D. W. Griffith produced his epic, *The Birth of a Nation*, which made him the outstanding director of motion pictures. He undoubtedly was a genius of the silent cinema. Though his work was melodramatic and at times outré and absurd, Griffith's pictures had an original touch that made each one worth seeing.

De Mille started with great promise with *The Whispering Chorus* and a version of *Carmen*, but after *Male and Female* his work never went beyond the chemise and the boudoir. Nevertheless, I was so impressed with his *Carmen* that I made a two-reel burlesque of it, my last film with Essanay. After I had left them they put in all the cut-outs and extended it to four reels, which prostrated me and sent me to bed for two days. Although this was a dishonest act, it rendered a service, for thereafter I had it stipulated in every contract that there should be no mutilating, extending or interfering with my finished work.

The approaching end of my contract brought Spoor back to the coast with a proposition, he said, that no one could match. He would give me three hundred and fifty thousand dollars if I delivered him twelve two-reel pictures, he to pay the cost of production. I told him that on signing any contract I wanted one hundred and fifty thousand dollars' bonus plonked down first. This terminated any further talks with Spoor.

The future, the future – the wonderful future! Where was it leading? The prospects were dazzling. Like an avalanche, money and success came with increasing momentum; it was all bewildering, frightening – but wonderful.

*

While Sydney was in New York reviewing various offers, I was completing the filming of *Carmen* and living at Santa Monica in a house facing the sea. Some evenings I dined at Nat Goodwin's Café at the end of Santa Monica pier. Nat Goodwin was considered the greatest actor and light comedian on the American stage. He had had a brilliant career both as a Shakespearian actor and a modern light comedian. He had been a close friend of Sir Henry Irving, and had married eight times, each wife celebrated for her beauty. His fifth wife was Maxine Elliott, whom he whimsically referred to as 'the Roman Senator'. 'But she was beautiful and remarkably intelligent,' he said. He was an amiable cultured man, advanced in years, with a profound sense of humour; and now he had retired. Although I had never seen him on the stage, I very much revered him and his great reputation.

We became very good friends and in the chill autumn evenings we would walk along the deserted ocean front together. The drear melancholy atmosphere accentuated a glow to my inner excitement. When he heard that I was going to New York at the completion of my picture, he gave me some excellent advice. 'You've made a remarkable success, and there's a wonderful life ahead of you if you know how to handle yourself. . . . When you get to New York keep off Broadway, keep out of the public's eye. The mistake with many successful actors is that they want to be seen and admired – it only destroys the illusion.' His voice was deep and resonant. 'You'll be invited everywhere,' he continued, 'but don't accept. Pick out one or two friends and be satisfied to imagine the rest. Many a great actor has made the mistake of accepting every social invitation. John Drew was an example; he was a great favourite with society and went to all their houses, but they would not go to his theatre. They had had him in their drawing-rooms. You've captivated the world, and you can continue doing so if you stand outside it,' he said wistfully.

They were wonderful talks, rather sad, as we walked in the

autumn twilight along the abandoned ocean front – Nat at the end of his career, I at the beginning of mine.

When I finished cutting *Carmen*, I hurriedly packed a small grip, and went directly from my dressing-room to the six o'clock train for New York, sending Sydney a telegram stating when I would leave and arrive.

It was a slow train which took five days to get there. I sat alone in an open compartment – in those days I was unrecognized without my comedy make-up. We were going the southern route through Amarillo, Texas, arriving there at seven in the evening. I had decided to shave, but other passengers were in the wash-room before me, so I had to wait. Consequently I was still in my underwear when we neared Amarillo. As we ploughed into the station, we were suddenly enveloped in babbling excitement. Peeking out of the wash-room window, I saw the station packed with a large milling crowd. Bunting and flags were wrapped and hung from pillar to post, and on the platform were several long tables set with refreshments. A celebration to welcome the arrival or departure of some local potentate, I thought. So I began to lather my face. But the excitement grew, then quite audibly I heard voices saying: 'Where is he?' Then a stampede entered the car, people running up and down the aisle shouting: 'Where is he? Where's Charlie Chaplin?'

'Yes?' I replied.

'On behalf of the Mayor of Amarillo, Texas, and all your fans, we invite you to have a drink and a light refreshment with us.'

I was seized with sudden panic. 'I can't, like this!' I said through shaving soap.

'Oh, don't bother about anything, Charlie. Just put on a dressing-gown and meet the folks.'

Hurriedly I washed my face, and, half-shaved, put on a shirt and tie and came out of the train buttoning my coat.

I was greeted with cheers. The mayor tried to speak: 'Mr Chaplin, on behalf of your fans of Amarillo –' but his voice was drowned by the continual cheering. He started again: 'Mr Chaplin, on behalf of your fans of Amarillo –' Then the crowd pressed forward, pushing the mayor into me and squashing us against the train, so that for a moment the welcoming speech was forgotten in quest of personal safety.

'Get back!' shouted the police, plunging through the crowd to make a way for us.

The Mayor lost his enthusiasm for the whole enterprise and spoke with slight asperity to the police and myself. 'All right, Charlie, let's get it over with, then you can get back on the train.'

After a general scramble to the tables, things quietened down and the mayor at last was able to make his address. He tapped the table with a spoon. 'Mr Chaplin, your friends of Amarillo, Texas, want to show their appreciation for all the happiness you have given them by asking you to join us in a sandwich and a Coca-Cola.'

After delivering his encomium, he asked if I would say a few words, urging me to get up on the table, where I mumbled something to the effect that I was happy to be in Amarillo and was so surprised by this wonderful, thrilling welcome that I would remember it for the rest of my life, etc. Then I sat down and tried to talk with the Mayor.

I asked him how he knew of my coming. 'Through the telegraph operators,' he said, explaining that the telegram I sent to Sydney had been relayed to Amarillo, then to Kansas City, Chicago and New York, and that the operators had given the news to the Press.

When I returned to the train I sat meekly in my seat, my mind for the moment a blank. Then the whole car became a turbulence of people passing up and down the aisle, staring and giggling. What had taken place in Amarillo I could not mentally digest or properly enjoy. I was too excited, I just sat tense, elated and depressed all at the same time.

Several telegrams were handed to me before the train departed. Said one: 'Welcome, Charlie, we're waiting for you in Kansas City.' Another: 'There will be a limousine at your disposal when you arrive in Chicago to take you from one station to the other.' A third: 'Will you stay over for the night and be the guest of the Blackstone Hotel?' As we neared Kansas City, people stood along the side of the railroad track, shouting and waving their hats.

The large railroad station in Kansas City was packed solidly with people. The police were having difficulty controlling further crowds accumulating outside. A ladder was placed against the train to enable me to mount it and show myself on the roof. I found myself repeating the same banal words as in Amarillo. More telegrams awaited me: would I visit schools and institutions? I stuffed them in my suitcase, to be answered in New York. From Kansas City to Chicago people were again standing at railroad junctions and in fields, waving as the train swept by. I wanted to enjoy it all without reservation, but I kept thinking the world had gone crazy! If a few slapstick comedies could arouse such excitement, was there not something bogus about all celebrity? I had always thought I would like the public's attention, and here it was – paradoxically isolating me with a depressing sense of loneliness.

In Chicago, where it was necessary to change trains and stations, crowds lined the exit and hoorayed me into a limousine. I was driven to the Blackstone Hotel and given a suite of rooms to rest in before embarking for New York.

At the Blackstone a telegram arrived from the Chief of Police of New York, requesting that I oblige him by putting off at 125th Street, instead of arriving at Grand Central Station as scheduled, as crowds were already gathering there in anticipation.

At 125th Street Sydney met me with a limousine, tense and excited. He spoke in whispers. 'What do you think of it?' he said. 'Crowds have been gathering from early morning at the station, and the Press has been issuing bulletins every day since you left Los Angeles.' He showed me a newspaper announcing in big black type: 'He's here!' Another headline: 'Charlie in hiding!' On the way to the hotel he told me that he had completed a deal with the Mutual Film Corporation amounting to six hundred and seventy thousand dollars payable at ten thousand a week, and after I had passed the insurance test, a hundred and fifty thousand bonus would be paid on my signing the contract. He had a lunch engagement with the lawyer which would occupy him for the rest of the day, so he would drop me off at the Plaza, where he had booked a room for me, and would see me in the morning.

As Hamlet said: 'Now I am alone.' That afternoon I walked the streets and looked into shop windows and paused aimlessly on street corners. Now what happens to me? Here I was at the apogee of my career – all dressed up and no place to go. How does one get to know people, interesting people? It seemed that everyone knew me, but I knew no one; I became introspective, full of self-pity, and a spell of melancholy beset me. I remember a successful Keystone comedian once saying: 'Now that we've arrived, Charlie, what's it all about?' 'Arrived where?' I answered.

I thought of Nat Goodwin's advice: 'Keep off Broadway.' Broadway was a desert as far as I was concerned. I thought of old friends whom I would like to meet framed in this success extravaganza – did I have old friends either in New York, London or elsewhere? I wanted a special audience – perhaps Hetty Kelly. I had not heard from her since my entry into movies – her reactions would be amusing.

She was then living in New York with her sister, Mrs Frank Gould. I took a walk up Fifth Avenue; 834 was her sister's address. I paused outside the house, wondering if she were there, but I had not the courage to call. However, she might come out and I could accidentally bump into her. I waited for about half an hour, sauntering up and down, but no one went in or came out of the house.

I went to Childs Restaurant at Columbus Circle and ordered wheat-cakes and a cup of coffee. I was served perfunctorily until I asked the waitress for an extra pat of butter; then she recognized me. From then on it was a chain reaction until everyone in the restaurant and from the kitchen was peering at me. Eventually I was obliged to propel my way through an immense crowd that had gathered both inside and out, and escape in a passing taxi.

For two days I walked about New York without meeting anyone I knew, vacillating between happy excitement and depression. Meanwhile the insurance doctors had examined me. A few days later, Sydney came to the hotel, elated. 'It's all settled, you've passed the insurance.'

The formalities of signing the contract followed. I was photographed receiving the one-hundred-and-fifty-thousand-dollar cheque. That evening I stood with the crowd in Times Square as the news flashed on the electric sign that runs round the Times building. It read: 'Chaplin signs with Mutual at six hundred and seventy thousand a year.' I stood and read it objectively as though it were about someone else. So much had happened to me, my emotions were spent.

# *twelve*

LONELINESS is repellent. It has a subtle aura of sadness, an inadequacy to attract or interest; one feels slightly ashamed of it. But, to a more or less degree, it is the theme of everyone. However, my loneliness was frustrating because I had all the requisite means for making friends; I was young, rich and celebrated, yet I was wandering about New York alone and embarrassed. I remember meeting the beautiful Josie Collins, the English musical comedy star, who suddenly came upon me walking along Fifth Avenue. 'Oh,' she said sympathetically, 'what are you doing all alone?' I felt I had been apprehended in some petty crime. I smiled and said that I was just on my way to have lunch with some friends; but I would like to have told her the truth – that I was lonely and would have loved to have taken her to lunch – only my shyness prevented it.

The same afternoon I took a stroll by the Metropolitan Opera House and ran into Maurice Guest, son-in-law of David Belasco. I had met Maurice in Los Angeles. He had started as a ticket-scalper, a business quite prevalent when I first arrived in New York. (A scalper was a man who bought up the best seats in the house, and stood outside the theatre selling them for a profit.) Maurice had a meteoric rise as a theatrical entrepreneur, climaxed by the great spectacle, *The Miracle*, directed by Max Reinhardt. Maurice – Slavic, pale face with large kidney eyes, a wide mouth and thick lips – looked like a coarse edition of Oscar Wilde. He was an emotional man who when he spoke seemed to bully you.

'Where the hell have you been?' Then before I could answer: 'Why in hell didn't you call me up?'

I told him that I was just taking a walk.

'What the hell! You shouldn't be alone! Where are you going?'

'Nowhere,' I answered meekly. 'Just getting some fresh air.'

'Come on!' he said, twisting me around in his direction and locking his arm through mine so that there was no escape. 'I'll introduce you to real people – the kind you should mix with.'

'Where are we going?' I asked anxiously.

'You're going to meet my friend Caruso,' said he.

My protestations were futile.

'There's a matinée of *Carmen* today with Caruso and Geraldine Farrar.'

'But I –'

'Christ's sake, you're not scared! Caruso's a wonderful guy – simple and human like yourself. He'll be crazy to meet you, draw your picture and everything.'

I tried to tell him that I wanted to walk and get some fresh air.

'This'll do you more good than fresh air!'

I found myself being marched through the lobby of the Metropolitan Opera House and swept down the aisle to two vacant seats.

'Sit there,' whispered Guest. 'I'll be back at the interval.' Then he strode up the aisle and disappeared.

I had heard the music of *Carmen* several times, but now it seemed unfamiliar. I looked at my programme; yes, it was Wednesday, and on that day it announced *Carmen*. But they were playing another aria which I thought familiar too and which sounded like *Rigoletto*. I was confused. About two minutes before the end of the act, Guest stole into his seat beside me.

'Is this *Carmen*?' I whispered.

'Yes,' he replied. 'Haven't you got a programme?'

He snatched it from me. 'Yes,' he whispered, 'Caruso and Geraldine Farrar, Wednesday matinée, *Carmen* – there it is!'

The curtain came down and he bundled me along the seats to the side entrance leading back stage.

Men in muffled boots were shifting scenery in such a fashion that I seemed always in the way. The atmosphere was like a troubled dream. Out of it loomed a tall, rangy man, solemn and austere, with a pointed beard and bloodhound eyes that peered down at me from a height. He stood in the centre of the stage, a worried man, as scenery went and came about him.

'How's my good friend Signor Gatti-Casazza?' said Maurice Guest, extending his hand.

Gatti-Casazza shook it and made a disparaging gesture, then mumbled something. Then Guest turned to me. 'You're right, it wasn't *Carmen*, it was *Rigoletto*. Geraldine Farrar called up at the last minute to say she had a cold. This is Charlie Chaplin,' said Guest. 'I'm taking him round to meet Caruso, maybe it'll cheer him up. Come with us.' But Gatti-Casazza shook his head mournfully.

'Where's his dressing-room?'

Gatti-Casazza called the stage-manager. 'He'll show you.'

My instinct warned me not to bother Caruso at such a time and I told Guest so.

'Don't be silly,' he answered.

We groped our way along the passage to his dressing-room. 'Somebody's turned off the light,' said the stage-manager. 'Just a moment and I'll find the switch.'

'Listen,' said Guest, 'I have people waiting for me, so I must run along.'

'You're not leaving?' I asked quickly.

'You'll be O.K.'

Before I could answer he disappeared, leaving me in utter darkness. The stage-manager struck a match. 'Here we are,' he said, and gently knocked at a door. A voice in Italian exploded from within.

My friend answered back in Italian, ending with 'Charlie Chaplin!'

There came another explosion.

'Listen,' I whispered, 'some other time.'

'No, no,' he said; now he had a mission to fulfil. The door opened a crack and the dresser peered through the darkness. My friend in an aggrieved tone explained who I was.

'Oh!' said the dresser, then closed the door again. The door re-opened. 'Come in, please!'

This little victory seemed to give my friend a lift. When we entered, Caruso was seated at his dressing-table before a mirror, his back towards us, clipping his moustache. 'Ah, signor,' said my friend cheerfully. 'It is my very great pleasure to present to you the Caruso of the cinema, Mr Charlie Chaplin.'

Caruso nodded into the mirror and continued clipping his moustache.

Eventually he got up and surveyed me as he fastened his belt. 'You have big success, eh? You make plenty of money.'

'Yes,' I smiled.

'You must be very 'appy.'

'Yes, indeed.' Then I looked at the stage-manager.

'So,' said he cheerfully, intimating that it was time to leave.

I stood up, then smiled at Caruso. 'I don't want to miss the Toreador scene.'

'That's *Carmen*, this is *Rigoletto*,' he said, shaking my hand.

'Oh yes, of course! Ha-Ha!'

*

I had assimilated as much of New York as was happily possible under the circumstances and thought it time to leave before the pleasures of vanity fair began to pall. Besides, I was anxious to start work under my new contract.

When I returned to Los Angeles I stayed at the Alexandria Hotel on Fifth Street and Main, the swankiest hotel in town. It was in the grand rococo style: marble columns and crystal chandeliers adorned the lobby, in the centre of which was the fabulous 'million-dollar carpet' – the mecca of big movie deals – humorously so named also because of the quidnuncs and quasi-promoters that stood about on it talking astronomical figures.

Nevertheless Abrahamson made a fortune on that carpet, selling cheap State Right pictures which he made economically by renting studio space and hiring unemployed actors. Such pictures were known as the products of 'Poverty Row'. The late Harry Cohn, head of Columbia Pictures, also started in Poverty Row.

Abrahamson was a realist, admitting that he was not interested in art, only in money. He had a thick Russian accent, and when directing his films would shout to the leading lady: 'All right, come in from de back side' (meaning from the back). 'Now you come to mirror and take a look at yourself. Ooh! Ain't I pretty!

Now monkey around for twenty feet' (meaning ad lib for twenty feet of film). The heroine was usually a bosomy young thing in a loose décolleté, showing plenty of cleavage. He would tell her to face the camera, bend over and tie her shoe, or rock a cradle or stroke a dog. Abrahamson made two million dollars this way, then wisely retired.

The million-dollar carpet brought Sid Grauman down from San Francisco to negotiate the building of his Los Angeles million-dollar theatres. As the town grew prosperous, so did Sid. He had a flair for bizarre publicity, and once startled Los Angeles with two taxis racing through town, the occupants shooting blank cartridges at each other, and on the back of the taxis placards announcing: '*The Underworld* at Grauman's Million Dollar Theatre.'

He was an innovator of gimcracks. A fantastic idea of Sid's was to get Hollywood stars to stick their hands and feet in wet cement outside his Chinese Theatre; for some reason they did it. It became an honour almost as important as receiving the Oscar.

The first day I arrived at the Alexandria Hotel the desk clerk handed me a letter from Miss Maude Fealy, the famous actress who had been leading lady to Sir Henry Irving and William Gillette, inviting me to a dinner she was giving for Pavlova, Wednesday, at the Hollywood Hotel. Of course, I was delighted. Although I had never met Miss Fealy, I had seen postcards of her all over London, and was an admirer of her beauty.

The day before the dinner I told my secretary to phone and inquire whether it was informal or I should wear a black tie.

'Who is calling?' Miss Fealy asked.

'This is Mr Chaplin's secretary, about his dining with you on Wednesday evening – .'

Miss Fealy seemed alarmed. 'Oh! By all means, informal,' she said.

Miss Fealy was on the porch of the Hollywood Hotel waiting to greet me. She was as lovely as ever. We sat for at least half an hour conversing irrelevantly, and I began wondering when the other guests would arrive.

Eventually she said: 'Shall we go in to dinner?'

To my surprise, I found we were dining alone!

Miss Fealy, besides being a lady of charm, was also very

reserved, and, looking across the table at her, I wondered what could be the motive for this *tête-à-tête*. Roguish and unworthy thoughts flashed through my mind – but she seemed too sensitive for my unseemly surmisings. Nevertheless, I began throwing out my antennae to find out what was expected of me. 'This is really fun,' I said ebulliently, 'dining alone this way!'

She smiled blandly.

'Let's do something amusing after dinner,' I said: 'go to a night-club or something.'

A look of mild alarm stole over her face, and she hesitated. 'I'm afraid I must retire early this evening, as I start rehearsing tomorrow morning for *Macbeth*.'

My antennae wavered. I was completely baffled. Fortunately, the first course arrived and for a moment we ate in silence. Something was wrong, and we both knew it. Miss Fealy hesitated. 'I'm afraid it's rather dull for you this evening.'

'It's perfectly delightful,' I replied.

'I'm sorry you weren't here three months ago at a dinner I gave for Pavlova, who, I know, is a friend of yours. But I understand you were in New York.'

'Excuse me,' I said quickly producing Miss Fealy's letter, and for the first time I looked at the date. Then I handed it to her. 'You see,' I laughed, 'I've arrived three months late!'

*

Los Angeles in 1910 was the end of an era of Western pioneers and tycoons, and I was entertained by most of them.

One was the late William A. Clark, multi-millionaire, railroad magnate and copper king, an amateur musician who donated $150,000 annually to the Philharmonic Symphony Orchestra in which he played second violin with the rest of the orchestra.

Death Valley Scottie was a phantom character, a jovial, fat-faced man who wore a ten-gallon hat, red shirt and dungarees, and spent thousands of dollars nightly along Spring Street's rathskellers and night-clubs, throwing parties, tipping waiters hundred-dollar bills, then mysteriously disappearing, to show up a month or so later and throw another party, which he did for years. No one knew where his money came from. Some believed he had a secret mine in Death Valley and tried to follow him there, but he always evaded them and no one, to this day, has ever learned his secret. Before he died in 1940 he built an enormous castle in Death Valley, in the middle of the desert, a fantastic structure costing over half a million. The building still stands rotting in the sun.

Mrs Craney-Gatts of Pasadena was a woman with forty million dollars, an ardent socialist who paid for the legal defence of many anarchists, socialists and members of the I.W.W.

Glenn Curtiss worked for Sennett in those days, doing aeroplane stunts, and was looking hungrily for capital to finance what is now the great Curtiss aircraft industry.

A. P. Giannini ran two small banks, which later developed into one of the greatest financial institutions in the United States: the Bank of America.

Howard Hughes inherited a large fortune from his father, the inventor of the modern oil-drill. Howard multiplied his millions by going into aircraft; he was an eccentric man who ran his large industrial enterprises over the telephone from a third-rate hotel room and was seldom seen. He also dabbled in motion pictures, achieving considerable success with such films as *Hell's Angels*, starring the late Jean Harlow.

In those days, my routine pleasures were watching Jack Doyle's Friday-night fights at Vernon; attending vaudeville at the Orpheum Theatre on Monday night; Morosco Theatre's stock company on Thursday; and, occasionally, a symphony at Clune's Philharmonic Auditorium.

*

The Los Angeles Athletic Club was a centre where the élite of local society and business gathered at the cocktail hour. It was like a foreign settlement.

A young man, a bit player, used to sit around the lounge, a lonely fellow who had come to Hollywood to try his luck but was not doing very well, named Valentino. He was introduced to me by another bit player, Jack Gilbert. I did not see Valentino again for a year or so; in the interim he jumped to stardom. When we met he was diffident, until I said: 'Since I last saw you you have joined the immortals.' Then he laughed and dropped his defences and became quite friendly.

186

Valentino had an air of sadness. He wore his success gracefully, appearing almost subdued by it. He was intelligent, quiet and without vanity, and had great allure for women, but had little success with them, and those whom he married treated him rather shabbily. Soon after one marriage, his wife started an affair with one of the men in the developing laboratory, with whom she would disappear into the dark-room. No man had greater attraction for women than Valentino; no man was more deceived by them.

I now began preparing to fulfil my $670,000 contract. Mr Caulfield, who represented the Mutual Film Corporation and attended to all the business, rented a studio in the heart of Hollywood. With a competent little stock company including Edna Purviance, Eric Campbell, Henry Bergman, Albert Austin, Lloyd Bacon, John Rand, Frank Jo Coleman and Leo White, I felt confident about starting to work.

My first picture, *The Floor Walker*, was happily a great success. It had a department store setting in which I did a chase on a moving staircase. When Sennett saw the film he commented: 'Why the hell didn't we ever think of a running staircase?'

Very soon I was in my stride, turning out a two-reel comedy every month. After *The Floor Walker* there followed *The Fireman*, *The Vagabond*, *One a.m.*, *The Count*, *The Pawnshop*, *Behind the Screen*, *The Rink*, *Easy Street*, *The Cure*, *The Immigrant*, *The Adventurer*. In all it took about sixteen months to complete these twelve comedies, which included time off for colds and minor impediments.

Sometimes a story would present a problem and I would have difficulty in solving it. At this juncture I would lay off work and try to think, striding up and down my dressing-room in torment or sitting for hours at the back of a set, struggling with the problem. The mere sight of the management or the actors gaping at me was embarrassing, especially as Mutual was paying the cost of production, and Mr Caulfield was there to see that things kept moving.

At a distance I would see him crossing the lot. By his mere outline I knew well what he was thinking: nothing accomplished and the overheads increasing. And I would intimate as gently as a sledge-hammer that I never liked people around when I was thinking, or to feel that they were worrying.

At the end of a fruitless day, he would meet me accidentally on purpose as I left the studio, and would greet me with a phoney levity and inquire: 'How's she coming?'

'Lousy! I guess I'm through! I can't think any more!'

And he would make a hollow sound, meant for a laugh. 'Don't worry, it'll come.'

Sometimes the solution came at the end of the day when I was in a state of despair, having thought of everything and discarded it; then the solution would suddenly reveal itself, as if a layer of dust had been swept off a marble floor – there it was, the beautiful mosaic I had been looking for. Tension was gone, the studio was set in motion, and how Mr Caulfield would laugh!

No member of my cast was injured in any of our pictures. Violence was carefully rehearsed and treated like choreography. A slap in the face was always tricked. No matter how much of a skirmish, everyone knew what he was doing, everything was timed. It was inexcusable to get hurt, because in films all effects – violence, earthquakes, shipwrecks, and catastrophes – can be faked.

We had only one accident in that whole series. It happened in *Easy Street*. While I was pulling a street-lamp over the big bully to gas him, the head of the lamp collapsed and its sharp metal edge fell across the bridge of my nose, necessitating two surgical stitches.

Fulfilling the Mutual contract, I suppose, was the happiest period of my career. I was light and unencumbered, twenty-seven years old, with fabulous prospects and a friendly, glamorous world before me. Within a short time I would be a millionaire – it all seemed slightly mad. Money was pouring into my coffers. The ten thousand dollars I received every week accumulated into hundreds of thousands. Now I was worth four hundred thousand, now five hundred thousand. I could never take it for granted.

I remember Maxine Elliott, a friend of J. P. Morgan, said to me once: 'Money is only good to forget.' But it is also something to remember say I.

There is no doubt that men of success live in a different world; when I met people their faces would light up with interest. Although I was a parvenu, my opinions were seriously considered. Acquaintances were willing to enter into the warmest of friendships and share my problems as though they were relatives. It was all very flattering, but my nature does not respond to such intimacy. I like friends as I like music – when I am in the mood. Such freedom, however, was at the price of occasional loneliness.

One day, towards the completion of my contract, my brother entered my bedroom at the Athletic Club and blithely announced: 'Well, Charlie, you're now in the millionaire class. I've just completed a deal for you to make eight two-reel comedies for First National for $1,200,000.'

I had just taken a bath and was wandering about the room with a towel around my loins, playing *The Tales of Hoffmann* on my violin. 'Hum-um, I suppose that's wonderful.'

Sydney suddenly burst into laughter. 'This goes into my memoirs: you with that towel around your hips, playing the violin, and your reaction to the news that I've signed up for a million and a quarter!'

I admit there was a tinge of pose because of the task it involved – the money had to be earned.

Notwithstanding, all this promise of wealth did not change my mode of living. I was reconciled to wealth but not to the use of it. This money I earned was legendary – a symbol in figures, for I had never actually seen it. I therefore had to do something to prove that I had it. So I procured a secretary, a valet, a car and a chaffeur. Walking by a show-room one day, I noticed a seven-passenger Locomobile, which, in those days, was considered the best car in America. The thing looked too magnificently elegant to be for sale. However, I walked into the shop and asked: 'How much?'

'Four thousand nine hundred dollars.'

'Wrap it up,' I said.

The man was astonished and tried to put up a resistance to such an immediate sale. 'Wouldn't you like to see the engine?' he asked.

'Wouldn't make any difference – I know nothing about them,'

I answered. However, I pressed the tyre with my thumb to show a professional touch.

The transaction was simple; it meant writing my name on a piece of paper and the car was mine.

Investing money was a problem and I knew little about it, but Sydney was familiar with all its nomenclature: he knew about book values, capital gains, preferred and common shares, A and B ratings, convertible stocks and bonds, industrial fiduciaries and legal securities of savings banks. Investment opportunities were rife in those days. A Los Angeles realtor pleaded with me to go into partnership with him, each of us putting up two hundred and fifty thousand dollars to buy a large tract of land in the Los Angeles Valley. Had I invested in his project my share would have amounted to fifty million dollars, for oil was discovered and it became one of the richest areas in California.

# *thirteen*

MANY illustrious visitors came to the studio at this time: Melba, Leopold Godowsky and Paderewski, Nijinsky and Pavlova.

Paderewski had great charm, but there was something bourgeois about him, an over-emphasis of dignity. He was impressive with his long hair, severe, slanting moustache and the small tuft of hair under his lower lip, which I thought revealed some form of mystic vanity. At his recitals, with house lights lowered and the atmosphere sombre and awesome when he was about to sit on the piano stool, I always felt someone should pull it from under him.

During the war I met him at the Ritz Hotel in New York and greeted him enthusiastically, asking if he were there to give a concert. With pontifical solemnity he replied: 'I do not give concerts when I am in the service of my country.'

Paderewski became Prime Minister of Poland, but I felt like Clemenceau, who said to him during a conference of the ill-fated Versailles Treaty: 'How is it that a gifted artist like you should stoop so low as to become a politician?'

On the other hand Leopold Godowsky, a greater pianist, was simple and humorous, a small man with a smiling, round face. After his concert in Los Angeles he rented a house there, and I visited him quite frequently. On Sundays I was privileged to listen to him practising and to witness the extraordinary facility and technique of his exceptionally small hands.

Nijinsky, with members of the Russian Ballet, also came to the studio. He was a serious man, beautiful-looking, with high cheekbones and sad eyes, who gave the impression of a monk dressed in civilian clothes. We were shooting *The Cure*. He sat behind the camera, watching me at work on a scene which I thought was funny, but he never smiled. Although the other onlookers laughed, Nijinsky sat looking sadder and sadder. Before leaving he came and shook hands, and in his hollow voice said how much he enjoyed my work and asked if he could come again. 'Of course,' I said. For two more days he sat lugubriously watching me. On the last day I told the cameraman not to put film in the camera, knowing Nijinsky's doleful presence would ruin my attempts to be funny. Nevertheless, at the end of each day he would compliment me. 'Your comedy is balletique, you are a dancer,' he said.

I had not yet seen the Russian Ballet, or any other ballet for that matter. But at the end of the week I was invited to attend the matinée.

At the theatre Diaghilev greeted me – a most vital and enthusiastic man. He apologized for not having the programme he thought I would most enjoy. 'Too bad it isn't *L'Après-midi d'un Faune*,' he said. 'I think you would have liked it.' Then quickly he turned to his manager. 'Tell Nijinsky we'll put on the *Faune* after the interval for Charlot.'

The first ballet was *Scheherazade*. My reaction was more or less negative. There was too much acting and too little dancing, and the music of Rimsky-Korsakov was repetitive, I thought. But the next was a *pas de deux* with Nijinsky. The moment he appeared I was electrified. I have seen few geniuses in the world, and Nijinsky was one of them. He was hypnotic, godlike, his sombreness suggesting moods of other worlds; every movement was poetry, every leap a flight into strange fancy.

He had asked Diaghilev to bring me to his dressing-room during the intermission. I was speechless. One cannot wring one's hand and express in words one's appreciation of great art. In his dressing-room I sat silent, watching the strange face in the mirror as he made up for the *Faune*, putting green circles around his cheeks. He was gauche in his attempt at conversation, asking inconsequential questions about my films, and I could only answer in monosyllables. The warning bell rang at the end of the interval, and I suggested returning to my seat.

'No, no, not yet,' he said.

There came a knock at the door. 'Mr Nijinsky, the overture is finished.'

I began to look anxious.

'That's all right,' he answered. 'There's plenty of time.'

I was shocked and at a loss to know why he was acting this way. 'Don't you think I had better go?'

'No, no, let them play another overture.'

Diaghilev eventually came bursting into the dressing-room. 'Come, come! The audience are applauding.'

'Let them wait, this is more interesting,' said Nijinsky, then began asking me more banal questions.

I was embarrassed. 'I really must get back to my seat,' I said.

No one has ever equalled Nijinsky in *L'Après-midi d'un Faune*. The mystic world he created, the tragic unseen lurking in the shadows of pastoral loveliness as he moved through its mystery, a god of passionate sadness – all this he conveyed in a few simple gestures without apparent effort.

Six months later Nijinsky went insane. There were signs of it that afternoon in his dressing-room, when he kept the audience waiting. I had witnessed the beginning of a sensitive mind on its way out of a brutal war-torn world into another of its own dreaming.

The sublime is rare in any vocation or art. And Pavlova was one of those rare artists who had it. She never failed to affect me profoundly. Her art, although brilliant, had a quality pale and luminous, as delicate as a white rose-petal. As she danced every move was the centre of gravity. The moment she made her entrance, no matter how gay or winsome she was, I wanted to weep.

I met 'Pav', as her friends called her, while she was in Hollywood making a picture at the Universal studios, and we became very good friends. It was a tragedy that the speed of the old cinema failed to capture the lyricism of her dancing, and because of that her great art has been lost to the world.

On one occasion the Russian Consulate gave her a testimonial dinner at which I was present. It was an international affair and quite a solemn one. During dinner there were many toasts and speeches, some in French and others in Russian. I believe I was the only Englishman called upon. Before my turn came to speak, however, a professor delivered a brilliant eulogy of Pavlova's art in Russian. At one moment the professor burst into tears, then went up to Pavlova and kissed her fervently. I knew that any attempt of mine would be tame after that, so I rose and said that as my English was totally inadequate to express the greatness of Pavlova's art I would speak in Chinese. I spoke in a Chinese jargon, building up to a crescendo as the professor had done, finishing by kissing Pavlova more fervently than the professor, taking a napkin and placing it over both our heads as I continually kissed her. The party roared with laughter, and it broke the solemnity of the occasion.

Sarah Bernhardt played at the Orpheum vaudeville theatre. She was, of course, very old and at the end of her career, and I cannot give a true appraisal of her acting. But when Duse came to Los Angeles, even her age and approaching end could not dim the brilliance of her genius. She was supported by an excellent Italian cast. One handsome young actor gave a superb performance before she came on, holding the centre of the stage magnificently. How could Duse excel this young man's remarkable performance? I wondered.

Then from extreme left up-stage Duse unobtrusively entered through an archway. She paused behind a basket of white chrysanthemums that stood on a grand piano, and began quietly rearranging them. A murmur went through the house, and my attention immediately left the young actor and centred on Duse. She looked neither at the young actor nor at any of the other characters, but continued quietly arranging the flowers and adding others which she had brought with her. When she had finished, she slowly walked diagonally down-stage and sat in an armchair by the fireplace and looked into the fire. Once, and only once, did she look at the young man, and all the wisdom and hurt of humanity was in that look. Then she continued listening and warming her hands – such beautiful, sensitive hands.

After his impassioned address, she spoke calmly as she looked into the fire. Her delivery had not the usual histrionics; her voice came from the embers of tragic passion. I did not understand a word, but I realized I was in the presence of the greatest actress I had ever seen.

*

Constance Collier, Sir Herbert Beerbohm Tree's leading lady, was engaged to play Lady Macbeth with Sir Herbert for the

Triangle Film Company. When a boy I had seen her many times from the gallery of His Majesty's Theatre and had admired her memorable performances in *The Eternal City* and as Nancy in *Oliver Twist*. So when a note came to my table at Levy's Café that Miss Collier would like to meet me and would I come over to her table, I was delighted to do so. From that meeting we became lifelong friends. She was a kindly soul who had a glowing warmth and a zest for living. She enjoyed bringing people together. Her desire was to have me meet Sir Herbert and a young man named Douglas Fairbanks, with whom she said I would have much in common.

Sir Herbert, I suppose, was the dean of the English theatre and the subtlest of actors, appealing to the mind as well as the emotions. His Fagin in *Oliver Twist* was both humorous and horrific. With little effort he could create tension that was almost unbearable. He had only to gently prod the Artful Dodger jokingly with a toasting-fork to evoke terror. Tree's conception of character was always brilliant. The ridiculous Svengali was an example; he made one believe in this absurd character and endowed him not only with humour but with poetry. Critics said Tree was beset with mannerisms; true, but he used them effectively. His acting was extremely modern. In *Julius Caesar* his interpretation was intellectual. His Mark Antony in the funeral scene, instead of haranguing the crowd with conventional passion, he spoke perfunctorily over their heads with cynicism and underlying contempt.

As a boy of fourteen I had seen Tree in many of his great productions, so when Constance arranged a small dinner for Sir Herbert, his daughter Iris and myself, I was indeed excited at the prospect. We were to meet in Tree's rooms at the Alexandria Hotel. I was deliberately late, hoping that Constance would be there to relieve pressure, but when Sir Herbert ushered me into his rooms he was alone, except for John Emerson, his film director.

'Ah, come in, Chaplin,' said Sir Herbert. 'I've heard so much about you from Constance!'

After introducing Emerson, he explained that they were going over some scenes of *Macbeth*. Soon Emerson left, and I was suddenly petrified with shyness.

195

'I am sorry to have kept you waiting,' said Sir Herbert, sitting in an armchair opposite me. 'We were discussing an effect for the witch scene.'

'Oh-h-h,' I stammered.

'I think it would be rather effective to hang gauze over balloons and have them float through the scene. What do you think?'

'Oh-h-h . . . wonderful!'

Sir Herbert paused and looked at me. 'You've had phenomenal success, haven't you?'

'Nothing at all,' I mumbled apologetically.

'But you're known all over the world! In England and France the soldiers even sing songs about you.'

'Is that so?' I said, feigning ignorance.

He looked at me again – I could see doubt and a reservation spreading all over his face. Then he got up. 'Constance is late. I'll telephone and find out what has happened. In the meantime you must meet my daughter Iris,' he said, as he left the room.

I was relieved, for I had visions of a child with whom I could talk on my own level about school and the movies. Then a tall young lady entered the room with a long cigarette-holder, saying in a sonorous low voice: 'How do you do, Mr Chaplin. I suppose I am the only person in the world who hasn't seen you on the screen.'

I grinned and nodded.

Iris looked Scandinavian, with blonde bobbed hair, snub nose and light blue eyes. She was then eighteen years old, very attractive with a bloom of Mayfair sophistication about her, having had a book of her poems published at the age of fifteen.

'Constance speaks so much about you,' she said.

I grinned and nodded again.

Eventually, Sir Herbert returned, announcing that Constance could not come as she had been delayed with costume fittings, and that we would dine without her.

Dear God! With these strangers how would I endure the night? With this burning thought in my mind, we left the room in silence and entered the lift in silence and in silence entered the dining-room and sat at table as though we had just returned from a funeral.

Poor Sir Herbert and Iris did their best to make conversation. Soon she gave up and just sat back scanning the dining-room. If only the food would come, eating might relieve my awful tension. . . . Father and daughter conversed a little and talked about the South of France, Rome and Salzburg – had I ever been there? Had I ever seen any of Max Reinhardt's productions?

I shook my head apologetically.

Tree now surveyed me. 'You know, you should travel.'

I told him that I had little time for that, then I came to: 'Look, Sir Herbert, my success has been so sudden that I have had little time to catch up with it. But as a boy of fourteen I saw you as Svengali, as Fagin, as Anthony, as Falstaff, some of them many times, and ever since you have been my idol. I never thought of you as existing off-stage. You were a legend. And to be dining with you tonight in Los Angeles overwhelms me.'

Tree was touched. 'Really!' he kept repeating. 'Really!'

From that night on we became very good friends. He would call me up occasionally and the three of us, Iris, Sir Herbert and I, would dine together. Sometimes Constance would come along, and we would go to Victor Hugo's restaurant and muse over our coffee and listen to sentimental chamber music.

*

From Constance I had heard much about Douglas Fairbanks's charm and ability, not only as a personality but as a brilliant after-dinner speaker. In those days I disliked brilliant young men – especially after-dinner speakers. However, a dinner was arranged at his house.

Both Douglas and I tell a story of that night. Before going I had made excuses to Constance that I was ill, but she would have none of it. So I made up my mind to feign a headache and leave early. Fairbanks said that he was also nervous, and that when the door-bell rang he quickly descended into the basement, where there was a billiard-table, and began playing pool. That night was the beginning of a lifelong friendship.

It was not for naught that Douglas captured the imagination and love of the public. The spirit of his pictures, their optimism and infallibility, were very much to the American taste, and indeed to the taste of the whole world. He had extraordinary magnetism and charm and a genuine boyish enthusiasm which he conveyed to the public. As I began to know him intimately I found him disarmingly honest because he admitted that he enjoyed being a snob and that successful people had allure for him.

Although Doug was tremendously popular, he generously praised other people's talent and was modest about his own. He often said that Mary Pickford and I had genius, while he had only a small talent. This of course was not so; Douglas was creative and did things in a big way.

He built a ten-acre set for *Robin Hood*, a castle with enormous ramparts and drawbridges, far bigger than any castle that ever existed. With great pride Douglas showed me the huge drawbridge. 'Magnificent,' I said. 'What a wonderful opening for one of my comedies: the drawbridge comes down, and I put out the cat and take in the milk.'

He had a varied assortment of friends, ranging from cowboys to kings, and found interesting qualities in them all. His friend Charlie Mack, a cowboy, a glib, verbose fellow, was highly amusing to Douglas. While we were at dinner, Charlie would frame himself in the doorway and talk: 'Nice place yer got here, Doug,' then looking around the dining-room: 'Only it's too far to spit from the table to the fireplace.' Then he would crouch on his heels and tell us about his wife suing him for 'di-vorce' on grounds of 'cruler-ty'. 'I says, Judge, that woman has more cruler-ty in her little finger than I have in ma whole body. And no baby ever toted a gun more than that gal did. She'd have me a-hopping and a-dodging behind that ole tree of ours till it was that perforated yer could see thru it!' I had an idea that Charlie's fanfaronade was rehearsed before visiting Doug.

Douglas's house had been a shooting lodge, a rather ugly two-storey bungalow set on a hill in the centre of what was then the scrubby, barren hills of Beverly. The alkali and the sagebrush gave off an odorous, sour tang that made the throat dry and the nostrils smart.

In those days Beverly Hills looked like an abandoned real estate development. Sidewalks ran along and disappeared into open fields and lamp-posts with white globes adorned empty streets; most of the globes were missing, shot off by passing revellers from roadhouses.

Douglas Fairbanks was the first film star to live in Beverly Hills, and often invited me to stay the week-end with him. At night from my bedroom I would listen to the coyotes howling, packs of them invading the garbage cans. Their howls were eerie, like the pealing of little bells.

He always had two or three stooges staying with him: Tom Geraghty, who wrote his scripts, Carl, an ex-Olympic athlete, and a couple of cowboys. Tom, Doug and I had a Three Musketeers relationship.

On Sunday morning Doug would organize a posse of cowponies and we would get up in the dark and ride over the hills to meet the dawn. The cowboys would stake the horses and make a camp-fire and prepare breakfast of coffee, hot cakes and 'sowbelly'. While we watched the dawn break, Doug would wax eloquent and I would joke about loss of sleep and argue that the only dawn worth seeing was with the opposite sex. Nevertheless, those early morning sorties were romantic. Douglas was the only man who could ever get me on a horse, in spite of my complaints that the world over-sentimentalized the beast and that it was mean and cantankerous with the mind of a half-wit.

At that time he was separated from his first wife. In the evening he would have friends to dinner, including Mary Pickford, of whom he was terrifically enamoured. They both acted like frightened rabbits about it. I used to advise them not to marry but just to live together and get it out of their systems, but they could not agree with my unconventional ideas. I had spoken so strongly against their marrying that when in the end they did so all their friends were invited to the wedding but me.

In those days Douglas and I often indulged in cliché philosophizing, and I would hold forth on the futility of life. Douglas believed that our lives were ordained and that our destiny was important. When Douglas was possessed with this mystic ebullience it usually had a cynical effect on me. I remember one warm summer's night both of us climbed to the top of a large water-tank and sat there talking in the wild grandeur of Beverly. The stars were mysteriously brilliant and the moon incandescent, and I had been saying that life was without reason.

'Look!' said Douglas, fervently, making an arc gesture

taking in all the heavens. 'The moon! And those myriads of stars! Surely there must be a reason for all this beauty? It must be fulfilling some destiny! It must be for some good and you and I are all part of it!' Then he turned to me, suddenly inspired. 'Why are you given this talent, this wonderful medium of motion pictures that reaches millions of people throughout the world?'

'Why is it given to Louis B. Mayer and the Warner Brothers?' I said. And Douglas laughed.

Douglas was incurably romantic. When spending week-ends with him I was sometimes awakened at three in the morning out of a sound sleep, and would see through the mist a Hawaiian orchestra playing on the lawn, serenading Mary. It was charming, but it was difficult to enter into the spirit of it when one was not personally involved. But these boyish attributes made him endearing.

Douglas was also the sportive type who had wolf-hounds and police dogs perched on the back seat of his open Cadillac. He genuinely liked that sort of thing.

*

Hollywood was fast becoming the Mecca of writers, actors and intellectuals. Celebrated authors came from all parts of the world: Sir Gilbert Parker, William J. Locke, Rex Beach, Joseph Hergesheimer, Somerset Maugham, Gouverneur Morris, Ibañez, Elinor Glyn, Edith Wharton, Kathleen Norris and many others.

Somerset Maugham never worked in Hollywood, though his stories were much in demand. He did, however, stay there a number of weeks prior to going to the South Sea islands, where he wrote those admirable short stories. At dinner he recounted one to Douglas and me, the story of *Sadie Thompson*, which he said was based on actual fact, and which was later dramatized as *Rain*. I have always considered *Rain* a model play. The Reverend Davidson and his wife are beautifully defined characters – more interesting than Sadie Thompson. How superb Tree would have been as the Reverend Davidson! He would have played him as gentle, ruthless, oily and terrifying.

Set in this Hollywood milieu was a fifth-rate, rambling, barnlike establishment known as the Hollywood Hotel. It had bounced into prominence like a bewildered country maiden bequeathed a fortune. Rooms were at a premium, only because the road from Los Angeles to Hollywood was almost impassable and these literary celebrities wanted to live in the vicinity of the studios. But everyone looked lost, as though they had come to the wrong address.

Elinor Glyn occupied two bedrooms there, converting one into a sitting-room by covering pillows with pastel-coloured material and spreading them over the bed to look like a sofa. Here she entertained her guests.

I first met Elinor when she gave a dinner for ten people. We were to meet in her rooms for cocktails before going into the dining-room and I was the first to arrive. 'Ah,' she said, cupping my face with her hands and gazing intently at me. 'Let me have a good look at you. How extraordinary! I thought your eyes were brown, but they're quite blue.' Though she was a little overwhelming at first, I became very fond of her.

Elinor, though a monument of English respectability, had shocked the Edwardian world with her novel *Three Weeks*. The hero, Paul, is a well-bred young Englishman who has an affair with a queen – her last fling before marrying the old king. The baby Crown Prince is, of course, secretly Paul's son. While we waited for her guests to arrive, Elinor took me into her other room, where framed on the walls were pictures of young English officers of the First World War. With a sweeping gesture she said: 'These are all my Pauls.'

She was ardently imbued with the occult. I remember one afternoon Mary Pickford complained of fatigue and sleeplessness. We were in Mary's bedroom. 'Show me the north,' commanded Elinor. Then she placed her finger gently on Mary's brow and repeated: 'Now she's fast asleep!' Douglas and I crept over and took a look at Mary, whose eyelids were fluttering. Mary told us later that she had to endure the pretence of sleeping for more than an hour, because Elinor stayed in the room and watched her.

Elinor had the reputation of being sensational, but no one was more staid. Her amorous conceptions for the movies were girlish and naïve – ladies brushing their eyelashes against the cheeks of their beloveds and languishing on tiger-rugs.

The trilogy she wrote for Hollywood was of a time-diminishing nature. The first was called *Three Weeks*, the second *His Hour*, and the third *Her Moment*. *Her Moment* had terrific implications. The plot concerns a distinguished lady, played by Gloria Swanson, who is to marry a man she does not love. They are stationed in a tropical jungle. One day she goes horse-back riding alone, and, being interested in botany, gets off her horse to inspect a rare flower. As she bends over it, a deadly viper strikes and bites her right on the bosom. Gloria clutches her breast and screams, and is heard by the man she really loves, who happens, opportunely, to be passing close by. It is handsome Tommy Meighan. Quickly he appears through the bush. 'What has happened?'

She points to the poisonous reptile. 'I have been bitten!'

'Where?'

She points to her bosom.

'That's the deadliest viper of all!' says Tommy, meaning of course the snake. 'Quick, something must be done! There is not a moment to spare!'

They are miles from a doctor, and the usual remedy of a tourniquet – twisting a handkerchief around the affected part to stop blood circulating – is unthinkable. Suddenly he picks her up, tears at her shirt-waist, and bares her gleaming white shoulders, then turns her from the vulgar glare of the camera, bends over her and with his mouth extracts the poison, spitting it out as he does so. As a result of this suctorial operation she marries him.

# *fourteen*

At the end of the Mutual contract I was anxious to get started with First National, but we had no studio. I decided to buy land in Hollywood and build one. The site was the corner of Sunset and La Brea and had a very fine ten-roomed house and five acres of lemon, orange and peach trees. We built a perfect unit, complete with developing plant, cutting-rooms and offices.

During the studio's construction, I took a trip to Honolulu with Edna Purviance, for a month's rest. Hawaii was a beautiful island in those days. Yet the thought of living there, two thousand miles from the mainland, was depressing; in spite of its effulgent beauty, its pineapples, sugar-cane, exotic fruits and flowers, I was glad to return, for I felt a subtle claustrophobia, as if imprisoned inside a lily.

It was inevitable that the propinquity of a beautiful girl like Edna Purviance would eventually involve my heart. When we first came to work in Los Angeles, Edna rented an apartment near the Athletic Club, and almost every night I would bring her there for dinner. We were serious about each other, and at the back of my mind I had an idea that some day we might marry, but I had reservations about Edna. I was uncertain of her, and for that matter uncertain of myself.

In 1916 we were inseparable and went to all the Red Cross fêtes and galas. At these affairs Edna would get jealous and had a gentle and insidious way of showing it. If someone paid too much attention to me, Edna would disappear and a message would come that she had fainted and was asking for me, and of course I would go and stay with her for the rest of the evening. On one occasion a pretty hostess, who was giving a garden fête in my honour, pranced me about from one society belle to another and eventually led me into an alcove. Again the message came that Edna had fainted. Although I was flattered that such a beautiful girl always asked for me after she came to, the habit was becoming a little annoying.

The dénouement came at Fanny Ward's party, where there was a galaxy of pretty girls and handsome young men. Again Edna fainted. But when she came to, she asked for Thomas Meighan, the tall, handsome leading man of Paramount. I knew nothing about it at the time. It was Fanny Ward who told me the next day; knowing my feelings for Edna, she did not wish to see me being made a fool of.

I could not believe it. My pride was hurt; I was outraged. If it were true it would be the end of our relationship. Yet I could not give her up so suddenly. The void would be too much. A resurgence of all that we had been to each other came over me.

The day after the incident I could not work. Towards afternoon I telephoned her for an explanation, intending to fume and fuss; but instead my ego took over and I became sarcastic. I even joked lightly about the matter: 'I understand you called for the wrong man at Fanny Ward's party – you must be losing your memory!'

She laughed and I detected a tinge of embarrassment. 'What are you talking about?' she said.

I was hoping she would fervently deny it. Instead she acted cleverly; she asked who had been telling me all this nonsense.

'What difference does it make who told me? But I think I should mean more to you than that you should openly make a fool of me.'

She was very calm, and insisted that I had been listening to a lot of lies.

I wanted to hurt her by a show of indifference. 'You don't have to make any pretence with me,' I said. 'You're free to do whatever you like. You're not married to me; so long as you're conscientious in your work, that's all that matters.'

To all this Edna was amiably in agreement, and wanted nothing to interfere with our working together. We could always be good friends, she said, which made me all the more desperately miserable.

I talked for an hour on the phone nervous and upset, wanting some excuse for a reconciliation. As is usual in such circumstances, I took a renewed and passionate interest in her, and the conversation tapered off by my asking her to dinner that evening on the pretext of talking over the situation.

She hesitated, but I insisted, in fact I pleaded and implored, all my pride and defences slipping away from me. Eventually she consented. . . . That night the two of us dined on ham and eggs, which she cooked in her apartment.

There was a reconciliation of a sort and I became less perturbed. At least I was able to work the next day. Nevertheless, there lingered a forlorn anguish and self-reproach. I blamed myself for having neglected her at times. I was cast into a dilemma. Should I completely break with her or not? Perhaps the story about Meighan was not true?

About three weeks later she called at the studio to get her cheque. As she was leaving I happened to bump into her. She was with a friend. 'You know Tommy Meighan?' she said blandly. I was somewhat shocked. In that brief moment Edna became a stranger as though I had just met her for the first time. 'Of course,' I said. 'How are you, Tommy?' He was a little embarrassed. We shook hands, and after we had exchanged one or two pleasantries they left the studio together.

However, life is another word for conflict which gives us little surcease. If it is not the problem of love it is something else. Success was wonderful, but with it grew the strain of trying to keep pace with that inconstant nymph, popularity. Nevertheless, my consolation was in work.

But writing, acting and directing fifty-two weeks in the year was strenuous, requiring an exorbitant expenditure of nervous energy. At the completion of a picture I would be left depressed and exhausted, so that I would have to rest in bed for a day.

Towards evening I would get up and go for a quiet walk. Feeling remote and melancholy, I would wander around town, looking vacantly into shop windows. I never tried to think on these occasions; my brain was numbed. But I was quick to recuperate. Usually the following morning, driving to the studio, my excitement would return and my mind would get activated again.

With a bare notion I would order sets, and during the building of them the art director would come to me for details, and I would bluff and give him particulars about where I wanted doors and archways. In this desperate way I started many a comedy.

Sometimes my mind would tighten like a twisted cord and would need some form of loosening. At this juncture a night out was efficacious. I never cared much for alcoholic stimulus. In fact, when working, I had a superstition that the slightest stimulus of any kind affected one's perspicacity. Nothing demanded more alertness of mind than contriving and directing comedy.

As for sex, most of it went in my work. When it did rear its delightful head, life was so inopportune that it was either a glut on the market or a serious shortage. However, I was a disciplinarian and took my work seriously. Like Balzac, who believed that a night of sex meant the loss of a good page of his novel, so I believed it meant the loss of a good day's work at the studio.

&ast;

A well-known lady novelist, hearing I was writing my autobiography, said: 'I hope you have the courage to tell the truth.' I thought she meant politically, but she was referring to my sex-life. I suppose a dissertation on one's libido is expected in an autobiography, although I do not know why. To me it contributes little to the understanding or revealing of character. Unlike Freud, I do not believe sex is the most important element in the complexity of behaviour. Cold, hunger and the shame of poverty are more likely to affect one's psychology.

Like everybody else's my sex-life went in cycles. Sometimes I was potent, other times disappointing. But it was not the all-absorbing interest in my life. I had creative interests which were just as all-absorbing. However, in this book I do not intend to give a blow-by-blow description of a sex bout: I find them inartistic, clinical and unpoetic. The circumstances that lead up to sex I find more interesting.

Apropos of that subject, a delightful impromptu occurred to me at the Alexandria Hotel the first night I arrived back in Los Angeles from New York. I had retired early to my room and started undressing, humming to myself one of the latest New York songs. Occasionally I paused, lost in thought, and when I did so a feminine voice from the next room took up the tune where I had left off. Then I took up where she left off, and so it became a joke. Eventually we finished the tune this way. Should I get acquainted? It was risky. Besides, I had no idea what she looked like. I whistled the tune again, and again the same thing happened.

'Ha, ha, ha! that's funny!' I laughed, tempering my intonation so that it could be addressed to her or to myself.

A voice came from the other room: 'I beg your pardon?'

Then I whispered through the key-hole: 'Evidently you have just arrived from New York.'

'I can't hear you,' she said.

'Then open the door,' I answered.

'I'll open it a little, but don't you dare come in.'

'I promise.'

She opened the door about four inches, and the most ravishing young blonde peered at me. I do not know exactly how she was dressed, but she was all silky negligée and the effect was dreamy.

'Don't come in or I'll beat you up!' she said charmingly, showing her pretty white teeth.

'How do you do,' I whispered, and introduced myself. She knew already who I was and that I had the room next door to hers.

Later that night she told me that under no circumstances was I to acknowledge her in public, or even nod if we passed each other in the hotel lobby. That was all she ever told me about herself.

The second night when I came to my room she frankly tapped on the door, and once more we embarked nocturnally. The third night I was getting rather weary; besides, I had work and a career to think about. So on the fourth night I surreptitiously opened my door and tiptoed into my room, hoping to get to bed unnoticed; but she had heard me, and began tapping on the door. This time I paid no attention and went straight to bed. Next day, when she passed me in the hotel lobby it was with an icy stare.

The following night she did not knock, but the handle of the door creaked and I saw it turning slowly. I had, however, locked it from my side. She turned the handle violently, then knocked impatiently. The next morning I thought it advisable to leave the hotel, so again I took up quarters at the Athletic Club.

*

My first picture in my new studio was *A Dog's Life*. The story had an element of satire, parallelling the life of a dog with that of a tramp. This leitmotif was the structure upon which I built sundry gags and slapstick routines. I was beginning to think of comedy in a structural sense, and to become conscious of its architectural form. Each sequence implied the next sequence, all of them relating to the whole.

The first sequence was rescuing a dog from a fight with other dogs. The next was rescuing a girl in a dance-hall who was also leading 'a dog's life'. There were many other sequences, all of which followed in a logical concatenation of events. As simple and obvious as these slapstick comedies were, a great deal of thought and invention went into them. If a gag interfered with the logic of events, no matter how funny it was, I would not use it.

In the Keystone days the tramp had been freer and less confined to plot. His brain was seldom active then – only his instincts, which were concerned with the basic essentials: food, warmth and shelter. But with each succeeding comedy the tramp was growing more complex. Sentiment was beginning to percolate through the character. This became a problem because he was bound by the limits of slapstick. This may sound pretentious, but slapstick demands a most exacting psychology.

The solution came when I thought of the tramp as a sort of Pierrot. With this conception I was freer to express and embellish the comedy with touches of sentiment. But logically it was difficult to get a beautiful girl interested in a tramp. This has always been a problem in my films. In *The Gold Rush* the girl's interest in the tramp started by her playing a joke on him, which later moves her to pity, which he mistakes for love. The girl in *City Lights* is blind. In this relationship he was romantic and wonderful to her until her sight is restored.

As my skill in story construction developed, so it restricted my comedy freedom. As a fan who preferred my early Keystone comedies to the more recent ones wrote to me: 'Then the public was your slave; now you are the public's slave.'

Even in those early comedies I strove for a mood; usually music created it. An old song called *Mrs Grundy* created the mood for *The Immigrant*. The tune had a wistful tenderness that suggested two lonely derelicts getting married on a doleful, rainy day.

The story shows Charlot en route to America. In the steerage he meets a girl and her mother who are as derelict as himself. When they arrive in New York they separate. Eventually he meets the girl again, but she is alone, and like himself is a failure. While they sit talking, she inadvertently uses a black-edged handkerchief, conveying the fact that her mother has passed on. And, of course, in the end they marry on a doleful, rainy day.

Simple little tunes gave me the image for other comedies. In one called *Twenty Minutes of Love*, full of rough stuff and nonsense in parks, with policemen and nursemaids, I weaved in and out of situations to the tune of *Too Much Mustard*, a popular two-step in 1914. The song *Violetera* set the mood for *City Lights*, and *Auld Lang Syne* the mood for *The Gold Rush*.

As far back as 1916 I had many ideas for feature pictures. One was a trip to the moon, a comic spectacle showing the Olympic Games there and the possibilities of playing about with the laws of gravity. It would have been a satire on progress. I thought of a feeding machine, and also a radio-electric hat that could register one's thoughts; and the trouble I get into when I put it on my head and am introduced to the moon-man's sexy wife. The feeding machine I eventually used in *Modern Times*.

Interviewers have asked me how I get ideas for pictures and to this day I am not able to answer satisfactorily. Over the years I have discovered that ideas come through an intense desire for them; continually desiring, the mind becomes a watch-tower on the look-out for incidents that may excite the imagination – music, a sunset, may give image to an idea.

I would say, pick a subject that will stimulate you, elaborate it and involve it, then, if you can't develop it further, discard it and pick another. Elimination from accumulation is the process of finding what you want.

How does one get ideas? By sheer perseverance to the point of madness. One must have a capacity to suffer anguish and sustain enthusiasm over a long period of time. Perhaps it's easier for some people than others, but I doubt it.

Of course every budding comic goes through philosophical generalizing about comedy. 'The element of surprise and suspense' was a phrase dropped every other day on the Keystone lot.

I will not attempt to sound the depths of psycho-analysis to explain human behaviour, which is as inexplicable as life itself. More than sex or infantile aberrations, I believe that most of our ideational compulsions stem from atavistic causes – however, I did not have to read books to know that the theme of life is conflict and pain. Instinctively, all my clowning was based on this. My means of contriving comedy plot was simple. It was the process of getting people in and out of trouble.

But humour is different and more subtle. Max Eastman analysed it in his book *A Sense of Humour*. He sums it up as being derived from playful pain. He writes that *Homo sapiens* is masochistic, enjoying pain in many forms and that the audience like to suffer vicariously – as children do when playing Indians; they enjoy being shot and going through the death throes.

With all this I agree. But it is more an analysis of drama than humour, although they are almost the same. But my own concept of humour is slightly different: it is the subtle discrepancy we discern in what appears to be normal behaviour. In other words, through humour we see in what seems rational, the irrational; in what seems important, the unimportant. It also heightens our sense of survival and preserves our sanity. Because of humour we are less overwhelmed by the vicissitudes of life. It activates our sense of proportion and reveals to us that in an over-statement of seriousness lurks the absurd.

For instance, at a funeral where friends and relatives are gathered in hushed reverence around the bier of the departed, a late arrival enters just as the service is about to begin and hurriedly tiptoes to his seat, where one of the mourners has left his top hat. In his hurry, the late arrival accidentally sits on it, then with a solemn look of mute apology, he hands it crushed to its owner, who takes it with mute annoyance and continues listening to the service. And the solemnity of the moment becomes ridiculous.

# *fifteen*

AT the beginning of the First World War, popular opinion was that it would not last more than four months, that the science of modern warfare would take such a ghastly toll of human life that mankind would demand cessation of such barbarism. But we were mistaken. We were caught in an avalanche of mad destruction and brutal slaughter that went on for four years to the bewilderment of humanity. We had started a haemorrhage of world proportion, and we could not stop it. Hundreds of thousands of human beings were fighting and dying and the people began wanting to know the reason why, and how the war started. Explanations were not too clear. Some said it was due to the assassination of an archduke; but this was hardly a reason for such a world conflagration. People needed a more realistic explanation. Then they said it was a war to make the world safe for democracy. Though some had less to fight for than others, the casualties were grimly democratic. As millions were mowed down the word 'democracy' loomed up. Consequently thrones toppled, republics were formed, and the whole face of Europe was changed.

But in 1915 the United States alleged that it was 'too proud to fight'. This gave the nation its cue for the song *I Didn't Raise My Boy to Be a Soldier*. This song went down very well with the public, until the *Lusitania* went down – which was the cue for a different song, *Over There*, and many other beguiling ditties. Until the sinking of the *Lusitania*, the burden of the European war had hardly been felt in California. There were no shortages, nothing was rationed. Garden fêtes and parties for the Red Cross were organized and were an excuse for social gatherings. At one gala a lady donated $20,000 to the Red Cross in order to sit next to me at a very posh dinner. But as time went on, the grim reality of war was brought home to everyone.

By 1918 America had already launched two Liberty Bond Drives, and now Mary Pickford, Douglas Fairbanks and I were requested to open officially the Third Liberty Bond campaign in Washington.

I had almost completed my first picture, *A Dog's Life*, for the First National. And as I had a commitment to release it at the same time as the Bond Drive, I stayed up three days and nights cutting the film. When it was finished I got on the train exhausted and slept for two days. When I came to, the three of us began to write our speeches. Never having made a serious one before, I was nervous about it, so Doug suggested that I should try it on the crowds who waited for us at the railroad stations. We had a stop somewhere and quite a crowd had gathered at the back of the observation car. And from there Doug introduced Mary who made a little speech, then introduced me, but no sooner had I started speaking than the train began to move; and as it drew away from the crowd, I became more eloquent and dramatic, my confidence growing as the crowd grew smaller and smaller.

In Washington we paraded through the streets like potentates, arriving at the football field where we were to give our initial address.

The speakers' platform was made of crude boards with flags and bunting around it. Among the representatives of the Army and Navy standing about was one tall, handsome young man who stood beside me, and we made conversation. I told him that I had never spoken before and was very anxious about it. 'There's nothing to be scared about,' he said confidently. 'Just give it to them from the shoulder; tell them to buy their Liberty Bonds; don't try to be funny.'

'Don't worry!' I said ironically.

Very soon I heard my introduction, so I bounded on to the platform in Fairbanksian style and without a pause let fly a verbal machine-gun barrage, hardly taking a breath: 'The Germans are at your door! We've got to stop them! And we *will* stop them if you buy Liberty Bonds! Remember, each bond you buy will save a soldier's life – a mother's son! – will bring this war to an early victory!' I spoke so rapidly and excitedly that I slipped off the platform, grabbed Marie Dressler and fell with her on top of my handsome young friend, who happened to be the then Assistant Secretary of the Navy, Franklin D. Roosevelt.

After the official ceremony, we were scheduled to meet President Wilson at the White House. Thrilled and excited, we were ushered into the Green Room. Suddenly the door opened and a secretary appeared and said briskly: 'Stand in a line, please, and all come one pace forward.' Then the President entered.

Mary Pickford took the initiative. 'The public's interest was most gratifying, Mr President, and I am sure the bond drive will go over the top.'

'It certainly was and will . . .' I butted in, completely confused.

The President glanced at me incredulously, then told a senatorial joke about a Cabinet Minister who liked his whisky. We all laughed politely, then left.

Douglas and Mary chose the northern states for their bond-selling tour and I the southern, as I had never been there. I invited a friend of mine from Los Angeles, Rob Wagner, a portrait painter and writer, to come along as my guest. The ballyhoo was enterprising and handled expertly and I sold millions of dollars' worth of bonds.

In one North Carolina city, the head of the reception committee was the big business man of the town. He confessed that he had had ten boys at the station with custard pies ready to throw at me, but seeing our serious entourage as we got off the train, he had thought better of it.

The same gentleman invited us to dinner, and several United States generals were there, including General Scott, who evidently disliked him. Said he during dinner: 'What's the difference between our host and a banana?' There was a slight tension. 'Well, you can skin a banana.'

As for the legend of the Southern gentleman, I met the perfect one in Augusta, Georgia – Judge Henshaw, head of the Bond Committee. We received a letter from him stating that, as we were to be in Augusta on my birthday, he had arranged a party for me at the country club. I had visions of being the centre of a large gathering with a lot of small talk, and, as I was exhausted, I made up my mind to refuse and to go straight to the hotel.

Usually when we arrived at a station there was an enormous crowd to greet us with the local brass-bands playing. But in Augusta there was no one but Judge Henshaw dressed in a black pongee coat and an old, sun-tanned panama hat. He was quiet and courteous, and after introducing himself he drove with Rob and me to the hotel in an old horse-drawn landau.

For a while we drove in silence. Suddenly the Judge broke it: 'What I like about your comedy is your knowledge of fundamentals – you know that the most undignified part of a man's anatomy is his arse, and your comedies prove it. When you kick a portly gentleman there, you strip him of all his dignity. Even the impressiveness of a presidential inauguration would collapse if you came up behind the President and kicked him in the rear.' As we drove along in the sunlight, he tilted his head whimsically, soliloquizing to himself, 'There's no doubt about it; the arse is the seat of self-consciousness.'

I nudged Rob and whispered: 'The birthday party's on.'

It took place on the same day as the meeting. Henshaw had invited only three other friends, and he apologized for the smallness of the party, saying that he was selfish and wanted to enjoy us exclusively.

The golf club was in a beautiful setting. Shadows of tall trees across the green lawn gave the scene a quiet elegance as we sat on the terrace, six of us, at a round table surrounding a candle-lit birthday cake.

As the Judge nibbled at a piece of celery, his eyes twinkling, he cast a look at Rob and me. 'I don't know whether you'll sell many bonds in Augusta . . . I'm not very good at arranging things. However, I think the townsfolk know you're here.'

I began extolling the beauty of the surroundings. 'Yes,' he said, 'there's only one thing missing – a mint julep.'

This brought us to the subject of the possibility of Prohibition, its evils and its benefits. 'According to medical reports,' said Rob, 'Prohibition will have a salutary effect on the public's health. The medical journals state that there will be fewer ulcerated stomachs if we stop drinking whisky.'

The Judge assumed a hurt expression. 'You don't talk of whisky in terms of the stomach; whisky is food for the soul!' Then he turned to me. 'Charlie, this is your twenty-ninth birthday and you're not married yet?'

'No,' I laughed. 'Are you?'

'No,' he sighed wistfully. 'I've listened to too many divorce cases. Nevertheless, if I were young again I'd marry; it's lonely being a bachelor. However, I believe in divorce. I suppose I'm the most criticized judge in Georgia. If people don't want to live together, I won't make them.'

After a while Rob looked at his watch. 'If the meeting starts at eight-thirty,' he said, 'we'll have to hurry.'

The Judge was leisurely nibbling at his piece of celery. 'There's plenty of time,' he said. 'Just dally with me. I like to dally.'

On the way to the meeting we passed through a small park. It must have had twenty or more statues of senators looking absurdly pompous, some with a hand behind the back and the other resting on the pelvis, holding a scroll. Jokingly I commented that they were the perfect foil for that comedy kick in the pants he had talked about.

'Yes,' he said airily, 'they do look full of piss and high purpose.'

He invited us to his home, a beautiful old Georgian house that Washington had 'actually slept' in, furnished with eighteenth-century American antiques.

'How beautiful,' I said.

'Yes, but without a wife, it's as empty as a jewel-case. So don't leave it too late, Charlie.'

In the South we visited several military training camps and saw many glum and bitter faces. The climax of our tour was a final bond drive in New York on Wall Street, outside the sub-Treasury, where Mary, Douglas and I sold more than two million dollars' worth of bonds.

New York was depressing; the ogre of militarism was everywhere. There was no escape from it. America was cast into a matrix of obedience and every thought was secondary to the religion of war. The false buoyancy of military bands along the gloomy canyon of Madison Avenue was also depressing as I heard them from the twelfth-storey window of my hotel, crawling along on their way to the Battery to embark overseas.

In spite of the atmosphere, a little humour occasionally crept in. Seven brass bands were to march through the Ball Park before the Governor of New York. Outside the stadium Wilson Mizner, with a phoney badge of some sort, stopped each band and told them to strike up the National Anthem before passing the Governor's grandstand. After the Governor and everyone had risen for the fourth time, he thought it necessary to inform the bands ahead to lay off the National Anthem.

*

Before leaving Los Angeles for the Third Liberty Loan Campaign, I had met Marie Doro. She had come to Hollywood to star in Paramount pictures. She was a Chaplin fan, and told Constance Collier that the one person she wanted to meet in Hollywood was Charlie Chaplin – not having the faintest idea that I had played with her in London at the Duke of York's Theatre.

So I met Marie Doro again. It was like the second act of a romantic play. After Constance had introduced me I said: 'But we've met before. You broke my heart. I was silently in love with you.' Marie, looking through her lorgnette at me and as beautiful as ever, said: 'How thrilling.' Then I explained that I was Billy in *Sherlock Holmes*. Later we dined in the garden. It was a warm summer's evening, and in the glow of candle-light I talked about the frustrations of a youth silently in love with her and told her that at the Duke of York's Theatre I would time the moment that she left her dressing-room so as to meet her on the stairs and gulp 'good-evening'. We talked of London and Paris; Marie loved Paris, and we talked of the bistros, of the cafés, of Maxim's and the Champs Èlysées . . .

And now Marie was in New York! And hearing I was staying at the Ritz, she had written a letter inviting me to dine at her apartment. It went as follows:

Charlie dear,

I have an apartment off the Champs Èlysées (Madison Avenue), where we can dine or go to Maxim's (The Colony). Then afterwards, if you wish it, we can drive through the Bois (Central Park) . . .

However, we did not do any of those things, but just dined quietly in Marie's apartment alone.

*

I returned to Los Angeles and again took up my quarters at the Athletic Club, and started to think about work. *A Dog's Life* had taken a little longer and cost more than I had anticipated. However, I was not worried because it would all average up by the end of my contract. But I was worried about getting an idea for my second picture. Then the thought came to me: why not a comedy about the war? I told several friends of my intention, but they shook their heads. Said De Mille: 'It's dangerous at this time to make fun of the war.' Dangerous or not, the idea excited me.

*Shoulder Arms* was originally planned to be five reels. The beginning was to be 'home life', the middle 'the war' and the end 'the banqueting', showing all the crowned heads of Europe celebrating my heroic act of capturing the Kaiser. And, of course, in the end I wake up.

The sequences before and after the war were discarded. The banquet was never photographed, but the beginning was. The comedy was by suggestion, showing Charlot walking home with his family of four children. He leaves them for a moment, then comes back wiping his mouth and belching. He enters the house and immediately a frying pan comes into the picture and hits him on the head. His wife is never seen, but an enormous chemise is hanging on the kitchen line, suggesting her size.

In the next sequence Charlot is examined for induction and made to strip down to the altogether. On a bevelled glass office-door he sees the name 'Dr Frances'. A shadow appears to open the door, and, thinking it is a woman, he escapes through another door and finds himself in a maze of glass-partitioned offices where lady clerks are engrossed in their work. As one lady looks up he dodges behind a desk, only to expose himself to another, eventually escaping through another door into more glass-partitioned offices, getting further and further away from his base, until he finds himself out on a balcony, nude, over-looking a busy thoroughfare below. This sequence, although photographed, was never used. I thought it better to keep

Charlot a nondescript with no background and to discover him already in the army.

*Shoulder Arms* was made in the middle of a sizzling heatwave. Working inside a camouflaged tree (as I did in one of the sequences) was anything but comfortable. I loathe working outside on location because of its distraction. One's concentration and inspiration blow away with the wind.

The picture took a long time to make and I was not satisfied with it, and I got everybody in the studio feeling the same way – and now Douglas Fairbanks wanted to see it. He came with a friend and I warned them that I was so discouraged I was thinking of throwing it in the ash-can. The three of us sat in the projection-room alone. From the beginning Fairbanks went into roars of laughter, stopping only for coughing spells. Sweet Douglas, he was my greatest audience. When it was over and we came out into the daylight, his eyes were wet from laughing.

'You really think it's that funny?' I said incredulously.

He turned to his friend. 'What do you think of him? He wants to throw it in the ash-can!' was Douglas's only comment.

*Shoulder Arms* was a smash hit and a great favourite with the soldiers during the war, but again the film had taken longer than I had anticipated besides costing more than *A Dog's Life*. Now I wanted to surpass myself and I thought First National might help me. Since I had joined them they were riding high, signing up producers and other stars and paying them $250,000 a picture and fifty per cent interest in the profits. Their films cost less and were easier to make than my comedies – and certainly grossed less at the box office.

When I spoke to Mr J. D. Williams, the president of First National about it, he said that he would put the matter before his directors. I did not want much, only enough to compensate for the extra cost, which would not have amounted to more than an additional ten or fifteen thousand dollars a picture. He said they would be meeting in Los Angeles within a week, and that I might talk to them myself.

Exhibitors were rugged merchants in those days and to them films were merchandise costing so much a yard. I thought I spoke well and sincerely in pleading my cause to them. I said that I needed a little extra because I was spending more than anticipated, but I might as well have been a lone factory worker asking General Motors for a raise. When I had finished talking there was a silence, then their spokesman stirred. 'Well, Charlie, this is business,' he said. 'You've signed a contract and we expect you to live up to it.'

Said I laconically: 'I could deliver the six pictures in a couple of months, if you want those kind of pictures.'

'That's up to you, Charlie,' said the calm voice.

I continued: 'I'm asking for an increase to keep up the standard of my work. Your indifference shows your lack of psychology and foresight. You're not dealing with sausages, you know, but with individual enthusiasm.' But nothing would move them. I could not understand their attitude, as I was considered the biggest drawing card in the country.

'I believe it has something to do with this motion picture convention,' said my brother Sydney. 'There are rumours that all the producing companies are merging.'

A day later Sydney saw Douglas and Mary. They, too, were perturbed because their contracts were expiring and Paramount had done nothing about it. Like Sydney, Douglas thought it had to do with this film merger. 'It would be a good idea to put a detective on their track just to know what's going on.'

We all agreed to hire a detective. We engaged a very clever girl, smart and attractive-looking. Soon she had made a date with an executive of an important producing company. Her report stated that she had passed the subject in the lobby of the Alexandria Hotel and had smiled at him, then made the excuse that she had mistaken him for an old friend. That evening he had asked her to have dinner with him. From her report we gathered that the subject was a glib braggart in an esurient state of libido. For three nights she went out with him, staving him off with promises and excuses. In the meantime she got a complete story of what was going on in the film industry. He and his associates were forming a forty-million-dollar merger of all the producing companies and were sewing up every exhibitor in the United States with a five-year contract. He told her they intended putting the industry on a proper business basis, instead of having it run by a bunch of crazy actors getting astronomical salaries. That was the gist of her story, and it was sufficient for our purposes. The four of us showed the report to D. W. Griffith and Bill Hart, and they had the same reaction as we did.

Sydney told us that we could defeat their merger if we announced to the exhibitors that we were forming our own production company and that we intended to sell our productions on the open market and remain independent. At the time we represented the top-drawer attraction of the industry. It was not our intention to go through with this project, however. Our objective was only to stop exhibitors from signing a five-year contract with this proposed merger, for without the stars it would be worthless. We decided that the night before their convention we would appear together in the main dining-room of the Alexandria Hotel for dinner, and then make an announcement to the Press.

On that night Mary Pickford, D. W. Griffith, W. S. Hart, Douglas Fairbanks and myself sat at a table in the main dining-room. The effect was electric. J. D. Williams unsuspectingly came in for dinner first, saw us, then hurried out again. One after another the producers came to the entrance, took a look, then hurried out, while we sat talking big business and marking the table-cloth with astronomical figures. Whenever one of the producers appeared in the dining-room, Douglas would suddenly talk a lot of nonsense. 'The cabbages on the peanuts and the groceries on the pork carry a great deal of weight these days,' he would say. Griffith and Bill Hart thought he had gone mad.

Very soon half a dozen members of the Press were sitting at our table taking notes as we issued our statement that we were forming a company of United Artists to protect our independence and to combat the forthcoming big merger. The story received front-page coverage.

The next day the heads of several production companies offered to resign their posts and become our president for a small salary and an interest in the new company. After such a reaction we decided to go through with our project. Thus the United Artists Corporation was formed.

*

We arranged a meeting at Mary Pickford's house. Each of us

turned up with a lawyer and manager. It was such a regal gathering that what we had to say was like public oratory. In fact, every time I spoke it made me quite·nervous. But I was astonished at the legal and business acumen of Mary. She knew all its nomenclature: the amortizations and the deferred stocks, etc. She understood all the articles of incorporation, the legal discrepancy on page 7, paragraph A, article 27, and coolly referred to the overlap and contradiction in paragraph D, article 24. On these occasions she saddened me more than amazed me, for this was an aspect of 'America's sweetheart' that I did not know. One phrase I have never forgotten. While solemnly haranguing our representative she came out with: 'It behoves us, gentlemen –' I broke into laughter and kept repeating: 'It behoves us! It behoves us!'

In spite of Mary's beauty in those days, she had the reputation of being quite astute in business. I remember Mabel Normand, who first introduced me to her, saying: 'This is Hetty Green* alias Mary Pickford.'

My participation at those business meetings was nil. Fortunately my brother was as shrewd in business as Mary; and Douglas, who assumed a debonair nonchalance, was more astute than any of us. While our lawyers haggled out legal technicalities, he would cut capers like a schoolboy – but when reading the articles of incorporation he never missed a comma.

Amongst the producers who were willing to resign and join our company was Adolph Zukor, president and founder of Paramount. He was a vivid personality, a sweet little man who looked like Napoleon and was just as intense. When talking business, he was compelling and dramatic. 'You,' he said in his Hungarian accent, 'you have every right to get the full benefits of your efforts because you are artists! You create! It is you that the people come to see.' We were modestly in accord. 'You,' he continued, 'have come to form what I consider the most formidable company in the business, if – *if*,' he emphasized, 'it is properly managed. You are creative at one end of the business, I am creative at the other. What could be sweeter?'

* Hetty Green, one of the richest women in the world, was reputed to have made over $100,000,000 through her business acumen.

He went on in this way, holding us absorbed, telling us of his visions and beliefs; he admitted he had plans to amalgamate both the theatres and the studios, but said he would be willing to give it all up to cast his lot with ours. He spoke in an intense, patriarchal way: 'You think I am your enemy! But I am your friend – the artist's friend. Remember, it was I who first had the vision! Who swept out your dirty nickelodeons? Who put in your plush seats? It was I who built your great theatres, who raised prices and made it possible for you to get large grosses for your pictures. Yet you, you are the people who want to crucify me!'

Zukor was both a great actor and business man. He had built up the largest circuit of theatres in the world. However, since he wanted stock in our company, nothing came of our negotiations.

Within six months Mary and Douglas were making pictures for the newly formed company, but I still had six more comedies to complete for First National. Their ruthless attitude had so embittered me that it impeded the progress of my work. I offered to buy up my contract and to give them a hundred thousand dollars' profit, but they refused.

As Mary and Doug were the only stars distributing their pictures through our company, they were continually complaining to me of the burden imposed upon them as a result of being without my product. They were distributing their pictures at a very low cost of twenty per cent, which ran the company into a deficit of a million dollars. However, with the release of my first film, *The Gold Rush*, the debt was wiped out, which rather softened Mary and Doug's grievances, and they never complained again.

*

The war was now grim. Ruthless slaughter and destruction were rife over Europe. In training camps men were taught how to attack with a bayonet – how to yell, rush and stick it in the enemy's guts, and, if the blade got stuck in his groin, to shoot into his guts to loosen it. Hysteria was excessive. Draft-dodgers were being sentenced to five years and every man was made to carry his registration card. Civilian apparel was a dress of shame,

223

for nearly every young man was in uniform and, if he was not, he was liable to be asked for his registration card, or a woman might present him with a white feather.

Some newspapers criticized my not being in the war. Others came to my defence, proclaiming my comedies were needed more than my soldiering.

The American army, new and fresh when it reached France, wanted immediate action, and against the seasoned advice of the English and French, who had had three years of bloody combat, it plunged into battle with courage and daring, but at the cost of hundreds of thousands of casualties. For weeks the news was depressing; long lists were printed of the American dead and wounded. Then came a lull and for months the Americans, like the rest of the Allies, settled down in the trenches to an ennui of mud and blood.

At last the Allies began to move. On the map our flags began edging up. Each day crowds watched those flags with eagerness. Then the break-through came, but at a tremendous sacrifice. Big black headlines followed: THE KAISER ESCAPES TO HOLLAND! Then a full front page with two words: ARMISTICE SIGNED! I was in my room at the Athletic Club when that news broke. In the streets below pandemonium broke loose; automobile horns, factory whistles, trumpets' began howling and went on all day and night. The world went mad with joy – singing, dancing, embracing, kissing and loving. Peace at last!

Living without a war was like being suddenly released from prison. We had been so drilled and disciplined that for months afterwards we were afraid to be without our registration cards. Nevertheless, the Allies had won – whatever that meant. But they were not sure that they had won the peace. One thing was sure, that civilization as we had known it would never be the same – that era had gone. Gone, too, were its so-called basic decencies – but, then, decency had never been prodigious in any era.

# *sixteen*

Tom Harrington sort of drifted into my service, but he was to play a part in a dramatic change in my life. He had been dresser and handyman to my friend Bert Clark, an English vaudeville comedian engaged by the Keystone Company. Bert, vague and impractical, an excellent pianist, had once talked me into going into partnership with him in the music-publishing business. We had rented a room three storeys up in a down-town office building and printed two thousand copies of two very bad songs and musical compositions of mine – then we waited for customers. The enterprise was collegiate and quite mad. I think we sold three copies, one to Charles Cadman, the American composer, and two to pedestrians who happened to pass our office on their way downstairs.

Clark had put Harrington in charge of the office, but a month later Clark went back to New York and the office was closed. Tom, however, stayed behind, saying he would like to work for me in the same capacity as he had worked for Clark. To my surprise he told me he had never received a salary from Clark, only his living expenses, which did not amount to more than seven or eight dollars a week; being a vegetarian, he lived only on tea, bread and butter and potatoes. Of course, this informa-tion appalled me and I gave him a proper salary for the time he had worked for the music company, and Tom became my handyman, my valet and my secretary.

He was a gentle soul, ageless-looking, with an enigmatic manner, the benign, ascetic face of St Francis, thin-lipped, with an elevated brow and eyes that looked upon the world with a sad objectivity. He was of Irish descent, a bohemian and a bit of a mystery, who came from the East Side of New York but

225

seemed more fitted for a monastery than for living on the froth of show business.

He would call in the morning at the Athletic Club with my mail and the newspapers and order my breakfast. Occasionally without comment he would leave books by my bedside – Lafcadio Hearn and Frank Harris, authors I had never heard of. Because of Tom I read Boswell's *Life of Johnson* – 'that's something to put you to sleep at night,' he giggled. He never spoke unless spoken to and had the gift of effacing himself while I had breakfast. Tom became the *sine qua non* of my existence. I would just tell him to do something and he would nod and it was done.

*

Had not the telephone rung just as I was leaving the Athletic Club, the course of my life might have been different. The call came from Sam Goldwyn. Would I come down to his beach-house for a swim? It was the latter part of 1917.

It was a gay, innocuous afternoon. I remember that the beautiful Olive Thomas and many other pretty girls were there. As the day wore on a girl by the name of Mildred Harris arrived. She came with an escort, a Mr Ham. She was pretty, I thought. Someone remarked that she had a crush on Elliott Dexter, who was also present, and I noticed her ogling him the whole afternoon. But he paid little attention to her. I thought no more about her until I was ready to leave and she asked me if I would drop her on the way into town, explaining that she had quarrelled with her friend and that he had already left.

In the car I remarked flippantly that perhaps her friend was jealous of Elliott Dexter. She confessed that she thought Elliott was quite wonderful.

I felt that her naïve banter was an intuitive feminine trick to create interest about herself. 'He's a very lucky man,' I said superciliously. It was all chit-chat to make conversation as we drove along. She told me she worked for Lois Weber and was now being starred in a Paramount picture. I dropped her off at her apartment, however, with the impression that she was a very silly young girl, and I returned to the Athletic Club with a sense of relief, for I was glad to be alone. But I was not more than five minutes in the room when the telephone rang. It was

Miss Harris. 'I just wanted to know what you were doing,' she said naïvely.

I was surprised at her attitude, as though we had been cosy sweethearts for a long time. I told her I was going to have dinner in my room, then go straight to bed and read a book.

'Oh!' she said mournfully and wanted to know what kind of a book, and what kind of a room I had. She could just picture me all alone, snugly tucked up in bed.

This fatuous conversation was catching, and I fell in with her wooing and cooing.

'When am I going to see you again?' she asked. And I found myself jokingly chiding her for betraying Elliott, and listening to her reassurance that she did not really care for him, which swept away my resolutions for the evening, and I invited her out for dinner.

Although she was pretty and pleasant that evening, I lacked the zest and enthusiasm that the presence of a pretty girl usually inspires. The only possible interest she had for me was sex; and to make a romantic approach to it, which I felt would be expected of me, was too much of an effort.

I did not think of her again until the middle of the week, when Harrington said she had telephoned. Had he not made a passing remark I might not have bothered to see her again, but he happened to mention that the chauffeur had told him that I had come away from Sam Goldwyn's house with the most beautiful girl he had ever seen. This absurd remark appealed to my vanity – and that was the beginning. There were dinners, dances, moonlit nights and ocean drives, and the inevitable happened – Mildred began to worry.

Whatever Tom Harrington thought he kept to himself. When one morning, after he brought in my breakfast, I announced casually that I wanted to get married, he never batted an eye. 'On what day?' he asked calmly.

'What day is this?'

'This is Tuesday.'

'Make it Friday,' I said, without looking up from my newspaper.

'I suppose it's Miss Harris.'

'Yes.'

227

He nodded matter-of-factly. 'Have you a ring?'

'No, you'd better get one and make all the preliminary arrangements – but have it done quietly.'

He nodded again and there was no further mention of it until the day of the wedding. He arranged that we should be married at eight o'clock, Friday evening.

On that day I worked late at the studio. At seven-thirty Tom came quietly on the set and whispered: 'Don't forget you have an appointment at eight.' With a sinking feeling I took off my make-up and dressed, Harrington helping me. Not a word passed between us until we were in the car. Then he explained that I was to meet Miss Harris at the house of Mr Sparks, the local registrar.

When we arrived there Mildred was seated in the hall. She smiled wistfully as we entered and I felt a little sorry for her. She was dressed in a simple dark grey suit and looked very pretty. Harrington quickly fumbled a ring into my hand as a tall, lean man appeared, warm and congenial, and ushered us into another room. It was Mr Sparks. 'Well, Charlie,' he said, 'you certainly have a remarkable secretary. I didn't know it was to be you until half an hour ago.'

The service was terribly simple and resolute. The ring Harrington had fumbled into my hand I placed on her finger. Now we were married. The ceremony was over. As we were about to leave, the voice of Mr Sparks said: 'Don't forget to kiss your bride, Charlie.'

'Oh yes, of course,' I smiled.

My emotions were mixed. I felt I had been caught in the mesh of a foolish circumstance which had been wanton and unnecessary – a union that had no vital basis. Yet I had always wanted a wife, and Mildred was young and pretty, not quite nineteen, and, though I was ten years older, perhaps it would work out all right.

The next morning I went to the studio with a heavy heart. Edna Purviance was there; she had read the morning papers, and as I passed her dressing-room she appeared at the door. 'Congratulations,' she said softly. 'Thank you,' I replied, and went on my way to my dressing-room. Edna made me feel embarrassed.

To Doug I confided that Mildred was no mental heavy-weight; I had no desire to marry an encyclopedia – I could get all my intellectual stimulus from a library. But this optimistic theory rested upon an underlying anxiety: would marriage interfere with my work? Although Mildred was young and pretty, was I to be always in close proximity to her? Did I want that? I was in a dilemma. Although I was not in love, now that I was married I wanted to be and wanted the marriage to be a success.

But to Mildred marriage was an adventure as thrilling as winning a beauty contest. It was something she had read about in story-books. She had no sense of reality. I would try to talk seriously to her about our plans, but nothing penetrated. She was in a continual state of dazzlement.

The second day after our marriage, Louis B. Mayer of the Metro-Goldwyn-Mayer Company began negotiating a contract offering Mildred $50,000 a year to make six pictures. I tried to persuade her not to sign. 'If you want to continue your film work, I can get you fifty thousand dollars for one picture.'

With a Mona Lisa smile she nodded to everything I said, but afterwards she signed the contract.

It was this acquiescing and nodding, then doing completely the opposite, that was frustrating. I was annoyed both with her and with Mayer, for he had pounced on her with a contract before the ink on our marriage licence had time to dry.

A month or so later she got into difficulties with the company and wanted me to meet Mayer to straighten out the matter. I told her that under no circumstances would I meet him. But she had already invited him to dinner, telling me only a few moments before his arrival. I was outraged and indignant. 'If you bring him here I shall insult him.' I had no sooner said this than the front-door bell rang. Like a rabbit I jumped into the conservatory adjoining the living-room, a glassed-in affair from which there was no way out.

For what seemed an interminable time I hid there while Mildred and Mayer sat in the living-room a few feet away, talking business. I had a feeling he knew I was hiding there, for his conversation seemed edited and paternal. After a moment of silence I was alluded to, and Mildred mentioned that perhaps

I would not be home, whereupon I heard them stir and was horrified they might come into the conservatory and find me there. I pretended to be asleep. However, Mayer made some excuse and left without staying for dinner.

*

After we were married Mildred's pregnancy turned out to be a false alarm. Several months had passed and I had completed only a three-reel comedy, *Sunnyside*, and that had been like pulling teeth. Without question marriage was having an effect on my creative faculties. After *Sunnyside* I was at my wits' end for an idea.

It was a relief in this state of despair to go to the Orpheum for distraction, and in this state of mind I saw an eccentric dancer – nothing extraordinary, but at the finish of his act he brought on his little boy, an infant of four, to take a bow with him. After bowing with his father he suddenly broke into a few amusing steps, then looked knowingly at the audience, waved to them and ran off. The audience went into an uproar, so that the child was made to come on again, this time doing quite a different dance. It could have been obnoxious in another child. But Jackie Coogan was charming and the audience thoroughly enjoyed it. Whatever he did, the little fellow had an engaging personality.

I didn't think of him again until a week later when I sat on the open stage with our stock company, still struggling to get an idea for the next picture. In those days I would often sit before them, because their presence and reactions were a stimulus. That day I was bogged down and listless and in spite of their polite smiles I knew my efforts were tame. My mind wandered, and I talked about the acts I had seen playing at the Orpheum and about the little boy, Jackie Coogan, who came on and bowed with his father.

Someone said that he had read in the morning paper that Jackie Coogan had been signed up by Roscoe Arbuckle for a film. The news struck me like fork-lightning. 'My God! Why didn't I think of that?' Of course he would be marvellous in films! Then I went on to enumerate his possibilities, the gags and the stories I could do with him.

230

Ideas flew at me. 'Can you imagine the tramp a window-mender, and the little kid going around the streets breaking windows, and the tramp coming by and mending them? The charm of the kid and the tramp living together, having all sorts of adventures!'

I sat and wasted a whole day elaborating on the story, describing one scene after another, while the cast looked askance, wondering why I was waxing so enthusiastic over a lost cause. For hours I went on inventing business and situations. Then I suddenly remembered: 'But what's the use? Arbuckle has signed him up and probably has ideas similar to mine. What an idiot I was not to have thought of it before!'

All that afternoon and all that night I could think of nothing but the possibilities of a story with that boy. The next morning, in a state of depression, I called the company for rehearsals – God knows for what reason, for I had nothing to rehearse, so I sat around with the cast on the stage in a state of mental doldrums.

Someone suggested that I should try and find another boy – perhaps a little Negro. But I shook my head dubiously. It would be hard to find a kid with as much personality as Jackie.

About eleven-thirty, Carlisle Robinson, our publicity man, came hurrying on to the stage, breathless and excited. 'It's not Jackie Coogan that Arbuckle's signed up, it's the father, Jack Coogan!'

I leaped out of my chair. 'Quick! Get the father on the phone and tell him to come here at once; it's very important!'

The news electrified us all. Some of the cast came up and slapped me on the back, they were so enthused. When the office staff heard about it, they came on to the stage and congratulated me. But I had not signed Jackie yet; there was still a possibility that Arbuckle might suddenly get the same notion. So I told Robinson to be cautious what he said over the phone, not to mention anything about the kid – 'not even to the father until he gets here; just tell him it's very urgent, that we must see him at once within the next half-hour. And if he can't get away, then go to his studio. But tell him nothing until he gets here.' They had difficulty finding the father – he was not at the studio – and for two hours I was in excruciating suspense.

At last, surprised and bewildered, Jackie's father showed up. I grabbed him by the arms. 'He'll be a sensation – the greatest thing that ever happened! All he has to make is this one picture!' I went on raving in this inarticulate way. He must have thought I was insane. 'This story will give your son the opportunity of his life!'

'My son!'

'Yes, your son, if you will let me have him for this one picture.'

'Why, of course you can have the little punk,' he said.

They say babies and dogs are the best actors in movies. Put a twelve-month-old baby in a bath-tub with a tablet of soap, and when he tries to pick it up he will create a riot of laughter. All children in some form or another have genius; the trick is to bring it out in them. With Jackie it was easy. There were a few basic rules to learn in pantomime and Jackie very soon mastered them. He could apply emotion to the action and action to the emotion, and could repeat it time and time again without losing the effect of spontaneity.

There is a scene in *The Kid* where the boy is about to throw a stone at a window. A policeman steals up behind him, and, as he brings his hand back to throw, it touches the policeman's coat. He looks up at the policeman, then playfully tosses the stone up and catches it, then innocently throws it away and ambles off, suddenly bursting into a sprint.

Having worked out the mechanics of the scene, I told Jackie to watch me, emphasizing the points: 'You have a stone; then you look at the window; then you prepare to throw the stone; you bring your hand back, but you feel the policeman's coat; you feel his buttons, then you look up and discover it's a policeman; you throw the stone playfully in the air, then throw it away, and casually walk off, suddenly bursting into a sprint.'

He rehearsed the scene three or four times. Eventually he was so sure of the mechanics that his emotion came with them. In other words, the mechanics induced the emotion. The scene was one of Jackie's best, and was one of the high spots in the picture.

Of course, not all the scenes were as easily accomplished. The simpler ones often gave him trouble, as simple scenes do. I once wanted him to swing naturally on a door, but, having nothing else on his mind, he became self-conscious, so we gave it up.

It is difficult to act naturally if no activity is going on in the mind. Listening on the stage is difficult; the amateur is inclined to be over-attentive. As long as Jackie's mind was at work, he was superb.

Jackie's father's contract with Arbuckle soon terminated, so he was able to be at our studio with his son, and later played the pickpocket in the flophouse scene. He was very helpful at times. There was a scene in which we wanted Jackie to actually cry when two workhouse officials take him away from me. I told him all sorts of harrowing stories, but Jackie was in a very gay and mischievous mood. After waiting for an hour, the father said: 'I'll make him cry.'

'Don't frighten or hurt the boy,' I said guiltily.

'Oh no, no,' said the father.

Jackie was in such a gay mood that I had not the courage to stay and watch what the father would do, so I went to my dressing-room. A few moments later I heard Jackie yelling and crying.

'He's all ready,' said the father.

It was a scene where I rescue the boy from the workhouse officials and while he is weeping I hug and kiss him. When it was over I asked the father: 'How did you get him to cry?'

'I just told him that if he didn't we'd take him away from the studio and really send him to the workhouse.'

I turned to Jackie and picked him up in my arms to console him. His cheeks were still wet with tears. 'They're not going to take you away,' I said.

'I knew it,' he whispered. 'Daddy was only fooling.'

Gouverneur Morris, author and short-story writer who had written many scripts for the cinema, often invited me to his house. 'Guvvy,' as we called him, was a charming, sympathetic fellow, and when I told him about *The Kid* and the form it was taking, keying slapstick with sentiment, he said: 'It won't work. The form must be pure, either slapstick or drama; you cannot mix them, otherwise one element of your story will fail.'

We had quite a dialectical discussion about it. I said that the transition from slapstick to sentiment was a matter of feeling and discretion in arranging sequences. I argued that form happened after one had created it, that if the artist thought of a world and sincerely believed in it, no matter what the admixture was, it would be convincing. Of course, I had no grounds for this theory other than intuition. There had been satire, farce, realism, naturalism, melodrama and fantasy, but raw slapstick and sentiment, the premise of *The Kid*, was something of an innovation.

❋

During the cutting of *The Kid*, Samuel Reshevsky, aged seven, the boy champion chess-player of the world, visited the studio. He was to give an exhibition at the Athletic Club, playing chess with twenty men at the same time, among them Dr Griffiths, the champion of California. He had a thin, pale, intense little face with large eyes that stared belligerently when he met people. I had been warned that he was temperamental and that he seldom shook hands with anybody.

After his manager had introduced us and spoken a few words, the boy stood staring at me in silence. I went on with my cutting, looking at strips of film.

A moment later I turned to him. 'Do you like peaches?'

'Yes,' he answered.

'Well, we have a tree full of them in the garden; you can climb up and get some – at the same time get one for me.'

His face lit up. 'Ooh good! Where's the tree?'

'Carl will show you,' I said, referring to my publicity man.

Fifteen minutes later he returned, elated, with several peaches. That was the beginning of our friendship.

'Can you play chess?' he asked.

I had to admit that I could not.

'I'll teach you. Come see me play tonight, I'm playing twenty men at the same time,' he said with braggadocio.

I promised and said I would take him to supper afterwards.

'Good, I'll get through early.'

It was not necessary to understand chess to appreciate the drama of that evening: twenty middle-aged men poring over their chessboards, thrown into a dilemma by an infant of seven who looked even less than his years. To watch him walking about in the centre of the 'U' table, going from one to another, was a drama in itself.

234

There was something surrealistic about the scene as an audience of three hundred or more sat in tiers on both sides of a hall, watching in silence a child pitting his brains against serious old men. Some looked condescending, studying with set Mona Lisa smiles.

The boy was amazing, yet he disturbed me, for I felt as I watched that concentrated little face flushing red, then draining white, that he was paying a price with his health.

'Here!' a player would call, and the child would walk over, study the board a few seconds, then abruptly make a move or call 'Checkmate!' And a murmur of laughter would go through the audience. I saw him checkmate eight players in rapid succession, which evoked laughter and applause.

And now he was studying the board of Dr Griffiths. The audience were silent. Suddenly he made a move, then turned away and saw me. His face lit up and he waved, indicating that he would not be long.

After checkmating several other players, he returned to Dr Griffiths, who was still deeply concentrating. 'Haven't you moved yet?' said the boy impatiently.

The Doctor shook his head.

'Oh come on, hurry up.'

Griffiths smiled.

The child looked at him fiercely. 'You can't beat me! If you move here, I'll move there! And if you move this, I'll move that!' He named in rapid succession seven or eight moves ahead. 'We'll be here all night, so let's call it a draw.'

The Doctor acquiesced.

*

Although I had grown fond of Mildred, we were irreconcilably mismated. Her character was not mean, but exasperatingly feline. I could never reach her mind. It was cluttered with pink-ribboned foolishness. She seemed in a dither, looking always for other horizons. After we had been married a year, a child was born but lived only three days. This began the withering of our marriage. Although we lived in the same house, we seldom saw each other, for she was as much occupied at her studio as I was at mine. It became a sad house. I would come home to find the dinner table laid for one, and would eat alone. Occasionally

235

she was away for a week without leaving word, and I would only know by seeing the door of her empty bedroom left open.

Sometimes, on a Sunday, we would meet accidentally as she was leaving the house, and she would tell me perfunctorily that she was going to spend the week-end with the Gishes or with some other girl-friends, and I would go to the Fairbankses'. Then the break came. It was during the cutting of *The Kid*. I was spending the week-end at the Fairbankses' (Douglas and Mary were now married). Douglas came to me with rumours concerning Mildred. 'I think you ought to know,' he said.

How true these rumours were I never wanted to find out, but they depressed me. When I confronted Mildred she coldly denied them.

'However, we can't continue living this way,' I said.

There was a pause and she looked at me coldly. 'What do you want to do?' she asked.

She spoke so dispassionately that I was a little shocked. 'I – I think we should divorce,' I said quietly, wondering what her reaction would be. But she did not answer, so after a silence I continued: 'I think we'll both be happier. You're young, you still have your life ahead of you, and of course we can do it in a friendly way. You can have your lawyer see my lawyer, so whatever you want can be arranged.'

'All I want is enough money to look after my mother,' she said.

'Perhaps you'd rather discuss it between ourselves,' I ventured.

She thought a moment, then concluded: 'I think I'd better see my lawyers.'

'Very well,' I answered. 'In the meantime you stay on at the house and I'll go back to the Athletic Club.'

We separated in a friendly way, agreeing that she was to get the divorce on grounds of mental cruelty, and that we would say nothing about it to the Press.

The following morning Tom Harrington moved my things to the Athletic Club. This was a mistake, for the rumour that we had separated quickly spread and the Press began telephoning Mildred. They also called at the Club, but I would neither see them nor make a statement. But she came out with a blast on the front page, saying that I had deserted her and that she

236

was seeking a divorce on the grounds of mental cruelty. Compared to modern standards the attack was mild. However, I called her up to know why she had seen the Press. She explained that at first she had refused, but they had told her that I had given out a strong statement. Of course, they had lied in an attempt to build up an antagonism between us and I told her so. She promised not to give out any more statements – but she did.

The Community Property Law in California legally entitled her to $25,000 and I offered her $100,000, which she agreed to accept as a complete settlement. But when the day came for signing the final papers she suddenly reneged without giving any reason.

My lawyer was surprised – 'there's something in the wind,' he said – and there was. I had been having disagreements with First National over The Kid; it was a seven-reel feature picture and they wanted to release it on a basis of three two-reel comedies. In this way they would have only paid me $405,000 for The Kid. As it had cost me almost half a million besides eighteen months' work I told them I would see hell freeze over first. Lawsuits were threatened. Legally they had little chance and they knew it. Therefore, they decided to operate through Mildred and try to attach The Kid.

As I had not finished cutting the film my instinct told me to cut it in another state. So I set out for Salt Lake City with a staff of two and over 400,000 feet of film, which consisted of five hundred rolls. We stayed at the Salt Lake City Hotel. In one of the bedrooms we laid out the film, using every piece of furniture – ledges, commodes and drawers – to put the rolls of film on. It being against the law to have anything dangerously inflammable in a hotel, we had to go about it secretly. Under these circumstances we continued cutting the picture. We had over two thousand takes to sort out, and, although they were numbered, one would occasionally get lost and we would be hours searching for it on the bed, under the bed, in the bathroom, until we found it. With such heartbreaking handicaps and without the proper facilities, by some miracle we finished the cutting.

And now I had the terrifying ordeal of previewing it before

an audience. I had only seen it with a small cutting machine, through which a picture no larger than a postcard was projected on to a towel. I was thankful that I had seen the rushes at my studio on a normal-size screen, but now I had the depressing feeling that fifteen months' work had been done in the dark.

Nobody had seen the picture except the studio staff. After running it a number of times on the cutting machine, nothing looked as funny or as interesting as we had imagined. We could only reassure ourselves by believing that our first enthusiasm had grown stale.

We decided to give it the acid test and arranged to show it at the local movie theatre without any announcement. It was a large theatre and three-quarters filled. In desperation I sat and waited for the film to come on. This particular audience seemed out of sympathy with anything I might present to them. I began to doubt my own judgement as to what an audience would like and react to in comedy. Perhaps I had made a mistake. Perhaps the whole enterprise would misfire and the audience would look upon it with bewilderment. Then the sickening thought came to me that a comedian can at times be so wrong in his ideas about comedy.

Suddenly my stomach jumped up into my throat as a slide appeared on the screen: 'Charlie Chaplin in his latest picture, *The Kid*'. A scream of delight went up from the audience and scattered applause. Paradoxically enough this worried me: they might be expecting too much and be disappointed.

The first scenes were exposition, slow and solemn, and threw me into an agony of suspense. A mother deserts her baby by leaving it in a limousine, the car is stolen and the thieves eventually leave the baby near an ash-can. Then I appeared – the tramp. There was a laugh that accumulated and increased. They saw the joke! From then on I could do no wrong. I discovered the baby and adopted it. They laughed at an improvised hammock made out of old sacking and yelled when I fed the child out of a teapot with a nipple on the spout, and screamed when I cut a hole through the seat of an old cane chair, placing it over a chamber-pot – in fact they laughed hysterically throughout the picture.

*

Now that we had had a showing of the picture, we felt that the cutting was completed, and so we packed up and left Salt Lake City for the East. At the Ritz in New York I was forced to stay in my room because I was being harassed by process-servers instigated by First National, who were using Mildred's divorce suit to attach the film. For three days the process-servers had kept a vigil around the hotel lobby, and I was getting bored by it. So that when Frank Harris invited me to dine at his house I could not resist the temptation. That evening a heavily veiled woman passed through the lobby of the Ritz and got into a taxi – it was me! I had borrowed my sister-in-law's clothes, which I wore over my suit, shedding them in the taxi before I arrived at Frank's house.

Frank Harris, whose books I had read and admired, was my idol. Frank was in a continual state of financial crisis; every other week his periodical, *Pearson's Magazine*, was about to fold. After one of his published appeals I had sent him a contribution and in gratitude he sent me two volumes of his book on Oscar Wilde, which he wrote in as follows:

To Charlie Chaplin – one of the few who has helped me without even knowing me, one whose rare artistry in humour I have often admired, for those who make men laugh are worthier than those who make them weep – from his friend, Frank Harris, sending this his *own* Copy, Aug. 1919. 'I praise and prize only that writer who tells the truth about men – with tears in his eyes' – *Pascal*.

That night I met Frank for the first time. He was a short, thick-set man with a noble head, strong, well-formed features, and a handle-bar moustache which was a little disconcerting. He had a deep, resonant voice and used it with great effect. He was then sixty-seven years old and had a beautiful young wife with red hair, who was devoted to him.

Frank, although a socialist, was a great admirer of Bismarck and was rather contemptuous of the socialist, Liebknecht. His imitation of Bismarck with his German effective pauses answering Liebknecht in the Reichstag was powerful histrionics. Frank could have been a great actor. We talked until four in the morning, Frank doing most of it.

That evening, I decided to stay at another hotel, in case, even at that hour, process-servers were hanging about, but every hotel in New York was filled. After driving round for over an hour, the taxi-driver, a rough-looking fellow about forty, turned and said: 'Listen, you ain't going to get into any hotel at this hour. You'd better come home to my place and sleep there until the morning.'

At first I had qualms, but when he mentioned his wife and family I knew it would be all right; besides, I would be safe from the process-servers.

'That's very kind of you,' I said and introduced myself.

He was surprised and laughed. 'My wife will get a kick out of this.'

We arrived somewhere in the Bronx in a congested neighbourhood. There were rows of brownstone houses. We entered one which was sparsely furnished but spotlessly clean. He led me to a back room where there was a large bed, in it a boy of twelve, his son, fast asleep. 'Wait,' he said, then lifted the boy and flopped him over to the edge of the bed, the boy sleeping soundly throughout. Then he turned to me. 'Get in there.'

I was about to reconsider, but this hospitality was so touching that I could not refuse. He gave me a clean night-shirt and gingerly I crept into bed, terrified of waking the boy.

I never slept a wink. When eventually he awoke, he got up and dressed, and through my half-closed eyes I saw him give me a casual look and without further reaction leave the room. A few minutes later he and a young lady of eight, evidently his sister, crept into the room. Still pretending to be asleep, I saw them peering at me, wide-eyed and excited. Then the little girl put her hands to her mouth to muffle a giggle, and the two of them left.

It wasn't long before audible murmurings were going on in the passage; then I heard the hushed whisper of the taxi-driver, who gently opened the door to see if I was awake. I assured him that I was.

'We've got yer bath ready,' he said. 'It's at the end of the landing.' He had brought in a dressing-gown and some slippers and a towel. 'What would you like for yer breakfast?'

'Anything,' I said apologetically.

'Whatever you want – bacon and eggs, toast and coffee?'

'Wonderful.'

They timed it perfectly. With the completion of my dressing, his wife came into the front room with a hot breakfast.

There was little furniture but a centre table, an armchair, and a couch; several framed photographs of family groups hung over the mantelpiece and upon the wall over the couch. While eating my breakfast alone I could hear a milling crowd of children and grown-ups outside the house.

'They're beginning to know you're here,' smiled his wife, bringing in the coffee. Then the taxi-driver entered, all excited. 'Look,' he said, 'there's a big crowd outside and it's getting bigger. If you let those kids get a peek at you, they'll go away, otherwise the Press'll get on to it and you're sunk!'

'By all means let them come in,' I replied.

And so the children came in, giggling, and filed around the table while I sipped my coffee. The taxi-driver outside was saying: 'All right, don't get excited, line up, two at a time.'

A young woman entered the room, her face tense and serious. She looked searchingly at me, then burst into weeping. 'No, it's not him, I thought it was him,' she sobbed.

It seems a friend had told her cryptically: 'Who do you think is here? You'll never believe it.' Then she had been led into my presence, expecting to see her brother who was reported missing in the war.

I decided to return to the Ritz whether served with papers or not. However, I encountered no process-servers. But a telegram awaited me from my lawyer in California stating that everything had been settled and Mildred had applied for her divorce.

The next day the taxi-driver and his wife, all dressed up, came to visit me. He said the Press had been bothering him to write a feature story for the Sunday papers about my staying at his house. 'But,' he said resolutely, 'I wouldn't tell them a thing unless I had your permission.'

'Go ahead,' I said.

*

And now the gentlemen of First National came to me metaphorically with their hats in their hands. Said one of the vice-presidents, Mr Gordon, a large owner of theatres in the eastern states: 'You want a million and a half dollars and we haven't even seen the picture.' I confessed they had something there, so a showing was arranged.

It was a grim evening. Twenty-five exhibitors of First National filed into the projection-room as though going to a coroner's inquest, an aggregation of graceless men, sceptical and unsympathetic.

Then the picture started. The opening title was: 'A picture with a smile and perhaps a tear.' 'Not bad,' said Mr Gordon by way of showing his magnanimity.

Since the preview in Salt Lake City I had become a little more confident, but before the showing was half through that confidence had collapsed: where the picture had got screams at the preview there were only one or two sniggers. When it was over and the lights went up, there was a momentary silence. Then they began to stretch and blink and talk about other matters.

'What are you doing tonight for dinner, Harry?'

'I'm taking the wife to the Plaza, then we're going on to the Ziegfeld show.'

'It's pretty good, I hear.'

'Do you want to come along?'

'No, I'm leaving New York tonight. I want to be back for my boy's graduation.'

All through this chatter, my nerves were on razor edge. Eventually I snapped: 'Well, what's the verdict, gentlemen?'

Some stirred self-consciously, others looked down at the ground. Mr Gordon, who evidently was their mouthpiece, began slowly walking up and down. He was a thick-set, heavy man with a round, owlish face and thick-lensed glasses. 'Well, Charlie,' he said, 'I'll have to get together with my associates.'

'Yes, I know,' I quickly interposed, 'but how do you like the picture?'

He hesitated, then grinned. 'Charlie, we're here to buy it, not to say how much we like it.' This remark evoked one or two loud guffaws.

'I won't charge you extra for liking it,' I said.

He hesitated. 'Frankly, I expected something else.'

'What did you expect?'

He spoke slowly. 'Well, Charlie, for a million and a half dollars – well, it hasn't got that big punch.'

'What do you want – London Bridge to fall down?'

'No. But for a million and a half. . . .' His voice cracked into a falsetto.

'Well, gentlemen, that's the price. You can take it or leave it,' I said impatiently.

J. D. Williams, the president, came over and got the drift and started to butter me up. 'Charlie, I think it's wonderful. It's human, different –' (I didn't like the 'different'). 'Just be patient and we'll iron this thing out.'

'There's nothing to iron out,' I said sharply. 'I'll give you a week to make up your minds.' After the way they had treated me, I had no respect for them. However, they quickly made up their minds and my lawyer drew up an agreement to the effect that I was to receive fifty per cent of the profits after they had recouped their million and a half. It was to be on a rental basis of five years, after which the film reverted to me, as did the rest of my films.

*

Having rid myself of the burden of domestic and business affairs, I felt I was stepping on air. Like a recluse I had lived in hiding for weeks, seeing nothing but the four walls of my room at the hotel. Having read the article about my adventure with the taxi-driver, my friends began to call up, and now a free and unencumbered, wonderful life began again.

New York's hospitality serenaded me. Frank Crowninshield, editor of *Vogue* and *Vanity Fair*, shepherded me through the glittering life of New York, and Condé Nast, owner and publisher of those magazines, gave the most glamorous parties. He lived in a large penthouse on Madison Avenue where the élite of the arts and wealth gathered, decorated with the pick of the Ziegfeld Follies Girls, including the lovely Olive Thomas and the beautiful Dolores.

At the Ritz, where I was staying, I rode on the crest of exciting events. All day long the telephone rang with invitations. Would I spend a week-end here, attend a horseshow there? It was all very town and countryish, but I loved it. New York was full of romantic intrigues, midnight suppers, luncheons, dinners crowding every moment – even to keeping breakfast engagements. Having skimmed over the surface of New York society, I now desired to penetrate the intellectual subcutaneous tissue of Greenwich Village.

Many comedians, clowns and crooners in capering through success arrive at a point of wanting to improve their minds; they hunger for intellectual manna. The student shows up among the unexpected: tailors, cigar-makers, prize-fighters, waiters, truck-drivers.

At a friend's house in Greenwich Village I remember talking of the frustration of trying to find the precise word for one's thoughts, saying that the ordinary dictionary was inadequate. 'Surely a system could be devised,' I said, 'of lexicographically charting ideas, from abstract words to concrete ones, and by deductive and inductive processes arriving at the right word for one's thought.' 'There is such a book,' said a Negro truck-driver: 'Roget's *Thesaurus*.'

A waiter working at the Alexandria Hotel used to quote his Karl Marx and William Blake with every course he served me.

A comedy acrobat with a Brooklyn 'dis', 'dem' and 'dose' accent recommended Burton's *Anatomy of Melancholy*, saying that Shakespeare was influenced by him and so was Sam Johnson. 'But you can skip the Latin.'

With the rest of them I was intellectually a fellow-traveller. Since my vaudeville days I have done a considerable amount of reading, but not thoroughly. Being a slow reader, I browse. Once I am familiar with the thesis and the style of an author, I invariably lose interest. I have read every word of five volumes of Plutarch's *Lives*; but I found them less edifying than the effort was worth. I read judiciously; some books over and over again. Over the years I have browsed through Plato, Locke, Kant, Burton's *Anatomy of Melancholy*, and in this piecemeal fashion I have gleaned as much as I have wanted.

In the village I met Waldo Frank, essayist, historian and novelist, Hart Crane, the poet, Max Eastman, editor of *The Masses*, Dudley Field Malone, brilliant lawyer and controller of the Port of New York, and his wife Margaret Foster, the suffragette. I also lunched at Christine's Restaurant, where I met several members of the Provincetown Players, who regularly lunched there during rehearsals of *Emperor Jones*, a drama written by a young playwright, Eugene O'Neill (later my father-in-law). I was shown over their theatre, a barnlike affair no bigger than a six-horse stable.

I came to know Waldo Frank through his book of essays, *Our America*, published in 1919. One essay about Mark Twain is a profound, penetrating analysis of the man; incidentally, Waldo was the first to write seriously about me. So, naturally, we became very good friends. Waldo is a combination of mystic and historian and his insight has penetrated deeply into the soul of the Americas, North and South.

In the Village we had interesting evenings together. Through Waldo I met Hart Crane, and we dined at Waldo's small flat in the Village, talking until breakfast-time the next morning. They were enthralling symposiums, the three of us reaching out mentally for the subtle definition of our thoughts.

Hart Crane was desperately poor. His father, a millionaire candy-manufacturer, wanted him to enter his business and tried to discourage his poetry by cutting him off financially. I have neither ear nor taste for modern poetry, but while writing this book I read Hart Crane's *The Bridge*, an emotional out-pouring, strange and dramatic, full of piercing anguish and a sharp diamond-cut imagery, for me a little too shrill. Perhaps the shrillness was in Hart Crane himself. Yet he had a gentle sweetness.

We discussed the purpose of poetry. I said it was a love letter to the world. 'A very small world,' said Hart ruefully. He spoke of my work as being in the tradition of the Greek comedies. I told him that I had tried to read an English translation of Aristophanes but could never finish it.

Hart eventually was awarded a Guggenheim Fellowship, but it was too late. After years of poverty and neglect he had turned to drink and dissipation, and when returning to the States from Mexico in a passenger boat he jumped into the sea.

A few years before he committed suicide he sent me a book of his short poems called *White Buildings*, published by Boni and Liveright. On the fly-leaf he wrote: 'To Charles Chaplin in memory of *The Kid* from Hart Crane. 20 January, '28'. One poem was titled *Chaplinesque*.

We make our meek adjustments,
Contented with such random consolations
As the wind deposits
In slithered and too ample pockets.

For we can still love the world, who find
A famished kitten on the step, and know
Recesses for it from the fury of the street,
A warm torn elbow coverts.

We will sidestep, and to the final smirk
Dally the doom of that inevitable thumb
That slowly chafes its puckered index towards us,
Facing the dull squint with what innocence
And what surprise!

And yet these fine collapses are not lies
More than the pirouettes of any pliant cane;
Our obsequies are, in a way, no enterprise.
We can evade you, and all else but the heart:
What blame to us if the heart live on?

The game enforces smirks; but we have seen
The moon in lonely alleys make
A grail of laughter of an empty ash can,
And through all sound of gaiety and quest
Have heard a kitten in the wilderness.

Dudley Field Malone gave an interesting party in the Village
and invited Jan Boissevain, the Dutch industrialist, Max Eastman
and others. One man, an interesting fellow introduced as
'George' (I never did know his real name), seemed highly
nervous and excited. Later somebody said that he had been a
great favourite with the King of Bulgaria, who had paid for his
education at Sofia University. But George overthrew his royal
patronage and became a Red, emigrated to the States and joined
the I.W.W. and eventually was sentenced to twenty years'
imprisonment. He had served two years of it and had won an
appeal for a new trial and was now out on bail.

He was playing charades, and as I watched him Dudley
Field Malone whispered: 'He hasn't a chance of winning his
appeal.'

George, with a tablecloth wrapped around him, was imitating,

Sarah Bernhardt. We laughed, but underneath many were thinking, as I was thinking, that he must go back to the penitentiary for eighteen more years.

It was a strange hectic evening and as I was leaving George called after me: 'What's the hurry, Charlie? Why going home so early?' I drew him aside. It was difficult to know what to say. 'Is there anything I can do?' I whispered. He waved his hand as if to sweep the thought aside, then gripped my hand and said emotionally: 'Don't worry about me, Charlie. I'll be all right.'

\*

I wanted to stay longer in New York, but I had work to do in California. First, I intended to hurry through my contract with First National, for I was anxious to get started with United Artists.

Returning to California was a let-down after the freedom, lightness and the intensely interesting time I had had in New York. The problem of completing four two-reel comedies for First National loomed up as an insuperable task. For several days I sat around the studio exercising the habit of thinking. Like playing the violin or the piano, thinking needs everyday practice and I had got out of the habit of it.

I had feasted too much on the kaleidoscopic life of New York and I could not get unwound. So with my English friend, Dr Cecil Reynolds, I decided to go to Catalina to do a little fishing.

If you were a fisherman, Catalina was a paradise. Avalon, its sleepy old village, had two small hotels. The fishing was good all the year round. If the tuna were running, there was not a boat to be hired. In the early morning, someone would shout: 'They're here!' Tuna, weighing from thirty to three hundred pounds apiece, would be thrashing and splashing about as far as the eye could see. The sleepy hotel was a sudden hum of excitement; there was hardly time for dressing, and, if you were one of the lucky ones who had ordered a boat in advance, you stumbled into it, still buttoning up your pants.

On one of these occasions the Doctor and I caught eight tuna before lunch, each weighing over thirty pounds. But as suddenly as they appeared they would disappear, and we would go back to normal fishing again. Sometimes we fished for tuna with a kite which was attached to the line and held the bait, a flying fish, flapping on the surface of the water. This type of fishing was exciting, for you could see the tuna strike, making a whirl of foam around the bait, then run with it for a couple of hundred feet or more.

Swordfish caught around Catalina are from one hundred up to six hundred odd pounds. This type of fishing is more delicate. The line is free and the swordfish gently takes the bait, a small albacore or a flying fish, and swims off with it for about a hundred yards. Then he stops and you stop the boat and wait a full minute to give him time to swallow the bait, reeling in slowly until the line is taut. Then you sock him hard with two or three jerks and the fun commences. He makes a run of a hundred yards or more, the reel screaming, then stops; quickly. you reel in the slack line, otherwise it would snap like cotton. Should he make a sudden turn while running, the friction of the water will cut the line. He begins to leap twenty to forty times out of the water, shaking his head like a bulldog. Eventually he sounds bottom. Then the hard work begins, pumping him up. My own catch weighed one hundred and seventy-six pounds and took me only twenty-two minutes to land.

They were halcyon days, the Doctor and I holding our rods and dozing in the stern of the boat on those beautiful mornings with the mist on the ocean and the horizon merging into infinity, the vast silence giving importance to the cry of seagulls and the lazy chugging of our motor-boat.

Dr Reynolds was a genius in brain surgery and had achieved miraculous results in that field. I had known many of his case histories. One was a child with a brain tumour; she was having twenty fits a day and degenerating into idiocy. Through Cecil's surgery she completely recovered her health and grew up to be a brilliant scholar.

But Cecil was a 'nut'. His obsession was acting. This insatiable passion drew him to me as a friend. 'The theatre sustains the soul,' he would say. I often argued that his medical work should be sustaining enough. What could be more dramatic than turning a drivelling idiot into a brilliant scholar?

'That's merely knowing where the brain fibres lie,' said

Reynolds, 'but acting is a psychic experience that expands the soul.'

I asked him why he had taken up brain surgery.

'For the sheer drama of it,' he replied.

He often took small parts at the Amateur Playhouse in Pasadena. He also played the parson who visits the jail in my comedy *Modern Times*.

When I returned from fishing news came that Mother's health had improved and now that the war had ended we could bring her safely to California. I sent Tom to England to accompany her on the boat-trip over. She was put on the passenger list under another name.

During the voyage she was perfectly normal. She dined every night in the main saloon and during the day participated in the deck games. On her arrival in New York she was quite charming and self-possessed until the head of Immigration greeted her: 'Well, well, Mrs Chaplin! This is indeed a pleasure! So you're the mother of our famous Charlie.'

'Yes,' said Mother sweetly, 'and you are Jesus Christ.'

The officer's face was a study. He hesitated, looked at Tom, then said politely: 'Would you mind stepping aside for a moment, Mrs Chaplin?'

Tom knew that they were in for trouble. However, after a lot of red tape the Immigration Department was kind enough to pass Mother through on a year-to-year permit on condition that she would not be dependent on the state.

I had not seen her since I was last in England, a period of ten years, so I was somewhat shocked when a little old lady stepped off the train at Pasadena. She recognized Sydney and me at once and was quite normal.

We arranged for her to live near us in a bungalow by the sea, with a married couple to run the house and a trained nurse for her personal care. Sydney and I would occasionally visit her and play games in the evening. During the day she liked going on picnics and excursions in her car. Sometimes she came to the studio and I would run my comedies for her.

Eventually *The Kid* opened in New York and was a tremendous success. And, as I had prophesied to his father the first day I met him, Jackie Coogan was sensational. As a result of his success in *The Kid*, Jackie earned in his career over four million dollars. Each day we would receive clippings of wonderful reviews: *The Kid* was proclaimed a classic. But I never had the courage to go to New York and see it, I much preferred to stay in California and hear about it.

\*

This discursive autobiography should not preclude essaying a few remarks about film-making. Although many worth-while books have been written on the subject, the trouble is that most of them impose the cinematic taste of the author. Such a book should be nothing more than a technical primer which teaches one to know the tools of the trade. Beyond that the imaginative student should use his own art sense about dramatic effects. If the amateur is creative he needs only the barest technical essentials. To an artist complete freedom to do the unorthodox is usually most exciting, and that is why many a director's first picture has freshness and originality.

The intellectualizing of line and space, composition, tempo, etc., is all very well, but it has little to do with acting, and is liable to fall into arid dogma. Simplicity of approach is always best.

Personally, I loathe tricky effects, photographing through the fireplace from the viewpoint of a piece of coal, or travelling with an actor through a hotel lobby as though escorting him on a bicycle; to me they are facile and obvious. As long as an audience is familiar with the set, it does not want the tedium of a travelling smear across the screen to see an actor move from one place to another. Such pompous effects slow up action, are boring and unpleasant, and have been mistaken for that tiresome word 'art'.

My own camera set-up is based on facilitating choreography for the actor's movements. When a camera is placed on the floor or moves about the player's nostrils, it is the camera that is giving the performance and not the actor. The camera should not obtrude.

Time-saving in films is still the basic virtue. Both Eisenstein and Griffith knew it. Quick cutting and dissolving from one scene to another are the dynamics of film technique.

I am surprised that some critics say that my camera technique is old-fashioned, that I have not kept up with the times. What times? My technique is the outcome of thinking for myself, of my own logic and approach; it is not borrowed from what others are doing. If in art one must keep up with the times, then Rembrandt would be a back number compared to Van Gogh.

While on the subject of films, a few brief words may be profitable for those contemplating making a super-duper special – which, as a matter of fact, is the easiest picture to make. It requires little imagination or talent in acting or directing. All one needs is ten million dollars, multitudinous crowds, costumes, elaborate sets and scenery. With a glorification of glue and canvas, one can float the languorous Cleopatra down the Nile, march twenty thousand extras into the Red Sea, or blow down the walls of Jericho; all of which is nothing but the virtuosity of building contractors. And while the field-marshal sits in his directorial chair with script and table chart, his drill sergeants sweat and grunt over the landscape, bawling out orders to the divisions: one whistle meaning 'ten thousand from the left', two whistles 'ten thousand from the right', and three, 'all on and go to it'.

The theme of most of these spectacles is Superman. The hero can out-jump, out-climb, out-shoot, out-fight and out-love anyone in the picture. In fact every human problem is solved by these methods – except thinking.

Also a brief word about directing. In handling actors in a scene, psychology is most helpful. For instance a member of the cast may join the company in the middle of a production. Although an excellent actor he may be nervous in his new surroundings. This is where a director's humility can be very helpful, as I have often found under these circumstances. Although knowing what I wanted, I would take the new member aside and confide in him that I was tired, worried and at a loss to know what to do with the scene. Very soon he would forget his own nervousness and try to help me and I would get a good performance out of him.

Marc Connelly, the playwright, once posed the question: what should an author's approach be in writing for the theatre? Should it be the intellectual or the emotional? I think primarily emotional, because it is more interesting in the theatre than intellect; the theatre is designed for it, its rostrum, its proscenium, its red curtains, its whole architectural flounce is addressed to the emotion. Naturally intellect participates but it is secondary. Chekhov knew this; so did Molnár and many other playwrights. They also knew the importance of theatricalism, which is basically the art in playwriting.

To me theatricalism means dramatic embellishment: the art of the aposiopesis; the abrupt closing of a book; the lighting of a cigarette; the effects off-stage, a pistol shot, a cry, a fall, a crash; an effective entrance, an effective exit – all of which may seem cheap and obvious, but if treated sensitively and with discretion, they are the poetry of the theatre.

An idea without theatrical sense is of little value. It is more important to be effective. With a theatrical sense one can be effective about nothing.

An example of what I mean was a prologue I put on in New York with my picture *A Woman of Paris*. In those days prologues went with all feature pictures and lasted about half an hour. I had no script or story but I remembered a sentimental coloured print captioned 'Beethoven's Sonata', depicting an artistic studio and a group of bohemians sitting moodily about in half-light, listening to a violinist. So I reproduced the scene on the stage, having only two days to prepare it.

I engaged a pianist, a violinist, apache dancers and a singer, then utilized every theatrical trick I knew. Guests sat around on settees or on the floor with their backs to the audience, ignoring them and drinking Scotch, while the violinist poured out his sonata, and in a musical pause a drunk snored. After the violinist had played, the apache dancers had danced, and the singer had sung *Auprès de ma Blonde* two lines were spoken. Said a guest: 'It's three o'clock, I must be going.' Said another: 'Yes, we must all be going,' ad libbing as they exited. When the last had gone, the host lit a cigarette and began turning out the lights of the studio as voices were heard singing down the street *Auprès de ma Blonde*. When the stage had darkened, except for the moonlight streaming in through the centre window, the host exited and, as the singing grew fainter, the curtain slowly descended.

During this nonsense you could have heard a pin drop from the audience. For half an hour nothing had been said, nothing but a few ordinary vaudeville acts had taken place on the stage. Yet on the opening night the cast took nine curtain calls.

I cannot pretend to enjoy Shakespeare in the theatre. My feeling is too contemporary. It requires a special panache type of acting which I do not like, and in which I am not interested. I feel I am listening to a scholarship oration.

> My gentle Puck, come hither. Thou remember'st
> Since once I sat upon a promontory,
> And heard a mermaid on a dolphin's back
> Uttering such dulcet and harmonious breath,
> That the rude sea grew civil at her song,
> And certain stars shot madly from their spheres
> To hear the sea-maid's music.

This may be eminently beautiful but I do not enjoy that kind of poetry in the theatre. Moreover, I dislike Shakespearean themes involving kings, queens, august people and their honour. Perhaps it is something psychological within me, possibly my peculiar solipsism. In my pursuit of bread and cheese, honour was seldom trafficked in. I cannot identify myself with a prince's problems. Hamlet's mother could have slept with everyone at court and I would still feel indifferent to the hurt it would have inflicted on Hamlet.

As for my preference in presenting a play, I like the conventional theatre, with its proscenium that separates the audience from the world of make-believe. I like the scene to be revealed by the lifting or parting of curtains. I dislike plays that come over the footlights and participate with an audience, in which a character leans against the proscenium and explains the plot. Besides being didactic, this device destroys the charm of the theatre, and is a prosaic way of getting over exposition.

In stage décor I prefer that which contributes reality to the scene and nothing more. If it is a modern play of everyday life, I do not want geometric design. These prodigious effects destroy my make-believe.

Some very fine artists have imposed their scenic effusions to the degree of subordinating both the actor and the play. On the

253

other hand just curtains and steps running up into infinity are worse intrusions. They reek of erudition and shout: 'We leave much to your noble sensibility and imagination!' I once saw Laurence Olivier in evening dress recite an excerpt from *Richard III* at a benefit. Although he achieved a medieval mood by his histrionics, his white tie and tails were rather incongruous.

Someone said that the art of acting is relaxing. Of course this basic principle can be applied to all the arts, but an actor especially must have restraint and an inner containment. No matter how frenzied the scene, the technician within the actor should be calm and relaxed, editing and guiding the rise and fall of his emotions – the outer man excited and the inner controlled. Only through relaxation can an actor achieve this. How does one relax? That is difficult. My own method is rather personal: before going on the stage, I am always extremely nervous and excited, and in this state I get so exhausted that by the time I make my entrance I am relaxed.

I do not believe acting can be taught. I have seen intelligent people fail at it and dullards act quite well. But acting essentially requires feeling. Wainewright, an authority on aesthetics, a friend of Charles Lamb and the literary lights of his time, was a ruthless, cold-blooded murderer who poisoned his cousin for mercenary reasons. Here is an example of an intelligent man who could never have been a good actor because he had little feeling.

All intellect and no feeling can be characteristic of the arch-criminal, and all feeling and no intellect exemplify the harmless idiot. But when intellect and feeling are perfectly balanced, then we get the superlative actor.

The basic essential of a great actor is that he loves himself in acting. I do not mean it in a derogatory sense. Often I have heard an actor say: 'How I'd love to play that part,' meaning he would love himself in the part. This may be egocentric; but the great actor is mainly preoccupied with his own virtuosity: Irving in *The Bells*, Tree as Svengali, Martin Harvey in *A Cigarette Maker's Romance*, all three very ordinary plays, but very good parts. Just a fervent love of the theatre is not sufficient; there must also be a fervent love of and belief in oneself.

The Method school of acting I know little about. I understand it concentrates on development of personality – which could very well be less developed in some actors. After all, acting is pretending to be other people. Personality is an indefinable thing that shines through a performance in any case. But there is something to all methods. Stanislavski, for example, strove for 'inner truth', which I understand, means 'being it' instead of 'acting it'. This requires empathy, a feeling into things: one should be able to feel what it is like to be a lion or an eagle, also to feel a character's soul instinctively, to know under all circumstances what his reactions will be. This part of acting cannot be taught.

In instructing a true actor or actress about a character, a word or a phrase will often suffice: 'This is Falstaffian' or 'This is a modern Madame Bovary'. Jed Harris is reported to have told an actress: 'This character has the mobility of a weaving black tulip.' This goes too far.

The theory that one must know a character's life story is unnecessary. No one could write into a play or a part those remarkable nuances that Duse conveyed to an audience. They must have been dimensions beyond the concept of the author. And Duse, I understand, was not an intellectual.

I abhor dramatic schools that indulge in reflections and intro-spections to evoke the right emotion. The mere fact that a student must be mentally operated upon is sufficient proof that he should give up acting.

As for that much-touted metaphysical word 'truth', there are different forms of it and one truth is as good as another. The classical acting at the Comédie Française is as believable as the so-called realistic acting in an Ibsen play; both are in the realm of artificiality and designed to give the illusion of truth – after all, in all truth there is the seed of falsehood.

I have never studied acting, but as a boy I was fortunate in living in an era of great actors, and I acquired an extension of their knowledge and experience. Although I was gifted, I was surprised at rehearsals to find how much I had to learn about technique. Even the beginner with talent must be taught tech-nique, for no matter how great his gifts, he must have the skill to make them effective.

I have found that orientation is the most important means of achieving this; that is, knowing where you are and what you're doing every moment you're on the stage. Walking into a scene one must have the authority of knowing where to stop; when to turn; where to stand; when and where to sit; whether to talk directly to a character or indirectly. Orientation gives authority and distinguishes the professional from the amateur. I have always insisted on this method of orientation with the cast when I'm directing my films.

In acting I like subtlety and restraint. John Drew was undoubtedly the epitome of this. He was debonair, humorous, subtle and had great charm. It is easy to be emotional – that is expected of a good actor – and of course diction and voice are necessary. Although David Warfield had a magnificent voice and ability to express emotion, somehow one felt that the Ten Commandments were in everything he said.

I have often been asked who were my favourite actors and actresses on the American stage. This is difficult to answer, for a choice implies that the rest were inferior, which was not so. My favourites were not all serious actors. Some were comedians, others even entertainers.

Al Jolson, for instance, was a great instinctive artist with magic and vitality. He was the most impressive entertainer on the American stage, a black-faced minstrel with a loud baritone voice, telling banal jokes and singing sentimental songs. Whatever he sang, he brought you up or down to his level; even his ridiculous song 'Mammy' enthralled everyone. Only a shadow of himself appeared in films, but in 1918 he was at the height of his fame and electrified an audience. He had a strange appeal, with his lithe body, large head and sunken piercing eyes. When he sang such songs as 'There's a Rainbow Round My Shoulder' and 'When I Leave the World Behind', he lifted the audience by unadulterated compulsion. He personified the poetry of Broadway, its vitality and vulgarity, its aims and dreams.

Sam Bernard, the Dutch comedian, another fine artist, was exasperated about everything. 'Eggs! Sixty cents a dozen – and rotten ones! And the price of corned beef! Two dollars you pay! Two dollars – for a tiny, little bit of corned beef!' Here he would exaggerate the tininess of it, as though threading a needle, then explode, expostulating and throwing himself in

1. At school in Kennington, aged seven and a half

2. My mother

3. My father

4. (*top*) Karno's Company hockey team. I am seated second from left. Stan Laurel is standing behind me

5. (*bottom*) Five companies outside Karno's office in Camberwell leaving for the music halls in and around London

*Thwarted ambitions, at sixteen, to be a dramatic actor*

6. (*top*) My imitation of Beerbohm Tree as Fagin
7. (*bottom*) As Dr Walford Bodie of bloodless surgery fame

8. (*top*) With Alf Reeves, his wife and Muriel Palmer on our way to America for the Karno Company
9. (*below left*) Before my success
10. (*below right*) ... and after

11. 'A gentleman, a poet, a dreamer – always hopeful of romance'

12. D. W. Griffith (*left*), whom I considered a genius, and Sid Grauman (*right*), a master showman

13. During a celebration at Mack Sennett's studios. From left to right: Thomas Ince, myself, Mack Sennett, D. W. Griffith

14. Ballet Américain – the Keystone Cops
15. Prosperity came to the Keystone studios after I left

16. (*right*)
G. M. Anderson,
known as Bronco
Billy, of the Essanay
Company, who gave
me my first bonus
of $600
17. (*below*) The studio
I built in Hollywood

*Selling bonds during the First World War*
18. Departing for Washington with Mary and Douglas

19. (*left*)
Photographer
Edward Steichen's
portrait of me
20. (*below*)
Maude Fealy

21. Edna Purviance, who remained with the Chaplin Company throughout her life

22. At the time of my marriage to Mildred Harris

23. With my mentors, Upton Sinclair (*left*) and Rob Wagner
24. Building a set with not an idea in my head

25- 27.Scenes from *The Kid*

28. In *Sunnyside*

29. In my salad days

30. My first meeting with Sir Philip Sassoon (*centre*) through Georges Carpentier, in Paris

31. With Amy Johnson (*left*), Lady Astor and Bernard Shaw

32. The meeting with Gandhi in London

*Visitors in Hollywood*
**33.** (*left*)
With Jascha Heifetz
**34.** (*below*)
A home-made movie.
The heroine, Lady
Mountbatten; the
villain with a gun, me

35. Pianist Godowsky and his family. The elder son, on my right, became one of the inventors of colour photography

36. Breaking the news to Lord Mountbatten that he is no actor

**37.** (*top*) Randolph and Millicent Hearst
**38.** (*bottom*) With Randolph Hearst and Marion Davies

39. (*left*) With Dr
Cecil Reynolds, brain
surgeon and friend
40. (*below*) The home
I built in Beverly
Hills when I returned
to bachelorhood in
1923

**41.** (*right*) With
Anna Pavlova at the
Chaplin studios
**42.** (*below*) With
Albert Einstein at
the opening night of
*City Lights*

*Leading Ladies*
43. (*left*) Virginia
Cherrill in *City Lights*
44. (*below*)
Paulette Goddard in
*The Great Dictator*

45. (*right*) Edna Purviance in
*A Woman of Paris*
46. (*below left*) Georgia Hale in
*The Gold Rush*
47. (*below right*) Merna Kennedy in
*The Circus*

48. The Dictator
49. The Dictator again

50. Lunch on location

51. (*left*)
Oona in 1942
52. (*below*)
A children's party
for Michael in the
Beverly Hills house:
Oona (*centre*) and
Judy Garland (*sitting
extreme left*)

53. (*right*) The clan
begins to increase.
Beverly Hills: with
Oona, Michael, and
Geraldine
54. (*below*) The last
picture I made in
America: Claire
Bloom in *Limelight*

55. (*right*) With the
Very Rev. Hewlett
Johnson, former
Dean of Canterbury
56. (*below*)
Watching a cabaret
with Winston
Churchill. The
former Duchess of
Rutland is on my
right and Sir Philip
Sassoon on her right

57. With Clara Haskil and Pablo Casals

58. Gathering of the clan for Christmas at Manoir de Ban. From left to right: Annette, Jane, Eugene, Victoria, Josephine, and Christopher. Geraldine and Michael were then in London

59. (*left*) Oona
60. (*below*) Snapshot
taken by Oona

all directions: 'I remember the time when you COULDN'T
CARRY TWO DOLLARS WORTH OF CORNED BEEF!'

Off-stage he was a philosopher. When Ford Sterling went to
him weeping about his wife having double-crossed him, said
Sam: 'So what? They double-crossed Napoleon!'

Frank Tinney I saw when I first came to New York. He was
a great favourite at the Winter Garden, and had a gregarious
intimacy with his audience. He would lean over the footlights
and whisper: 'The leading lady's kind of stuck on me,' then
surreptitiously look off-stage to see that no one was listening,
then back at the audience and confide: 'It's pathetic; as she was
coming through the stage door tonight I said "good-evening",
but she's so stuck on me she couldn't answer.'

At this point the leading lady crosses the stage, and Tinney
quickly puts his finger on his lips, warning the audience not to
betray him. Cheerily he hails her: 'Hi, kiddo!' She turns indignantly and in a huff struts off the stage, dropping her haircomb.

Then he whispers to the audience: 'What did I tell you?
But in private we are just like that.' He crosses his two fingers.
Picking up her comb, he calls to the stage-manager: 'Harry,
put this in *our* dressing-room, will you, please?'

I saw him again on the stage a few years later and was shocked,
for the comic Muse had left him. He was so self-conscious that
I could not believe it was the same man. It was this change in
him that gave me the idea years later for my film *Limelight*. I
wanted to know why he had lost his spirit and his assurance. In
*Limelight* the case was age; Calvero grew old and introspective
and acquired a feeling of dignity, and this divorced him from
all intimacy with the audience.

Among the American actresses I most admired were Mrs
Fiske, ebullient, humorous and intelligent, and her niece, Emily
Stevens, a gifted actress with style and lightness of touch. Jane
Cowl had projection and intensity, and Mrs Leslie Carter was
equally arresting. Among the comediennes, I enjoyed Trixie
Friganza and, of course, Fanny Brice, whose great talent for
burlesque was enriched by her sense of histrionics. We English
had our great actresses: Ellen Terry, Ada Reeve, Irene Vanbrugh,
Sybil Thorndike and the sagacious Mrs Pat Campbell – all of
whom I saw except Mrs Pat.

John Barrymore stood out as having the true tradition of the theatre, but John had the vulgarity of wearing his talent like silk socks without garters – a nonchalance that treated everything rather contemptuously; whether it was a performance of *Hamlet* or sleeping with a duchess, it was all a joke to him.

In his biography by Gene Fowler there is a story about him getting out of a warm bed after a terrific champagne binge and being pushed on to play Hamlet, which he did between sporadic vomitings at the side of the wings and alcoholic restoratives. The English critics were supposed to have hailed his performance that night as the greatest Hamlet of the age. Such a ridiculous story insults everyone's intelligence.

I first met John at the height of his success sitting broodingly in an office in the United Artists building. After being introduced, we were left alone and I began to talk about his triumph as Hamlet. I said that Hamlet gave a greater account of himself than any other character of Shakespeare.

He mused a moment. 'The King is not a bad part either. In fact, I prefer it to Hamlet.'

I thought this odd and wondered how sincere he was. Had he been less vain and more simple he could have been in line with the greatest actors: Booth, Irving, Mansfield and Tree. But they had the noble spirit and the sensitive outlook. The trouble with Jack was that he had a naïve, romantic conception of himself as a genius doomed to self-destruction – which he eventually achieved in a vulgar, boisterous way by drinking himself to death.

Although *The Kid* was a great success my problems were not yet over: I still had four pictures to deliver to First National. In a state of quiet desperation, I wandered through the property room in the hope of finding an old prop that might give me an idea: remnants of old sets, a jail door, a piano or a mangle. My eye caught a set of old golf-clubs. That's it! The tramp plays golf – *The Idle Class*.

The plot was simple. The tramp indulges in all the pleasures of the rich. He goes south for the warm weather, but travels under the trains instead of inside them. He plays golf with balls he finds on the golf-course. At a fancy-dress ball he mingles with the rich, dressed as a tramp, and becomes involved with a beautiful girl. After a romantic misadventure he escapes from the irate guests and is on his way again.

During one of the scenes I had a slight accident with a blow-torch. The heat of it went through my asbestos pants, so we added another layer of asbestos. Carl Robinson saw an opportunity for publicity and gave the story to the Press. That evening I was shocked to read headlines that I had been severely burnt about the face, hands and body. Hundreds of letters, wires and telephone calls swamped the studio. I issued a denial, but few newspapers printed it. As a consequence amongst my English mail was a letter from H. G. Wells, stating that it affected him with a great deal of shock to read of my accident. He went on to say how much he admired my work and how regrettable it would be if I were unable to continue. I immediately wired back stating the true facts.

At the completion of *The Idle Class* I intended starting another two-reeler and toyed with an idea of a burlesque on the prosperous occupation of plumbers. The first scene was to show their arrival in a chauffeured limousine with Mack Swain and me stepping out of it. We are lavishly entertained by the beautiful mistress of the house, Edna Purviance, and after she wines and dines us we are shown the bathroom, where I immediately go to work with a stethoscope, placing it on the floor, listening to the pipes, and tapping them as a doctor would a patient.

This was as far as I got. I could concentrate no further. I did not realize how tired I was. Besides in the last two months I had developed an insatiable desire to visit London – I had dreamed about it, and H. G. Wells's letter was an added inducement. And after ten years I had received a letter from Hetty Kelly. She wrote: 'Do you remember a silly young girl'. . . . She was now married and living in Portman Square, and if ever I came to London would I look her up? The letter was without tone and could arouse little, if any, emotional resurgence. After all, in the interim of ten years I had been in and out of love several times. However, I would certainly look her up.

I told Tom to pack my things, and Reeves to close the studio and give the company a holiday. I intended going to England.

# *seventeen*

THE night before sailing from New York, I gave a party at the Élysée Café for about forty guests, among them Mary Pickford, Douglas Fairbanks and Madame Maeterlinck. We played charades. Douglas and Mary acted the first one. Douglas, a street-car conductor, punched a ticket and gave it to Mary. For the second syllable they pantomimed a rescue, Mary screaming for help and Douglas swimming to her and bringing her safely to the side of the river. Of course, all of us yelled: 'Fairbanks!'

As the evening grew merry Madame Maeterlinck and I did the death scene from *Camille*, Madame Maeterlinck playing Camille and I playing Armand. As she was dying in my arms, she started coughing, slightly at first, then with increasing momentum. Her coughing became so infectious that I caught it from her. Then it became a coughing contest between us. Eventually it was I who did the dying in Camille's arms.

The day of sailing I was painfully awakened at eight-thirty in the morning. After a bath, I was rid of all dissipation and filled with excitement, leaving for England. Edward Knoblock, my friend, author of *Kismet* and other plays, was leaving on the *Olympic* with me.

A crowd of newspaper men came aboard and I had a depressing feeling that they were going to remain with us throughout the voyage – two of them did, but the others got off with the pilot.

At last I was alone in my cabin which was stocked with flowers and baskets of fruit from my friends. . . . It had been ten years since I had left England, and on this very boat with the Karno Company; then we had travelled second class. I remember the steward taking us on a hurried tour through the first class, to give us a glimpse of how the other half lived. He had talked of the luxury of the private suites and their prohibitive price, and now I was occupying one of them, and was on my way to England. I had known London as a struggling young nondescript from Lambeth; now as a man celebrated and rich I would be seeing London as though for the first time.

A few hours out and the atmosphere was already English. Each night Eddie Knoblock and I would dine in the Ritz restaurant instead of the main dining-room. The Ritz was *à la carte*, with champagne, caviar, duck *à la presse*, grouse and pheasant, wines, sauces, and crêpes suzette. With time on my hands I enjoyed the nonsense of dressing each evening in black tie. Such luxury and indulgence brought home to me the delights of money.

I thought I would be able to relax. But there were bulletins on the *Olympic* notice board about my anticipated arrival in London. Half-way across the Atlantic an avalanche of telegrams with invitations and requests began piling up. Hysteria gathered like a storm. The *Olympic* bulletin quoted articles from the *United News* and the *Morning Telegraph*. One read: 'Chaplin returns like a Conqueror! Progress from Southampton to London will resemble a Roman triumph.'

Another read: 'The daily bulletins on the ship's run and Charlie's activities on board have been superseded by hourly flashes from the boat, and special editions of the newspapers are on the streets telling about this great little man with the preposterous feet.'

Another read: 'The old Jacobite song, *Charlie is My Darling*, epitomizes the Chaplin madness that has run through England this last week, becoming more acute every hour as the *Olympic* shoves the knots behind her, bearing Charlie home.'

Another read: 'The *Olympic* was fog-bound outside Southampton tonight and in the city there waited a huge army of worshippers come to welcome the little comedian. The police were busy making special arrangements to handle the crowd at the docks and at the civic ceremony in which Charlie is to be received by the Mayor. . . . The newspapers, as in the days preceding the victory parade, are pointing out the best points from which the people may see Chaplin.'

*

I was not prepared for this kind of welcome. Wonderful and extraordinary as it was, I would have postponed my visit until I felt more equal to it. What I yearned for was the sight of old familiar places. To go around quietly and look about London, to look around Kennington and Brixton, to look up at the window at 3 Pownall Terrace, to peer in at the darkened wood shed where I had helped the wood-choppers, to look up at the second-floor window of 287 Kennington Road where I had lived with Louise and my father; this desire had suddenly developed almost into an obsession.

At last we reached Cherbourg! Many were getting off and many getting on – cameramen and newspaper men. What message had I for England? What message for France? Would I visit Ireland? What did I think of the Irish question? Metaphorically, I was being devoured.

We left Cherbourg and were on our way to England, but crawling, crawling ever so slowly. Sleep was out of the question. One, two, three o'clock and I was still awake. The engines stopped, then started in reverse, then completely stopped. I could hear hollow footsteps running up and down the passage outside. Tense and wide awake, I looked through the porthole. But it was dark, I could see nothing; nevertheless, I could hear English voices!

The dawn broke and from sheer exhaustion I fell asleep, but only for two hours. After the steward had brought me some hot coffee and the morning papers, I was up like a lark.

One headline stated:

HOMECOMING OF COMEDIAN TO RIVAL
ARMISTICE DAY

Another:

ALL LONDON TALKS OF CHAPLIN'S VISIT

Another:

CHAPLIN GOING TO LONDON ASSURED MIGHTY
WELCOME

And another in big type:

Of course there were a few critical comments:

### A CALL FOR SANITY

In heaven's name, let us recover our sanity. I daresay Mr Chaplin is a most estimable person, and I am not much interested to inquire why the home-sickness which so touchingly affects him at this juncture did not manifest itself during the black years when the homes of Great Britain were in danger through the menace of the Hun. It may be true, as has been argued, that Charlie Chaplin was better employed playing funny tricks in front of a camera than he would have been doing manly things behind a gun.

At the dockside I was greeted by the Mayor of Southampton, then hurried on to the train. Eventually, we were on our way to London! Arthur Kelly, Hetty's brother, was in my compartment. I remember looking out at the revolving panorama of green fields as Arthur and I sat together trying to make conversation. I told him that I had received a letter from his sister inviting me to dinner at their house in Portman Square.

He looked at me strangely and seemed embarrassed. 'Hetty died, you know.'

I was shocked, but at that moment I could not assimilate the full tragedy of it; too many events were crowding in; but I felt I had been robbed of an experience. Hetty was the one audience from the past I should have liked to meet again, especially under these fantastic circumstances.

\*

We were coming into the suburbs of London. Eagerly I looked out of the window, trying vainly to recognize a passing street. Mingling with my excitement lurked a fear that perhaps London had greatly changed since the war.

Now the excitement intensified. Nothing seemed to be registering but anticipation. Anticipation of what? My mind was chaotic. I could not think. I could only see objectively the roof-tops of London, but the reality was not there. It was all anticipation, anticipation!

At last we were entering that enclosing sound of a railway station – Waterloo! As I stepped off the train I could see at the end of the platform vast crowds roped off, and lines of policemen. Everything was high tension, vibrant. And although I was beyond assimilating anything but excitement, I was conscious of being grabbed and marched down the platform as though under arrest. As we approached the roped-off crowds, the tension began to loosen: 'Here he is! Here he is!' 'Good old Charlie!' Then they burst into cheers. In the midst of it I was bundled into a limousine with my cousin Aubrey, whom I had not seen in fifteen years. I had not the presence of mind to object to being hidden from the crowds, who had waited so long to see me.

I asked Aubrey to be sure we went over Westminster Bridge. Passing out of Waterloo and down York Road, I noticed the old houses had gone and in their place was a new structure, the L.C.C. building. But when we turned the corner of York Road, like a sunburst Westminster Bridge came into view! It was exactly the same, its solemn Houses of Parliament still erect and eternal. The whole scene was just as I had left it. I was on the verge of tears.

I chose the Ritz Hotel because it had just been built when I was a boy and, passing its entrance, I had caught a glimpse of the gilt and splendour inside, and ever since I had had a curiosity to know how the rest of it looked.

An enormous crowd was waiting outside the hotel and I made a little speech. When at last I was settled in the rooms my impatience to get out alone was excruciating. But the milling crowds were outside, shouting their greetings, and I was obliged to go on the balcony several times and, like royalty, acknowledge their cheers. It is hard to describe what went on under such extraordinary circumstances.

My suite was crowded with friends, but my one desire was to get away from them. It was four o'clock in the afternoon, so I told them I would take a nap and would see them that evening for dinner.

As soon as they had gone, I hurriedly changed my clothes, took the freight elevator and left unnoticed by the back entrance. Immediately I made my way down Jermyn Street, hired a taxi and was off, down the Haymarket, through Trafalgar Square, down Parliament Street and over Westminster Bridge.

The taxi turned a corner, and at last Kennington Road! There it was! Incredible! Nothing had changed, There was Christ Church at the corner of Westminster Bridge Road! There was the Tankard at the corner of Brook Street!

I stopped the taxi a little before 3 Pownall Terrace. A strange calm came over me as I walked towards the house. I stood a moment, taking in the scene. 3 Pownall Terrace! There it was, looking like a gaunt old skull. I looked up at the two top windows – the garret where Mother had sat, weak and under-nourished, losing her mind. The windows were closed tight. They were telling no secrets and seemed indifferent to the man who stood gazing up at them so long, yet their silence communicated more than words. Eventually some little children came up and surrounded me. I was obliged to move on.

I walked towards the mews at the back of Kennington Road, where I used to help the wood-choppers. But the mews had been bricked in, the wood-choppers had gone.

Then on to 287 Kennington Road, where Sydney and I had lived with my father and Louise and their little boy. I gazed up at the second-floor windows of the room that was so familiar with my childhood despair. How innocuous they looked now, calm and enigmatic.

Then on to Kennington Park, passing the post office in which I had a savings account of sixty pounds: money I had skimped to save since the year 1908, and it was still there.

Kennington Park! In spite of the years, it still bloomed green with sadness. Then to Kennington Gate, my first trysting place with Hetty. I paused a moment and watched a tram-car stop. Someone got on, but no one got off.

Then on to Brixton Road, to 15 Glenshaw Mansions, the flat which Sydney and I had furnished. But my emotions were spent; only my curiosity was left.

On my way back I stopped at the Horns for a drink. It had been rather elegant in its day, with its polished mahogany bar, fine mirrors and billiard-room. The large assembly room was where my father had had his last benefit. Now the Horns was a little seedy, but it was all intact. Near by was the seat of my two years' learning, the Kennington Road County Council School. I peered into the playground: its grey patch of asphalt had shrunk with additional buildings.

As I wandered through Kennington, all that had happened to me there seemed like a dream, and what had happened to me in the States was the reality. Yet I had a feeling of slight uneasiness that perhaps those gentle streets of poverty still had the power to trap me in the quicksands of their hopelessness.

*

Much nonsense has been written about my profound melancholy and loneliness. Perhaps I have never needed too many friends – celebrity attracts them indiscriminately. To help a friend in need is easy, but to give him your time is not always opportune. At the height of my popularity, friends and acquaintances crowded in upon me excessively. And, being both extrovert and introvert, when the latter prevailed I would have to get away from it all. This might account for those articles written about my being elusive, lonely and incapable of true friendship. This is nonsense. I have one or two very good friends who brighten my horizon, and when I am with them I usually have an enjoyable time.

Yet my personality has been high-lighted and low-lighted according to the disposition of the writer. For example, Somerset Maugham has written:

Charlie Chaplin . . . his fun is simple and sweet and spontaneous. And yet all the time you have a feeling that at the back of all is a profound melancholy. He is a creature of moods and it does not require his facetious assertion: 'Gee, I had such a fit of the blues last night I didn't hardly know what to do with myself' to warn you that his humour is lined with sadness. He does not give you the impression of a happy man. I have a notion that he suffers from a nostalgia of the slums. The celebrity he enjoys, his wealth, imprison him in a way of life in which he finds only constraint. I think he looks back to the freedom of his struggling youth, with its poverty and bitter privation, with a longing which knows it can never be satisfied. To him the streets of southern London are the scene of frolic, gaiety and extravagant adventure . . . I can imagine him going into his own house and wondering what on earth he is doing in this strange man's dwelling. I suspect that the only home he can ever look upon as such is a second-floor back in the Kennington Road. One night I walked with him in Los Angeles and presently our steps took us into the poorest quarter of the city. There were sordid tenement houses and the shabby, gaudy shops in which are

266

sold the various goods that the poor buy from day to day. His face lit up and a buoyant tone came into his voice as he exclaimed: 'Say, this is the real life, isn't it? All the rest is just sham.'*

This attitude of wanting to make poverty attractive for the other person is annoying. I have yet to know a poor man who has nostalgia for poverty, or who finds freedom in it. Nor could Mr Maugham convince any poor man that celebrity and extreme wealth mean constraint. I find no constraint in wealth – on the contrary I find much freedom in it. I do not think Maugham would ascribe such false notions to any character in his novels – even in the least of them. Such glibness as 'the streets of southern London are the scene of frolic, gaiety and extravagant adventure' has a tinge of Marie-Antoinette's airy persiflage.

I found poverty neither attractive nor edifying. It taught me nothing but a distortion of values, an over-rating of the virtues and graces of the rich and the so-called better classes.

Wealth and celebrity, on the contrary, taught me to view the world in proper perspective, to discover that men of eminence, when I came close to them, were as deficient in their way as the rest of us. Wealth and celebrity also taught me to spurn the insignia of the sword, the walking-stick and the riding whip as something synonymous with snobbery, to know the fallacy of the college accent in estimating the merit and intelligence of a man, and the paralysing influence this myth has wrought on the minds of the English middle classes, to know that intelligence is not necessarily a result of education or a knowledge of the classics.

In spite of Maugham's assumptions, like everyone else I am what I am: an individual, unique and different, with a lineal history of ancestral promptings and urgings; a history of dreams, desires, and of special experiences, all of which I am the sum total.

*

After my arrival in London, I found myself constantly in the company of Hollywood friends. I wanted change, new experiences, new faces; I wanted to cash in on this business of being a celebrity. I had just one date, and that was with H. G.

* This accredited remark is not true. We happened to be in the Mexican quarter, and my remark was: 'There is more vitality here than in Beverly Hills.'

Wells. After that, I was free-lancing, with the dubious hope of meeting other people.

'I have arranged a dinner for you at the Garrick Club,' said Eddie Knoblock.

'Actors, artists and authors,' I said jokingly. 'But where is this exclusive English set, these country homes and house parties that I'm not invited to?' I wanted that rarer sphere of ducal living. Not that I was a snob, but I was a tourist sight-seeing.

The Garrick Club had a chiaroscuro atmosphere of dark oak walls and oil paintings – a sombre haven, in which I met Sir James Barrie, E. V. Lucas, Walter Hackett, George Frampton, Edwin Lutyens, Squire Bancroft and other illustrious gentlemen. Although it was a dull affair, I was extremely moved by the touching tribute of the presence of these distinguished gentlemen.

But I felt the evening did not quite come off. When the illustrious forgather, the occasion calls for an easy congeniality, and this was rather difficult to achieve when the guest of honour was a celebrated parvenu who had insisted on no after-dinner speeches; perhaps that was what was lacking. During dinner, Frampton, the sculptor, attempted levity and was charming; but he had difficulty in scintillating in the gloom of the Garrick Club, as the rest of us sat eating boiled ham and treacle pudding.

In my first interview with the English Press, I had inadvertently said I had come back to revisit the environs of my English boyhood, to savour again stewed eels and treacle pudding. As a consequence, they gave my treacle pudding at the Garrick Club, at the Ritz, at H. G. Wells's; even at Sir Philip Sassoon's opulent dinner the dessert was treacle pudding.

The party soon dispersed, and Eddie Knoblock whispered that Sir James Barrie would like us to come to his apartment in Adelphi Terrace for a cup of tea.

Barrie's apartment was like an *atelier*, a large room with a beautiful view of the river Thames. In the centre of the room was a round stove with a chimney-pipe ascending to the ceiling. He took us to a window that looked out on a narrow side-street with a window directly opposite. 'That's Shaw's bedroom,' he said mischievously with his Scotch accent. 'When I see a light on, I flip cherry-stones or plum-stones at the window. If he wants to chat, he opens it and we do a little back-yard gossiping, and, if he doesn't, then he pays no attention or turns out the light. Usually I flip about three times, then give up.'

Paramount was going to film *Peter Pan* in Hollywood. '*Peter Pan*,' I told Barrie, 'has even greater possibilities as a film than a play,' and he agreed. He expressly desired a scene showing Wendy sweeping up some fairies into the bark of a tree. Said Barrie also that evening: 'Why did you interpose a dream sequence in *The Kid*? It interrupted the flow of the story.'

'Because I was influenced by *A Kiss for Cinderella*,' I answered frankly.

The following day, Eddie Knoblock and I went shopping, and afterwards he suggested that we call on Bernard Shaw. No appointment had been made. 'We could just drop in on him,' said Eddie. At four o'clock Eddie pressed the doorbell at Adelphi Terrace. While we waited I suddenly developed a blue funk. 'Some other time,' I said, and ran up the street with Eddie running after me, vainly assuring me that everything would be all right. It was not until 1931 that I had the pleasure of meeting Shaw.

The next morning I was awakened by the telephone ringing in the sitting-room, and then heard the metallic voice of my American secretary: 'Who? . . . The Prince of Wales!'

Eddie was there and, since he claimed to be versed in protocol, took the phone. I could hear Eddie's voice saying: 'Are you there? Oh yes. Tonight? Thank you!'

He announced excitedly to my secretary that the Prince of Wales would like Mr Chaplin to dine with him that night and started for my bedroom.

'Don't wake him now,' said my secretary.

'Good God, man, this is the Prince of Wales!' said Eddie indignantly, and launched into a tirade on British etiquette.

A moment later I heard the handle of my bedroom door turn, so I pretended to be just waking. Eddie came in and announced with suppressed excitement and a phoney nonchalance: 'You must keep tonight open; you're invited to dine with the Prince of Wales.'

Assuming a similar nonchalance, I told him it would be

awkward, as this evening I had a previous engagement to dine with H. G. Wells. Eddie ignored what I said and repeated the message. Naturally I was thrilled – the thought of dining with the Prince at Buckingham Palace! 'But I think someone must be spoofing us,' I said, 'because only last night I read that the Prince was up in Scotland, shooting.'

Eddie suddenly looked foolish. 'Perhaps I'd better telephone the Palace and find out.'

He returned with an inscrutable look and announced unemotionally: 'It's true, he's still in Scotland.'

That morning news came that Fatty Arbuckle, my associate at the Keystone Company, had been charged with murder. This was preposterous; I knew Roscoe to be a genial, easy-going type who would not harm a fly, and expressed this view to the Press when they interviewed me about it. Eventually, Arbuckle was completely exonerated, but it ruined his career: although he was reinstated with the public, the ordeal took its toll, and within a year or so he died.

I was to meet Wells in the afternoon at the offices of Oswald Stoll Theatres, where we were to see a film based on one of Wells's stories. As we drew near I noticed a dense crowd. Very soon I was pushed and propelled and shot into an elevator and swept up into a small office where there were more people.

I was bewildered that our first meeting should be under such auspices. Wells was seated calmly by a desk, his violet-blue eyes kindly and twinkling, looking a little embarrassed. Before we could shake hands, a barrage of flashlights and photographers appeared from everywhere. Wells leaned over and whispered: 'You and I are the goats.'

Then we were ushered into a projection-room and towards the end of the film Wells whispered: 'How do you like it?' I told him frankly that it was not good. When the lights went up, Wells quickly leaned over. 'Say something nice about the boy.' As a matter of fact, the boy, George K. Arthur, was the only redeeming feature of the picture.

Wells's attitude to movies was an affected tolerance. 'There is no such thing as a bad film,' he said; 'the fact that they move is wonderful!'

There was no chance to get acquainted on that occasion, but later that day I received a message:

Don't forget dinner. You can wrap up in an overcoat if you deem it advisable, and slip in about 7.30 and we can dine in peace.

That evening Rebecca West was there. Conversation was a little stiff at first. But eventually we began to thaw out. Wells talked of Russia, for he had recently been there.

'Progress is slow,' he said. 'It is easy to issue ideal manifestoes but difficult to carry them out.'

'What's the solution?' I asked.

'Education.'

I told him that I was not well informed about socialism, and said jestingly that I saw little virtue in a system in which man must work to live. 'Frankly, I prefer one that enables him to live without work.'

He laughed. 'What about your films?'

'That isn't work – that's child's play,' I said, facetiously.

He asked me what I intended doing during my holiday in Europe. I told him I thought of going to Paris, then on to Spain to see a bullfight. 'I've been told that the technique is dramatic and beautiful.'

'Quite so, but it's very cruel to horses,' he said.

'Why be sentimental about horses?' I could have kicked myself for making such a silly remark; it was my nerves. But I could see that Wells understood. However, all the way home I reproached myself for being such an ass.

The next day Eddie Knoblock's friend, Sir Edwin Lutyens, the celebrated architect, came to the hotel. He was working on the plans of a new Government building for Delhi, and had just returned from Buckingham Palace after an interview with King George V. He had taken with him a workable miniature toilet; it was about six inches high with a cistern that held a small wine-glass full of water, and when the chain was pulled it flushed like a regular toilet. Both the King and Queen had been so charmed and amused by it, pulling its chain and refilling its cistern, that Lutyens had suggested building a dolls' house around it. Later he arranged for various important English artists to paint miniature pictures for the principal rooms. Every domestic installation was made in miniature. When it was finished, the Queen permitted it to be exhibited to the public, and collected large sums of money for charity.

*

After a while the tide of my social activity began to recede. I had met the literati and the illustrious and had visited the scenes of my boyhood; now there seemed little left but to jump in and out of taxis to escape the crowds; and as Eddie Knoblock had left for Brighton, I suddenly decided to pack up and go to Paris and get away from it all.

We left without publicity – so I thought – but at Calais a large crowd greeted us. '*Vive* Charlot!' they cried as I came down the gangplank. We had had a rough crossing, and half of me had been left in the Channel; nevertheless, I waved and smiled weakly. I was pushed, shoved and pressured into the train. On arriving in Paris I was greeted by a large crowd and a cordon of police. Again I was pushed and massaged with enthusiasm and, with the help of the police, I was lifted and bundled into a taxi. It was fun and I frankly enjoyed it. But it was more than I had bargained for. Although it was a stirring reception, the excitement of it left me exhausted.

At Claridge's, the telephone rang persistently every ten minutes. It was Miss Anne Morgan's secretary calling. I knew this would be for some request or other, as she was the daughter of J. P. Morgan. So we put the secretary off. But the secretary would not be put off: would I meet Miss Anne Morgan? She would not take up much of my time. I succumbed, promising to meet her at my hotel at a quarter to four. But Miss Morgan was late, so after ten minutes I started to leave. As I went through the lobby the manager came running after me, very concerned. 'Miss Anne Morgan is here to see you, sir.'

I was nettled by Miss Morgan's persistence and assurance – and then to be late! I greeted her smilingly. 'I'm sorry, I have an appointment at four.'

'Oh really?' she said. 'Well, I won't detain you more than five minutes.'

I looked at the clock; it was five minutes to four.

'Perhaps we could sit down for a moment,' she said, and

began talking while we were looking for a place to sit in the lobby. 'I am helping to raise funds for the rebuilding of devastated France and if we could have your picture, *The Kid*, for a gala at the Trocadero and you could appear with it we could raise thousands of dollars.'

I told her that she could have the picture for that occasion, but that I would not appear with it.

'But your presence will add extra thousands of dollars,' she insisted, 'and I am sure you will be decorated.'

Something devilish came over me and I looked at her steadily. 'Are you sure?'

Miss Morgan laughed. 'One can only make recommendations to the Government,' she said, 'and of course I'll do my best.'

I looked at the clock and extended my hand. 'I am awfully sorry but I must go. However, I shall be in Berlin for the next three days, so perhaps you can let me know.' And with this cryptic remark I said good-bye. I know it was naughty of me and the moment I left the hotel I regretted such brashness.

*

An introduction to the social set usually comes about by one incident, which, like a spark from a flint, ignites a conflagration of social activities – and you're 'in'.

I remember two ladies from Venezuela – simple girls – telling me how they broke into New York society. On an ocean liner they had met one of the Rockefellers, who gave them a letter of introduction to friends, and that started the ball rolling. The secret of their success, one told me years later, was that they never made a play for the married men; consequently New York hostesses adored them and invited them everywhere – and even found husbands for them.

As for myself, my entrée into the English set came unexpectedly, while I was taking a bath at Claridge's. Georges Carpentier, whom I had met in New York before his fight with Jack Dempsey, was announced and entered the bathroom. After a warm greeting, he whispered that he had a friend waiting in the sitting-room whom he would like me to meet, an Englishman who was '*très important en Angleterre*'. So I slipped on a bathrobe and met Sir Philip Sassoon. That was the beginning of a very dear friendship that lasted for over thirty years. That evening I had dinner with Sir Philip and his sister, who was then Lady Rocksavage, and the following day I left for Berlin.

The reaction of the public in Berlin was amusing. I was stripped of everything but my personality, and that could not get me even a decent table in a night-club, for my pictures had not yet been shown there. It was not until I was recognized by an American officer, who indignantly informed the bewildered proprietor who I was, that at least we were placed out of a draught. It was also amusing to see the management's reaction when those who recognized me gathered about our table. One, a German who had been a prisoner in England and had seen two or three of my comedies there, suddenly screamed 'Schaarlie!' and turned to the bewildered customers. 'Do you know who this is? Schaarlie!' Then hysterically he embraced and kissed me. But his excitement caused little stir. It was not until Pola Negri, the German film star, who was the cynosure of all eyes, asked if I would join her table that mild interest was aroused.

The day after my arrival, I received a mysterious message. It read:

Dear friend Charlie,

So much has happened to me since we met in New York at Dudley Field Malone's party. At present I am very ill in a hospital, so please do come and see me. It will cheer me up so much . . .

The writer gave the address of the hospital and signed himself 'George'.

At first I did not realize who it was. Then it occurred to me: of course, it was George the Bulgarian, who had been due to go back to prison for eighteen years. It seemed obvious from the tone of the letter that it was all leading up to a 'touch'. So I thought I would take along $500. To my surprise, at the hospital I was ushered into a spacious room with a desk and two telephones, where I was greeted by two well-dressed civilians who, I learnt later, were George's secretaries. One of them ushered me into the next room, where George was in bed. 'My friend!' he said, greeting me emotionally. 'I am so glad you have come. I've never forgotten your sympathy and kindness at Dudley Malone's party!' Then he gave a perfunctory order to his secretary and we were left alone. As he never proffered any explanation about his departure from the States, I felt it would be indiscreet to ask him about it; besides, he was too interested in inquiring about his friends in New York. I was bewildered; I could not make sense of the situation; it was like skipping several chapters of a book. The dénouement came when he explained that he was now the purchasing agent for the Bolshevik Government and was in Berlin buying railway engines and steel bridges. I left with my $500 intact.

*

Berlin was depressing. It still had an atmosphere of defeat, with its tragic aftermath of armless and legless soldiers begging on almost every street corner. Now I began to receive telegrams from Miss Anne Morgan's secretary, fraught with anxiety, for already the Press was announcing my appearance at the Trocadero. I wired back that I had made no promise to attend, and that to keep faith with the French public I would have to apprise them of the fact.

Eventually a telegram arrived: 'Have absolute assurance that you will be decorated if you are present, but it has been a veritable series of manoeuvres and crises – Anne Morgan.' So after three days in Berlin I returned to Paris.

On the night of the Trocadero première I was in the box with Cécile Sorel, Anne Morgan and several others. Cécile leaned close to impart a deep secret. 'Tonight you are going to be decorated.'

'How wonderful!' I said with modesty.

A dreary documentary film went on endlessly up to the intermission. After I had suffered interminable ennui the lights went up and two officials escorted me to the Minister's box. Several journalists accompanied us; one, an astute American correspondent, kept continually whispering down my neck: 'You're getting the Legion of Honour, kid.' As the Minister was delivering his encomium, my friend kept up a stream of whispering: 'They've double-crossed you, kid; that's the wrong colour – that's what they give to school-teachers; you don't get the smackeroos on the cheek for that one; you want the red ribbon, kid.'

Actually, I was very happy to be honoured in a class with

school-teachers. The certificate stated: 'Charles Chaplin, dramatist, artist, an Officier de l'Instruction Publique . . .' etc.

I received a charming letter of thanks from Anne Morgan and an invitation to lunch next day at the Villa Trianon, Versailles, saying that she would see me there. It was an affluent pot-pourri. – Prince George of Greece, Lady Sarah Wilson, the Marquis de Talleyrand-Périgord, Commandant Paul-Louis Weiller, Elsa Maxwell and others. Whatever incident or conversation took place on that matutinal occasion I do not remember, for I was too busy exercising my charm.

The next day my friend Waldo Frank came to the hotel with Jacques Copeau, the leader of a new movement in the French theatre. Together we went to the circus that evening and saw some excellent clowns, then later we supped with Copeau's company in the Latin Quarter.

The day following I was due in London for a lunch with Sir Philip Sassoon and Lord and Lady Rocksavage, to meet Lloyd George. But the plane was forced to land on the French coast because of a fog over the Channel, and we arrived three hours too late.

A word about Sir Philip Sassoon. He had been official secretary to Lloyd George during the war. A man about my own age, he was a picturesque personality, handsome and exotic-looking. He had a seat in Parliament representing Brighton and Hove, and, although one of the wealthiest men in England, he was not satisfied to be idle, but worked hard and made an interesting life for himself.

When I first met him in Paris I had said that I was exhausted and needed to get away from people and was moreover extremely nervous, complaining that even the colour of the hotel walls was getting on my nerves.

He laughed. 'What coloured walls would you like?'

'Yellow and gold,' I said jokingly.

He then suggested my going to his estate in Lympne, where I would be quiet and away from people. To my astonishment, when I arrived there I discovered my room had pastel curtains of yellow and gold.

His estate was extraordinarily beautiful, the house furnished with flamboyant daring. Philip could do this successfully because he had great taste. I remember how impressed I was with my luxurious suite: the lighted chafing-dish to keep soup warm in case I was hungry during the night and in the morning two stalwart butlers wheeling into the room a veritable cafeteria, with a choice of American cereals, fish cutlets, and bacon and eggs. I had remarked that since visiting Europe I missed American wheat-cakes, and there they were, brought to my bedside, all hot, with butter and maple syrup. It was something out of the *Arabian Nights*.

Sir Philip went about conducting his household affairs with one hand in his coat pocket, fingering his mother's pearls – a string over a yard long, and each pearl the size of a thumbnail. 'I carry them around to keep them alive,' he said.

After I had recovered from my fatigue, he asked if I would accompany him to a hospital in Brighton to visit the incurable spastic cases who had been wounded during the war. It was terribly sad to look into those young faces and to see the lost hope there. One young man was so paralysed that he painted with a brush in his mouth, the only part of his body he could use. Another had fists so clenched that he had to be given an anaesthetic in order to cut his finger-nails to prevent them from growing into the palms of his hands. Some patients were in such a terrible state that I was not allowed to see them – but Sir Philip did.

After Lympne we drove together back to London to his house in Park Lane, where he was holding his annual Four Georges Exhibition of paintings for charity. It was a magnificent house with a large conservatory carpeted with blue hyacinths. On the second day I lunched there, the hyacinths had been changed and were of another colour.

We visited Sir William Orpen's studio and saw a portrait of Philip's sister, Lady Rocksavage, which was beautifully luminous. I had a rather negative reaction to Orpen, for he affected a dumb, incredulous expression which I thought was supercilious.

Another visit was to H. G. Wells's country house on the Countess of Warwick's estate, where he lived with his wife and their two sons, who had just come down from Cambridge. I had been invited to stay the night.

In the afternoon over thirty members of the Cambridge

faculty showed up and sat cloistered together in the garden like a school group being photographed, mutely observing me as they would a species from another planet.

In the evening, the Wells family played a game called 'Animal, Vegetable or Mineral' which made me feel that I was taking an I.Q. test. Paramount in my memory are the icy sheets and going to bed by candle-light. It was the coldest night I ever spent in England. After I had thawed out the next morning, H.G. asked me how I had slept.

'Quite well,' I said politely.

'So many of our guests complain about the room being cold,' he said innocently.

'I wouldn't say it was cold, just icy!'

He laughed.

A few more memories of that visit to H.G. His small, simple study dimmed by the shade of the trees outside, by the window his old-fashioned, slanting writing desk; his pretty, dainty wife showing me around an eleventh-century church; our talk with an old engraver who was taking brass impressions from some of the gravestones; the deer that roamed in herds near the house; St John Ervine's remark at lunch about the thrilling aspect of coloured photography, and my expressing an abhorrence of it; H.G. reading a paper from a Cambridge professor's lecture and my saying that its prolix style sounded as though a monk had written it in the fifteenth century; and Wells's story about Frank Harris. Wells said that as a struggling young writer he had written one of the first scientific articles touching on the fourth dimension, which he submitted to several magazine editors without success. Eventually he received a note from Frank Harris requesting him to call at his office.

'Although I was hard up,' said Wells, 'I had bought a second-hand top hat for the occasion. Harris greeted me with: "Where the hell did you get that hat? And why the hell do you think you can sell articles of this nature to magazines?" He threw my manuscript on the desk. "It's too intelligent – there's no market for intelligence in this business!" I had carefully placed my hat on the corner of his desk, and during the interview Frank kept slamming his hand on the desk for emphasis, so that my top hat bounced around. I was terrified that at any moment his fist might come down squarely on it. However, he bought the article and gave me other assignments.'

In London I met Thomas Burke, author of *Limehouse Nights*. Burke was a quiet, inscrutable little man with a face reminding me of the portrait of Keats. He would sit immobile, rarely looking at the person talking. Yet he drew me out. I felt I wanted to unburden my soul to him, and I did. I was at my best with Burke, more than with Wells. Burke and I strolled around the streets of Limehouse and Chinatown without his saying a word. It was his way of showing them to me. He was a diffident man, and I never quite knew what he thought of me until three or four years later when he sent me his semi-auto-biographical book *The Wind and the Rain*. His youth had been similar to my own. Then I knew he liked me.

When the excitement tapered off I had dinner with my cousin Aubrey and his family, and a day later visited Jimmy Russell of the Karno days, who had a pub. Then I began to think about returning to the States.

I had now reached the moment when I realized that if I stayed longer in London, I would begin to feel idle. I was reluctant to leave England. But celebrity could give me no more. I was returning with complete satisfaction – though somewhat sad, for I was leaving behind not alone the noise of acclaim or the accolades of the rich and celebrated who had entertained me, but the sincere affection and enthusiasm of the English and the French crowds that had waited to welcome me at Waterloo and at the Gare du Nord; the frustration of being hustled past them and bundled into a taxi without being able to respond hurt as if I were treading on flowers. I was also leaving behind my past. That visit to Kennington, 3 Pownall Terrace, had completed something within me; now I was satisfied to return to California and get back to work, for in work was orientation, all else was chimerical.

# *eighteen*

WHEN I arrived in New York Marie Doro telephoned. Marie Doro telephoning – what that would have meant a few years ago! I took her to lunch and afterwards went to the matinée of the play in which she was performing: *Lilies of the Field*.

In the evening I dined with Max Eastman, his sister Crystal Eastman, and Claude McKay, the Jamaican poet and longshoreman.

The last day in New York, I visited Sing-Sing with Frank Harris. On the way he told me he was working on his autobiography, but thought he had left it too late. 'I'm getting old,' he said.

'Age has its compensations,' I ventured. 'It is less apt to be brow-beaten by discretion.'

Jim Larkin, the Irish rebel and labour union organizer, was serving five years in Sing-Sing, and Frank wanted to see him. Larkin was a brilliant orator who had been sentenced by a prejudiced judge and jury on false charges of attempting to overthrow the Government, so Frank claimed, and this was proved later when Governor Al Smith quashed the sentence, though Larkin had already served years of it.

Prisons have a strange atmosphere, as if the human spirit were suspended. At Sing-Sing the old cell blocks were grimly medieval: small, narrow stone chambers crowded with four to six inmates sleeping in each cell. What fiendish brain could conceive of building such horrors! The cells were vacant for the moment, the inmates being in the exercise yard, except one, a young man, who leant against his open cell door looking mournfully pre-occupied. The warder explained that new arrivals with long sentences spent the first year in the old cell blocks before occupying the more modern ones. I stepped past the young man into his cell and was appalled by the horror of claustrophobia. 'My God!' I said, quickly stepping out. 'It's inhuman!' 'You're right,' whispered the young man with bitterness.

The warder, a kindly man, explained that Sing-Sing was overcrowded and needed appropriations to build more cells. 'But we are the last to be considered in that respect; no politician is too concerned about prison conditions.'

The old death-house was like a school-room, long and narrow with a low ceiling, with forms and desks for reporters and, facing them, a cheap wooden structure, the electric chair. A stark electric wire from the ceiling descended over it. The horror of the room was its simplicity, its lack of drama, which was more sinister than the grim scaffold. Directly behind the chair was a wooden partition. Here the victim was carried immediately after execution and an autopsy performed. 'In case the chair hasn't quite completed the job, the body is surgically decapitated,' the doctor told us, and added that the temperature of the blood in the brain directly after execution was something like 212° Fahrenheit. We came away from the death-house reeling.

Frank inquired about Jim Larkin and the warder agreed that he could see him; although it was against the rules, he would make an exception. Larkin was in the shoe factory, and here he greeted us, a tall, handsome man, about six feet four, with piercing blue eyes but a gentle smile.

Although happy to see Frank, he was nervous and disturbed and was anxious to get back to his bench. Even the warder's assurance would not allay his uneasiness. 'It's bad morally for the other prisoners if I'm privileged to see visitors during working hours,' said Larkin. Frank asked him how he was treated and if there was anything he could do for him. He said he was treated reasonably well, but he was worried about his wife and family in Ireland, whom he had not heard from since his confinement. Frank promised to help him. After we left, Frank said it depressed him to see a courageous, flamboyant character like Jim Larkin reduced to prison discipline.

*

When I returned to Hollywood, I dropped by to see Mother.

She seemed very gay and happy, and had heard all about my triumphant visit to London. 'Well, what do you think of your son and all this nonsense?' I said whimsically.

'It's wonderful, but wouldn't you rather be yourself than live in this theatrical world of unreality?'

'You should talk,' I laughed. 'You're responsible for this unreality.'

She paused. 'If only you had put your talent in the service of the Lord – think of the thousands of souls you could have saved.'

I smiled. 'I might have saved souls but not money.'

On the way home Mrs Reeves, my manager's wife, who adored Mother, told me that since I had been away Mother had been in excellent health and had rarely had any mental lapses. She was gay and happy, and had no sense of responsibility. Mrs Reeves enjoyed visiting Mother because she was so entertaining, and would have her in roars of laughter with anecdotes of the past. Of course, there were times when she was stubborn. Mrs Reeves told me of the day she and the nurse took Mother down town to fit her for some new dresses. A sudden whim possessed Mother: she would not get out of the car. 'Let them come to me,' she insisted. 'In England they come to your carriage.'

Eventually she got out. A nice young girl waited on them, showing them several bolts of cloth; one was a drab brown colour which Mrs Reeves and the nurse thought suitable, but Mother hated it.

And in a most cultured English voice she said: 'No, no! that's a shit colour – show me something gayer.'

The startled young girl obeyed, not quite believing her ears.

Mrs Reeves also told me of taking Mother to the ostrich farm. The keeper, a friendly, courteous man, had shown them around the hatcheries. 'This,' he said, holding an ostrich egg, 'is about to be hatched in the next week or so.' Then he was called to the telephone, and, handing the egg to the nurse, excused himself. No sooner had he left than Mother snatched the egg from the nurse, saying: 'Give it back to the poor bloody ostrich!' and threw it over into the corral, where it exploded with a loud report. Quickly they bundled Mother out of the ostrich farm before the keeper returned.

'On a hot sunny day,' said Mrs Reeves, 'she insists on buying the chauffeur and all of us ice-cream cones.' Once, as they were slowly driving past a man-hole, a workman's head popped up. Mother leaned out of the car intending to give the man her cone, but tossed it full in his face. 'There, son, that'll keep you cool,' she said, waving back to him from the car.

Although I tried to keep my personal matters from her, she seemed to know all that was going on. During my domestic troubles with my second wife, she suddenly remarked during a game of draughts (incidentally, she always won): 'Why don't you shed yourself of all these annoyances? Take a trip to the Orient and enjoy yourself.'

I was surprised and asked her what she meant.

'All this heckling in the Press about your private affairs,' she said.

I laughed. 'What do you know about my private affairs?'

She shrugged. 'If you weren't so diffident, I might be able to give you a little advice.'

Such remarks she would let slip and say no more.

She often came to the house in Beverly Hills to see my children, Charlie and Sydney. I remember her first visit. I had just built the house, which was nicely furnished and fully staffed – butlers, maids, etc. She looked about the room, then out of the window at the distant view of the Pacific Ocean four miles away. We waited for her reaction.

'It's a pity to disturb the silence,' she said.

She seemed to take my wealth and success for granted, never once commenting on them, until one day we were alone on the lawn; she was admiring the garden and how well it was kept.

'We have two gardeners,' I told her.

She paused and looked at me. 'You must be quite rich,' she said.

'Mother, as of this moment I'm worth five million dollars.'

She nodded thoughtfully. 'So long as you're able to keep your health and enjoy it,' was her only comment.

Mother enjoyed good health for the next two years. But during the making of *The Circus* I received a message that she was ill. She had suffered a previous gall-bladder attack and had recovered. This time the doctors warned me that her relapse was serious. She had been taken to Glendale Hospital, but the doctors thought it advisable not to operate because of the weak condition of her heart.

When I arrived at the hospital, she was in a semi-coma, having been given a drug to relieve the pain. 'Mother, this is Charlie,' I whispered, then gently took her hand. She responded feebly by squeezing mine, then opened her eyes. She wanted to sit up, but was too weak. She was restless and complained of the pains. I tried to assure her that she would get well. 'Perhaps,' she said wearily, then squeezed my hand again and lapsed into unconsciousness.

The following day in the middle of work I was told that she had passed on. I was prepared for it, for the doctor had warned me. I stopped work, took off my make-up, and with Harry Crocker, my assistant director, went to the hospital.

Harry waited outside, and I entered the room and sat in a chair between the window and the bed. The shades were half drawn. The sunlight outside was intense, as was the silence of the room. I sat and gazed at that small figure on the bed, the face tilted upwards, the eyes closed. Even in death her expression looked troubled, as though anticipating further woes to come. How strange that her life should end here, in the environs of Hollywood, with all its absurd values – seven thousand miles from Lambeth, the soil of her heart-break. Then a flood of memories surged in upon me of her life-long struggle, her suffering, her courage and her tragic, wasted life . . . and I wept.

It was an hour before I could recover and leave the room. Harry Crocker was still there and I apologized for keeping him waiting so long; of course he understood, and in silence we drove home.

Sydney was in Europe, ill, at the time and unable to attend the funeral. My sons, Charlie and Sydney, were there with their mother, but I did not see them. I was asked if I wanted her cremated. Such a thought horrified me! No, I preferred her buried in the green earth, where she still lies, in Hollywood Cemetery.

I do not know if I have given a portrait worthy of Mother. But I do know that she carried her burden cheerfully. Kindness and sympathy were her outstanding virtues. Although religious, she loved sinners and always identified herself with them. Not an atom of vulgarity was in her nature. Whatever Rabelaisian expression she used, it was always rhetorically appropriate. And in spite of the squalor in which we were forced to live, she had kept Sydney and me off the streets and made us feel we were not the ordinary product of poverty, but unique and distinguished.

*

When Clare Sheridan, the sculptress, who created quite a sensation with her book *From Mayfair to Moscow*, came to Hollywood, Sam Goldwyn gave a dinner for her and I was invited.

Clare, tall and good-looking, was the niece of Winston Churchill and wife of a direct descendant of Richard Brinsley Sheridan. She was the first Englishwoman to enter Russia after the Revolution, and had been commissioned to do busts of the principal heads of the Bolshevik party, including Lenin and Trotsky.

Although pro-Bolshevik, her book aroused only mild antagonism; Americans were confused by it because the writer was reputed to be an English aristocrat. She was entertained by New York society and did several busts of them. She also did busts of Bayard Swope and Bernard Baruch and others. When I met her she was lecturing across the country, her son Dicky, six years old, travelling with her. She complained that in the States it was difficult earning a living sculpting. 'American men don't mind their wives sitting for busts, but are reluctant to pose themselves, they are so modest.'

'I'm not modest,' I said.

So arrangements were made to bring her clay and tools to my house, and after lunch I would sit for her into the late afternoon. Clare had a faculty of stimulating conversation and I found myself intellectually showing off. Near the completion of the bust, I examined it. 'This could be the head of a criminal,' I said.

'On the contrary,' she answered with mock solemnity, 'it's the head of a genius.'

I laughed and developed a theory about the genius and the criminal being closely allied, both being extreme individualists.

She told me that since lecturing about Russia she had felt

ostracized. I knew Clare was no pamphleteer, nor a political fanatic. 'You wrote a very interesting book about Russia – let it go at that,' I said. 'Why enter the political arena? You are bound to get hurt.'

'I am lecturing for a living,' she said, 'but they don't want to hear the truth, and when I speak spontaneously I can only be guided by truth. Besides,' she added airily, 'I love my darling Bolsheviks.'

'My darling Bolsheviks,' I repeated and laughed. Nevertheless, I felt that underneath Clare had a clear, realistic attitude about her circumstances, for when I met her later in 1931 she told me she was living outside Tunis.

'But why do you live there?' I asked.

'It's cheaper,' she answered quickly. 'In London, with my limited income, I would be living in two small rooms in Bloomsbury, but in Tunis I can have a house and servants, with a beautiful garden for Dicky.'

Dicky died at the age of nineteen, a sad and terrible blow from which she never recovered. She became a Catholic and lived for a while in a convent, turning to religion, I suppose as a solace.

I once saw on a tombstone in the South of France a photograph of a smiling young girl of fourteen, and engraved below, one word: '*Pourquoi?*' In such bewilderment of grief it is futile to seek an answer. It only leads to false moralizing and torment – yet it does not mean that there is no answer. I cannot believe that our existence is meaningless or accidental, as some scientists would tell us. Life and death are too resolute, too implacable to be accidental.

The ways of life and death – genius cut down in its prime, world upheavals, holocausts and catastrophes – may seem futile and meaningless. But the fact that these things have happened are demonstrable of a resolute, fixed purpose beyond the comprehension of our three-dimensional minds.

There are philosophers who postulate that all is matter in some form of action, and that in all existence nothing can be added or taken away. If matter is action, it must be governed by the laws of cause and effect. If I accept this, then every action is preordained. If so, is not the scratching of my nose predestined as much as a shooting star? The cat walks round the house, the leaf falls from the tree, the child stumbles. Are not these actions traceable back into infinity? Are not they predestined and continuous into eternity? We know the immediate cause of the fallen leaf, the child stumbling, but we cannot trace its beginning or its end.

I am not religious in the dogmatic sense. My views are similar to those of Macaulay, who wrote to the effect that the same religious arguments were debated in the sixteenth century with the same philosophical astuteness as they are today; and in spite of accumulated knowledge and scientific progress, no philosopher, past or present, has contributed any further illuminating facts on the matter.

I neither believe nor disbelieve in anything. That which can be imagined is as much an approximation to truth as that which can be proved by mathematics. One cannot always approach truth through reason; it confines us to a geometric cast of thought that calls for logic and credibility. We see the dead in our dreams and accept them as living, knowing at the same time they are dead. And although this dream mind is without reason, has it not its own credibility? There are things beyond reason. How can we comprehend a thousand billionth part of a second? Yet it must exist according to the system of mathematics.

As I grow older I am becoming more preoccupied with faith. We live by it more than we think and achieve by it more than we realize. I believe that faith is a precursor of all our ideas. Without faith, there never could have evolved hypothesis, theory, science or mathematics. I believe that faith is an extension of the mind. It is the key that negates the impossible. To deny faith is to refute oneself and the spirit that generates all our creative forces.

My faith is in the unknown, in all that we do not understand by reason; I believe that what is beyond our comprehension is a simple fact in other dimensions, and that in the realm of the unknown there is an infinite power for good.

*

In Hollywood I was still a lone wolf, working in my own studio, so I had little chance of meeting people from other studios;

therefore it was difficult to make new friends. Douglas and Mary were my social salvation.

Since their marriage they were extremely happy. Douglas had rebuilt his old house and had refurbished it attractively and had added several guest-rooms. They lived in grand style, and had excellent service, excellent cuisine, and Douglas was an excellent host.

At the studio he had elaborate quarters, a dressing-room with a Turkish bath, and a swimming pool. It was there that he entertained the illustrious, lunching them at the studio, taking them on a sight-seeing tour round the lot, showing them how movies were made, then inviting them to a steam bath and a swim. Afterwards they sat around his dressing-room, wrapped in bath towels like Roman senators.

It was indeed odd to be presented to the King of Siam just as one had emerged from the steam-room and was about to plunge into the swimming pool. In fact I met many eminent gentlemen in the Turkish bath, including the Duke of Alba, the Duke of Sutherland, Austen Chamberlain, the Marquis of Vienna, the Duke of Panaranda and many others. When a man is stripped of all worldly insignia, one can appraise him for what he is truly worth – the Duke of Alba went up a great deal in my estimation.

Whenever Douglas was visited by these potentates I was invited, for I was one of the showpieces. It was customary that after a steam one would arrive at Pickfair about eight, dine at eight-thirty and after dinner see a movie. So I never got down to knowing the guests too intimately. Occasionally, however, I would relieve the Fairbankses of their social overflow and put some of them up at my house. But I confess I could not 'host' them as well as the Fairbankses.

When entertaining the exalted, Douglas and Mary were at their best. They could assume a *dégagé* familiarity with them, which was difficult for me. Of course, when entertaining dukes, on the first night the formal appellation of 'Your Grace' was constantly heard; but it was not long before 'Your Grace' became the familiar 'Georgie' or 'Jimmy'.

At dinner, Douglas's little mongrel dog often appeared and Douglas, with an easy diverting manner, would make it perform foolish little tricks, which would loosen up what could have been a stiff and formal affair. I was often the recipient of whispered compliments paid to Douglas by the guests. 'Such a delightful person!' said the ladies confidingly. And of course he was. No one could charm them more than Douglas.

But on one occasion he met his Waterloo. I am not mentioning names for obvious reasons, but the entourage was exclusive, abounding in exalted titles, and Douglas devoted a whole week to their pleasure and entertainment. The guests of honour were a honeymoon couple. Everything imaginable was done to entertain them. There was a fishing expedition on a private yacht to Catalina, where Douglas had had a steer killed and sunk in the sea to attract the fish (but they did not catch any), then a private rodeo on the studio grounds. But the beautiful, tall, young bride, though gracious, was extemely reticent and showed little enthusiasm.

Each night at dinner Douglas tried his best to entertain her, but all his wit and ebullience could not rouse her from her cool demeanour. On the fourth night Douglas took me aside. 'She baffles me, I can't talk to her,' he said, 'so at dinner tonight I've arranged for you to sit next to her.' He chuckled. 'I've told her how brilliant and amusing you are.'

After Douglas's build-up, I felt as comfortable as a paratrooper about to jump as I took my seat at dinner. However, I thought I would try the esoteric approach. So, taking my napkin from the table, I leant over and whispered to the lady: 'Cheer up.'

She turned, not quite sure of what I had said. 'I beg your pardon?'

'Cheer up!' I repeated, cryptically.

She looked surprised. 'Cheer up?'

'Yes,' I replied, adjusting my napkin over my knee and looking straight ahead.

She paused, studying me a moment. 'Why do you say that?'

I took a chance. 'Because you are very sad,' and before she could answer I continued: 'You see, I'm part gipsy and know these things – what month were you born in?'

'April.'

'Of course, Aries! I should have known.'

She became animated, which was most becoming to her. 'Know what?' she smiled.

'This month is the low ebb of your vitality.'

She thought a moment. 'It's extraordinary you should say that.'

'It's simple if one is intuitive – your aura at the moment is an unhappy one.'

'Is it that apparent?'

'Perhaps not to others.'

She smiled, then studied a moment and said thoughtfully: 'So strange you should say that. Of course it is true. I'm very depressed.'

I nodded sympathetically. 'This is your worst month.'

'I'm so despondent, I feel utterly desperate,' she continued.

'I think I understand,' I said, not realizing what was coming next.

She continued mournfully: 'If only I could run away – away from everything and everybody ... I'd do anything – get a job – do extra work in films, but it would hurt everyone concerned and they are too fine for that.'

She spoke in the plural – but of course I knew she was speaking of her husband. Now I became alarmed, so I dropped all pose of the esoteric and tried to give her serious advice, which, of course, was banal. 'It's futile to run away; responsibilities always pursue you,' I said. 'Life is an expression of want, no one is ever satisfied, so don't do anything rash – something you may regret all your life.'

'I suppose you're right,' she said wistfully. 'However, I'm so relieved to talk to someone who understands.'

Every so often during the chatter of the other guests Douglas threw a glance in our direction. Now she turned to him and smiled.

After dinner, Douglas took me aside. 'What on earth were you two talking about? I thought you were going to bite each other's ears off!'

'Oh, just the usual fundamentals,' I said smugly.

# nineteen

I WAS now entering the last mile of my contract with First National and looking forward to its termination. They were inconsiderate, unsympathetic and short-sighted, and I wanted to be rid of them. Moreover, ideas for feature films were nagging at me.

Completing the last three pictures seemed an insuperable task. I worked on *Pay Day*, a two-reeler, then I had only two more films to go. *The Pilgrim*, my next comedy, took on the proportions of a feature-length film. This again meant more irksome negotiations with First National. But as Sam Goldwyn said of me: 'Chaplin is no business man – all he knows is that he can't take anything less.' The negotiations terminated satisfactorily. After the phenomenal success of *The Kid*, I met little resistance to my terms for *The Pilgrim*: it would take the place of two films and they would give me a guarantee of $400,000 and an interest in the profits. At last I was free to join my associates in United Artists.

At the suggestion of Douglas and Mary, Honest Joe, as we called Joseph Schenck, joined United Artists with his wife Norma Talmadge, whose films were to be released through our company. Joe was to be made president. Although I was fond of Joe, I did not think his contribution was valuable enough to justify his presidency. Although his wife was a star of some magnitude, she could not match the box-office receipts of Mary or Douglas. We had already refused to give Adolph Zukor stock in our company, so why give it to Joe Schenck, who was not as important as Zukor? Nevertheless, Douglas and Mary's enthusiasm won the day, and Joe became president and an equal stockholder in United Artists.

Shortly after, I received an urgent letter requiring my presence at a meeting concerning the future of United Artists. After the formal and optimistic remarks of our president, Mary solemnly addressed us. She said that she was alarmed at what was going on in the industry – she was always alarmed – theatre circuits were merging, and, unless we took measures to counteract these moves, the future of United Artists would be in jeopardy.

This pronouncement did not bother me, because I believed that the excellence of our films was the answer to all such competition. But the others would not be reassured. Joe Schenck warned us gravely that, although the company was fundamentally healthy, we should insure our future by not taking all the risks ourselves, but letting others participate a little in our profits. He had approached Dillon Read and Company of Wall Street, who were willing to put up $40,000,000 for an issue of stock and an interest in our company. I said frankly that I was opposed to Wall Street having anything to do with my work, and again contended that we had nothing to fear from mergers as long as we made good pictures. Joe, repressing his irritation, said in a calm, lofty way that he was trying to do something constructive for the company and that we should take advantage of it.

Mary again took over. She had a reproving way of talking business, addressing me not directly but through the others, that made me feel guilty of gross selfishness. She extolled the virtues of Joe, stressing how hard he had worked and to what trouble he had gone in building up our company. 'We must all try to be constructive,' she said.

But I was adamant, maintaining that I did not want anyone else participating in my personal efforts; I was confident and willing to invest my own money in those efforts. The meeting developed into a heated discussion – more heat than discussion – but I stood my ground, saying that if the rest wished to go ahead without me, they could do so and I would retire from the company. This brought about a solemn avowal of loyalty among us all, and an affirmation from Joe that he did not wish to do anything that would disrupt our friendship or the harmony of our company. And so the matter of Wall Street was dropped.

*

Before starting on my first picture for United Artists, I intended launching Edna Purviance in a star role. Although Edna and I were emotionally estranged, I was still interested in her career. But, looking objectively at Edna, I realized she was growing rather matronly, which would not be suitable for the feminine confection necessary for my future pictures. Besides, I did not wish to confine my ideas and characters to the limits of a comedy stock company, for I had vague, ambitious ideas about feature comedies which would require more general casting.

For months I had toyed with the idea of doing *The Trojan Women* with Edna, using my own adaptation of it. But the more research we did, the more it developed into an expensive production, so the idea was abandoned.

Then I began to think of other interesting women that Edna might portray. Of course, Josephine! The fact that it would involve period costumes and cost twice as much as *The Trojan Women* was of little consequence. I was enthusiastic.

We began extensive research, reading Bourrienne's *Memoirs of Napoleon Bonaparte* and the Memoirs of Constant, Napoleon's valet. But the further we delved into the life of Josephine, the more Napoleon got in the way. So fascinated was I with this flamboyant genius that a film about Josephine ended in a pale cast of thought, and Napoleon loomed up as a part I might play myself. The film would be a record of his Italian campaign: an epic story of the will and courage of a young man of twenty-six, overcoming stupendous opposition and the jealousies of old, experienced generals. But, alas, my enthusiasm subsided and so the enterprise of both Napoleon and Josephine went away.

About this time Peggy Hopkins Joyce, the celebrated matrimonial beauty, appeared on the Hollywood scene, bedecked in jewels and with a collected bank-roll of three million dollars from her five husbands – so she told me. Peggy was of humble origin: a barber's daughter who became a Ziegfeld chorus girl and had married five millionaires. Although Peggy was still a beauty, she was a little tired-looking. She came direct from Paris, attractively gowned in black, for a young man had recently committed suicide over her. In this funereal chic, she invaded Hollywood.

During a quiet dinner together, she confided to me that she

hated notoriety. 'All I want is to marry and have babies. At heart I'm a simple woman,' she said, adjusting the twenty-carat diamond and emerald bracelets that mounted up her arm. When not in a serious mood, Peggy referred to them as 'my service stripes'.

Of one husband, she said that on her bridal night she had locked herself in her bedroom and would not let him in unless he put a $500,000 cheque under the door.

'And did he?' I asked.

'Yes,' she said petulantly and not without humour, 'and I cashed it the first thing in the morning before he was awake. But he was a fool and drank a lot. Once I hit him over the head with a bottle of champagne and sent him to the hospital.'

'And that's how you parted?'

'No,' she laughed, 'he seemed to like it, and was even more crazy about me.'

Thomas Ince invited us on to his yacht. There were just three of us, Peggy, Tom and I, sitting at a table in the stateroom drinking champagne. It was in the evening and a champagne bottle was in close proximity to Peggy. As the night wore on, I could see Peggy's interest veering from me over to Tom Ince, and she began to grow a little ugly, reminding me that what she had done to her husband with a champagne bottle she might do to me.

Although I had drunk a little champagne, I was sober, and told her gently that if I saw the slightest suspicion of such a notion cross her pretty brow, I would toss her overboard. After that I was dropped from her coterie, and Irving Thalberg of M.G.M. became the next focal point of her affection. For a while, her notoriety dazzled Irving, for he was very young. At the M.G.M. studios there were alarming rumours of marriage, but the fever left him and nothing came of it.

During our bizarre, though brief, relationship, Peggy told me several anecdotes about her association with a well-known French publisher. These inspired me to write the story *A Woman of Paris* for Edna Purviance to star in. I had no intention of appearing in the film but I directed it.

Some critics declared that psychology could not be expressed on the silent screen, that obvious action, such as heroes bending ladies over tree-trunks and breathing fervently down into their tonsils, or chair-swinging, knock-out rough stuff, was its only means of expression. *A Woman of Paris* was a challenge. I intended to convey psychology by subtle action. For example, Edna plays a *demi-mondaine*, Edna's girl-friend enters and shows her a society magazine which announces the marriage of Edna's lover. Edna nonchalantly takes the magazine, looks at it, then quickly casts it aside, acting with indifference, and lights a cigarette. But the audience can see that she has been shocked. After smilingly bidding her friend adieu at the door, she quickly goes back to the magazine and reads it with dramatic intensity. The film was full of subtle suggestion. In a scene in Edna's bedroom, a maid opens a chest of drawers and a man's collar accidentally falls to the floor, which reveals her relationship with the leading man (played by Adolphe Menjou).

The film was a great success with discriminating audiences. It was the first of the silent pictures to articulate irony and psychology. Other films of the same nature followed, including Ernst Lubitsch's *The Marriage Circle*, with Menjou playing almost the same character again.

Adolphe Menjou became a star overnight, but Edna did not quite make the grade. Nevertheless, she got an offer of $10,000 for five weeks' work to make a film in Italy, and asked my advice about accepting it. Of course, I was enthusiastic; but Edna was reluctant to sever her ties completely. So I suggested that she should take the offer, and, if it did not work out, she could return and continue with me and still be $10,000 to the good. Edna made the picture, but it was not a success, and so she returned to the company.

*

Before I completed *A Woman of Paris*, Pola Negri made her American début in true Hollywood fashion. The Paramount publicity department went beyond even its usual asinine excesses. In a mélange of cooked-up jealousies and quarrels, Gloria Swanson and Pola were publicized and glamorized. Headlines announced: 'Negri demands Swanson's dressing-room.' 'Gloria Swanson refuses to meet Pola Negri.' 'Negri accedes to Swanson's request for a social visit.' And so the Press went on, *ad nauseam*.

Neither Gloria nor Pola was to blame for those invented stories. In fact, they were very good friends from the start. But the twisted feline angle was manna to the publicity department. Parties and receptions were given in Pola's honour. During this cooked-up festival I met Pola at a symphony concert at the Hollywood Bowl. She was seated next to my box with her suite of publicity men and Paramount executives.

'Chaarlee! Why haven't I heard from you? You never called me up. Don't you realize I have come all the way from Germany to see you?'

I was flattered, even though I could hardly believe her last remark, for I had seen her only once in Berlin for twenty minutes.

'You are very cruel, Chaarlee, not to have telephoned. I have been waiting so long to hear from you. Where is it you work? Give me your number and I will call you,' she said.

I was sceptical about all this ardour, but attention from the beautiful Pola had its effect on me. A few days later, I was invited to a party she gave at her rented house in Beverly Hills. It was a magnificent affair even by Hollywood standards, and in spite of the presence of other male stars she concentrated most of her attention on me. Sincere or not, I enjoyed it. This was the beginning of our exotic relationship. For several weeks we were seen together in public, and, of course, this was aphrodisiac to the columnists. Very soon there were headlines: 'Pola engaged to Charlie.' This was most upsetting to Pola, and she said that I should make a statement of some kind.

'That should come from the lady,' I answered.

'What should I tell them?'

I shrugged non-committally.

The following day I received a message to say that Miss Negri could not see me, giving no explanation. But the same evening her maid frantically telephoned to say that her mistress was very ill and would I come at once? When I arrived, I was ushered by a tearful maid into the drawing-room, and found Mistress Pola supine upon a settee, her eyes closed. When she opened them, she moaned: 'You are cruel!' And I found myself in the role of a Casanova.

A day or so later, Charlie Hyton, manager of the Paramount

studios, telephoned. 'You are causing us a lot of trouble, Charlie. I'd like to talk to you about it.'

'By all means. Come on up to the house,' I said.

So up he came. It was almost midnight when he arrived. Hyton, a heavy-set, prosaic type of man, who would have looked at home in a wholesale warehouse, sat down and without any preliminaries started: 'Charlie, all these rumours in the Press are making Pola ill. Why don't you make a statement and stop them?'

Confronted in such a blatant manner, I looked at him squarely. 'What do you want me to say?'

With humorous audacity he tried to hide his embarrassment. 'You're fond of her, aren't you?'

'I don't think that's anyone's business,' I answered.

'But we have millions invested in this woman! And this publicity is bad for her.' He paused. 'Charlie, if you're fond of her, why don't you marry her?'

At the moment I saw little humour in this incredible affront. 'If you think I am going to marry someone just to safeguard Paramount's investment, you're very much mistaken!'

'Then don't see her again,' he said.

'That's up to Pola,' I answered.

The conversation that followed ended on a dry, humorous note to the effect that as I had no stock in the Paramount Company, I did not see why I should marry her. And as suddenly as my relationship with Pola had begun, so it ended. She never called me again.

During this hectic association with Pola, a young Mexican girl arrived at the studio; she had walked all the way from Mexico City to meet Charlie Chaplin. Having had several experiences with nuts and cranks, I told my manager to 'get rid of her in a nice way'.

I thought nothing more about it until a telephone message from the house informing me that the lady was sitting on the front-door step. This made my hair stand on end. I told the butler to get rid of the girl and that I would wait at the studio until the coast was clear. Ten minutes later a message came that she had gone.

That evening Pola, Dr Reynolds and his wife dined at my

297

house and I told them of the incident. We opened the front door and looked around to make sure the girl had not returned. But half-way through dinner the butler came bursting into the dining-room, looking white. 'She's upstairs in your bed!' He said that he had gone to prepare my room for the night and had discovered her in bed in my pyjamas.

I was at a loss what to do.

'I'll see her,' said Reynolds, getting up from the table and hurrying upstairs. The rest of us sat awaiting developments. A little later, he came down. 'I've had a long talk with her,' he said. 'She's young and good-looking – and talks quite intelligently. I asked her what she was doing in your bed. "I want to meet Mr Chaplin," she said. "Do you know," I told her, "your conduct might be considered insane and possibly you could be put in a mental institution for it?" She was not in the least perturbed. "I'm not insane," she said, "I'm just an admirer of Mr Chaplin's art and I've come all the way from Mexico to meet him." I told her that she had better take off your pyjamas and get dressed and leave at once, otherwise we'd call the police.'

'I would like to see this girl,' said Pola airily. 'Have her come downstairs to the sitting-room.' I demurred, feeling it would be embarrassing for everyone. However, the girl entered the room with great poise. Reynolds was right: she was young and attractive. She told us she had been hanging around outside the studio all day. We offered her dinner, but she would only take a glass of milk.

As she sat sipping it, Pola plied her with questions. 'Are you in love with Mr Chaplin?' (I winced).

The girl laughed. 'In love! Oh no, I only admire him because he is a great artist.'

Proffered Pola: 'Have you seen any of my pictures?'

'Oh yes,' she said casually.

'What do you think of them?'

'Very good – but you are not as great an artist as Mr Chaplin.' Pola's expression was a study.

I warned the girl that her actions could be misunderstood, then asked her if she had any means of getting back to Mexico City. She said that she had; and after Reynolds had given her more advice she left the house.

But the following midday, the butler again came rushing into the room, saying she was lying in the middle of the road, having poisoned herself. Without further ado, we telephoned the police and she was taken away in an ambulance.

There was quite a spread in the newspapers the following day, with photographs of her sitting up in bed in hospital. She had been given the stomach-pump and was now receiving the Press. She declared that she had not taken poison but had only wanted to attract attention, that she was not in love with Charlie Chaplin, but had come to Hollywood only to try and get into movies.

After her discharge from hospital she was placed in the custody of the Welfare League, who wrote a nice letter to me, asking if I would care to help in getting her back to Mexico City. 'She is harmless and not a bad sort,' they declared, so we paid her fare home.

*

I was now free to make my first comedy for United Artists and anxious to top the success of *The Kid*. For weeks I strove, thought and brooded, trying to get an idea. I kept saying to myself: 'This next film must be an epic! The greatest!' But nothing would come. Then one Sunday morning, while spending the week-end at the Fairbankses, I sat with Douglas after breakfast, looking at stereoscopic views. Some were of Alaska and the Klondike; one a view of the Chilkoot Pass, with a long line of prospectors climbing up over its frozen mountain, with a caption printed on the back describing the trials and hardships endured in surmounting it. This was a wonderful theme, I thought, enough to stimulate my imagination. Immediately ideas and comedy business began to develop, and, although I had no story, the image of one began to grow.

In the creation of comedy, it is paradoxical that tragedy stimulates the spirit of ridicule; because ridicule, I suppose, is an attitude of defiance: we must laugh in the face of our helplessness against the forces of nature – or go insane. I read a book about the Donner party who, on the way to California, missed the route and were snowbound in the mountains of Sierra Nevada. Out of one hundred and sixty pioneers only eighteen survived, most of them dying of hunger and cold. Some resorted to cannibalism, eating their dead, others roasted their moccasins to relieve their hunger. Out of this harrowing tragedy I conceived one of our funniest scenes. In dire hunger I boil my shoe and eat it, picking the nails as though they were bones of a delicious capon, and eating the shoe-laces as though they were spaghetti. In this delirium of hunger, my partner is convinced I am a chicken and wants to eat me.

For six months I developed a series of comedy sequences and began shooting without a script, feeling that a story would evolve from comedy routines and business. Of course, I was led up many a blind alley, and many amusing sequences were discarded. One was a love scene with an Eskimo girl who teaches the tramp to kiss in Eskimo fashion by rubbing noses together. When he departs in quest of gold, he passionately rubs his nose against hers in a fond farewell. And as he walks away he turns and touches his nose with his middle finger and throws her a last fond kiss, then surreptitiously wipes his finger on his trousers, for he has a bit of a cold. But the Eskimo part was cut out because it conflicted with the more important story of the dance-hall girl.

During the filming of *The Gold Rush* I married for the second time. Because we have two grown sons of whom I am very fond, I will not go into any details. For two years we were married and tried to make a go of it, but it was hopeless and ended in a great deal of bitterness.

*The Gold Rush* opened at the Strand Theatre in New York and I attended its première. From the moment the film started, showing me blithely rounding a precipice unconscious of a bear following, the audience yelled and applauded. Throughout the laughter there was sporadic applause till the end of the picture. Hiram Abrams, the United Artists sales manager, later came up and embraced me. 'Charlie, I guarantee that it will gross at least six million dollars' – and it did!

After the première, I had a collapse. I was staying at the Ritz Hotel and I could not breathe, so I frantically telephoned a friend. 'I'm dying,' I gasped. 'Call my lawyer!'

'Lawyer! You want a doctor,' said he, alarmed.

'No, no, my lawyer, I want to make a will.'

My friend, shocked and alarmed, called both, but, as my lawyer happened to be in Europe, only the doctor arrived.

After a perfunctory examination he found nothing wrong but

an attack of nerves. 'It's the heat,' he said. 'Get out of New York and down by the ocean where you can be quiet and get the sea air.'

Within half an hour I was bundled off to Brighton Beach. On the way I wept for no reason. However, I procured a front room at a hotel facing the ocean and sat at the window breathing in deep draughts of sea air. But crowds began to gather outside the hotel: 'Hi, Charlie!' 'Attaboy, Charlie!' so that I had to move back from my window in order not to be seen.

Suddenly there was a yell like the barking of a dog. It was a man drowning. The lifeguards brought him in, right in front of my window, and gave him first aid, but it was too late; he was dead. No sooner had the ambulance taken him away than another barked. In all there were three brought in: the other two recovered. I was in a worse state than ever, so I decided to return to New York. Two days later I was well enough to return to California.

# *twenty*

BACK in Beverly Hills, I received an invitation to meet Gertrude Stein at the house of a friend of mine. When I arrived, Miss Stein was seated on a chair in the centre of the drawing-room, dressed in brown, wearing a lace collar, her hands on her lap. For some reason she looked like Van Gogh's portrait of Madam Roulin, only instead of red hair with a bun on top Gertrude had short-cropped brown hair.

The guests stood around at a respectful distance, forming a circle. A lady-in-waiting whispered something to Gertrude, then came to me. 'Miss Gertrude Stein would like to meet you.' I hopped forward. There was little opportunity to talk at that moment because others were arriving and waiting to be introduced.

At lunch the hostess placed me next to her and in some way or other we got on to the subject of art. I believe it started by my admiring the view from the dining-room window. But Gertrude showed little enthusiasm. 'Nature,' she said, 'is commonplace; imitation is more interesting.' She enlarged on this thesis, stating that imitation marble looked more beautiful than the real thing, and that a Turner sunset was lovelier than any real sky. Although these pronouncements were rather derivative, I politely agreed with her.

She theorized about cinema plots: 'They are too hackneyed, complicated and contrived.' She would like to see me in a movie just walking up the street and turning a corner, then another corner, and another. I thought of saying that her idea was a paraphrase of that mystic emphasis of hers: 'Rose is a rose is a rose' – but an instinct stopped me.

The luncheon was served on a beautiful Belgian lace table-

cloth, which evoked several compliments from the guests. During
our confab, coffee was served in very light lacquer cups and
mine was placed too near my sleeve, so that when I slightly
moved my hand I upset my coffee over the table-cloth. I was
mortified! In the middle of my profuse apologies to my hostess,
Gertrude did exactly the same thing, upsetting her coffee. I
was inwardly relieved, for now I was not alone in my embarrassment. But Gertrude never dropped a spangle. Said she: 'It's
all right, it didn't spill on my dress.'

John Masefield visited the studio; he was a tall, handsome,
gentle man, kindly and understanding. But for some reason
these qualities made me extremely shy. Fortunately I had just
read *The Widow in the Bye Street* which I admired, so I was not
entirely mum and quoted some of my favourite lines from it:

> There was a group outside the prison gate,
> Waiting to hear them ring the passing bell,
> Waiting as empty people always wait,
> For the strong toxic of another's hell.

*

During the production of *The Gold Rush*, I received a telephone call from Elinor Glyn: 'My dear Charlie, you must meet
Marion Davies; she is really a dear, and would adore meeting
you, so will you dine with us at the Ambassador Hotel and
afterwards come with us to Pasadena to see your picture, *The
Idle Class?*'

I had never met Marion, but had encountered her bizarre
publicity. It was in every Hearst newspaper and magazine and hit
one full in the face *ad nauseam*. It was so overdone that the name
Marion Davies became the target of many jokes. There was
Beatrice Lillie's remark when someone showed her the clustered
lights of Los Angeles. 'How wonderful!' said Beatrice. 'I suppose later they all merge and spell "Marion Davies"!' One
could not open a Hearst magazine or newspaper without a large
picture of Marion. All this only kept the public away from the
box office.

But one evening at the Fairbankses' they ran a Marion Davies
film, *When Knighthood Was in Flower*. To my surprise she was
quite a comedienne, with charm and appeal, and would have

been a star in her own right without the Hearst cyclonic publicity. At Elinor Glyn's dinner I found her simple and charming and from that moment we struck up a great friendship.

The relationship between Hearst and Marion is legendary in the United States, and throughout the world for that matter. It was an association of over thirty years, lasting until the day he died.

If I were asked what personality in my life has made the deepest impression on me, I would say the late William Randolph Hearst. I should explain that the impression was not always a pleasant one – although he had commendable qualities. It was the enigma of his personality that fascinated me, his boyishness, his shrewdness, his kindness, his ruthlessness, his immense power and wealth, and above all his genuine naturalness. In worldly values, he was the freest man I have ever known. His business empire was fabulous and diversified, consisting of hundreds of publications, large holdings in New York real estate, mining, and vast tracts of land in Mexico. His secretary told me that Hearst's enterprises were worth $400,000,000 – a lot of money in those days.

There are conflicting opinions about Hearst. Some maintain that he was a sincere American patriot, others that he was an opportunist merely interested in the circulation of his newspapers and enlarging his fortune. But as a young man he was adventurous and liberal. Moreover, the parental exchequer was always at hand. The story goes that Russell Sage, the financier, met Hearst's mother, Phoebe Hearst, on Fifth Avenue. Said he: 'If your son persists in attacking Wall Street his newspaper will lose a million dollars a year.'

'At that rate, Mr Sage, he can stay in business for another eighty years,' said his mother.

The first time I met Hearst I committed a *faux pas*. Sime Silverman, editor and publisher of *Variety*, took me up to Hearst's apartment on Riverside Drive for lunch. It was the conventional rich man's home, a duplex affair, with rare paintings, high ceilings, mahogany panelling and built-in cases displaying porcelain. After I had been introduced to the Hearst family, we all sat down to lunch.

Mrs Hearst was an attractive woman with a kindly, easy

manner. Hearst, on the other hand, was wide-eyed and let me do the talking.

'The first time I saw you, Mr Hearst,' I said, 'was at the Beaux Arts Restaurant, sitting with two ladies. You were pointed out to me by a friend.'

From under the table I felt a pressure on my foot. I gathered it was Sime Silverman.

'Oh!' said Hearst with a humorous expression.

I began to falter. 'Well, if it wasn't you, it was someone very much like you – of course my friend was not quite sure,' I said naïvely.

'Well,' said Hearst with a twinkle. 'it's very convenient to have a double.'

'Yes,' I laughed, perhaps a little too loudly.

Mrs Hearst rescued me. 'Yes,' she emphasized humorously, 'it's very convenient.'

However, it passed off lightly and I thought the lunch went very well.

Marion Davies came to Hollywood to star in Hearst's Cosmopolitan Productions. She rented a house in Beverly Hills and Hearst brought his two-hundred-and-eighty-foot cruiser through the Panama Canal into Californian waters. From then on the film colony enjoyed an era of Arabian Nights. Two or three times a week, Marion gave stupendous dinner parties with as many as a hundred guests, a mélange of actors, actresses, senators, polo-players, chorus boys, foreign potentates and Hearst's executives and editorial staff to boot. It was a curious atmosphere of tension and frivolity, for no one could predict the mercurial temper of the powerful Hearst, which was the barometer of whether the evening would go or not.

I remember an incident at a dinner Marion gave in her rented house. About fifty of us were standing about, while Hearst, looking saturnine, was seated in a high-backed chair surrounded by his editorial staff. Marion, gowned *à la* Madame Recamier, reclined on a settee, looking radiantly beautiful, but growing more taciturn as Hearst continued his business. Suddenly she shouted indignantly: 'Hey! You!'

Hearst looked up: 'Are you referring to me?' he said.

'Yes, you! Come here!' she answered, keeping her large blue

orbs on him. His staff backed away and the room hardened into silence.

Hearst's eyes narrowed as he sat sphinx-like, his scowl growing darker, his lips disappearing into a thin line as his fingers tapped nervously on the arm of his throne-like chair, undecided whether to burst into fury or not. I felt like reaching for my hat. But suddenly he stood up. 'Well, I suppose I shall have to go,' he said, oafishly hobbling over to her. 'And what does my lady want?'

'Do your business down town,' said Marion disdainfully, 'not in my house. My guests are waiting for a drink, so hurry up and get them one.'

'All right, all right,' he said, clownishly hobbling off into the kitchen, and everyone smiled with relief.

Journeying on a train once from Los Angeles to New York to attend to some urgent business, I received a wire from Hearst inviting me to go with him to Mexico. I wired back, regretting that I had business to attend to in New York. In Kansas City, however, I was met by two of Hearst's agents. 'We've come to take you off the train,' they said, smiling, explaining that Mr Hearst would have his New York lawyers attend to all my business there. But I could not go.

I have never known a person throw wealth around in such a *dégagé* manner as did Hearst. Rockefeller felt the moral burden of money, Pierpont Morgan was imbued with the power of it, but Hearst spent millions nonchalantly as though it were weekly pocket money.

The beach-house that Hearst gave Marion at Santa Monica was a palace built, symbolically, on the sands by imported Italian artisans, a seventy-roomed Georgian structure, three hundred feet wide and three storeys high, with a gold-leaf-gilded ballroom and dining-room. Paintings by Reynolds, Lawrence and others were hung everywhere – some fakes. In the spacious oak-panelled library, when a button was pressed, a section of the floor rose up and became a screen for moving pictures.

Marion's dining-room could seat fifty guests comfortably. Several elaborate suites accommodated at least twenty guests. An Italian marble swimming pool, over one hundred feet long with a Venetian marble bridge across the centre of it, was set in an enclosed garden facing the ocean. Adjacent to the swimming pool was a combination bar-room and small cabaret dance floor.

The Santa Monica authorities wanted to build a harbour for small naval craft and pleasure boats, a project supported by the Los Angeles *Times*. Owning a small cruiser myself, I thought it a good idea and told Hearst so at breakfast one morning. 'It would demoralize the whole neighbourhood,' said he indignantly, 'having sailors peeking in these windows as though the place was a brothel!' Nothing further was said on the subject.

Hearst was remarkably natural. If in the mood he would do his favourite Charleston dance with charming gaucheness, regardless of what people thought of him. He was nothing of the *poseur* and was activated only by what interested him. He gave me the impression of being a dull man – perhaps he was, but he made no effort to be otherwise. Many people thought that the daily editorials signed by Hearst were written by Arthur Brisbane, but Brisbane himself told me that Hearst was the most brilliant editorial writer in the country.

At times he was surprisingly childish and his feelings could be easily hurt. I remember one evening while we were choosing sides for a game of charades, he complained that he had been left out. 'Well,' said Jack Gilbert facetiously, 'we'll play a charade on our own, and act out the word "pill-box" – I'll be the box and you can be the pill.' But W.R. took it the wrong way; his voice quivered. 'I don't want to play your old charades,' he said, and with that he left the room, slamming the door behind him.

Hearst's four-hundred-thousand-acre ranch at San Simeon extended thirty miles along the Pacific Coast. The living quarters were set back on a plateau like a citadel, five hundred feet above sea level and four miles from the ocean. The main château was built from several castles shipped over in crates from Europe. The façade looked like a combination of Rheims Cathedral and a gigantic Swiss chalet. Surrounding it like vanguards were five Italian villas, set in on the edge of the plateau, each housing six guests. They were furnished in Italian style with baroque ceilings from which carved seraphs and cherubs smiled down at you. In the main château were rooms for thirty more guests. The reception room was about ninety by fifty feet, hung with Gobelin tapestries, some genuine, others faked. In this baronial atmosphere were backgammon tables and pin-ball games at each end of the room. The dining-room was a small replica of the nave of Westminster Abbey and seated comfortably eighty guests. The house personnel numbered sixty.

Within hearing distance of the château was a zoo, containing lions, tigers, bears, apes, orang-outangs, birds and reptiles. From the lodge gates to the château was a five-mile drive flanked with notices: 'Animals have the right of way.' One waited in one's car while a brace of ostriches made up their minds to get off the roads. Ewes, deer, elks and buffaloes roamed the estate in herds and impeded one's progress.

There were cars to meet the guests at the railway station, or, if you came by plane, there was a private landing field. If you happened to arrive between meals, you were shown your quarters and instructed that dinner was at eight and cocktails would be served in the main hall at seven-thirty.

For amusement, there was swimming, horseback riding, tennis and games of every description, or a visit to the zoo. Hearst made a rigid rule that no one could get a cocktail until six in the evening. But Marion would gather her friends in her quarters, where cocktails were served surreptitiously.

The dinners were elaborate; the menu read like a Charles the First banquet. There was game of the season: pheasant, wild duck, partridge and venison. Yet amidst this opulence we were served paper napkins, and it was only when Mrs Hearst was in residence that the guests were given linen ones.

Mrs Hearst visited San Simeon annually, and nothing conflicted. The coexistence between Marion and Mrs Hearst was mutually understood: when it was nearing time for Mrs Hearst's arrival, Marion and the rest of us would discreetly leave or return to Marion's Santa Monica beach-house. I had known Millicent Hearst since 1916 and we were very good friends, so I had a visa to both establishments. When ensconced at the ranch with her San Francisco society friends, she would ask me for the week-end and I would show up as though it were my first visit of the season. But Millicent had no illusions. Although feigning ignorance of the recent exodus, she had a sense of humour about it. 'If it weren't Marion it would be someone else,' she said. She often talked confidentially with me about the relationship of Marion and W.R., but never with bitterness. 'He still acts as though nothing had ever happened between us and as if Marion doesn't exist,' she said. 'When I arrive he is always sweet and charming, but never stays more than a few hours. And it's always the same routine: in the middle of dinner the butler hands him a note, then he excuses himself and leaves the table. When he returns, he sheepishly mentions that some urgent business matter needs his immediate attention in Los Angeles, and we all pretend to believe him. And of course we all know he returns to join Marion.'

One evening after dinner I accompanied Millicent on a walk about the grounds. The château was drenched in moonlight, looking wondrous and ghostly against the wild setting of the seven mountain tops; the stars pierced an intensely clear sky. We stood a moment taking in the panoramic beauty. From the zoo the occasional roar of a lion could be heard and the continual scream of an enormous orang-outang, that echoed and bounced about the mountain tops. It was eerie and terrifying, for each evening at sundown the orang-outang would start, quietly at first, then working up to horrific screaming, which lasted on into the night.

'That wretched animal must be insane,' I said.

'The whole place is crazy. Look at it!' she said, viewing the château. 'The creation of mad Otto . . . and he'll go on building and adding to it till the day he dies. Then what use will it be? No one can afford to keep it up. As an hotel it's useless, and if he leaves it to the State I doubt whether they could make any use of it – even as a university.'

Millicent always spoke of Hearst in a maternal way, which made me suspect she was still emotionally involved with him. She was a kindly, understanding woman, but in later years, after I became politically *de trop*, she snubbed me.

*

One evening when I arrived at San Simeon for a week-end, Marion met me, nervous and excited. One of the guests had been attacked with a razor as he was crossing the grounds.

Marion stuttered whenever excited, which added to her charm and gave her a lady-in-distress quality. 'We d-d-don't know yet who did it,' she whispered, 'but W.R. has several detectives searching the grounds, and we're trying to keep the news away from the other guests. Some think that the attacker was a Filipino, so W.R. has had every Filipino put off the ranch until a proper investigation is made.'

'Who is the man that's been attacked?' I asked.

'You'll see him this evening at dinner,' she said.

At dinner I sat opposite a young man whose face was swathed in bandages; all that could be seen were his gleaming eyes and white teeth, which he bared in a perpetual smile.

Marion nudged me under the table. 'That's him,' she whispered.

He seemed none the worse for the attack and had a very good appetite. To all inquiries about the matter he just shrugged and grinned.

After dinner Marion showed me where the assault had taken place. 'It was behind that statue,' she said, pointing to a marble replica of 'Winged Victory'. 'Here are the blood-stains.'

'What was he doing behind the statue?' I asked.

'T-t-trying to get away from the a-t-t-tacker,' she answered.

Suddenly out of the night our guest appeared again, his face dripping with blood, as he staggered past us. Marion screamed and I jumped three feet. In a moment twenty men from nowhere surrounded him. 'I've been attacked again,' he moaned. He was borne on the arms of two detectives and taken back to his room, where they questioned him. Marion disappeared, but I saw her in the main hall an hour later. 'What happened?' I asked.

She looked sceptical. 'They say he did it himself. He's a nut and just wants attention.' Without further compunction the eccentric was bundled off the hill that night and the poor Filipinos returned to their work in the morning.

Sir Thomas Lipton was a guest at San Simeon and Marion's beach-house, a delightful, verbose old Scotsman with a charming brogue. He talked interminably and reminisced.

Said he: 'Charlie, you came to America and made good – so did I. The first time I arrived was in a cattle boat. And I said to myself: "The next time, I'll arrive on my own yacht" – and I did.' He complained to me that he was being robbed of millions of pounds in his Lipton tea business. Alexander Moore, Ambassador to Spain, Sir Thomas Lipton and I often dined together in Los Angeles, and Alex and Sir Thomas would reminisce, each in turn dropping royal names like cigarette butts, leaving me with the impression that royalty uttered nothing but epigrams.

At this time I saw a great deal of Hearst and Marion as I enjoyed the extravagant life they lived, and having an open invitation to spend every week-end at Marion's beach-house I often took advantage of it, especially as Doug and Mary were in Europe. One morning, at breakfast, with several others, Marion asked my advice about her script, but what I said was not to W.R.'s liking. The theme of the story was feminism, and I mentioned that women chose their men and that men had little to do about it.

W.R. thought otherwise. 'Oh, no,' said he, 'it is always the man who makes the choice.'

'We think we do,' I replied, 'but some little damsel points her finger at you and says: "I'll take that one" and you're taken.'

'You're entirely wrong,' said Hearst confidently.

'The trouble is,' I went on, 'their technique is so well hidden that we are made to believe we do the choosing.'

Hearst suddenly slammed the table with the palm of his hand, making all the breakfast things jump. 'If I say a thing is white, you say it's black!' he shouted.

I believed I paled slightly. The butler happened to be serving my coffee. I looked up and said: 'Will you please have someone pack my things and order me a taxi?' Then without a word I got up and went into the ballroom and began strutting up and down, speechless with rage. A moment later Marion appeared. 'What's wrong, Charlie?'

My voice quivered. 'No man can shout at me like that. Who does he think he is? Nero? Napoleon?'

Without answering she turned and hurriedly left the room. A moment later W.R. appeared, pretending nothing had happened. 'What's the matter, Charlie?'

'I am not used to being shouted at, especially when I am a guest in the house. So I'm leaving. I –' My voice disappeared into my throat and I could not finish my sentence.

311

W.R. thought a moment, then he too began pacing the floor. 'Let's talk it over,' he said, his voice also tremulous.

I followed him into the hall to a recess where there was an antique Chippendale double chair. Hearst was six foot four and quite large. He sat in it and pointed to what space was left. 'Sit down, Charlie, and we'll talk it over.' I sat beside him, but it was a tight squeeze. Without a word he suddenly extended his hand which, although unable to move in my seat, I managed to shake. Then he began to explain, his voice still tremulous. 'You see, Charlie, I really don't want Marion to do this script – and she respects your opinion. And when you approved of it – well, that's probably why I was a little short with you.'

Immediately I melted and was all placating, insisting that it was all my fault; as a final gesture we managed to shake hands again, then started to rise, but found ourselves wedged in the Chippendale, which began to creak alarmingly. After several efforts, we eventually released ourselves with the chair intact.

It appears that after Marion left me she had gone straight to Hearst and upbraided him for being so rude and told him to go and apologize. Marion knew when to choose her moment and when to keep silent, as she sometimes did. 'In his ugly mood,' said Marion, 'the storm comes up like th-th-thunder.'

Marion was gay and charming; and when W.R.'s business called him to New York, she would gather all her friends at her house in Beverly Hills (this was before the beach-house was built), and we would have parties and play charades into the small hours. Then Rudolph Valentino would reciprocate at his house and I would do the same at mine. Sometimes we hired a public omnibus and stacked it with victuals and hired a concertina-player, and ten or twenty of us would go to Malibu Beach, where we built a bonfire and had midnight picnics and caught grunnion.

Invariably Louella Parsons, the Hearst columnist, would come along, escorted by Harry Crocker, who eventually became one of my assistant directors. After such expeditions we would not get home until four or five in the morning. Marion would say to Louella: 'If W.R. hears about this, one of us is going to lose his job, an-an-and it won't be me.'

During our merry dinner party at Marion's house, W.R. telephoned from New York. When Marion returned from the phone she was furious. 'Can you imagine?' she said indignantly. 'W.R. has had me watched!'

Over the phone Hearst read her a detective's report of what she had been doing since he had been away, saying that she had been seen leaving subject A's house at four in the morning and subject B's house at five, and so forth. She told me later that he was returning immediately to Los Angeles to settle up all his affairs with her and that they would part. Of course Marion was indignant, because she had done nothing but enjoy herself among friends. The detective's report was true in effect, but distorted to give the wrong impression. At Kansas City W.R. sent a wire: 'I have changed my mind and will not return to California because I cannot face going back to those places where I have had so much happiness in the past, so I am returning to New York'. But soon after he sent another wire saying that he was arriving in Los Angeles.

It was a tense moment for all concerned when W.R. returned. However, Marion's interview with him had a salutary effect which resulted in an enormous banquet to welcome W.R. back to Beverly Hills. Marion built a temporary dining-room on to her rented house to seat one hundred and sixty guests. It was completed in two days – decorated, electrically lit, including the building of a dance floor. Marion had only to rub the magic lamp and it was done. That evening she appeared with a new $75,000 emerald ring – a present from W.R. – and, incidentally, nobody lost his job.

As a change from San Simeon and Marion's beach-house, we occasionally spent a week-end on Hearst's yacht and cruised over to Catalina or south to San Diego. It was during one of these cruises that Thomas H. Ince, who had taken over Hearst's Cosmopolitan Film Productions, had to be carried off the boat in San Diego. I was not present on that trip, but Elinor Glyn, who was aboard, told me that Ince had been gay and debonair, but during lunch had been suddenly stricken with paralysing pain and forced to leave the table. Everyone thought it was an attack of indigestion, but he became so ill that it seemed advisable to put him ashore and get him to a hospital. There it was discovered he had suffered a heart-attack, and he was sent to his home in Beverly Hills, where three weeks later he had a second attack and died.

Ugly rumours began to spread that Ince had been shot and, Hearst was implicated. These rumours were completely untrue. I know this because Hearst, Marion and I went to see Ince at his home two weeks before he died; he was very happy to see the three of us and believed that he would soon be well.

Ince's death upset Hearst's Cosmopolitan Productions' plans, so they were taken over by Warner Brothers. But after two years Hearst Productions moved over to M.G.M., where an elaborate bungalow dressing-room was built for Marion (I called it the Trianon).

Here Hearst transacted most of his newspaper business. Many times I saw him seated in the centre of Marion's reception room, with twenty or more newspapers spread all over the floor. From his chair he would scan the various headlines. 'That's a feeble set-up,' he would say in his high voice, pointing to one paper. 'And why is so-and-so featuring that story?' He would pick up a magazine and thumb its pages, weighing it appraisingly with both hands. 'What's the matter with the *Redbook*'s advertising? – pretty light this month. Wire Ray Long to come here at once.' In the midst of this scene, Marion would appear in all her finery, having just left the movie set, and in her *moqueuse* way deliberately walk over the newspapers, saying: 'Get rid of all this junk, it's cluttering up my dressing-room.'

Hearst could be extremely naïve. When going to a première of one of Marion's pictures, he would invite me to drive with them, and before arriving at the entrance of the theatre he would get out so as not to be seen arriving with Marion. Yet when the *Hearst Examiner* and the Los Angeles *Times* were embroiled in a political fight, Hearst attacking vigorously and the *Times* coming off second best, the *Times* resorted to a personal attack, accusing Hearst of leading a double life and maintaining a love-nest at Santa Monica beach and mentioning Marion. Hearst did not answer the attack in his newspaper, but came to me a day later (Marion's mother had just died) and said: 'Charlie, will you be a principal pall-bearer with me at Mrs Davies's funeral?' And, of course, I accepted.

In 1933 or thereabouts, Hearst invited me to take a trip with him to Europe. He had engaged the whole side of one of the Cunard liners for his party. But I declined, for it meant trailing along with twenty others, lingering where Hearst wanted to linger, and hurrying where he wanted to hurry.

I had had a taste of that experience on a trip to Mexico with him, when my second wife was pregnant. A parade of ten cars followed Hearst and Marion over bumpy roads and I was cursing the whole outfit because of it. So impassable were the roads that we had to abandon our destination and put up at a Mexican farmhouse for the night. There were only two rooms for twenty of us; one was graciously allotted to my wife, Elinor Glyn and myself. Some slept on tables and chairs, others in chicken coops and in the kitchen. It was a fantastic scene in that small room, my wife in the only bed, I propped up on two chairs, and Elinor, dressed as though going to the Ritz, sleeping on a broken-down couch, wearing her hat, her veil and gloves. She lay with her hands folded across her chest like a supine figure on a tomb, and slept undisturbed in that one position. I knew, for I did not sleep a wink all night. In the morning, from the corner of my eye, I watched her get up as she had lain down, with everything intact, not one hair out of place, her skin white and enamelled, as ebullient and spry as if she were walking through the tea-room of the Plaza Hotel.

On the trip to Europe, Hearst took Harry Crocker, my former assistant director, with him. Harry had now become Hearst's social secretary, and asked if I would give W.R. a letter of introduction to Sir Philip Sassoon, which I did.

Philip gave Hearst a very good time. Knowing that Hearst had been flagrantly anti-British for many years, he arranged for him to meet the Prince of Wales. He got the two of them closeted in his library, where, according to Philip's story, the Prince asked Hearst point-blank why he was so anti-British. They were there for two hours, he said, and Philip believed that the Prince's interview had a salutary effect.

I could never understand Hearst's anti-British feeling, for he had valuable holdings in England and enjoyed large profits from them. His pro-German tendencies dated back to the First World War, at which critical time his association and friendship with Count Bernstorff – then the German Ambassador – verged on a scandal. Even Hearst's immense power could hardly suppress it. Then, too, his American foreign correspondent, Karl von Wiegand, always wrote favourably of Germany up to the very edge of the Second World War.

During Hearst's trip to Europe, he visited Germany and had an interview with Hitler. At that time no one knew much about Hitler's concentration camps. The first intimation of them came from articles written by my friend Cornelius Vanderbilt, who had, on some pretext, got into one and written of the Nazi tortures there. But his stories of degenerate brutality were so fantastic that few people believed them.

Vanderbilt sent me a series of picture postcards showing Hitler making a speech. The face was obscenely comic – a bad imitation of me, with its absurd moustache, unruly, stringy hair and disgusting, thin, little mouth. I could not take Hitler seriously. Each postcard showed a different posture of him: one with his hands claw-like haranguing the crowds, another with one arm up and the other down, like a cricketer about to bowl, and another with hands clenched in front of him as though lifting an imaginary dumb-bell. The salute with the hand thrown back over the shoulder, the palm upwards, made me want to put a tray of dirty dishes on it. 'This is a nut!' I thought. But when Einstein and Thomas Mann were forced to leave Germany, this face of Hitler was no longer comic but sinister.

*

I first met Einstein in 1926, when he came to California to lecture. I have a theory that scientists and philosophers are sublimated romanticists who channel their passions in another direction. This theory fitted well the personality of Einstein. He looked the typical Alpine German in the nicest sense, jovial and friendly. And although his manner was calm and gentle, I felt it concealed a highly emotional temperament, and that from this source came his extraordinary intellectual energy.

Carl Laemmle of the Universal studios phoned to say that Professor Einstein would like to meet me. I was thrilled. So we met at the Universal studios for lunch, the Professor, his wife, his secretary, Helene Dukas, and his Assistant Professor, Walter Meyer. Mrs Einstein spoke English very well, in fact better than the Professor. She was a square-framed woman with abundant vitality; she frankly enjoyed being the wife of the great man and made no attempt to hide the fact; her enthusiasm was endearing.

After lunch, while Mr Laemmle showed them around the studio, Mrs Einstein drew me aside and whispered: 'Why don't you invite the Professor to your house? I know he would be delighted to have a nice quiet chat with just ourselves.' As Mrs Einstein had requested it should be a small affair, I invited only two other friends. At dinner she told me the story of the morning he conceived the theory of relativity.

'The Doctor came down in his dressing-gown as usual for breakfast but he hardly touched a thing. I thought something was wrong, so I asked what was troubling him. "Darling," he said, "I have a wonderful idea." And after drinking his coffee, he went to the piano and started playing. Now and again he would stop, making a few notes then repeat: "I've got a wonderful idea, a marvellous idea!"'

'I said: "Then for goodness' sake tell me what it is, don't keep me in suspense."'

'He said: "It's difficult, I still have to work it out." '

She told me he continued playing the piano and making notes for about half an hour, then went upstairs to his study, telling her that he did not wish to be disturbed, and remained there for two weeks. 'Each day I sent him up his meals,' she said, 'and in the evening he would walk a little for exercise, then return to his work again.'

'Eventually,' she said, 'he came down from his study looking very pale. "That's it," he told me, wearily putting two sheets of paper on the table. And that was his theory of relativity.'

Dr Reynolds, whom I had invited that evening because he had a smattering of physics, asked the Professor during dinner whether he had ever read Dunne's *Experiment with Time.*

Einstein shook his head.

Said Reynolds airily: 'He has an interesting theory about dimensions, a sort of a' – here he hesitated – 'a sort of an extension of a dimension.'

Einstein turned to me quickly and mischievously whispered 'An extension of a dimension, *was ist das*?'

Reynolds got off the dimensions after that and asked Einstein if he believed in ghosts. Einstein confessed that he had never seen one, and added: 'When twelve other persons have witnessed the same phenomenon at the same time, then I might believe.' He smiled.

At that time psychic phenomena were rife and ectoplasm loomed over Hollywood like smog, especially in the homes of the movie stars, where spiritualist meetings and demonstrations of levitation and psychic phenomena took place. I did not attend these affairs, but Fanny Brice, the celebrated comedienne, swore that at a spiritualist meeting she had seen a table rise and float about the room. I asked the Professor if he had ever witnessed such phenomena. He smiled blandly and shook his head. I also asked him whether his theory of relativity conflicted with the Newtonian hypothesis.

'On the contrary,' he said, 'it is an extension of it.'

During dinner I told Mrs Einstein that after the opening of my next picture I intended going to Europe.

'Then you must come to Berlin and visit us,' she said. 'We have not a big place – the Professor is not rich although he has access to over a million dollars for his scientific work from the Rockefeller Foundation – but he has never used it.'

Later when I went to Berlin I visited them in their modest little flat. It was like something you might find in the Bronx, a sitting-room and dining-room in one, covered with old worn carpets. The most expensive piece of furniture was the black piano upon which he made those historical preliminary notes on the fourth dimension. I have often wondered what became of the piano. Possibly it is in the Smithsonian Institution or the Metropolitan Museum – possibly used as kindling wood by the Nazis.

When the Nazi terror came to Germany, the Einsteins took refuge in the United States. Mrs Einstein tells an interesting story of the Professor's ignorance of money matters. Princeton University wanted him to join their faculty and wrote about terms; the Professor submitted such a modest figure that the heads of Princeton replied that the terms he asked would not be adequate for living in the United States, and that he would require at least three times the amount.

When the Einsteins came again to California in 1937, they visited me. He embraced me affectionately and warned me that he was bringing three musicians. 'We are going to play for you after dinner.' That evening Einstein was one of a Mozart quartet. Although his bowing was not too assured and his technique a little stiff, nevertheless he played rapturously, closing his eyes and swaying. The three musicians, who did not show too much enthusiasm for the Professor's participation, discreetly suggested giving him a rest and playing something on their own. He acquiesced and sat with the rest of us and listened. But after they had played several pieces, he turned and whispered to me: 'When do I play again?' When the musicians left, Mrs Einstein, slightly indignant, assured her husband: 'You played better than all of them!'

A few nights later the Einsteins came again for dinner and I invited Mary Pickford, Douglas Fairbanks, Marion Davies, W. R. Hearst, and one or two others. Marion Davies sat next to Einstein, and Mrs Einstein sat on my right next to Hearst. Before dinner everything seemed to be going pretty well; Hearst was amiable and Einstein polite. But as dinner progressed I could feel a slow freeze-up until neither one of them exchanged a word. I did my best to enliven conversation, but nothing would make them talk. The dining-room became charged with an ominous silence and I saw Hearst looking mournfully into his dessert plate and the Professor smiling, calmly engrossed in thought.

Marion in her flippant way had been making quips and asides to everyone at the table but Einstein. Suddenly she turned to the Professor and said elfishly: 'Hallo!' then twiddled her middle fingers over his head, saying: 'Why don't you get your hair cut?'

Einstein smiled and I though it time to disperse for coffee in the drawing-room.

*

Eisenstein, the Russian film director, came to Hollywood with his staff, including Grigor Alexandrov and also a young Englishman named Ivor Montagu, a friend of Eisenstein. I saw a lot of them. They used to play very bad tennis on my court – at least Alexandrov did.

Eisenstein was to make a picture for the Paramount Company. He came with the fame of *Potemkin* and *Ten Days That Shook the World*; Paramount had thought it good business to engage him to direct and write his own script. He wrote a very fine one, *Sutter's*

*Gold*, taken from an interesting document about California's early days. There was no propaganda in it, but because Eisenstein was from Russia Paramount later grew fearful, and nothing came of it.

Discussing Communism with him one day, I asked if he thought that the educated proletarian was mentally equal to the aristocrat with his generations of cultural background. I think he was surprised at my ignorance. Eisenstein, who came from a Russian middle-class family of engineers, said: 'If educated, the cerebral strength of the masses is like rich new soil.'

His film *Ivan the Terrible*, which I saw after the Second World War, was the acme of all historical pictures. He dealt with history poetically – an excellent way of dealing with it. When I realize how distorted even recent events have become, history as such only arouses my scepticism. Whereas a poetic interpretation achieves a general effect of the period. After all, there are more valid facts and details in works of art than there are in history books.

# *twenty-one*

WHILE I was in New York, a friend told me that he had witnessed the synchronization of sound in films and predicted that it would shortly revolutionize the whole film industry.

I did not think of it again until months later when the Warner Brothers produced their first talking sequence. It was a costume picture, showing a very lovely actress – who shall be nameless – emoting silently over some great sorrow, her big, soulful eyes imparting anguish beyond the eloquence of Shakespeare. Then suddenly a new element entered the film – the noise that one hears when putting a sea-shell to one's ear. Then the lovely princess spoke as if talking through sand: 'I shall marry Gregory, even at the cost of giving up the throne.' It was a terrible shock, for until then the princess had enthralled us. As the picture progressed the dialogue became funnier, but not as funny as the sound effects. When the handle of the boudoir door turned I thought someone had cranked up a farm tractor, and when the door closed it sounded like the collision of two lumber trucks. At the beginning they knew nothing about controlling sound: a knight-errant in armour clanged like the noise in a steel factory, a simple family dinner sounded like the rush hour in a cheap restaurant, and the pouring of water into a glass made a peculiar tone that ran up the scale to high C. I came away from the theatre believing the days of sound were numbered.

But a month later M.G.M. produced *The Broadway Melody*, a full-length sound musical, and a cheap dull affair it was, but a stupendous box-office success. That started it; overnight every theatre began wiring for sound. That was the twilight of silent films. It was a pity, for they were beginning to improve. Murnau, the German director, had used the medium effectively, and some of our American directors were beginning to do the same. A good silent picture had universal appeal both to the intellectual and the rank and file. Now it was all to be lost.

But I was determined to continue making silent films, for I believed there was room for all types of entertainment. Besides, I was a pantomimist and in that medium I was unique and, without false modesty, a master. So I continued with the production of another silent picture, *City Lights*.

It evolved from a story of a clown who, through an accident at the circus, has lost his sight. He has a little daughter, a sick, nervous child, and when he returns from the hospital the doctor warns him that he must hide his blindness from her until she is well and strong enough to understand, as the shock might be too much for her. His stumblings and bumpings into things make the little girl laugh joyously. But that was too 'icky'. However, the blindness of the clown was transferred to the flower-girl in *City Lights*.

The sub-plot was a notion I had been toying with for years: two members of a rich man's club, discussing the instability of human consciousness, decide to experiment with a tramp whom they find asleep on the Embankment. They take him to their palatial apartment and lavish him with wine, women and song, and when he is dead drunk and asleep they put him back where they found him and he wakes up, thinking it has all been a dream. From this idea came the story of the millionaire of *City Lights* who befriends the tramp when he is drunk and ignores him when he is sober. This theme motivates the plot and enables the tramp to keep up the pretence with the blind girl that he is rich.

After a day's work on *City Lights*, I used to go to Doug's studio and take a steam bath. Many of his friends – actors, producers and directors – gathered there and we would sit around sipping our gin and tonics, gossiping and discussing talking pictures. The fact that I was making another silent film surprised most of them. 'You have a lot of courage,' they said.

In the past my work had usually stimulated interest among producers. But now they were too preoccupied with the success of the talkies, and as time went on I began to feel outside of things; I guess I had been spoiled.

Joe Schenck, who had publicly expressed his dislike for talkies, was now won over to them. 'They're here to stay, I'm afraid, Charlie,' and he would hypothesize that only Chaplin could pull off a successful silent picture. This was complimentary but not very comforting, as I did not wish to be the only adherent of the art of silent pictures. Neither was it reassuring to read magazine articles expressing doubts and fears for the future of Charlie Chaplin's film career.

Nevertheless, *City Lights* was an ideal silent picture, and nothing could deter me from making it. But I was up against several problems. Since the advent of talkies, which had now been established for three years, the actors had almost forgotten how to pantomime. All their timing had gone into talk and not action. Another difficulty was to find a girl who could look blind without detracting from her beauty. So many applicants looked upwards, showing the whites of their eyes, which was too distressing. Fate, however, played into my hands. One day I saw a film company at work on the Santa Monica beach. There were many pretty girls in bathing suits. One waved to me. It was Virginia Cherrill, whom I had met before.

'When am I going to work for you?' she said.

Her shapely form in a blue bathing suit did not inspire the thought of her playing such a spiritual part as the blind girl. But after making one or two tests with other actresses, in sheer desperation I called her up. To my surprise she had the faculty of looking blind. I instructed her to look at me but to look inwardly and not to see me, and she could do it. Miss Cherrill was beautiful and photogenic, but she had little acting experience. This is sometimes an advantage, especially in silent pictures where technique is all-important. Experienced actresses are sometimes too set in their habits, and in pantomime the technique of movement is so mechanical that it disturbs them. Those with less experience are more apt to adapt themselves to the mechanics.

I had a scene of the tramp avoiding a traffic jam by walking through a limousine and getting out the other side. When he slams the door, the blind flower-girl hears it and offers her flowers, thinking he is the owner of the car. With his last half-crown he buys a button-hole. Accidentally he knocks the flower from her hand and it falls to the pavement. On one knee she gropes around to pick it up. He points to where it is. But she continues groping. Impatiently he picks it up himself and looks at her incredulously. But suddenly it dawns on him that she cannot see, and, passing the flower before her eyes, he realizes she is blind and apologetically helps her to her feet.

The whole scene lasted seventy seconds, but it took five days of retaking to get it right. This was not the girl's fault, but partly my own, for I had worked myself into a neurotic state of wanting perfection. *City Lights* took more than a year to make.

During the filming of it the stock market crashed. Fortunately, I was not involved because I had read Major H. Douglas's *Social Credit*, which analysed and diagrammed our economic system, stating that basically all profit came out of wages. Therefore, unemployment meant loss of profit and a diminishing of capital. I was so impressed with his theory that in 1928, when unemployment in the United States reached 14,000,000, I sold all my stocks and bonds and kept my capital fluid.

The day before the crash I dined with Irving Berlin, who was full of optimism about the stock market. He said a waitress where he dined had made $40,000 in less than a year by doubling up her investments. He himself had an equity in several million dollars' worth of stocks which showed him over a million profit. He asked me if I were playing the market. I told him I could not believe in stocks when 14,000,000 were unemployed. When I advised him to sell his stocks and get out while he had a profit, he became indignant. We had quite an argument. 'Why, you're selling America short!' he said, and accused me of being very unpatriotic. The next day the market dropped fifty points and Irving's fortune was wiped out. A couple of days later he came round to my studio, stunned and apologetic, and wanted to know where I had got my information.

At last *City Lights* was finished; only the music was to be recorded. One happy thing about sound was that I could control the music, so I composed my own.

I tried to compose elegant and romantic music to frame my comedies in contrast to the tramp character, for elegant music gave my comedies an emotional dimension. Musical arrangers rarely understood this. They wanted the music to be funny. But I would explain that I wanted no competition, I wanted the music to be a counterpoint of grace and charm, to express sentiment, without which, as Hazlitt says, a work of art is incomplete. Sometimes a musician would get pompous with me and talk of the restricted intervals of the chromatic and the diatonic scale, and I would cut him short with a layman's remark: 'Whatever the melody is, the rest is just a vamp.' After putting music to one or two pictures I began to look at a conductor's score with a professional eye and to know whether a composition was over-orchestrated or not. If I saw a lot of notes in the brass and woodwind section, I would say: 'That's too black in the brass,' or 'too busy in the woodwinds.'

Nothing is more adventurous and exciting than to hear the tunes one has composed played for the first time by a fifty-piece orchestra.

When at last *City Lights* was synchronized, I was anxious to know its fate. So, unannounced, we had a preview in a down-town theatre.

It was a ghastly experience, because our film was thrown on the screen to a half-empty house. The audience had come to see a drama and not a comedy, and they did not recover from their bewilderment until half-way through the picture. There were laughs, but feeble ones. And before the picture was through I saw shadowy figures going up the aisle. I nudged my assistant director. 'They're walking out on it.'

'Maybe they're going to the toilet,' he whispered.

After that I could not concentrate on the picture, but waited to see if those who had walked up the aisle would come back. After a few minutes I whispered: 'They haven't come back.'

'Some have to catch trains,' said he.

I left the theatre with a feeling of two years' work and two million dollars having gone down the drain. As I came out of the theatre the manager was standing in the lobby and greeted me. 'It's very good,' he said smilingly, and as a back-handed compliment added: 'Now I want to see you make a talkie, Charlie – that's what the whole world's waiting for.'

I tried to smile. Our staff had trailed out of the theatre and were standing about the sidewalk. I joined them. Reeves, my manager, always serious, greeted me with a lilt in his voice: 'Went over pretty well, I thought, considering –' His last word was an ominous reservation, but I nodded confidently. 'With a full house it'll be great – of course it needs one or two cuts,' I added.

Then the disquieting thought loomed up like thunder that we had not yet attempted to sell the picture. But I was not too concerned about that, for the kudos of my name was still box-office – I hoped. Joe Schenck, our United Artists president, warned me that the exhibitors were not prepared to give me the same terms as they had done for *The Gold Rush*, and that the big circuits were holding off and had a wait-and-see attitude. In the past exhibitors had always had a lively interest in a new film of mine; now their interest was only lukewarm. Moreover, difficulties arose about getting a New York showing. All the New York movie houses were booked up, I was told. So I would have to wait my turn.

The only one available in New York was the George M. Cohan theatre with a seating capacity of eleven hundred and fifty, and that was off the beaten path and considered a white elephant. It was not even a cinema house. I could hire the four walls for seven thousand dollars a week, guaranteeing eight weeks' rental, and I would have to supply everything else: manager, cashier, ushers, projectionist, stage-hands and the expense of electric signs and publicity. As I was financially involved to the extent of two million dollars – and my own money at that – I might as well take the full gamble and hire the theatre.

Meanwhile Reeves had closed a deal in Los Angeles to open in a new theatre which had just been built. As the Einsteins were still there, they expressed a desire to go to the opening – but I do not think they realized what they had let themselves in for. On the eve of the première they dined at my house, then we all went down town. The main street was packed with people for several blocks. Police cars and ambulances were attempting to plough through the crowds, which had smashed in the shop windows next to the theatre. With the help of a squadron of police, we were propelled into the foyer. How I loathe first nights: the personal tension, the mixture of perfumes, musk and carbona – the effect is nauseating and nerve-racking.

The proprietor had built a beautiful theatre but, like many exhibitors in those days, he knew little about the presentation of films. The picture started. It showed the credit titles, to the usual first-night applause. Then at last the first scene opened. My heart pounded. It was a comedy scene of the unveiling of a statue.

326

They began to laugh! The laughter increased into roars. I had got them! All my doubts and fears began to evaporate. And I wanted to weep. For three reels they laughed. And from sheer nerves and excitement I was laughing with them.

Then a most incredible thing happened. Suddenly in the middle of the laughter the picture was turned off! The house lights went up and a voice over a loud-speaker announced: 'Before continuing further with this wonderful comedy, we would like to take five minutes of your time and point out to you the merits of this beautiful new theatre.' I could not believe my ears. I went mad. I leaped from my seat and raced up the aisle: 'Where's that stupid son of a bitch of a manager? I'll kill him!'

The audience were with me and began stamping their feet and applauding as the idiot went on speaking about the beautiful appointments of the theatre. However, he soon stopped when the audience began booing. It took a reel before the laughter got back into its stride. Under the circumstances I thought the picture went well. During the final scene I noticed Einstein wiping his eyes – further evidence that scientists are incurable sentimentalists.

The following day I left for New York without waiting for the reviews, for I would get there only four days before the opening. When I arrived, to my horror I discovered that hardly any publicity had been given the picture other than a perfunctory ad announcing: 'Our old friend is with us again,' and other feeble phrases. So I read the riot act to our United Artists staff: 'Never mind the sentiment, give them information; we are opening in a non-movie house that's off the beaten track.'

I took half-page advertisements, staggering them each day in the most prominent New York newspapers, announcing in the same size letters:

CHARLES CHAPLIN
AT THE COHAN THEATRE
IN
CITY LIGHTS
CONTINUOUS ALL DAY AT 50 CENTS AND ONE DOLLAR

I spent $30,000 extra with the newspapers, then rented an electric sign for the front of the theatre costing another $30,000. As there was little time and we had to hustle, I was up all night, experimenting with projection of the film, deciding size of picture and correcting distortion. The next day I met the Press and told them the whys and wherefores of my making a silent picture.

The United Artists staff were doubtful about my admission prices because I was charging one dollar top and fifty cents, whereas all the important first-run cinemas only charged eighty-five cents top down to thirty-five cents – and with talkies and a live show to boot. My psychology rested on the eminent fact that it was a silent film and that called for raising the prices, and that if the public wanted to see the picture the difference between eighty-five cents and one dollar would not stop them. So I refused to compromise.

At the première the picture went off very well. But premières are not indicative. It was the ordinary public that would count. Would they be interested in a silent picture? These thoughts kept me awake half the night. In the morning, however, I was awakened by my publicity man, who came bursting into my bedroom at eleven o'clock, shrieking with excitement: 'Boy, you've done it! What a hit! There's been a line running round the block ever since ten o'clock this morning and it's stopping the traffic. There are about ten cops trying to keep order. They're fighting to get in. And you should hear them yell!'

A happy, relaxed feeling stole over me and I ordered breakfast and dressed. 'Tell me where the biggest laughs were,' I said. And he gave a minute description of where they laughed, belly-laughed and yelled. 'Come and see for yourself,' he said; 'it'll do your heart good.'

I was reluctant to go, for nothing could live up to his enthusiasm. However, I saw half an hour of it, standing with the crowds at the back of the theatre, in the midst of happy intensity relieved continuously by sudden outbursts of laughter. That was enough. I came away satisfied and gave vent to my feelings by walking all over New York for four hours. At intervals I passed the theatre and saw the long unbroken line that went round the block. The picture also received unanimous rave reviews.

In a 1150-seat house we took in $80,000 a week for three weeks. The Paramount directly opposite, with 3,000 seats, showing a talkie and with Maurice Chevalier in person, took in only $38,000 the same week. *City Lights* stayed twelve weeks, making a net profit, after all expenses, of over $400,000. The only reason it was taken off was because of the request of the New York theatre circuits, which had booked the picture at a very good price and did not want to have it played out before it reached their circuits.

Now I intended to go to London and launch *City Lights* there. While in New York I saw a lot of my friend Ralph Barton, one of the editors of the *New Yorker*, who had just illustrated a new edition of Balzac's *Droll Stories*. Ralph was only thirty-seven years old, a highly civilized and eccentric fellow who had been married five times. He had been depressed of late and had attempted suicide by taking an overdose of something. I suggested that he should come to Europe as my guest, that the change would do him good. So the two of us set off on the *Olympic* – the same boat on which I had travelled to England on the first trip.

# *twenty-two*

AFTER ten years, I was sensitive as to what my reception would be in London. I would rather have stolen in quietly without any fuss. But I had come to attend the première of *City Lights* and it meant publicity for the picture. However, I was not disappointed by the size of the crowd that welcomed me.

This time I stayed at the Carlton, for it was an older landmark than the Ritz and made London more familiar to me. My suite was exquisite. The saddest thing I can imagine is to get used to luxury. Each day I stepped into the Carlton was like entering a golden paradise. Being rich in London made life an exciting adventure every moment. The world was an entertainment. The performance started the first thing in the morning.

I glanced out of the window of my room and saw several placards down on the street. One read: 'Charlie is still their darling.' I smiled, thoughtfully at the connotation. The Press were extremely nice, for in an interview I made quite a *faux pas* when asked if I intended visiting Elstree. 'Where's that?' I inquired innocently. They looked and smiled at each other, then told me it was the centre of the English film industry. My embarrassment was so genuine that they didn't take offence.

This second visit was almost as soul-stirring and exciting as the first, and undoubtedly it was more interesting, for I was fortunate in meeting many more interesting people.

Sir Philip Sassoon rang up and invited Ralph and me to several dinners at his town house in Park Lane and his country house at Lympne. We also lunched with him at the House of Commons, where we met Lady Astor in the Lobby. A day or so later she invited us to lunch at No. 1 St James's Square.

As we entered the reception room, it was like stepping into the

Hall of Fame at Madame Tussaud's – we were confronted with Bernard Shaw, John Maynard Keynes, Lloyd George and others, but all in the flesh. Lady Astor kept the conversation alive with her unfailing resourcefulness until she was suddenly called away, and then there came an embarrassing silence. But Bernard Shaw took over and told an amusing anecdote about Dean Inge, who, expressing his indignation over the teaching of St Paul, said: 'He so distorted the teachings of our Saviour as metaphorically to crucify Him head downwards.' This kindness and geniality in helping to keep the ball rolling was most amiable and attractive in Shaw.

During lunch I talked to Maynard Keynes, the economist, and told him that I had read in an English magazine about the functioning of credit in the Bank of England, which then was a private corporation: that during the war the Bank had been drained of its gold reserves, having only £400,000,000 of foreign securities left, and that when the Government wanted a loan of £500,000,000 from the Bank, the Bank merely brought out its foreign securities, looked at them, put them back in the vault, and issued the loan to the Government, and that this transaction was repeated several times. Keynes nodded and said: 'That is about what took place.'

'But,' I asked politely, 'how were those loans redeemed?'

'With the same fiduciary money,' said Keynes.

Towards the end of lunch Lady Astor put in some comedy buck teeth that covered her own and gave an imitation of a Victorian lady speaking at an equestrian club. The teeth distorted her face with a most comical expression. Said she fervently: 'In our day we British women followed the hounds in proper lady-like fashion – not in the vulgar cross-legged style of those Western hussies in America. We rode side-saddle hard and fast with dignity and womanly comeliness.'

Lady Astor would have made a wonderful actress. She was a charming hostess and I have to thank her for many wonderful parties, which gave me the opportunity of meeting many of the illustrious of England.

After lunch when everyone else had dispersed, Lord Astor took us to see his portrait, painted by Munnings. When we arrived at the studio, Munnings was reluctant to let us in, until Lord Astor earnestly persuaded him to do so. The portrait was of Lord Astor, on a hunter, surrounded by a pack of hounds. I made a hit with Munnings, for I admired several of the preliminary, quick studies he had made of the movement of the dogs as much as the finished portrait. 'The action is music,' I said. Munnings brightened and showed me several other quick sketches.

A day or so later we lunched at Bernard Shaw's. Afterwards G.B. took me into his library – just the two of us – leaving Lady Astor and the other guests in the living-room. The library was a bright cheerful room that looked out on the Thames. And, lo and behold, I found myself confronted with a shelf of Shaw's books over the mantelpiece, and like a fool, having read little of Shaw, I went over to them with an exclamation of 'Ah, all your works!' Then it occurred to me that he might have brought about this opportune moment to explore my mind through discussing his books. I imagined our being so engrossed that the other guests would have to come in and break it up. How I should have liked this to happen. But instead there was a mincing moment of silence as I smiled and turned away and looked about the room and made some banal comment on its cheerfulness. Then we rejoined the other guests.

I met Mrs Shaw several times after that. I remember discussing with her G.B.'s play *The Applecart*, which had received indifferent reviews. Mrs Shaw was indignant. Said she: 'I told G.B. he should not write any more plays; the public and the critics don't deserve them!'

For the next three weeks we were kept busy with invitations. One was from the Prime Minister, Ramsay MacDonald, another from Winston Churchill, others from Lady Astor, Sir Philip Sassoon and so on down the regal line.

I first met Winston Churchill at Marion Davies's beach-house. About fifty guests were milling about between the ballroom and the reception room when he appeared in the doorway with Hearst and stood Napoleon-like with his hand in his waistcoat, watching the dancing. He seemed lost and out of place. W.R. saw me and beckoned me over and we were introduced.

Churchill's manner, though intimate, was abrupt. Hearst left us and for a while we stood exchanging the usual comments while people milled about us. Not until I talked about the English

Labour Government did he brighten up. 'What I don't understand,' I said, 'is that in England the election of a socialist government does not alter the status of a king and queen.'

His glance was quick and humourously challenging. 'Of course not,' he said.

'I thought socialists were opposed to a monarchy.'

He laughed. 'If you were in England we'd cut your head off for that remark.'

An evening or so later he invited me to dinner in his suite at the hotel. Two other guests were there, also his son Randolph, a handsome stripling of sixteen, who was esurient for intellectual argument and had the criticism of intolerant youth. I could see that Winston was very proud of him. It was a delightful evening in which father and son bantered about inconsequential things. We met several times after that at Marion's beach-house before he returned to England.

And now we were in London Mr Churchill invited Ralph and me to Chartwell for the week-end. We had a cold, bitter drive getting there. Chartwell is a lovely old house, modestly furnished, but in good taste, with a family feeling about it. It was not until this second visit to London that I really began to know Churchill. At this period he was a back-bencher in the House of Commons.

Sir Winston, I should imagine, has had more fun than most of us. On the stage of life he has played many parts with courage, zest and a remarkable enthusiasm. He has missed very few pleasures in this world. Life has been good to him. He has lived well and played well – and for the highest stakes and won. He has enjoyed power but has never been obsessed by it. In his busy life he has found time for hobbies: brick-laying, horse-racing and painting. In the dining-room I noticed a still-life painting over the fireplace. Winston saw me showing a keen interest in it.

'I did that.'

'But how remarkable!' I said enthusiastically.

'Nothing to it – saw a man painting a landscape in the South of France and said: "I can do that".'

The next morning he showed me the walls around Chartwell which he himself had built. I was astonished and said something about brick-laying not being as easy as it looks.

'I'll show you how and you'll do it in five minutes.'

At dinner the first night there were several young Members of Parliament who, metaphorically, sat at his feet, including Mr Boothby, now Lord Boothby, and the late Brendan Bracken, who became Lord Bracken, both charming and interesting talkers. I told them I was going to meet Gandhi, who was in London at that time.

'We've catered to this man long enough,' said Bracken. 'Hunger strikes or no, they should put him in jail and keep him there. Unless we are firm we shall lose India.'

'Jailing him would be a very simple solution if it would work,' I interposed, 'but if you imprison one Gandhi, another will arise. He is a symbol of what the Indian people want, and until they get what they want they will produce one Gandhi after another.'

Churchill turned to me and smiled. 'You would make a good Labour Member.'

The charm of Churchill is in his tolerance and respect for other people's opinions. He seems not to bear malice with those who disagree with him.

Bracken and Boothby left that first night and the next day I saw Winston intimately with his family. It was a day of political tumult, Lord Beaverbrook telephoning Chartwell all day and Winston being interrupted several times during dinner. This was during the election and in the midst of the economic crisis. .

I was amused at meal-times, for Winston would politically perorate at the dinner table, while the family sat complacently unmoved. One felt it was a frequent procedure and they were used to it.

'The Ministry talks of the difficulties of balancing the Budget,' said Churchill, casting a furtive glance at his family, then at me, 'of having reached the limit of its appropriations, of having nothing further to tax, when England is stirring its tea like syrup.' He paused for the effect.

'Is it possible that the Budget could be balanced by an additional tax on tea?' I asked.

He looked at me and hesitated. 'Yes,' he answered – but not with conviction, I thought.

I was charmed by the simplicity and almost spartan taste at Chartwell. His bedroom was a combined library with an overflow of books stacked up against the walls on all sides. One side was devoted entirely to Hansard's Parliamentary Reports. There were also many volumes on Napoleon. 'Yes,' he admitted, 'I'm a great admirer of him.'

'I hear you are interested in filming Napoleon,' said he. 'You should do it – great comedy possibilities: Napoleon taking a bath, his brother Jerome bursting in upon him, arrayed in gold-braided uniform, using the moment to embarrass Napoleon and make him acquiesce to his demands. But Napoleon deliberately slips in the tub and splashes the water all over his brother's uniform, telling him to get out. He exits ignominiously – a wonderful comedy scene.'

I remember Mr and Mrs Churchill lunching at Quaglino's restaurant. Winston sat looking boyishly disgruntled. I went over to their table to greet them. 'You look as though you have swallowed the weight of the world,' I said, smilingly.

He said he had just come from a debate in the House of Commons and did not like what was being discussed about Germany. I made an airy comment, but he shook his head. 'Oh no, it's very serious, very serious indeed.'

\*

I met Gandhi shortly after my stay with Churchill. I have always respected and admired Gandhi for his political astuteness and his iron will. But I thought his visit to London was a mistake. His legendary significance evaporated in the London scene, and his religious display fell short of impressiveness. In the cold dank climate of England, wearing his traditional loin-cloth, which he gathered about him in disorderly fashion, he seemed incongruous. It made his presence in London food for glibness and caricature. One's impressiveness is greater at a distance. I had been asked if I would like to meet him. Of course I was thrilled.

I met him in a humble little house in the slum district off the East India Dock Road. Crowds filled the streets and the Press and the photographers packed both floors. The interview took place in an upstairs front room about twelve feet square. The Mahatma had not yet arrived; and as I waited I began to think of what I would say to him. I had heard of his imprisonment and hunger strikes, and his fight for the freedom of India, and vaguely knew of his opposition to the use of machinery.

When at last he arrived there was hooraying and cheering as he

335

stepped out of the taxi, gathering about him the folds of his loin-cloth. It was a strange scene in that crowded little slum street, that alien figure entering a humble house, accompanied by cheering throngs. He came upstairs and showed himself at the window, then beckoned to me, and together we waved to the crowds below.

The room was suddenly attacked by flash-lights from the cameras as we sat on the sofa. I was on the Mahatma's right. Now came that uneasy, terrifying moment when I should say something astutely intelligent upon a subject I knew little about. Seated on my right was a persistant young lady telling me a long story of which I did not hear a word, but I nodded approvingly, wondering all the time what I would say to Gandhi. I knew I had to start the ball rolling, that it was not up to the Mahatma to tell me how much he enjoyed my last film, and so forth – I doubted if he had ever seen a film. However, an Indian lady's commanding voice suddenly interrupted the verbose young woman: 'Miss, will you kindly finish your conversation and let Mr Chaplin talk to Gandhi?'

The packed room grew suddenly silent. And as the Mahatma's mask-like expression was one of waiting, I felt that all India was also waiting on my words. So I cleared my throat. 'Naturally I am in sympathy with India's aspirations and struggle for freedom,' I said. 'Nonetheless, I am somewhat confused by your abhorrence of machinery.'

The Mahatma nodded and smiled as I continued: 'After all, if machinery is used in the altruistic sense, it should help to release man from the bondage of slavery, and give him shorter hours of labour and time to improve his mind and enjoy life.'

'I understand,' he said, speaking calmly, 'but before India can achieve those aims she must first rid herself of English rule. Machinery in the past has made us dependent on England, and the only way we can rid ourselves of that dependence is to boycott all goods made by machinery. That is why we have made it the patriotic duty of every Indian to spin his own cotton and weave his own cloth. That is our form of attacking a very powerful nation like England – and, of course, there are other reasons. India has a different climate from England; and her habits and wants are different. In England the cold weather necessitates arduous industry and an involved economy. You need the industry of eating utensils; we use our fingers. And so it translates into manifold differences.'

I got a lucid object lesson in tactical manoeuvring in India's fight for freedom, inspired, paradoxically, by a realistic, virile-minded visionary with a will of iron to carry it out. He also told me that supreme independence is to shed oneself of unnecessary things, and that violence eventually destroys itself.

When the room cleared, he asked me if I would like to remain and see them at prayers. The Mahatma sat cross-legged on the floor while five others sat in a circle with him. It was a curious sight: six figures squatting on the floor in that small room, in the heart of the London slums, as a saffron sun was rapidly sinking behind the roof-tops, and myself sitting on a sofa looking down at them, while they humbly intoned their prayer. What a paradox, I thought, as I watched this extremely realistic man, with his astute legal mind and his profound sense of political reality, all of which seemed to vanish in a sing-song chant.

\*

At the opening of *City Lights* it rained torrents, but the goodly crowd was there and the picture went over very well. I took my seat in the circle next to Bernard Shaw, which caused much laughter and applause. We were made to stand up together and bow. This caused renewed laughter.

Churchill came to the première and to the supper party after-wards. He made a speech to the effect that he wished to toast a man who had started out as a lad from across the river and had achieved the world's affection – Charlie Chaplin! It was un-expected and I was a little bowled over, especially when he prefaced his remark with 'My Lords, Ladies and Gentlemen.' However, imbued with the formality of the occasion – besides other things – I responded in like manner: 'My Lords, Ladies and Gentlemen, as my friend the late Chancellor of the Exchequer – ' I got no further. There was quite a gahoff. And I heard a booming voice repeating: 'The late, the late! I like that, the late!' Of course it was Churchill. When I recovered I remarked: 'Well, it seems peculiar to say the "ex-Chancellor of the Exchequer".'

Malcolm MacDonald, son of the Labour Prime Minister, Ramsay MacDonald, invited Ralph and me to meet his father and spend the night at Chequers. We met the Prime Minister along the road as he was taking his constitutional walk in his plus-fours, his scarf, his cap, his pipe and walking stick, a typical country squire, the last person to look like a leader of the Labour Party. My first impression was of a gentleman of great dignity, extremely conscious of the burden of premiership, with a noble countenance which was not without humour.

The first part of the evening was somewhat restrained. But after dinner we went to the famous historical Long Room for coffee, and after viewing the original Cromwellian death mask and other historical objects we got down to a cosy chat. I told him that since my first visit there was a great change for the better. In 1921 I had seen much poverty in London, grey-haired old ladies sleeping on the Thames Embankment, but now those old ladies were gone; no more were derelicts sleeping there. The shops looked well stocked and the children well shod, and that, surely, must be to the credit of the Labour Government.

He wore an inscrutable expression and let me go on without interruption. I asked him if the Labour Government, which I understood to be a socialist government, had the power to alter basically the constitution of the country. His eyes twinkled and he replied humourously: 'It should do, but that is the paradox of British politics: the moment one appropriates power one becomes impotent.' He reflected a moment, then told the story of his being first called to Buckingham Palace as Prime Minister. Said His Majesty, greeting him cordially: 'Well, what are you socialists going to do about me?'

The Prime Minister laughed and said: 'Nothing but try to serve Your Majesty and the country's best interest.'

During the election, Lady Astor invited Ralph and me to spend the week-end at her house in Plymouth and to meet T. E. Lawrence, who was also to spend the week-end there. But for some reason Lawrence did not show up. However, she invited us to her constituency and to a meeting at the dock-side where she was to speak before some fishermen. She asked if I would say a few words. I warned her that I was for Labour and could not really endorse her politics.

'It doesn't matter,' she said; 'it is only that they would like to see you, that's all.'

It was an open-air meeting and we spoke from a large truck. The bishop of her constituency was there and seemed in a rather irritable mood and greeted us perfunctorily, I thought. After Lady Astor's short introductory speech, I got up on the truck. 'How do you do, friends,' I said. 'It's all very well for us millionaires to tell you how to vote, but our circumstances are quite different from yours.'

Suddenly I heard an exclamation from the bishop. 'Bravo!' said he.

I continued: 'Lady Astor and yourselves may have something in common – what it is I don't know. I think you know better than I do.'

'Excellent! Very good!' exclaimed the bishop.

'As to her politics and past record in representing this eh – eh –'

'Constituency,' said the bishop – any time I hesitated he would give me the word – 'Lady Astor's record must be very satisfactory,' and I finished by saying that I knew her to be a very sweet and kindly woman with the best of intentions. When I stepped down, the bishop was all glowing and smiles and shook my hand heartily.

There is a strong sense of frankness and sincerity about the English clergy that is a reflection of England at its best. It is men like Dr Hewlett Johnson and Canon Collins and many other prelates that give vitality to the English Church.

\*

My friend Ralph Barton was acting strangely. I noticed the electric clock in the sitting-room had stopped – the wires had been cut. When I told Ralph about it he said: 'Yes, I cut them. I hate the ticking of clocks.' I was dismayed and slightly annoyed, but dismissed the matter as one of Ralph's idiosyncrasies. Since leaving New York he had seemed fully recovered from his depression. Now he had decided to return to the States.

Before leaving he asked if I would go with him to visit his daughter, who had only a year previously taken the veil and was now in a Catholic convent in Hackney. She was his eldest daughter by his first wife. Ralph had often spoken about her, saying that since the age of fourteen she had felt the call to become a nun, although he and his wife had done everything they could

339

to dissuade her. He showed me a photograph of her taken when she was sixteen, and I was instantly struck by her beauty: two large dark eyes, a full sensitive mouth and an engaging smile looked out of the picture.

Ralph explained that they had taken her round Paris to many dances and night-clubs, hoping to wean her away from her ecclesiastic desire. They had introduced her to beaux and given her the gayest time, which she seemed to have enjoyed. But nothing could deter her from becoming a nun. Ralph had not seen her in eighteen months. She had now graduated from novice-hood and had fully embraced the order.

The convent was a gloomy, dark building in the heart of a slum district in Hackney. When we arrived there, we were greeted by the Mother Superior and ushered into a small, dismal room. Here we sat and waited for what seemed an interminable time. Eventually his daughter entered. I was immediately struck with sadness, for she was just as beautiful as her picture. Only, when she smiled, two teeth were missing at the side.

The scene was incongruous: the three of us sitting in that small gloomy room, this debonair, urbane father of thirty-seven, his legs crossed, smoking a cigarette, and his daughter, this pretty young nun of nineteen, sitting across from us. I wanted to excuse myself and wait outside in the car. But neither would hear of it.

Although she was bright and vivacious, I could see that she was detached from life. Her actions were nervous and jerky and showed strain as she talked of her duties as a school-teacher. 'Young children are so difficult to teach,' she said, 'but I'll get used to it.'

Ralph's eyes twinkled with pride as he talked to her and smoked his cigarette. Pagan that he was, I could see he rather enjoyed the idea of his daughter being a nun.

There was a wistful detachment about their meeting. Undoubtedly she had been through a spiritual trial. As beautiful and as youthful as she was, her face was sad and dedicated. She talked of the glowing accounts of our reception in London, and inquired about Germaine Taillfer, Ralph's fifth wife. Ralph told her that they were separated. 'Of course,' she said humorously turning to me, 'I can't keep up with Daddy's wives.' Both Ralph and I laughed self-consciously.

Ralph asked if she were staying long in Hackney. She shook her head thoughtfully and said she might be sent to Central America. 'But they never let us know when or where.'

'Well, you can write to your father when you get there,' I interposed.

She hesitated. 'We're not supposed to communicate with anyone.'

'Not even with your parents?' I asked.

'No,' she said, attempting to be matter-of-fact, then smiled at her father. There was a moment's silence.

When it was time to leave she took her father's hand and held it long and affectionately, as though some intuition were at work. As we drove away Ralph was subdued, though still nonchalant. Two weeks later, in his apartment in New York, he committed suicide by shooting himself while he lay in his bed with a sheet over his head.

\*

I now saw H. G. Wells frequently. He had an apartment in Baker Street. When I visited him there, he had four lady secretaries inundated in books of reference, checking and making notes from encyclopedias, technical books, documents and papers. 'That's *The Anatomy of Money*, my new book,' said he – 'quite an industry.'

'It strikes me they're doing most of the work,' I remarked jokingly. What appeared to be large biscuit-tins were ranged on a high shelf round his library, each labelled 'Biographical Material', 'Personal Letters', 'Philosophy', 'Scientific Data', and so forth.

After dinner friends arrived, among them Professor Laski, who was still very young-looking. Harold was a most brilliant orator. I heard him speak to the American Bar Association in California, and he talked unhesitantly and brilliantly for an hour without a note. At H.G.'s flat that night, Harold told me of the amazing innovations in the philosophy of socialism. He said that the slightest acceleration in speed translates into terrific social differences. The conversation was most interesting until H.G.'s bedtime, which, with little subtlety, he indicated by looking at the guests, then at his watch, until everybody left.

When Wells visited me in 1935 in California, I took him to task about his criticism of Russia. I had read of his disparaging reports, so I wanted a first-hand account and was surprised to find him almost bitter about it.

'But is it not too early to judge?' I argued. 'They have had a difficult task, opposition and conspiracy from within and from without. Surely in time good results should follow?'

At that time Wells was enthusiastic about what Roosevelt had accomplished with the New Deal, and was of the opinion that a quasi-socialism in America would come out of a dying capitalism. He seemed especially critical of Stalin, whom he had interviewed, and said that under his rule Russia had become a tyrannical dictatorship.

'If you, a socialist, believe that capitalism is doomed,' I said, 'what hope is there for the world if socialism fails in Russia?'

'Socialism won't fail in Russia, or anywhere else,' he said, 'but this particular development of it has grown into a dictatorship.'

'Of course Russia has made mistakes,' I said, 'and like other nations she will continue to do so. The biggest one, I think, was the repudiation of her foreign loans, Russian bonds, etc., and calling them the Tsar's debts after the Revolution. Although she might have been justified in not paying them, I think she made a great mistake, because it resulted in world antagonism, boycotts and military invasions. In the long run, it cost her twice as much as if she had paid them.'

Wells partially agreed and said that my comment was good in theory but not in fact; for the repudiation of the Tsar's debts was one of the edicts that had inspired the spirit of the Revolution. The people would have been outraged at having to pay off the debts of the old régime.

'But,' I argued, 'had Russia played the game and been less idealistic, she might have borrowed large sums of money from the capitalist countries and built up her economy more rapidly – what with the vicissitudes of capitalism since the war, inflation and the like, she might have liquidated her debts easily and retained the world's good-will.'

Wells laughed. 'It's too late now.'

I saw a lot of H.G. under different auspices. In the South of France he had built a house for his Russian mistress, a very temperamental lady. And over the mantelpiece was inscribed in

Gothic letters: 'Two lovers built this house.' 'Yes,' he said, after my commenting on it. 'We've had it put on and taken off a number of times. Whenever we quarrel, I instruct the mason to take if off and when we make up she instructs the mason to put it back. It had been put on and taken off so many times that the mason finally ignored us and left it there.'

In 1931 Wells completed *The Anatomy of Money*, a two years' work, and he looked rather tired.

'Now what are you going to do?' I asked.

'Write another book.' He smiled wearily.

'Good heavens,' I exclaimed, 'wouldn't you like to take a rest or do something else?'

'What else is there to do?'

Wells's humble origin had left its mark, not in his work or outlook, but as in my own case, in an over-emphasis of personal sensitiveness. I remember once he aspirated an 'h' in the wrong place and blushed to the roots of his hair. Such a little thing for a great man to blush about. I remember him talking about an uncle who had been head gardener of a titled Englishman's estate. His uncle's ambition had been that Wells should go into domestic service. Said H. G. ironically: 'But for the grace of God I might have been a second butler!'

Wells wanted to know how I became interested in socialism. It was not until I came to the United States and met Upton Sinclair, I told him. We were driving to his house in Pasadena for lunch and he asked me in his soft-spoken way if I believed in the profit system. I said facetiously that it required an accountant to answer that. It was a disarming question, but instinctively I felt it went to the very root of the matter, and from that moment I became interested and saw politics not as history but as an economic problem.

Wells questioned my having, as I thought, extrasensory perception. I told him of an incident which might have been more than a coincidence. Henri Cochet, the tennis player, another friend and I went into a cocktail bar in Biarritz. Three gambling wheels were on the bar-room wall, each with numbers from one to ten. Dramatically I announced, half in fun, that I felt possessed with psychic power, that I would spin the three wheels, and that the first wheel would stop at nine, the second at four and the third at seven. And, lo, the first wheel stopped at nine, the second at four and the third at seven – a million-to-one chance.

Wells said it was purely a coincidence. 'But the repetition of coincidence is worthy of examination,' I said, and related a story that happened to me as a boy. I was passing a grocer's shop in Camberwell Road and noticed the shutters were up, which was unusual. Something prompted me to climb on the window-ledge and look through the diamond hole of the shutter. Inside it was dark and deserted, but the groceries were all there, and there was a large packing-case in the centre of the floor. I jumped from the ledge with a sense of repugnance and went on my way. Soon after, a murder case exploded. Edgar Edwards, an affable old gentleman of sixty-five, had acquired five grocery stores by simply bludgeoning the owners to death with a sash-weight and then taking over their business. In that grocery shop in Camberwell, in that packing-case, were his three last victims, Mr and Mrs Darby and their baby.

But Wells would have none of it; he said that it was commonplace in everyone's life to have many coincidences, and that it proved nothing. That was the end of the discussion, but I could have told him of another experience, of the time when I as a boy stopped at a saloon in the London Bridge Road and asked for a glass of water. A bluff, amiable gentleman with a dark moustache served me. For some reason I could not drink the water. I pretended to, but as soon as the man turned to talk to a customer I put the glass down and left. Two weeks later, George Chapman, proprietor of the Crown public house in the London Bridge Road, was charged with murdering five wives by poisoning them with strychnine. His latest victim had been dying in a room above the saloon the day he gave me the glass of water. Both Chapman and Edwards were hanged.

Apropos of the esoteric, about a year before I built my house in Beverly Hills I received an anonymous letter stating that the writer was a clairvoyant and in a dream had seen a house perched on a hill-top, fronted by a lawn that came to a point like the bow of a boat, a house with forty windows and a large music room with a tall ceiling. The ground was the sacred site upon which ancient Indian tribes had made human sacrifice two thousand years ago. The house was haunted and must never be left in darkness. The letter stated that so long as I was never alone in it and there was light, there would be no visitations.

At the time, I dismissed the letter as being written by a crank and put it aside as something odd and amusing. But going through my desk two years later, I came upon the letter and re-read it. Strangely enough, the description of the house and lawn was accurate. I had not counted the windows and thought I would do so, and to my astonishment I found there were exactly forty.

Although not a believer in ghosts, I decided to experiment. Wednesday was the staff's night off and the house was empty, so I dined out. Immediately after dinner I returned home and went into the organ room, which was long and narrow like the nave of a church, and had a Gothic ceiling. After drawing the curtains I turned out every light. Then, groping my way to an armchair, I sat in silence for at least ten minutes. The heavy darkness stimulated my senses and I imagined shapeless forms floating before my eyes; but I rationalized that it was the moonlight coming through a slight crack in the curtains, reflected on a crystal decanter.

I pulled the curtains closer and the floating forms disappeared. Then again I waited in the darkness – it must have been five minutes. As nothing happened, I began talking audibly: 'If there are spirits here, please give me a manifestation.' I waited for some time, but nothing happened. Then I continued: 'Isn't there some way of communicating? Perhaps through a sign – a tap, or, if not that way, perhaps through my mind, which might prompt me to write something; or perhaps a cold draught of wind would indicate a presence.'

Then I sat for another five minutes, but there was no draught or manifestation of any kind. The silence was deafening, and my mind was a blank. Finally I gave it up as a lost cause and turned on a light. Then I went into the living-room. The curtains had not been drawn, and outlined in the moonlight was the piano. I sat down and began running my fingers over the keys. Eventually I came upon a chord that fascinated me, and repeated it several times until it vibrated the whole room. Why was I doing this? Perhaps this was a manifestation! I kept repeating the one chord. Suddenly a white band of light embraced me around the waist;

like a shot I leaped from the piano and stood, my heart pounding like a drum.

When I had recovered, I tried to reason. The piano was in a recess by the window. Then I realized that what I thought was a belt of ectoplasm was the light from an automobile coming down the mountain-side. To satisfy myself, I sat at the piano and again struck the same chord several times. At the far end of the living-room was a dark passage and, across from it, the door of the dining-room. From the corner of my eye I saw the door open and something come from the dining-room and pass along the dark passage, a grotesque, dwarfish-looking monster with clownish white circles around its eyes, waddling towards the organ room. Before I could turn my head, it had gone. Horrified, I got up and tried to follow it, but it had vanished. Believing that in my highly nervous state a moving eyelash might have created the illusion, I went back to playing the piano. But nothing further happened, so I decided to go to bed.

I changed into my pyjamas and entered the bathroom. When I turned on the light, there was the phantom sitting up in the bath-tub looking at me! I leaped out of the bathroom almost horizontally. It was a skunk! The same little fellow I had seen from the corner of my eye, only downstairs it had seemed magnified.

In the morning, the butler put the bewildered little animal in a cage and we eventually made a pet of it. But one day it disappeared and we never saw it again.

❖

Before I left London the Duke and Duchess of York invited me to lunch. It was an intimate affair, just the Duke, the Duchess, her father and mother and her brother, a young chap about thirteen. Sir Philip Sassoon called later, and he and I were assigned to return the Duchess's little brother to Eton. He was a quiet little fellow who trailed along as Sir Philip and I were escorted around the school by two prefects, who, with several others, invited us to tea.

When we entered the tuck-shop, an ordinary place selling candy and serving sixpenny teas, he remained outside with about a hundred other Etonians. Four of us sat at a small table in a crowded little upstairs room. Everything was going splendidly until I was asked if I would like another cup of tea and inadvertently said 'Yes.' This caused a financial crisis, as our host was short of money and was obliged to go into a huddle with several other boys.

Philip whispered: 'I'm afraid we've caught them short for an extra twopence and there's nothing we can do about it.'

However, between them they managed to order another pot of tea, which we had to drink hurriedly because the school bell rang, giving them only a minute to get within the school gates, so there was quite a scamper. Inside, we were greeted by the headmaster, who showed us the hall where Shelley and many of the illustrious had inscribed their names. Eventually the headmaster turned us back to the two prefects, who ushered us into the holiest of holy sanctums, the room that Shelley had once occupied. But our little Bowes-Lyon friend remained outside.

Said our young host in a most imperious voice to him: 'What is it you want?'

'Oh, he's with us,' interposed Philip, explaining that we had brought him down from London.

'All right,' said our young host impatiently. 'Come in.'

Whispered Sir Philip: 'They're making a great concession allowing him in; it would imperil another boy's career to trespass on such holy ground.'

Not until I later visited Eton with Lady Astor was I aware of its spartan discipline. It was bitterly cold and quite dark as we groped our way along the dimly-lit, brown corridor which had footbaths hanging on the walls next to each room-door. At last we found the right door and knocked.

Her son, a pale-faced little chap, opened the door. Inside his two companions were huddled over a handful of coals in a small fireplace, warming their hands. The atmosphere was indeed drear.

Lady Astor said: 'I want to see if I can have you up for the week-end.'

We talked a moment, then suddenly there was a rap on the door and before we could say 'Come in' the handle turned and the housemaster entered, a handsome, blond man, well built, about forty. 'Good evening,' he said curtly to Lady Astor and nodded to me. He then leant his elbow on the small mantelpiece and began smoking his pipe. Her visit was evidently inopportune, so Lady

347

Astor began explaining: 'I've come to see if I could take the young one back for the week-end.'

'I'm very sorry, but you can't,' was the abrupt answer.

'Oh, come now,' said Lady Astor in her cosy way. 'Don't be so recalcitrant.'

'I'm not recalcitrant, I'm merely stating a fact.'

'But he looks so pale.'

'Nonsense, there's nothing wrong with him.'

She got up from the boy's bed, upon which we were sitting, and went over to the housemaster. 'Oh, come on!' she cried beguilingly, giving him a slight characteristic push which I had often seen her give Lloyd George and others whom she wished to persuade.

'Lady Astor,' said the housemaster, 'you have an unfortunate habit of pushing people off their balance. I wish you wouldn't do it.'

At this Lady Astor's *savoir faire* deserted her.

Somehow the conversation turned to politics, which the housemaster cut short with the laconic remark: 'The trouble with English politics is that women interfere too much in them, and with that I shall say good-night, Lady Astor.' Then he nodded curtly to both of us and left.

'What a disgruntled man,' said Lady Astor.

But the boy spoke up for him. 'Oh no, Mother, he's really very nice.'

I could not but admire the man, in spite of his anti-feminism, for there was an honesty and forthrightness about him; humourless but nevertheless sincere.

*

As I had not seen my brother Sydney for a number of years, I left England to spend a little time with him in Nice. Sydney had always said that when he had saved $250,000 he would retire. I might add that he saved considerably more than that. Besides being a shrewd business man he was an excellent comedian and had made many successful pictures, *Submarine Pilot*, *The Better 'Ole*, *Man in the Box* and *Charley's Aunt* among others, which added to his substantial fortune. And now Sydney had retired, as he said he would, and with his wife was living in Nice.

When Frank J. Gould, who also lived in Nice, heard that I was coming to visit my brother he invited me to be his guest at Juan-les-Pins, so I accepted.

Before going to Nice I stopped off in Paris for two days and went to the Folies Bergère, because Alfred Jackson, of the original Eight Lancashire Lads, was working there; he was one of the sons of the original troupe. When I met Alfred, he told me that the Jackson family had grown fairly prosperous, having eight troupes of dancing girls working for them, and that his father was still alive. If I came down to the Folies Bergère, where they were rehearsing, I could meet him there. Although past eighty, the old chap was still lithe and healthy-looking. We spoke of old times with exclamations of 'Who would have thought it!'

'You know, Charlie,' he said, 'the outstanding memory I have of you as a little boy was your gentleness.'

*

It is a mistake to dally long in the public's adulation; like a soufflé, if left standing, it bogs down. So with this welcome of mine: it suddenly cooled off. The first draught came from the Press. After their hyperboles of praise they took an opposite slant. I suppose it made interesting reading.

The excitement of London and Paris had taken its toll. I was tired and needed a rest. While recuperating in Juan-les-Pins I was asked to appear at a Command Performance at the Palladium in London. Instead, I sent a cheque for two hundred pounds. That started a rumpus. I had offended the King and slighted the Royal Command. I did not regard a note from the manager of the Palladium as a royal edict. Besides, I was unprepared to perform at a moment's notice.

The next attack came a few weeks later. I happened to be waiting on the tennis court for my partner, when a young gentleman introduced himself as a friend of a friend of mine. After an exchange of pleasantries, we drifted on to mutual opinions. He was an engaging young man and extremely sympathetic. Having a weakness for taking a sudden liking to people – especially if they are good listeners – I talked on many subjects. On the state of world affairs, I wallowed pessimistically, telling him that the situation in Europe was leading up to another war.

'Well, they won't get me in the next one,' said my friend.

'I don't blame you,' I replied. 'I have no respect for those who get us into trouble; I dislike being told whom to kill and what to die for – and all in the name of patriotism.'

We parted in a cordial way. I believe I made a date with him to dine the next evening, but he never showed up. And lo! instead of talking to a friend, I discovered I had been talking to a news reporter; and the next day a front-page spread was in the newspapers: 'Charlie Chaplin no patriot!', etc.

This is true, but at the time I did not want my private views aired in the Press. The fact is I am no patriot – not for moral or intellectual reasons alone, but because I have no feeling for it. How can one tolerate patriotism when six million Jews were murdered in its name? Some might say that was in Germany; nevertheless, these murderous cells lie dormant in every nation.

I cannot vociferate about national pride. If one is steeped in family tradition, home and garden, a happy childhood, family and friends, I can understand this feeling – but I have not that background. At best patriotism to me is nurtured in local habits; horse-racing, hunting, Yorkshire pudding, American hamburgers and Coca-Cola, but today such native yams have become worldwide. Naturally, if the country in which I lived were to be invaded, like most of us, I believe I would be capable of an act of supreme sacrifice. But I am incapable of a fervent love of homeland, for it has only to turn Nazi and I would leave it without compunction – and from what I have observed, the cells of Nazism, although dormant at the moment, can be activated very quickly in every country. Therefore, I do not wish to make any sacrifice for a political cause unless I personally believe in it. I am no martyr for nationalism – neither do I wish to die for a president, a prime minister or a dictator.

A day or so later Sir Philip Sassoon took me to Consuelo Vanderbilt Balsan's house for lunch. It was a beautiful place in the South of France. One guest stands out, a tall, lean man, dark-haired with cropped moustache, pleasant and engaging, to whom I found myself addressing my conversation at lunch. I was discussing Major Douglas's book, *Economic Democracy*, and said how aptly his credit theory might solve the present world crisis – to quote Consuelo Balsan about that afternoon: 'I found Chaplin interesting to talk to and noted his strong socialist tendencies.'

I must have said something that particularly appealed to the tall gentleman, for his face lit up and his eyes opened so wide that I could see the whites of them. He seemed to be endorsing everything I said until I reached the climax of my thesis, which must have veered in a direction contrary to his own, for he looked disappointed. I had been talking to Sir Oswald Mosley, little realizing that this man was to be the future head of the blackshirts of England – but those eyes with the whites showing over the pupils and the broad grinning mouth stand out in my memory vividly as an expression most peculiar – if not a little frightening.

I also met Emil Ludwig in the South of France, voluminous biographer of Napoleon, Bismarck, Balzac and others. He wrote interestingly about Napoleon, but he over-applied psychoanalysis to the point of detracting from the interest of the narrative.

He sent me a telegram saying how much he admired *City Lights* and that he would like to meet me. He was entirely different from what I had imagined. He looked like a refined Oscar Wilde, with rather long hair and a feminine curve to a full mouth. We met at my hotel, where he presented himself in a rather florid, dramatic manner, handing me a bay leaf, saying: 'When a Roman had achieved greatness he was presented with a laurel crown made of bay leaves. I therefore present one to you.'

It took a moment to get adjusted to this effusion; then I realized he was covering a shyness. When he came to I met a very clever and interesting man. I asked him what he considered most essential in writing a biography. He said an attitude. 'Then a biography is a biased and censored account,' I said.

'Sixty-five per cent of the story is never told,' he answered, 'because it involves other people.'

During dinner he asked what I considered the most beautiful sight I had ever seen. Off-handedly I said the movement of Helen Wills playing tennis: it had grace and economy of action as well as a healthy appeal to sex. Another was a newsreel scene, soon after the Armistice, of a farmer ploughing a field in Flanders where thousands had died. Ludwig described a sunset on a Florida beach, an open sports car lazily travelling along filled with pretty girls in bathing suits, one perched on the back fender, her leg dangling, her toe touching the sand and making a continuous line as they drove along.

Since then I can recall other beautiful sights: Benvenuto Cellini's 'Perseus' in the Piazza della Signoria in Florence. It was night, with the square lit up, and I was drawn there by the figure of Michelangelo's 'David'. But as soon as I saw 'Perseus', all else was secondary. I was enthralled by its impalpable beauty of grace and form. Perseus, holding high the head of Medusa with her pathetic twisted body at his feet, is the epitome of sadness, and made me think of Oscar Wilde's mystic line: 'For each man kills the thing he loves.' In the combat of that eternal mystery, good and evil, his cause was ended.

I received a telegram from the Duke of Alba inviting me to Spain. But the following day large headlines appeared in all the newspapers: 'Revolution in Spain'. So instead I went to Vienna – sad, sensuous Vienna. My predominant memory of it is a romance I had with a beautiful girl. It was like the last chapter of a Victorian novel: we made passionate vows of affection and kissed good-bye, knowing that we would never see each other again.

After Vienna, I went on to Venice. It was autumn and the place was deserted. I like it better when the tourists are there, because they give warmth and vitality to what could easily be a graveyard without them. In fact I like sightseers because the people seem more agreeable on holiday than when banging through revolving doors into office buildings.

Although Venice was beautiful it was melancholy, and I stayed only two nights, having nothing to do but play phonograph records – and that under cover, as Mussolini forbade dancing or playing records on Sunday.

I should have liked to return to Vienna to enact a sequel to my amour there. But I had an engagement in Paris that I did not want to miss, a lunch with Aristide Briand, implementer and patron of the idea of the United States of Europe. When I met him, Monsieur Briand seemed delicate in health, disillusioned and embittered. The luncheon took place at the house of Monsieur Balbi, publisher of the Paris *l'Intransigeant*, and was most interesting although I did not speak French. Countess Noailles, a bright, birdlike little woman, spoke English and was extremely witty and charming. Monsieur Briand greeted her by saying: 'I see so little of you these days; your presence is as rare as that of one's discarded mistress.'

After lunch I was taken to the Élysée and there made a Chevalier of the Légion d'Honneur.

*

I shall not describe the wild enthusiasm of multitudinous crowds that attended my second arrival in Berlin – although the temptation is almost irresistible.

Apropos of this I am reminded of Mary and Douglas showing a film record of their trip abroad. I was all prepared to enjoy an interesting travelogue. The film started with Mary and Doug's arrival in London with enormous enthusiastic crowds at the station and enormous enthusiastic crowds outside the hotel, then their arrival in Paris with even more enormous crowds. After being shown the exterior of hotels and railroad stations of London, Paris, Moscow, Vienna and Budapest, I innocently asked: 'When are we going to see a little of the town and country?' They both laughed. I confess I have not been overly modest in describing my own welcoming crowds.

In Berlin I was the guest of the democratic government, and Countess York, a very attractive German girl, was assigned my attaché, as it were. It was 1931, soon after the Nazis had emerged as a power in the Reichstag, and I was not aware that half the Press was against me, objecting that I was a foreigner and that the Germans were making themselves ridiculous by such a fanatical demonstration. Of course that was the Nazi Press, and I was innocently oblivious of all this, and had a wonderful time.

A cousin of the Kaiser kindly conducted me around Potsdam and Sans Souci. To me all palaces are preposterous, a tasteless, dreary expression of ostentation. In spite of their historic interest, when I think of Versailles, the Kremlin, Potsdam, Buckingham Palace, and the rest of those mausoleums, I realize what pompous egos must have created them. The cousin of the Kaiser told me that Sans Souci was in better taste, small and more human; but to me it had the feeling of a vanity case and left me cold.

Frightening and depressing was my visit to the Berlin Police Museum – photographs of murder victims, suicides, degenerates and human abnormalities of every kind. I was thankful to leave the building and to breathe the fresh air again.

Dr von Fulmuller, author of *The Miracle*, entertained me at his house, where I met German representatives of the arts and the theatre. Another evening I spent with the Einsteins in their small apartment. Arrangements were made for me to dine with General von Hindenburg, but at the last moment he was indisposed, so I went to the South of France again.

*

Elsewhere I have said that sex will be mentioned but not stressed, as I can add nothing new to the subject. However, procreation is nature's principal occupation, and every man, whether he be young or old, when meeting every woman measures the potentiality of sex between them. Thus it has always been with me.

During work, women never interested me; it was only between pictures, when I had nothing to do, that I was vulnerable. As H. G. Wells said: 'There comes a moment in the day when you have written your pages in the morning, attended to your correspondence in the afternoon, and have nothing further to do. Then comes that hour when you are bored; that's the time for sex.'

So, having nothing to do on the Côte d'Azur, I had the good fortune to be introduced to a very charming girl who had all the requisites to alleviate that blue hour of boredom. She was footloose like myself and we accepted each other at face value. She confided in me that she had just recovered from an unhappy love affair with a young Egyptian. Our relationship, though not discussed, was understood; she knew that eventually I would return to America. I gave her a weekly allowance and together we went the rounds of casinos, restaurants and galas. We dined and tangoed and did all the usual foru-foru. But propinquity caught me in the meshes of her charm and the inevitable happened, my emotions became involved; and thinking about returning to America, I was not too sure about leaving her behind. The mere thought of leaving her excited my pity; she was gay, charming and sympathetic. Nevertheless, there were occasions that provoked my mistrust.

One afternoon at a *thé dansant* at the casino, she suddenly clutched by hand. There was 'S—', her Egyptian lover, whom she had told me so much about. I was nettled; however, a few moments later we left. As we neared the hotel, she suddenly discovered that she had left her gloves behind and must go back for them, telling me to go on ahead. Her excuse was too obvious. I put up no resistance and made no comment but went on to the hotel. When she had not returned after two hours, I came to the conclusion that there was more than a pair of gloves involved. That evening I had invited some friends for dinner, and when the time drew near she was still missing. As I was about to leave the room without her, she showed up, looking pale and dishevelled.

'You've left it too late for dinner,' I said, 'so you'd better go back to your nice warm bed.'

She denied, pleaded, implored, but could give no plausible excuse for being absent so long. I was convinced that she had been with her Egyptian lover, and after a tirade of invectives I went off without her.

Who has not sat talking above the noise of sobbing saxophones and the humdrum and clatter of a night-club, depressed with sudden loneliness? You sit with others, acting the host, but you are inwardly tormented. When I returned to the hotel she was not there. This threw me into a panic. Had she gone already? So quickly! I went into her bedroom and to my great relief her clothes and other things were still there. She came in ten minutes later, bright and cheerful, and said she had been to a movie. Coldly I told her that as I was leaving for Paris the next day, I would settle up my accounts with her and this was definitely the end. To all this she acquiesced, but still denied having been with her Egyptian lover.

'Whatever friendship there's left,' I said, 'you kill it by keeping up this deception.' Then I lied and told her that I had had her followed and that she had left the casino and had gone with her Egyptian friend to his hotel. To my surprise she broke down and confessed it was true, and made vows and promises that she would never see him again.

The following morning while I was packing and getting ready to leave, she began quietly to weep. I was going in the car of a friend who came up to announce that everything was ready and that he would be waiting downstairs. She bit her index finger and now began weeping bitterly. 'Please don't leave me, please don't – don't.'

'What do you expect me to do?' I asked coldly.

'Just let me go with you as far as Paris; after that I promise never to bother you again,' she replied.

She looked such an object of pity that I weakened. I warned her that it would be an unhappy journey and that it did not make sense, because the moment we arrived in Paris we would separate. She agreed to everything. That morning the three of us left for Paris in my friend's car.

It started out a solemn journey, she quiet and subdued, I cold and polite. But this attitude was difficult to keep up, for as we travelled along something of mutual interest would catch our eye, and one of us would comment. But it was all outside of our previous intimacy.

We drove directly to her hotel, then said good-bye. Her pretence that this was her final farewell was pitifully transparent. She thanked me for all I had done for her, shook my hand and with a dramatic good-bye disappeared into the hotel.

The next day she rang up and asked if I would take her to lunch. I refused. But as my friend and I left the hotel, there she was outside all dressed in furs and what-have-you. So the three of us had lunch together and afterwards visited Malmaison, where Josephine had lived and died after Napoleon had divorced her. It was a beautiful house, in which Josephine had shed many tears; a bleak autumn day befitted the melancholy of our situation. Suddenly I missed my lady friend; then I found her in the garden sitting on a stone seat dissolved in tears – imbued, it seemed, with the spirit of the whole atmosphere. My heart would have relented had I allowed it, but I could not forget her Egyptian lover. So we parted in Paris and I left for London.

*

Back in London I saw the Prince of Wales several times. The first time I had met him was in Biarritz through a friend of mine, Lady Furness. Cochet, the tennis player, two others and myself were at a popular restaurant when the Prince and Lady Furness came in. Thelma sent a message over to our table asking if we would join them later at the Russian Club.

It was a perfunctory meeting, I thought. After we were introduced, his Royal Highness ordered drinks, then got up and danced with Lady Furness. When he came back to the table, the

Prince sat down beside me and began to catechize: 'You are an American, of course?' he remarked.

'No, I'm English.'

He looked surprised. 'How long have you been in the States?'

'Since 1910.'

'Oh.' He nodded thoughtfully. 'Before the war?'

'I think so.'

He laughed.

In the course of conversation that night I said that Chaliapin was giving a party for me. Quite boyishly the Prince remarked that he would like to come along. 'I am sure, Sir,' I said, 'Chaliapin would be honoured and delighted,' and I asked permission to arrange it.

The Prince won my esteem that evening by sitting with Chaliapin's mother, who was in her late eighties, until she retired. Then he joined the rest of us and had fun.

And now the Prince of Wales was in London and had invited me down to Fort Belvedere, his house in the country. It was an old castle that had been renovated and furnished in rather ordinary taste, but the cuisine was excellent and the Prince a charming host. He showed me over the house; his bedroom was simple and naïve with a modern red silk tapestry with the royal ensign at the head of his bed. Another bedroom quite bowled me over, a pink and white affair with a four-poster bed that had three pink feathers at the top of each post. Then I remembered; of course, the feathers were the Prince's royal coat of arms.

Someone that evening introduced a game that was prevalent in America, called 'Frank Estimations'. The guests were each given a card with ten qualifications on it: charm, intelligence, personality, sex appeal, good looks, sincerity, sense of humour, adaptability, and so forth. A guest left the room and marked up his card with a frank estimation of his own qualifications, giving himself from one to the maximum of ten – for instance, I gave myself seven for a sense of humour, six for sex appeal, six for good looks, eight for adaptability, four for sincerity. Meanwhile, each guest gave an appraisal of the victim who had left the room, marking his card secretly. Then the victim entered and read off the marks he had given himself, and a spokesman read aloud the cards of the guests to see how they tallied.

357

When the Prince's turn came he announced three for sex appeal, the guests averaged him four, I gave him five, some cards read only two. For good looks, the Prince gave himself six, the guests averaged him eight, and I marked him seven. For charm he announced five, the guests gave him eight, and I gave him eight. For sincerity the Prince announced the limit, ten, the guests averaged him three and a half, I gave him four. The Prince was indignant. 'Sincerity is the most important qualification I think I have,' he said.

As a boy I had once lived in Manchester for several months. And now that I had little to do, I thought I would run up there and look around. In spite of its grimness, Manchester had a romantic appeal to me, something of an intangible glow through fog and rain; perhaps it was the memory of a Lancashire kitchen fire – or it was in the spirit of the people. So I hired a limousine and went north.

On the way to Manchester I stopped at Stratford-on-Avon, a place I had never visited. I arrived late Saturday night, and after supper took a walk, hoping to find Shakespeare's cottage. The night was pitch-black but I instinctively turned down a street and stopped outside a house, lit a match and saw a sign: 'Shakespeare's Cottage'. No doubt a kindred spirit had led the way – possibly the Bard!

In the morning Sir Archibald Flower, the Mayor of Stratford, called at the hotel and conducted me over Shakespeare's cottage. I can by no means associate the Bard with it; that such a mind ever dwelt or had its beginnings there, seems incredible. It is easy to imagine a farmer's boy emigrating to London and becoming a successful actor and theatre-owner; but for him to have become the great poet and dramatist, and to have had such knowledge of foreign courts, cardinals and kings, is inconceivable to me. I am not concerned with who wrote the works of Shakespeare, whether Bacon, Southampton or Richmond, but I can hardly think it was the Stratford boy. Whoever wrote them had an aristocratic attitude. His utter disregard for grammar could only have been the attitude of a princely, gifted mind. And after seeing the cottage and hearing the scant bits of local information concerning his desultory boyhood, his indifferent school record, his poaching and his country bumpkin point of view, I cannot believe he went through such a mental metamorphosis as to become the greatest of all poets. In the work of the greatest of geniuses humble beginnings will reveal themselves somewhere – but one cannot trace the slightest sign of them in Shakespeare.

From Stratford I motored up to Manchester and arrived about three in the afternoon. It was Sunday and Manchester was cataleptic; hardly a soul stirred on the streets. So I was happy to get back to the car and be on my way to Blackburn.

When touring as a boy in *Sherlock Holmes*, Blackburn had been one of my favourite towns. I used to stay at a little pub there for fourteen shillings a week, board and lodging, and in the off hours play on their small billiard-table. Billington, England's hangman, used to frequent the place and it was my boast that I had played billiards with him.

Although it was only five o'clock and quite dark when we arrived in Blackburn, I found my pub and had a drink there unrecognized. The ownership had changed hands, but my old friend the billiard-table was still there.

Later I groped my way to the market square, about three acres of blackness which could not have been lit by more than three or four street-lamps. Several groups were listening to political speakers. At the time it was the depth of England's depression. I walked from one group to another, listening to the various speeches: some were sharp and bitter; one talked of socialism, another of Communism and another of the Douglas Plan, which, unfortunately, was too involved for the average worker to understand. Listening to the smaller groups that formed after the meeting, I was surprised to find an old Victorian conservative airing his views. Said he: 'The trouble is that England has been living off our own fat too long; the dole is ruining England!' In the dark I could not resist my twopence worth, so I piped in: 'Without the dole there'd be no England,' and I was supported by a few 'hear, hears!'

The political outlook was cynical. England had almost four million unemployed – and the number was increasing – yet the Labour Party had little to offer that was different from the Conservative Party.

I went down to Woolwich and heard an election address by Mr Cunningham Reid on behalf of the Liberal contestant.

Although he spoke a lot of political sophistry, he promised nothing and made little impression on that constituency. Shouted a young cockney girl, sitting next to me: 'Never mind all that high-class chatter, tell us what you're going to do for four million unemployed, then we'll know whether to vote for your party or not.'

If she was an example of the political rank and file, there was hope for Labour winning the election, I thought – but I was mistaken. After Snowden's speech over the radio, it was a landslide for the Conservatives and a peerage for Snowden. Thus I left England with a Conservative government on the way in and arrived in America with a Conservative government on the way out.

*

A holiday at best is an empty pursuit. I had dilly-dallied around the resorts of Europe too long – and I knew why. I was aimless and frustrated. Since the innovation of sound in movies, I could not determine my future plans. Although *City Lights* was a great triumph and had made more money than any talking picture at that time, I felt that to make another silent film would be giving myself a handicap – also I was obsessed by a depressing fear of being old-fashioned. Although a good silent film was more artistic, I had to admit that sound made characters more present.

Occasionally I mused over the possibility of making a sound film, but the thought sickened me, for I realized I could never achieve the excellence of my silent pictures. It would mean giving up my tramp character entirely. Some people suggested that the tramp might talk. This was unthinkable, for the first word he ever uttered would transform him into another person. Besides, the matrix out of which he was born was as mute as the rags he wore.

It was these melancholy thoughts that kept me on a prolonged holiday, but my conscience kept nagging at me: 'Get back to Hollywood and work!'

After my trip up north, I returned to the Carlton in London, intending to make reservations for returning to California via New York, when a telegram from Douglas Fairbanks in St Moritz altered my plans. It read: 'Come to St Moritz. Will order fresh snow for your arrival. Shall be waiting for you. Love Douglas.'

No sooner had I read it than a timid rap came at the door. 'Come in!' I said, expecting a waiter. Instead, the face of my lady friend from the Côte d'Azur peered in. I was surprised, irritated and resigned. 'Come in,' I said, coldly.

We went shopping at Harrods and purchased ski-ing outfits, then on to a jeweller's in Bond Street to buy a bracelet, with which she was highly pleased. A day or so later we arrived in St Moritz, where seeing Douglas brightened my horizon. Although Doug was in the same dilemma as I was about his career, neither of us spoke about it. He was alone – I believe Mary and he had separated. However, meeting in the mountains of Switzerland dissipated our melancholy. We ski-ed together – at least we learnt to ski together.

The German ex-Crown Prince, son of the Kaiser, was in the hotel, but I never met him, although when I happened to find myself with him in the same elevator I smiled primly, thinking of my comedy *Shoulder Arms*, in which the Crown Prince was a comedy character.

While in St Moritz I invited my brother Sydney to join us. As there was no vital hurry to get back to Beverly Hills, I decided to return to California via the Orient, and Sydney agreed to accompany me as far as Japan.

We left for Naples, where I said good-bye to my lady friend. But this time she was in a gay mood. There were no tears. I think she was resigned and somewhat relieved, for since our sojourn in Switzerland our alchemy of attraction had become somewhat diluted, and we both knew it. So we parted good friends. As the boat pulled out, she was imitating my tramp walk along the quáy. That was the last I saw of her.

# *twenty-three*

MANY excellent travel books have already been written about the Orient, so I will not encroach on the reader's patience. I have an excuse, however, to write about Japan because of the weird circumstances in which I became involved there. I had read a book about Japan by Lafcadio Hearn, and what he wrote about Japanese culture and their theatre aroused my desire to go there.

We sailed on a Japanese boat, leaving the icy winds of January to enter the sunny climate of the Suez Canal. At Alexandria we took on new passengers, Arabs and Hindus – in fact we took on a new world! At sunset the Arabs would place their mats on deck and face Mecca and chant prayers.

The next morning we were in the Red Sea, so we peeled off our 'Nordics' and wore white shorts and light silk shirts. We had taken on tropical fruits and coconuts at Alexandria, so for breakfast we had mangoes and at dinner iced coconut milk. One night we went Japanese and had dinner on the floor of the deck. I learnt from a ship's officer that pouring a little tea over my rice complemented its flavour. As the boat drew nearer to the next southern port, the thrill increased. The Japanese captain calmly announced we were arriving at Colombo in the morning. Although Ceylon was an exotic experience, our one desire was to get to Bali and Japan.

Our next port was Singapore, where we entered the atmosphere of a Chinese willow-pattern plate – banyan trees growing out of the ocean. My outstanding memory of Singapore is of the Chinese actors who performed at the New World Amusement Park, children who were extraordinarily gifted and well read, for their plays consisted of many Chinese classics by the great

Chinese poets. The actors performed on a pagoda in the traditional fashion. The play I saw lasted three nights. The principal actor of the cast, a girl of fifteen, played the prince, and sang in a high, rasping voice. The third night was the final climax. Sometimes it is better not to understand the language, for nothing could have affected me more poignantly than the last act, the ironic tones of the music, the whining strings, the thundering clash of gongs and the piercing, husky voice of the banished young prince crying out in the anguish of a lost soul in lonely spheres as he made his final exit.

It was Sydney who had recommended visiting the island of Bali, saying how untouched it was by civilization and describing its beautiful women with their exposed bosoms. These aroused my interest. Our first glimpse of the island was in the morning – white puff clouds encircled green mountains leaving their peaks looking like floating islands. In those days there was no port or airfield; one landed at an old wooden dock by row-boat.

We passed through compounds with beautifully built walls and imposing entrances where ten or twenty families lived. The farther we travelled the more beautiful the country became; silvery mirrored steps of green rice-fields led down to a winding stream. Suddenly Sudney nudged me. Along the roadside was a line of stately young women, dressed only in batiks wrapped around their waists, their breasts bare, carrying baskets on their heads laden with fruit. From then on we were continually nudging. Some were quite pretty. Our guide, an American Turk who sat in front with the chauffeur, was most annoying, for he would turn with lecherous interest to see our reactions – as though he had put on the show for us.

The hotel in Denpasar had only recently been built. Each sitting-room was open like a veranda, partitioned off, with sleeping quarters at the back which were clean and comfortable.

Hirschfeld, the American water-colour artist, and his wife had been living in Bali for two months and invited us to his house, where Miguel Covarrubias, the Mexican artist, had stayed before them. They had rented it from a Balinese nobleman, and lived there like landed aristocrats for fifteen dollars a week. After dinner the Hirschfelds, Sydney and I took a walk. The night was dark and sultry. Not a breath of wind stirred, then suddenly a sea of fire-flies, acre upon acre of them, raced over the rice-fields in undulating waves of blue light. From another direction came sounds of jingling tambourines and clashing gongs in rhythmic tonal patterns. 'A dance going on somewhere,' said Hirschfeld; 'let's go.'

About two hundred yards away a group of natives were standing and squatting around, and maidens sat cross-legged with baskets and small flares selling dainty edibles. We edged through the crowd and saw two girls about ten years old wrapped in embroidered sarongs, with elaborate gold tinsel head-dresses that flickered sparklingly in the lamplight as they danced mosaic patterns to treble high notes, accompanied by deep bass tones from large gongs; their heads swayed, their eyes flickered, their fingers quivered to the devilish music, which developed to a crescendo like a raging torrent, then calmed down again into a placid river. The finish was anticlimactic; the dancers stopped abruptly and sank back into the crowd. There was no applause – the Balinese never applaud; nor have they a word for love or thank you.

Walter Spies, the musician and painter, called and had lunch with us at the hotel. He had lived in Bali for fifteen years, and spoke Balinese. He had transcribed some of their music for piano, which he played for us; the effect was like a Bach concerto played in double time. Their musical taste was quite sophisticated, he said; our modern jazz they dismissed as dull and too slow. Mozart they considered sentimental, and only Bach interested them because his patterns and rhythms were similar to their own. I found their music cold, ruthless and slightly disturbing; even the deep doleful passages had the sinister yearning of a hungry minotaur.

After lunch Spies took us into the interior of the jungle, where a ceremony of flagellation was to take place. We were obliged to walk four miles along a jungle path to get there. When we arrived, we came upon a large crowd surrounding an altar about twelve feet long. Young maidens in beautiful sarongs, their breasts bare, were queueing up with baskets laden with fruit and other offerings, which a priest, looking like a dervish with long hair down to his waist and dressed in a white gown, blessed and laid upon the altar. After the priests had intoned prayers, giggling youths broke through and ransacked the altar, grabbing what they could as the priests lashed violently out at them with whips. Some were forced to drop their spoils because of the severity of the lashings, which were supposed to rid them of evil spirits that tempted them to rob.

We went in and out of temples and compounds as we pleased, and saw cock-fights and attended festivals and religious cere-monies which took place all hours of the day and night. I left one at five in the morning. Their gods are pleasure-loving, and the Balinese worship them not with awe, but with affection.

Late one night Spies and I came upon a tall Amazon woman dancing by torchlight, her little son imitating her in the back-ground. A young-looking man occasionally instructed her. We discovered later that he was her father. Spies asked him his age.

'When was the earthquake?' he asked.

'Twelve years ago,' said Spies.

'Well, I had three married children then.' Seemingly not satisfied with this answer, he added: 'I am two thousand dollars old,' declaring that in his lifetime he had spent that sum.

In many compounds I saw brand-new limousines used as chicken-coops. I asked Spies the reason. Said he: 'A compound is run on communistic lines, and the money it makes by exporting a few cattle they put into a savings fund which over the years amounts to a considerable sum. One day an enterprising auto-mobile salesman talked them into buying Cadillac limousines. For the first couple of days they rode around having great fun, until they ran out of gasoline. Then they discovered that the cost of running a car for a day was as much as they earned in a month, so they left them in the compounds for the chickens to roost in.'

Balinese humour is like our own and abounds in sex jokes, truisms and play on words. I tested the humour of our young waiter at the hotel. 'Why does a chicken cross the road?' I asked.

His reaction was supercilious. 'Everyone knows that one,' said he to the interpreter.

'Very well then, which came first, the chicken or the egg?'

This stumped him. 'The chicken – no –' he shook his head, '– the egg – no,' he pushed back his turban and thought a while; then announced with final assurance: 'The egg.'

'But who laid the egg?'

'The turtle, because the turtle is supreme and lays all the eggs.'

Bali then was a paradise. Natives worked four months in the rice-fields and devoted the other eight to their art and culture. Entertainment was free all over the island, one village performing for the other. But now paradise is on the way out. Education has taught them to cover their breasts and forsake their pleasure-loving gods for Western ones.

Before leaving for Japan, my Japanese secretary, Kono, expressed a desire to go ahead and prepare for our arrival. We were to be the guests of the Government. In Kobe harbour we were greeted by aeroplanes circling over our ship dropping leaflets of welcome, while thousands cheered on the docks. The sight of numerous brightly coloured kimonos against the background of smoke-stacks and the drab grey docks was paradoxically beautiful. There was little of the reputed mystery or restraint in that Japanese demonstration. It was as excited and emotional as any crowd I have ever seen anywhere.

The Government put a special train at our disposal to take us on to Tokyo. At each station the crowds and excitement increased, and the platforms were crammed with a galaxy of pretty girls who loaded us with presents. The effect, as they stood waiting in their kimonos, was like a flower show. In Tokyo an estimated crowd of forty thousand waited to greet us at the station. In the rush Sydney stumbled and fell and was almost trampled upon.

The mystery of the Orient is legendary. I had always thought we Europeans exaggerated it. But it was in the air the moment we stepped ashore at Kobe, and now in Tokyo it began to envelop us. On the way to the hotel we turned into a quiet part of the city. Suddenly the car slowed down to a stop near the Emperor's palace. Kono looked back anxiously through the limousine window, then turned to me and made a strange request. Would I get out of the car and bow towards the palace?

'Is this customary?' I asked.

'Yes,' he said casually. 'You don't have to bow, just step out of the car, that will be enough.'

This request somewhat bewildered me, because no one was around except the two or three cars that had followed us. If it were customary, the public would have known and a crowd would have been there, if only a small one. However, I got out and bowed.

When I got back in the car, Kono looked relieved. Sydney thought this was a strange request, and thought Kono had acted strangely. He looked worried ever since we arrived at Kobe. I dismissed the matter and said that perhaps he had been working too hard.

Nothing happened that night, but the following morning Sydney came into the sitting-room very excited. 'I don't like it,' he said; 'my bags have been searched and all my papers have been disturbed!' I told him that even if it were true it was not important. But nothing would allay Sydney's apprehension. 'There's something fishy going on!' he said. But I laughed and accused him of being overly suspicious.

That morning a Government agent was assigned to look after us, explaining that if we wished to go anywhere we should let him know through Kono. Sydney insisted that we were being watched and that Kono was holding back something. I must admit that Kono was looking more worried and harassed every hour.

Sydney's suspicions were not unfounded, because a peculiar thing happened that day. Kono said that a merchant had some pornographic pictures painted on silk which he would like me to come and see at his house. I told Kono to tell the man I was not interested. Kono looked worried. 'Supposing I ask him to leave them at the hotel?' he suggested.

'Under no circumstances,' I said. 'Just tell him not to waste his time.'

He hesitated. 'These people don't take no for an answer.'

'What are you talking about?' I asked.

'Well, they've been threatening me for several days; there's a tough element here in Tokyo.'

'What nonsense!' I answered. 'We'll put the police on their tracks.'

But Kono shook his head.

The next night, while my brother, Kono and I were dining in a private room in a restaurant, six young men entered. One sat down next to Kono and folded his arms, while the others backed up a pace and remained standing. The seated man began talking in Japanese to Kono with suppressed anger. Something he said made Kono suddenly blanch.

I was unarmed. Nevertheless, I put my hand in my coat-pocket

367

as though I had a revolver, and shouted: 'What's the meaning of this?'

Kono, without looking up from his plate, mumbled: 'He says you've insulted his ancestors by refusing to see his pictures.'

I sprang to my feet and, keeping my hand in my pocket, looked fiercely at the young man. 'What's all this about?' Then I said to Sydney: 'Let's get out of here. And you, Kono, order a cab.'

Once we were safely in the street we were all relieved. A taxi was waiting for us and we drove away.

The culmination of the mystery came the following day when the Prime Minister's son invited us as his guests to the Suomi wrestling matches. As we sat and watched them, an attendant tapped Mr Ken Inukai on the shoulder and whispered something. He turned to us and excused himself, saying that something urgent had arisen and that he had to leave, but he would come back later. Towards the end of the wrestling he returned, looking white and shaken. I asked him if he were ill. He shook his head, then suddenly covered his face with his hands. 'My father has just been assassinated,' he said.

We took him back to our rooms and offered him some brandy. Then he told us what had happened: six naval cadets had killed the guards outside the Prime Minister's palace and had broken into his private quarters, where they found him with his wife and daughter. His mother had told him the rest of the story: the assassins stood over his father for twenty minutes pointing their guns, while the Prime Minister tried to reason with them, but to no avail. Without a word they were about to shoot. But he begged them not to kill him in the presence of his family. So they allowed him to take leave of his wife and daughter. Calmly he got up and led the assassins to another room – where he must have tried to reason with them again, for the family sat in agonizing suspense before they heard the shots that killed their father.

The murder had occurred while his son was at the wrestling matches. Had he not been with us, he said, he would have been killed with his father.

I accompanied him back to his home and saw the room in which two hours previously his father had been murdered. The stain of a large pool of blood was still wet on the matting. A battery of cameramen and reporters were there, but they had the decency not to take photographs. They nevertheless prevailed upon me to make a statement. I could only say that it was a shocking tragedy for the family and for the country.

The day after the tragedy I was to have met the late Prime Minister at an official reception, which was, of course, called off.

Sydney declared that the murder was all a part of the mystery and that in some way we were involved. Said he: 'It is more than a coincidence that six assassins murdered the Prime Minister and that six men came into the restaurant that night while we were dining.'

It was not until Hugh Byas had written his most interesting and informative book *Government by Assassination*, published by Alfred A. Knopf, that the whole mystery, as far as I was involved, was clarified. It appears that the society called The Black Dragon was active at that moment, and it was they who had demanded that I bow to the palace. I quote from Hugh Byas's book the following account of the trial of those who had assassinated the Prime Minister:

Lieutenant Seishi Koga, naval ringleader of the plot, afterwards told the court martial that the conspirators had discussed a plan to bring about martial law by bombing the House of Representatives. Civilians who could easily get passes were to throw bombs from the public gallery while young officers waited at the doors to kill the members as they rushed out. Another plan, which might be too grotesque for credence if it had not been told in court, proposed the killing of Charles Chaplin, then visiting Japan. The Prime Minister invited Mr Chaplin to a tea and the young officers considered a scheme for raiding the official residence while the party was in progress.

JUDGE: What was the significance of killing Chaplin?

KOGA: Chaplin is a popular figure in the United States and the darling of the capitalist class. We believed that killing him would cause a war with America, and thus we could kill two birds with a single stone.

JUDGE: Then why did you give up your splendid plan?

KOGA: Because the newspapers later reported that the projected reception was still uncertain.

JUDGE: What was the motive of planning to attack the official residence of the Prime Minister?

KOGA: It was to overthrow the Premier, who was also the president of a political party; in other words to overthrow the very centre of government.

JUDGE: Did you intend to kill the Premier?
KOGA: Yes, I did. However, I had no personal grudge against him.

The same prisoner said that the plan to kill Chaplin was abandoned because 'it was disputed whether it was advisable to kill the comedian on the slight chance that it might bring about war with the United States and increase the power of the military'.

I can imagine the assassins having carried out their plan, then discovering that I was not an American but an Englishman – 'Oh, so sorry!'

However, it was not all mystery and unpleasantness in Japan; for the most part I had an interesting time there. The Kabuki theatre was a pleasure that went beyond my expectations. The Kabuki is not a purely formal theatre, but a mixture of the ancient and modern. An actor's virtuosity is the most important consideration, and the play is merely the material with which he performs. According to our Western standards their technique has sharp limitations. Realism is ignored where it cannot be effectively achieved. For instance, we occidentals cannot stage a sword fight without a touch of the absurd, for no matter how fierce the fighting one detects a modicum of caution. The Japanese on the other hand make no pretence of realism. They fight at a distance apart from each other, making sweeping panache gestures with their swords, one attempting to cut off the head of his opponent, the other slashing at his opponent's legs. Each in his own sphere jumps, dances and pirouettes. It is like ballet. The combat is impressionistic, terminating in a posture of victor and vanquished. From this impressionism the actors merge into realism during the death scene.

Irony is the theme of many of their plays. I saw what was comparable to *Romeo and Juliet*, a drama of two young lovers whose marriage is opposed by their parents. It was performed on a revolving stage, which the Japanese have used for three hundred years. The first scene was the interior of the bridal chamber showing the young couple just married. During the act, couriers intercede with the parents for the young lovers, who are hoping there may be a reconciliation. But tradition is too strong. The parents are adamant. So the lovers decide to commit suicide in the traditional Japanese way, each one bestrewing a carpet of

flower petals upon which to die; the bridegroom to kill his bride
first, then to fall upon his sword.

The comments of the lovers, as they scatter flower petals on the
floor preparing for death, created laughter from the audience. My
interpreter told me that the humour was ironic in such lines as:
'To live after such a night of love would be anti-climax.' For ten
minutes they continue such ironic banter. Then the bride kneels
on her mat of flowers, which is at a distance away from his, and
bares her throat; and as the bridegroom draws his sword and
slowly walks towards her, the revolving stage begins to move, and
before the point of his sword reaches his young wife's throat, the
scene turns out of sight of the audience and shows the exterior of
the house, drenched in moonlight. The audience sits through
what seems an interminable silence. Eventually, voices are heard
approaching. They are friends of the dead couple come to bring
them the happy news that their parents have forgiven them. They
are tipsy and argue about which of them should break the news.
Then they commence to serenade them and, getting no response,
they beat on the door.

'Don't disturb them,' says one; 'they're either asleep or too
busy.' So they go on their way, continuing their serenade, accompanied by a tick-tock, boxlike sound, signalling the end of the
play, as the curtain draws slowly across the stage.

How long Japan will survive the virus of Western civilization is
a moot question. Her people's appreciation of those simple
moments in life so characteristic of their culture – a lingering look
at a moonbeam, a pilgrimage to view cherry blossom, the quiet
meditation of the tea ceremony – seems destined to disappear in
the smog of Western enterprise.

My holiday was at an end, and although I had enjoyed many
aspects of it, some had been depressing. I saw food rotting, goods
piled high while people wandered hungrily about them, millions
of unemployed and their services going to waste.

I actually heard a man say at a dinner that nothing could save
the situation unless we found more gold. When I discussed the
problem of automation doing away with jobs, someone said that
the problem would solve itself because labour would eventually
be so cheap that it would be able to compete with automation.
The Depression was deeply cruel.

# *twenty-four*

WHEN I arrived home in Beverly Hills, I stood in the centre of the living-room. It was late afternoon and a carpet of long shadows lay across the lawn and streaks of golden sunlight streamed across the room. How serene it all looked. I could have wept. I had been away eight months, yet I wondered whether I was happy to be back. I was confused and without plan, restless and conscious of an extreme loneliness.

I had had in Europe a vague hope of meeting someone who might orient my life. But nothing had come of it. Of all the women I met, few fitted into that category – those that might have done were not interested. And now back again in California I had returned to a graveyard. Douglas and Mary had separated, so that world was no more.

That evening I was to dine alone, something I never liked doing in that big house. So I cancelled dinner, drove to Hollywood, parked the car and took a walk down Hollywood Boulevard. It seemed that I had never been away. There were the same long lines of one-storey shops, the stale-looking Army and Navy stores, the cut-rate drug-stores, Woolworth's and Kresge's, all of it depressing and lacking sophistication. Hollywood had not outgrown the look of a boom town.

As I walked the boulevards I began to deliberate whether I should retire, sell everything and go to China. There was no further incentive to stay in Hollywood. Without doubt silent pictures were finished and I did not feel like combating the talkies. Besides, I was out of circulation. I tried to think of someone whom I knew intimately enough to phone and invite for dinner without feeling embarrassed, but there was no one. When I returned to the house, Reeves, my manager, had called up to say that everything was okay. But no one else had called.

It was like jumping into cold water, putting in appearances at the studio to attend to irksome business affairs. However, I was delighted to hear that *City Lights* was doing extremely well, and that we already had $3,000,000 (net) in the kitty, and cheques of more than $100,000 were still coming in every month. Reeves suggested that I should go to the Hollywood bank and meet the new manager, just to get acquainted. Not having entered a bank in seven years, I declined.

Prince Louis Ferdinand, grandson of the Kaiser, called at the studio and later we dined at my house and had an interesting talk. The Prince, charming and very intelligent, spoke of the German revolution after the First World War as being comic opera. 'My grandfather had gone to Holland,' he said, 'but some of my relatives remained in the palace at Potsdam, too terrified to move. When at last the revolutionists marched on the palace, they sent a note asking my relatives if they would receive them, and in that interview assured them that they would be given every protection and that, if they needed anything, they had only to telephone the Socialist headquarters. They could not believe their ears. But when later the Government approached them about a settlement of their estates, my relatives began to equivocate and want more.' In summing up he said: 'The Russian Revolution was a tragedy – ours was a joke.'

Since my return to the States something quite wonderful was happening. The economic reverses, although drastic, brought out the greatness of the American people. Conditions had gone from bad to worse. Some states went so far as to print a fiduciary currency on wood in order to distribute unsold goods. Meanwhile the lugubrious Hoover sat and sulked, because his disastrous economic sophistry of allocating money at the top in the belief that it would percolate down to the common people had failed. And amidst all this tragedy he ranted in the election campaign that if Franklin Roosevelt got into office the very foundations of the American system – not an infallible system at that moment – would be imperilled.

However, Franklin D. Roosevelt did get into office, and the country was not imperilled. His 'Forgotten Man' speech lifted American politics out of its cynical drowse and established the

373

most inspiring era in American history. I heard the speech over the radio at Sam Goldwyn's beach-house. Several of us sat around, including Bill Paley of the Columbia Broadcasting System, Joe Schenck, Fred Astaire, his wife and other guests. 'The only thing we have to fear is fear itself' came over the air like a ray of sunlight. But I was sceptical, as were most of us. 'Too good to be true,' I said.

No sooner had Roosevelt taken office than he began to fit actions to his words, ordering a ten-day bank holiday to stop the banks from collapsing. That was a moment when America was at its best. Shops and stores of all kinds continued to do business on credit, even the cinemas sold tickets on credit, and for ten days, while Roosevelt and his so-called brains trust formulated the New Deal, the people acted magnificently.

Legislation was ordered for every kind of emergency: reestablishing farm credit to stop the wholesale robbery of foreclosures, financing big public projects, establishing the National Recovery Act, raising the minimum wage, spreading out jobs by shortening working hours, and encouraging the organization of labour unions. This was going too far; this was socialism, the opposition shouted. Whether it was or not, it saved capitalism from complete collapse. It also inaugurated some of the finest reforms in the history of the United States. It was inspiring to see how quickly the American citizen reacted to constructive government.

Hollywood was also going through a change of life. Most of the silent screen stars had disappeared – only a few of us were left. Now that the talkies had taken hold, the charm and insouciance of Hollywood were gone. Overnight it had become a cold and serious industry. Sound technicians were renovating studios and building elaborate sound devices. Cameras the size of a room lumbered about the stage like juggernauts. Elaborate radio equipment was installed, involving thousands of electrical wires. Men, geared like warriors from Mars, sat with earphones while the actors performed, with microphones hovering above them like fishing rods. It was all very complicated and depressing. How could anyone be creative with all that junk around them? I hated the whole idea of it. Then someone found that all this elaborate junk could be made portable, and the cameras more mobile, and that equipment could be rented for a reasonable sum. Notwithstanding these improvements, I found little inducement to start work again.

I still toyed with the idea of pulling up stakes and settling in China. In Hong Kong I could live well and forget motion pictures, instead of languishing here in Hollywood, rotting on the vine.

For three weeks I dallied about, then one day Joe Schenck telephoned me to save the week-end for his yacht – a beautiful sailing boat, a hundred and thirty-eight feet long, that could comfortably accommodate fourteen people. Joe usually moored around Catalina Island near Avalon. His guests were seldom exciting, usually poker-players, and poker did not interest me. But there were other interests. Joe usually embarked with a bevy of pretty girls, and being desperately lonely, I hoped I might find a pretty little ray of sunlight.

That is precisely what happened. I met Paulette Goddard. She was gay and amusing and during the course of the evening told me she was going to invest $50,000, part of her alimony from her ex-husband, in a film venture. She had brought aboard all the documents ready to sign. I almost took her by the throat to prevent her. The company was obviously a Hollywood gyp enterprise. I told her that I had been in the movie business almost since its inception and with my knowledge of it I would not invest one penny except in my own pictures – and even that was a risk. I argued that if Hearst, with a literary staff and access to the most popular stories in the States, had lost $7,000,000 investing in movies, what chance had she? Eventually I talked her out of it. This was the beginning of our friendship.

The bond between Paulette and me was loneliness. She was just out from New York and knew no one. It was a case of Robinson Crusoe discovering Friday for both of us. During the week there was plenty to do, for Paulette was working in a Sam Goldwyn movie and I attended to business. But Sunday was a forlorn day. In desperation we would take long drives, in fact we combed the whole coastline of California. There seemed to be nothing to do. Our most thrilling adventure was to go to San Pedro harbour to look at the pleasure boats. One was for sale, a fifty-five-foot motor cruiser which had three state-rooms, a galley and an attractive wheel-house – the kind of boat I would have liked.

'Now if you had something like that,' Paulette said, 'we could have lots of fun on Sundays, and go to Catalina.' So I made inquiries about purchasing it. It was owned by a Mr Mitchell, manufacturer of the motion picture cameras, who showed us over the boat. Three times within a week we looked it over until our presence became embarrassing. However, Mr Mitchell said that until it was sold we were welcome to come aboard and look at it.

Unbeknown to Paulette I bought the boat and provisioned it for a cruise to Catalina, taking aboard my own cook, and an ex-Keystone Cop, Andy Anderson, who had been a licensed captain. The following Sunday everything was ready. Paulette and I started out very early, as she thought, for a long drive, agreeing that we would just have a cup of coffee and go somewhere later for breakfast. Then she discovered we were on our way to San Pedro. 'Surely you are not going to look at that boat again?'

'I'd like to go over it once more just to make up my mind,' I answered.

'Then you'll have to go alone, it's too embarrassing,' she said mournfully. 'I'll sit in the car and wait for you.'

When we pulled up at the boat landing-stage, nothing would induce her to get out of the car. 'No, you'll have to go alone. But hurry – we haven't had breakfast yet.'

After two minutes I returned to the car and persuaded her much against her will to come aboard. The cabin was gaily decorated with a pink and blue table-cloth and pink and blue china to match. A delectable aroma of bacon and eggs frying came up from the galley. 'The captain has kindly invited us to breakfast,' I said. 'We have wheat-cakes, bacon and eggs, toast and coffee.' Paulette looked down into the galley and recognized our cook. 'Well,' I said, 'you wanted some place to go on Sunday so after breakfast we're going to Catalina for a swim.' Then I told her I had bought the boat.

Her reaction was funny. 'Wait a minute,' she said. She got up, left the boat and ran about fifty yards along the harbour and covered her face with her hands.

'Hey! Come and get your breakfast,' I shouted.

When she came aboard again she said: 'I had to do that to get over the shock of it.'

Then Freddy, the Japanese cook, came up all grinning with the breakfast. And afterwards we warmed up the engines, cruised down towards the harbour and out into the Pacific Ocean towards Catalina, twenty-two miles away, where we moored for nine days.

*

Still no immediate plans for work. With Paulette I did all the witless things: attended race meetings, night spots and all the public functions – anything to kill time. I did not want to be alone or to think. But underlying these pleasures was a continual sense of guilt: What am I doing here? Why aren't I at work?

Furthermore, I was depressed by the remark of a young critic who said that *City Lights* was very good, but that it verged on the sentimental, and that in my future films I should try to approximate realism. I found myself agreeing with him. Had I known what I do now, I could have told him that so-called realism is often artificial, phoney, prosaic and dull; and that it is not reality that matters in a film but what the imagination can make of it.

It was curious how by accident, and when I least expected it, I was suddenly stimulated to make another silent picture. Paulette and I went to Tijuana race-track in Mexico, where the winner of the Kentucky something or other was to be presented with a silver cup. Paulette was asked if she would present the cup to the winning jockey and say a few words with a Southern accent. She needed little persuasion. I was astonished to hear her over the loudspeaker. Although from Brooklyn, she gave a remarkable imitation of a Kentucky society belle. This convinced me that she could act.

Thus I was stimulated. Paulette struck me as being somewhat of a *gamine*. This would be a wonderful quality for me to get on the screen. I could imagine us meeting in a crowded patrol wagon, the tramp and this gamine, and the tramp being very gallant and offering her his seat. This was the basis on which I could build plot and sundry gags.

Then I remembered an interview I had had with a bright young reporter on the New York *World*. Hearing that I was visiting Detroit, he had told me of the factory-belt system there – a harrowing story of big industry luring healthy young men off the farms who, after four or five years at the belt system, became nervous wrecks.

It was that conversation that gave me the idea for *Modern*

377

*Times*. I used a feeding machine as a time-saving device, so that the workers could continue working during the lunch time. The factory sequence resolved itself in the tramp having a nervous breakdown. The plot developed out of the natural sequence of events. After his cure, he gets arrested and meets a *gamine* who has also been arrested for stealing bread. They meet in a police patrol car packed with offenders. From then on, the theme is about two nondescripts trying to get along in modern times. They are involved in the Depression, strikes, riots and unemployment. Paulette was dressed in rags. She almost wept when I put smudges on her face to make her look dirty. 'Those smudges are beauty spots,' I insisted.

It is easy to dress an actress attractively in fashionable clothes, but to dress a flower-girl and have her look attractive, as in *City Lights*, was difficult. The girl's costume in *The Gold Rush* was not such a problem. But Paulette's outfit in *Modern Times* required as much thought and finesse as a Dior creation. If a *gamine* costume is treated without care, the patches look theatrical and unconvincing. In dressing an actress as a street urchin or a flower-girl I aimed to create a poetic effect and not to detract from her personality.

Before the opening of *Modern Times* a few columnists wrote that they had heard rumours the picture was communistic. I suppose this was because of a summary of the story that had already appeared in the Press. However, the liberal reviewers wrote that it was neither for nor against communism and that metaphorically I had sat on the fence.

Nothing is more nerve-racking than to receive bulletins informing one that the first week's attendance broke all records and that the second week fell off slightly. Therefore, after the premières in New York and Los Angeles, my one desire was to get as far away as possible from any news of the picture; so I decided to go to Honolulu, taking Paulette and her mother with me, leaving instructions with the office not to send messages of any kind.

*

We embarked at Los Angeles, arriving in San Francisco in pouring rain. However, nothing dampened our spirits; we had time for a little shopping, then returned to the boat. Passing by warehouses, I saw stamped on some of the freight the word 'China'. 'Let's go there!'

'Where?' said Paulette.

'China.'

'Are you kidding?'

'Let's do it now or we never will,' I said.

'But I haven't any clothes.'

'You can buy all you want in Honolulu,' I said.

All boats should be called *Panacea*, for nothing is more recuperative than a sea-voyage. Your worries are adjourned, the boat adopts you, and cures you and, when finally she enters port, reluctantly gives you back again to the humdrum world.

But when we arrived in Honolulu, to my horror I saw large posters advertising *Modern Times*, and the Press waiting on the dock ready to devour me. There was no escape.

However, I was not apprehended in Tokyo, for the captain had obligingly registered me under another name. The Japanese authorities took it big when they saw my passport. 'Why didn't you let us know you were coming?' they said. Since there had just been a military coup in which several hundreds had been killed, it was just as well, I thought. During our stay in Japan an official of the Government never left our side. From San Francisco on through to Hong Kong we hardly spoke to a passenger; but when we arrived in Hong Kong the austerity thawed. It came about through a Catholic priest. 'Charlie,' said a tall, reserved-looking business man, 'I want you to meet an American priest from Connecticut who's been stationed out here for five years in a leper colony. It's pretty lonesome for the Father, so every Saturday he comes to Hong Kong just to meet the American boats.'

The priest was a tall, handsome man in his late thirties with rosy cheeks and an ingratiating smile. I bought a drink, then my friend bought a drink, then the Father bought a drink. It was a small circle at first, but as the evening progressed it enlarged to about twenty-five people, everyone buying drinks. The party increased to about thirty-five and the drinks kept coming; many were carried aboard unconscious, but the priest, who did not miss a drink, was still smiling and soberly administering to everyone. Eventually I reared up to bid him good-bye. And as he held me up solicitously I shook his hand. It felt rough, so I turned it over and examined the palm. There were cracks and crevices and in the centre a white spot. 'That's not leprosy, I hope,' I said jokingly. He grinned and shook his head. A year later we heard that he had died of it.

We stayed away from Hollywood for five months. During this trip Paulette and I were married. Afterwards we returned to the States, boarding a Japanese boat in Singapore.

The first day out I received a note which read that the writer and I had many mutual friends, that for years we had just missed meeting each other and that now, in the centre of the South China Sea, was an excellent opportunity. Signed 'Jean Cocteau'. Then P.S.: perhaps he could come to my cabin for an aperitif before dinner. Immediately I suspected an imposter. What could this urbane Parisian be doing in the middle of the South China Sea? However, it was true, for Cocteau was doing an assignment for the French newspaper *Figaro*.

Cocteau could not speak a word of English, neither could I speak French, but his secretary spoke a little English, though not too well, and he acted as interpreter for us. That night we sat up into the small hours, discussing our theories of life and art. Our interpreter spoke slowly and hesitantly while Cocteau, his beautiful hands spread on his chest, spoke with the rapidity of a machine gun – his eyes flashing an appealing look at me, then at the interpreter, who spoke unemotionally: 'Mr Cocteau – he say – you are a poet – of zer sunshine – and he is a poet of zer – night.'

Immediately Cocteau turned from the interpreter to me with a quick, birdlike nod, and continued. Then I would take over, getting deeply involved in philosophy and art. In moments of agreement we would embrace, while our cool-eyed interpreter looked on. Thus, in this exalted way, we carried on through the night until four in the morning, promising to meet at one o'clock for lunch.

But our enthusiasm had reached a climax; we had had it! Neither of us showed up. In the afternoon our letters of apology must have crossed, for their contents were identical, both profuse with apologies but careful not to make any more dates – we had had more than a glut of each other.

At dinner-time, when we entered the dining-room, Cocteau was seated in the far corner, his back towards us. But his secretary could not help but see us, and with a weak gesture indicated our presence to Cocteau, who hesitated, then turned and feigned surprise, and gaily waved the letter I had sent him; I gaily waved his and we both laughed. Then we turned soberly from each other and became deeply engrossed in our menus. Cocteau finished dinner first, and as the stewards were serving our main course he discreetly passed our table in a hurry. However he turned before exiting and pointed outside, indicating 'We'll see you there.' I vigorously nodded approval. But later I was relieved to find he'd vanished.

The following morning I promenaded the deck alone. Suddenly, to my horror, Cocteau appeared around the corner in the distance coming towards me! My God! I quickly looked for an escape, then he saw me and to my relief darted through the main saloon door. That finished our morning promenade. Throughout the day we kept up a game of hide-and-seek avoiding each other. However, by the time we reached Hong Kong we had recovered enough to meet momentarily. Still there were four more days to go before reaching Tokyo.

During the voyage Cocteau told an amazing story: he had seen in the interior of China a living Buddha, a man about fifty, who had lived his whole life floating in a jar of oil, with just his head exposed out of the neck of it. Through years of soaking in oil, the body had remained embryonic and was so soft that one could put a finger through it. In what part of China he saw this was never made clear, and eventually he admitted that he had not seen it himself but had heard about it.

In the various stopping-off places we rarely saw each other, unless for a brief how-do-you-do and farewell. But when news broke that we were both sailing on the *President Coolidge* going back to the States, we became resigned, making no further attempts at enthusiasm.

In Tokyo Cocteau had bought a pet grasshopper which he kept in a little cage and often brought ceremoniously to my cabin. 'He is very intelligent,' he said, 'and sings every time I talk to him.' He built up such an interest in it that it became our topic of conversation. 'How is Pilou this morning?' I would ask.

'Not very well,' he would say solemnly. 'I have him on a diet.'

When we arrived in San Francisco I insisted on him driving

with us to Los Angeles, as we had a limousine waiting. Pilou came along. During the journey he began to sing. 'You see,' said Cocteau, 'he likes America.' Suddenly he opened the car window, then opened the door of the little cage and shook Pilou out of it.

I was shocked and asked: 'Why did you do that?'

'He gives him freedom,' said the interpreter.

'But,' I answered, 'he's a stranger in a foreign country – and can't speak the language.'

Cocteau shrugged. 'He's smart, he'll soon pick it up.'

*

When we arrived home in Beverly Hills, news from the studio was encouraging. *Modern Times* was a great success.

But again I was faced with the depressing question: should I make another silent picture? I knew I'd be taking a great chance if I did. The whole of Hollywood had deserted silent pictures and I was the only one left. I had been lucky so far, but to continue with a feeling that the art of pantomime was gradually becoming obsolete was a discouraging thought. Besides, it was not easy to contrive silent action for an hour and forty minutes, translating wit into action and creating visual jokes every twenty feet of film, for seven or eight thousand feet. Another thought was that, if I did make a talking picture, no matter how good I was I could never surpass the artistry of my pantomime. I had thought of possible voices for the tramp; whether he should speak in monosyllables or just mumble. But it was no use. If I talked I would become like any other comedian. These were the melancholy problems that confronted me.

Paulette and I had now been married for a year, but a breach was widening between us. It was partly due to my being worried and absorbed in trying to work. However, on the success of *Modern Times* Paulette was signed up to make several pictures for Paramount. But I could neither work nor play. In this melancholy frame of mind I decided to go to Pebble Beach with my friend Tim Durant. Perhaps I could work better there.

Pebble Beach, a hundred-odd miles south of San Francisco, was wild, baneful and slightly sinister. I called it 'the abode of stranded souls'. It was known as the Seventeen-mile Drive; it had deer roaming through its wooded sections, and many pretentious houses unoccupied and for sale; there were fallen trees rotting in fields full of wood ticks, poison ivy, oleander bushes and deadly nightshade – a setting for banshees. Fronting the ocean, built on the rocks, were several elaborate houses occupied by millionaires; this section was known as the Gold Coast.

I had met Tim Durant when someone brought him to one of our Sunday tennis parties. Tim was very good at tennis, and we played a lot together. He had just divorced his wife, the daughter of E. F. Hutton, and had come to California to get away from it all. Tim was sympathetic, and we became very good friends.

We rented a house set back from the ocean half a mile. It was dank and miserable, and when we lit a fire it would fill the room with volumes of smoke. Tim knew many of the social set of Pebble Beach, and while he visited them I tried to work. For days and days I sat alone in the library and walked in the garden, trying to get an idea, but nothing would come. Eventually, I deferred worrying, joined Tim and met some of our neighbours. I often thought they were good material for short stories – typical de Maupassant. One large house, although comfortable, was slightly eerie and sad. The host, an agreeable chap, talked loudly and incessantly while his wife sat without uttering a word. Since her baby had died five years ago, she seldom spoke or smiled. Her only utterance was good-evening and good-night.

At another house built on the high cliffs overlooking the sea, a novelist had lost his wife. It appears she had been in the garden taking photographs and must have stepped backwards too far. When her husband went to look for her, he found only a tripod. She was never seen again.

Wilson Mizner's sister disliked her neighbours, whose tennis court overlooked her house, and whenever her neighbours played tennis she would build a fire and volumes of smoke would cover the court.

The Fagans, an old couple, immensely rich, entertained elaborately on Sundays. The Nazi Consul, whom I met there, a blond, smooth-mannered young man, did his best to be engaging. But I gave him a wide-berth.

Occasionally we spent a week-end at the John Steinbecks'. They had a small house near Monterey. He was just on the threshold of fame, having written *Tortilla Flat* and a series of short stories. John worked in the morning and averaged about two thousand words a day. I was amazed at how neat were his pages, with hardly a correction. I envy him.

I like to know the way writers work and how much they turn out a day. Thomas Mann averaged about 400 words a day. Lion Feuchtwanger dictated 2,000 words, which averaged 600 written words a day. Somerset Maugham wrote 400 words a day just to keep in practice. H. G. Wells averaged 1,000 words a day, Hannen Swaffer, the English journalist, wrote from 4,000 to 5,000 words a day. The American critic, Alexander Woollcott, wrote a 700-word review in fifteen minutes, then joined a poker game – I was there when he did it. Hearst would write a 2,000-word editorial in an evening. Georges Simenon has written a short novel in a month – and of excellent literary quality. Georges tells me that he gets up at five in the morning, brews his own coffee, then sits at his desk and rolls a golden ball, the size of a tennis ball, and thinks. He writes with a pen and when I asked him why he wrote in such small handwriting, he said: 'It requires less effort of the wrist.' As for myself I dictate about 1,000 words a day, which averages me about 300 in finished dialogue for my films

The Steinbecks had no servants, his wife did all the housework. It was a wonderful ménage and I was very fond of her.

We had many a discourse and in discussing Russia John said that one thing the Communists had done was to abolish prostitution. 'That's about the last of private enterprise,' I said. 'Too bad, it's about the only profession that gives full value for your money, and a most honest one – why not unionize it?'

An attractive married lady, whose husband was flagrantly unfaithful, arranged a *pas de deux* with me at her large house. I went there with every adulterous intention. But when the lady confided tearfully that she had had no sexual relations with her husband in eight years and that she still loved him, her tears dampened my ardour, and I found myself giving her philosophical advice – the whole thing became cerebral. Later it was rumoured that she had turned Lesbian.

Robinson Jeffers, the poet, lived near Pebble Beach. The first time Tim and I met him was at a friend's house. He was aloof and silent, and in my usual glib way I started to carp about the ills

384

and evils of the day just to make the evening go. But Jeffers never said a word. I came away rather annoyed at myself for having monopolized the conversation. I felt that he disliked me, but I was wrong, for a week later he invited Tim and me to tea.

Robinson Jeffers and his wife lived in a small medieval stone castle called Tor, which he had built himself on a slab of rock on the shores of the Pacific Ocean. It looked rather boyishly indulgent, I thought. The largest room was not more than twelve feet square. A few feet away from the house was a medieval-looking round stone tower, eighteen feet high and four feet in diameter. Narrow stone steps led up to a little round dungeon with slits for windows. This was his study. It was here that *Roan Stallion* was written. Tim maintained that this sepulchral taste was a psychological desire for death. But I saw Robinson Jeffers walking with his dog at sunset, enjoying the evening, his face set in an ineffable expression of peace as though immersed in some far-off reverie. I feel sure that no such person as Robinson Jeffers desires death.

# twenty-five

WAR was in the air again. The Nazis were on the march. How soon we forgot the First World War and its torturous four years of dying. How soon we forgot the appalling human debris: the basket cases – the armless, the legless, the sightless, the jawless, the twisted spastic cripples. Those that were not killed or wounded did not escape, for many were left with deformed minds. Like a minotaur war had gobbled up the youth, leaving cynical old men to survive. But we soon forget and glamorize war with popular Tin Pan Alley ditties:

> How're you going to keep them down on the farm,
> After they've seen Paree –

and so forth. War in many ways was a good thing, some said. It expanded industry and advanced techniques and gave people new jobs. How could we think of the millions that lay dead when millions were being made on the stock market? At the height of the market Arthur Brisbane of the *Hearst Examiner* said: 'U.S. Steel will jump up to five hundred dollars a share.' Instead it was the speculators that jumped out of windows.

And now another war was brewing and I was trying to write a story for Paulette; but I could make no progress. How could I throw myself into feminine whimsy or think of romance or the problems of love when madness was being stirred up by a hideous grotesque, Adolf Hitler?

Alexander Korda in 1937 had suggested I should do a Hitler story based on mistaken identity, Hitler having the same moustache as the tramp: I could play both characters, he said. I did not think too much about the idea then, but now it was topical, and I was desperate to get working again. Then it suddenly struck me. Of course! As Hitler I could harangue the crowds in jargon and talk all I wanted to. And as the tramp I could remain more or less silent. A Hitler story was an opportunity for burlesque and pantomime. So with this enthusiasm I went hurrying back to Hollywood and set to work writing a script. The story took two years to develop.

I thought of the opening sequence, which would start with a battle scene of the First World War, showing Big Bertha, with its shooting range of seventy-five miles, with which the Germans intended to awe the Allies. It is supposed to destroy Rheims Cathedral – instead it misses its mark and destroys an outside water-closet.

Paulette was to be in the picture. In the last two years she had had quite a success with Paramount. Although we were somewhat estranged we were friends and still married. But Paulette was a creature of whims. One would have been quite amusing if it had not come at an inopportune time. One day she arrived in my dressing-room at the studio with a slim, well-tailored young man, who looked poured into his clothes. I had had a difficult day with the script and was rather surprised at this interruption. But Paulette said it was very important; then she sat down and invited the young man to pull up a chair and sit down beside her.

'This is my agent,' said Paulette.

Then she looked at him to take over. He spoke rapidly with clipped enunciation, as though enjoying his words. 'As you know, Mr Chaplin, since *Modern Times* you're paying Paulette two thousand five hundred dollars a week. But what we haven't straightened out with you, Mr Chaplin, is her billing, which should be featured seventy-five per cent on all posters – ' He got no further. 'What the hell is this?' I shouted. 'Don't tell me what billing she's to get! I have her interests at heart more than you have! Get out, the pair of you!'

Half-way through making *The Great Dictator* I began receiving alarming messages from United Artists. They had been advised by the Hays Office that I would run into censorship trouble. Also the English office was very concerned about an anti-Hitler picture and doubted whether it could be shown in Britain. But I was determined to go ahead, for Hitler must be laughed at. Had I known of the actual horrors of the German concentration camps,

I could not have made *The Great Dictator*; I could not have made fun of the homicidal insanity of the Nazis. However, I was determined to ridicule their mystic bilge about a pure-blooded race: As though such a thing ever existed outside of the Australian Aborigines!

While I was making *The Great Dictator*, Sir Stafford Cripps came to California *en route* from Russia. He came to dinner with a young man just down from Oxford whose name escapes my memory, but not the remark he made that evening. Said he: 'The way things are going in Germany and elsewhere, I have a small chance of living more than five years.' Sir Stafford had been on a fact-finding tour in Russia and was profoundly impressed with what he had seen. He described their vast projects and of course their terrific problems. He seemed to think that war was inevitable.

More worrying letters came from the New York office imploring me not to make the film, declaring it would never be shown in England or America. But I was determined to make it, even if I had to hire halls myself to show it.

Before I had finished *The Dictator* England declared war on the Nazis. I was in Catalina on my boat over the week-end and heard the depressing news over the radio. In the beginning there was inaction on all fronts. 'The Germans will never break through the Maginot Line,' we said. Then suddenly the holocaust began: the break-through in Belgium, the collapse of the Maginot Line, the stark and ghastly fact of Dunkirk – and France was occupied. The news was growing gloomier. England was fighting with her back to the wall. Now our New York office was wiring frantically: 'Hurry up with your film, everyone is waiting for it.'

*The Great Dictator* was difficult to make; it involved miniature models and props, which took a year's preparation. Without these devices it would have cost five times as much. However, I had spent $500,000 before I began turning the camera.

Then Hitler decided to invade Russia! This was proof that his inevitable dementia had set in. The United States had not yet entered the war, but there was a feeling of great relief both in England and America.

Near the completion of *The Dictator*, Douglas Fairbanks and his wife, Sylvia, visited us on location. Douglas had been inactive for the last five years and I had rarely seen him, for he had been travelling to and from England. I thought he had aged and grown a little stouter and seemed preoccupied. Nevertheless, he was still the same enthusiastic Douglas. He laughed uproariously during the taking of one of our scenes. 'I can't wait to see it,' he said.

Doug stayed about an hour. When he left I stood gazing after him, watching him help his wife up a steep incline; and as they walked away along the footpath, the distance growing between us, I felt a sudden tinge of sadness. Doug turned and I waved, and he waved back. That was the last I ever saw of him. A month later Douglas Junior telephoned to say his father had died in the night of a heart-attack. It was a terrible shock, for he belonged so much to life.

I have missed Douglas – I have missed the warmth of his enthusiasm and charm; I have missed his friendly voice over the telephone, that used to call me up on a bleak and lonely Sunday morning: 'Charlie, coming up for lunch – then for a swim – then for dinner – then afterwards, see a picture?' Yes, I have missed his delightful friendship.

In what society of men would I prefer to associate? I suppose my own profession should be my choice. Yet Douglas was the only actor of whom I ever made a friend. Meeting the stars at various Hollywood parties, I have come away sceptical – maybe there were too many of us. The atmosphere was more challenging than friendly, and one ran many gauntlets to and from the buffet in vying for special attention. No, stars amongst stars gave little light – or warmth.

Writers are nice people but not very giving; whatever they know they seldom impart to others; most of them keep it between the covers of their books. Scientists might be excellent company, but their mere appearance in a drawing-room mentally paralyses the rest of us. Painters are a bore because most of them would have you believe they are philosophers more than painters. Poets are undoubtedly the superior class and as individuals are pleasant, tolerant and excellent companions. But I think musicians in the aggregate are more cooperative than any other class. There is nothing so warm and moving as the sight of a symphony orchestra. The romantic lights of their music stands, the tuning up and the sudden silence as the conductor makes his entrance, affirms the social, cooperative feeling. I remember Horowitz, the pianist, dining at my house, and the guests discussing the state of the world, saying that the Depression and unemployment would bring about a spiritual renaissance. Suddenly he got up and said: 'This conversation makes me want to play the piano.' Of course nobody objected and he played Schumann's Sonata No. 2. I doubted if it would ever be played as well again.

Just before the war I dined at his house with his wife, the daughter of Toscanini. Rachmaninov and Barbirolli were there. Rachmaninov was a strange-looking man, with something aesthetic and cloistral about him. It was an intimate dinner, just five of us.

It seems that each time art is discussed I have a different explanation of it. Why not? That evening I said that art was an additional emotion applied to skilful technique. Someone brought the topic round to religion and I confessed I was not a believer. Rachmaninov quickly interposed: 'But how can you have art without religion?'

I was stumped for a moment. 'I don't think we are talking about the same thing,' I said. 'My concept of religion is a belief in a dogma – and art is a feeling more than a belief.'

'So is religion,' he answered. After that I shut up.

\*

While dining at my house, Igor Stravinsky suggested we should do a film together. I invented a story. It should be surrealistic, I said – a decadent night-club with tables around the dance floor, at each table groups and couples representing the mundane world – at one table greed, at another hypocrisy, at another ruthlessness. The floor show is the passion play, and while the crucifixion of the Saviour is going on, groups at each table watch it indifferently, some ordering meals, others talking business, others showing little interest. The mob, the High Priests and the Pharisees are shaking their fists up at the Cross, shouting: 'If Thou be the Son of God come down and save Thyself.' At a nearby table a group of business men are talking excitedly about a big deal. One draws nervously on his cigarette, looking up at the Saviour and blowing his smoke absent-mindedly in His direction.

At another table a business man and his wife sit studying the menu. She looks up, then nervously moves her chair back from the floor. 'I can't understand why people come here,' she says uncomfortably; 'it's depressing.'

'It's good entertainment,' says the business man. 'The place was bankrupt until they put on this show. Now they are out of the red.'

'I think it's sacrilegious,' says his wife.

'It does a lot of good,' says the man. 'People who have never been inside a church come here and get the story of Christianity.'

As the show progresses, a drunk, being under the influence of alcohol, is on a different plane; he is seated alone and begins to weep and shout loudly: 'Look, they're crucifying Him! And nobody cares!' He staggers to his feet and stretches his arms appealingly towards the Cross. The wife of a minister sitting nearby complains to the head waiter, and the drunk is escorted out of the place still weeping and remonstrating: 'Look, nobody cares! A fine lot of Christians you are!'

'You see,' I told Stravinsky, 'they throw him out because he is upsetting the show.' I explained that putting a passion play on the dance floor of a night-club was to show how cynical and conventional the world has become in professing Christianity.

The maestro's face became very grave. 'But that's sacrilegious!' he said.

I was rather astonished and a little embarrassed. 'Is it?' I said. 'I never intended it to be. I thought it was a criticism of the world's attitude towards Christianity – perhaps, having made up the story as I went along, I haven't made that very clear.' And so the subject was dropped. But several weeks later, Stravinsky wrote, wanting to know if I still considered the idea of our doing a film together. However, my enthusiasm has cooled off and I become interested in making a film of my own.

Hanns Eisler brought Schoenberg to my studio, a frank and abrupt little man whose music I much admired, and whom I had seen regularly at the Los Angeles tennis tournaments sitting alone in the bleachers wearing a white cap and a T-shirt. After seeing my film *Modern Times*, he told me that he enjoyed the comedy but my music was very bad – and I had partly to agree with him. In discussing music one remark of his was indelible: 'I like sounds, beautiful sounds.'

Hanns Eisler tells an amusing story about the great man. Hanns, studing harmony under him, would walk in the depth of winter five miles in the snow to receive a lesson from the master at eight o'clock. Schoenberg, who was inclined to baldness, would sit at the piano while Hanns looked over his shoulder, reading and whistling the music. 'Young man,' said the master, 'don't whistle. Your icy breath is very cold on my head.'

During the making of *The Dictator* I began receiving crank letters, and now that it was finished they started to increase. Some threatened to throw stink bombs in the theatre and shoot up the screen wherever it would be shown, others threatening to create riots. At first I thought of going to the police, but such publicity might keep the public away from the theatre. A friend of mine suggested having a talk with Harry Bridges, head of the longshoreman's union. So I invited him to the house for dinner.

I told him frankly my reason for wanting to see him. I knew Bridges was anti-Nazi so I explained that I was making an anti-Nazi comedy and that I had been receiving threatening letters. I said: 'If I could invite, say, twenty or thirty of your longshoremen to my opening, and have them scattered amongst the audience, then if any of these pro-Nazi fellows started a rumpus, your folks might gently stamp on their toes before anything got seriously going.'

Bridges laughed. 'I don't think it will come to that, Charlie. You'll have enough defenders with your own public to take care of any cranks. And if these letters are from Nazis, they'll be afraid to show up in the daylight anyway.'

That night Harry told an interesting story of the San Francisco strike. At that time he had practically commanded the whole city, controlling all its supplies. But he never interfered with the necessary supplies for hospitals and for children. In telling me about the strike he said: 'When the cause is justified, you don't have to persuade people; all you do is to tell them the facts, they they decide for themselves. I told my men that if they decided to strike there'd be plenty of trouble; some might never know the results. But whatever they decided, I would abide by their decision. If it's to strike, I'll be there on the front line,

I said – and the five thousand voted unanimously to strike.'

*The Great Dictator* was booked to play two theatres in New York, the Astor and the Capitol. At the Astor we previewed it for the Press. Harry Hopkins, Franklin Roosevelt's chief adviser, dined with me that night. Afterwards we went to the Press showing and arrived half-way through the picture.

A Press preview of a comedy has a very definite characteristic – the laughter sounds in spite of itself. At that preview, what laughter there was sounded the same.

'It's a great picture,' said Harry as we left the theatre, 'a very worth-while thing to do, but it hasn't a chance. It will lose money.' Since $2,000,000 of my own money and two years' work were involved, I was not frantically ebullient about his prognostications. However, I nodded soberly. Thank God Hopkins was wrong. *The Great Dictator* opened at the Capital to a glamorous audience who were elated and enthused. It stayed fifteen weeks in New York, playing two theatres, and turned out to be the biggest grosser of all my pictures up to that time.

But the reviews were mixed. Most of the critics objected to the last speech. The New York *Daily News* said I pointed a finger of Communism at the audience. Although the majority of the critics objected to the speech and said it was not in character, the public as a whole loved it, and I had many wonderful letters eulogizing it.

Archie L. Mayo, one of Hollywood's important directors, asked permission to print the speech on his Christmas card. What follows is his introduction to it and the speech:

Had I lived at the time of Lincoln, I believe I would have sent you his Gettysburg speech, because it was the greatest inspirational message of his period. Today we face new crises, and another man has spoken from the depth of an earnest and sincere heart. Although I know him but slightly, what he says has moved me deeply . . . I am inspired to send you the full text of the speech written by Charles Chaplin that you, too, may share the expression of Hope.

### The Concluding Speech of
#### THE DICTATOR

I'm sorry, but I don't want to be an emperor. That's not my business. I don't want to rule or conquer anyone. I should like to help everyone – if possible – Jew, Gentile – black men – white.

We all want to help one another. Human beings are like that. We want to live by each other's happiness – not by each other's misery. We don't want to hate and despise one another. In this world there is room for everyone. And the good earth is rich and can provide for everyone.

The way of life can be free and beautiful, but we have lost the way. Greed has poisoned men's souls – has barricaded the world with hate – has goose-stepped us into misery and bloodshed. We have developed speed, but we have shut ourselves in. Machinery that gives abundance has left us in want. Our knowledge has made us cynical; our cleverness, hard and unkind. We think too much and feel too little. More than machinery we need humanity. More than cleverness, we need kindness and gentleness. Without these qualities, life will be violent and all will be lost.

The aeroplane and the radio have brought us closer together. The very nature of these things cries out for the goodness in man – cries out for universal brotherhood – for the unity of us all. Even now my voice is reaching millions throughout the world – millions of despairing men, women, and little children – victims of a system that makes men torture and imprison innocent people. To those who can hear me, I say: 'Do not despair.' The misery that has come upon us is but the passing of greed – the bitterness of men who fear the way of human progress. The hate of men will pass, and dictators die, and the power they took from the people will return to the people. And so long as men die, liberty will never perish.

Soldiers! Don't give yourselves to these brutes – who despise you – enslave you – who regiment your lives – tell you what to do – what to think and what to feel! Who drill you – diet you – treat you like cattle and use you as cannon fodder. Don't give yourselves to these unnatural men – machine men with machine minds and machine hearts! You are not machines! You are men! With the love of humanity in your hearts! Don't hate! Only the unloved hate – the unloved and the unnatural!

Soldiers! Don't fight for slavery! Fight for liberty! In the seventeenth chapter of St Luke, it is written that the kingdom of God is within man – not one man nor a group of men, but in all men! In you! You, the people, have the power – the power to create machines. The power to create happiness! You, the people, have the power to make this life free and beautiful – to make this life a wonderful adventure. Then – in the name of democracy – let us use that power – let us all unite. Let us fight for a new world – a decent world that will give men a chance to work – that will give youth a future and old age a security.

By the promise of these things, brutes have risen to power. But they lie! They do not fulfil that promise. They never will! Dictators free themselves but they enslave the people. Now let us fight to free the world – to do away with national barriers – to do away with greed, with hate and intolerance. Let us fight for a world of reason – a world where science and progress will lead to the happiness of us all. Soldiers, in the name of democracy, let us unite!

Hannah, can you hear me? Wherever you are, look up! Look up, Hannah! The clouds are lifting! The sun is breaking through! We are coming out of the darkness into the light! We are coming into a new world – a kindlier world, where men will rise above their greed, their hate and their brutality. Look up, Hannah! The soul of man has been given wings and at last he is beginning to fly. He is flying into the rainbow – into the light of hope. Look up, Hannah! Look up!

*

A week after the première I was invited to a luncheon given by Arthur Sulzberger, the owner of the *New York Times*. When I arrived, I was taken to the top floor of the *Times* building and ushered into a domestic suite, a drawing-room furnished with paintings, photographs and leather upholstery. Gracing the fireplace with his august presence was the ex-President of the United States, Mr Herbert Hoover, a towering man of saintly demeanour and small eyes.

'This, Mr President, is Charlie Chaplin,' said Mr Sulzberger, leading me up to the great man.

Mr Hoover's face smiled through many wrinkles. 'Oh yes,' he said, beamingly, 'we've met before many years ago.'

I was surprised that Mr Hoover should remember, because at the time he had seemed intensely preoccupied with grooming himself for the White House. He was attending a Press dinner at the Astor Hotel, and I had been brought in by one of the members as a side-dish, as it were, before Mr Hoover's speech. I was in the throes of being divorced and believe I mumbled something to the effect of knowing little about state affairs – in fact, knowing very little about my own affairs. After rambling on this way for a couple of minutes I sat down. Later, I was introduced to Mr Hoover. I think I said 'how do you do,' and that was about all.

He had spoken from a loose manuscript, about four inches high, lifting off page after page as he read. After an hour and a half, everyone watched those pages wistfully. After two hours the pages were evenly divided. Sometimes he skipped a dozen or more and laid them aside. Those, indeed, were gracious moments. As nothing is permanent in life the speech came to an end. As he gathered up his agenda in a most businesslike way, I smiled and was about to congratulate him on his speech, but he brushed by without noticing me.

And now, after many years, an interim in which he had been President, he was standing in front of the fireplace looking unusually genial. We sat down to lunch at a large round table, twelve of us. I was told that these lunches were exclusively inner sanctum affairs.

There is a type of American business executive that makes me feel inadequate. They are very tall, good-looking, immaculately dressed, unruffled, clear-thinking men with facts clearly before them. They have amplified metallic voices and speak in geometrical terms about human affairs, such as: 'The organizational processes occurring in the yearly unemployment pattern,' etc. Such were the types that sat around the table at lunch, looking formidable and most stalwart – like towering skyscrapers. The only human influence was Anne O'Hare McCormick, a brilliant and charming lady, the celebrated political columnist of the *New York Times*.

At lunch the atmosphere was formal and conversation was difficult. Everyone addressed Mr Hoover as 'Mr President', somewhat more than necessary I thought. As lunch went on I began to feel that it was not for nought that I had been invited. A moment later Mr Sulzberger left no doubt about it. During a propitious silence he said: 'Mr President, I wish you would explain to us your proposed mission to Europe.'

Mr Hoover put down his knife and fork, thoughtfully chewed, then swallowed and began to speak of what had been evidently occupying his mind throughout lunch. He talked into his plate and as he spoke threw furtive glances at Mr Sulzberger and at me. 'We are all aware of the deplorable state of Europe at the moment, of the misery and famine rapidly growing there since the war. The condition is so urgent that I have prevailed upon Washington that it should immediately relieve the situation.' (I assumed Washington meant President Roosevelt.) Here he enumerated the facts and figures and results of his last mission in the First World War, when 'we fed the whole of Europe'. 'Such a mission,' he continued, 'would be non-partisan, purely for humanitarian purposes – you're somewhat interested in that,' he said, throwing me a side-glance.

I nodded solemnly.

'When do you propose to launch this project, Mr President?' Mr Sulzberger asked.

'As soon as we can get Washington's approval,' said Mr Hoover. 'Washington needs urging by public demand and support of well-known public figures' – again another side-glance at me, and again I nodded. 'In occupied France,' he went on, 'there are millions in want. In Norway, Denmark, Holland, Belgium, all through Europe famine is growing!' He spoke eloquently, marshalling his facts and endowing them with faith, hope and charity.

Then came a silence. I cleared my throat. 'Of course, the situation is not exactly the same as in the First World War. France is completely occupied as well as many other countries – naturally we don't want this food to fall into the hands of the Nazis.'

Mr Hoover frowned slightly, and a slight stir went through the assembled group, all of whom looked across at Mr Hoover, then at me.

Mr Hoover frowned again into his plate. 'We would set up a non-partisan commission in cooperation with the American Red Cross and work through the Hague Agreement, under paragraph twenty-seven, section forty-three, which allows a Commission of Mercy to administer to the sick and needy of both sides, belligerent or not. I think you as a humanitarian will endorse such a commission.' This is not accurately what he said – only an impression of it.

I held my ground. 'I am whole-heartedly in agreement with the idea, providing the food does not get into the Nazis' hands,' I said.

This remark created another stir round the table.

'We did this sort of thing before.' said Mr Hoover with an air of nettled modesty. The towering skyline of young men now directed their attention to me. One of them smiled. 'I think Mr President can handle that situation,' he said.

'It's an excellent idea,' said Mr Sulzberger authoritatively.

'I quite agree,' I answered meekly, 'and would endorse it one hundred per cent, if the physical administration of it could be handled by Jews only!'

'Oh,' said Mr Hoover curtly, 'that wouldn't be possible.'

*

It was strange to listen to slick young Nazis along Fifth Avenue haranguing small gatherings from little mahogany pulpits. One spiel went as follows: 'The philosophy of Hitler is a profound and thoughtful study of the problems of this industrial age, in which there is little room for the middleman or the Jew.'

A woman interrupted. 'What kind of talk is that!' she exclaimed. 'This is America. Where do you think you are?'

The young man, an obsequious, good-looking type, smiled blandly. 'I'm in the United States and I happen to be an American citizen,' he said smoothly.

'Well,' she said, 'I'm an American citizen, and a Jew, and if I were a man I'd knock your block off!'

One or two endorsed the lady's threat, but most of them stood apathetically silent. A policeman standing by quietened the woman. I came away astonished, hardly believing my ears.

A day or so later I was at a country house and a pale, anaemic-looking young Frenchman, Count Chambrun, husband of Pierre Laval's daughter, pursued me continually before lunch. He had seen *The Great Dictator* the opening night in New York. Said he magnanimously: 'But of course, your point of view is not to be taken seriously.'

'After all, it's a comedy,' I answered.

Had I been aware of the bestial murders and tortures that went on in the Nazi concentration camps, I would not have been so polite. About fifty guests were present and we sat four at a table. He joined ours and tried to draw me into a political argument, but I told him I much preferred good food to politics. His conversation was such that I lifted my glass and said: 'I seem to be drinking in a lot of "Vichy".' I had no sooner said this than a violent altercation broke out at another table, and two women went at it hammer and tongs. It became so violent that I thought they would resort to hair-pulling. One shouted to

398

the other: 'I won't listen to that kind of talk. You're a goddam Nazi!'

A young New York scion asked me in a benign way why I was so anti-Nazi. I said because they were anti-people. 'Of course,' he said, as though making a sudden discovery, 'you're a Jew, aren't you?'

'One doesn't have to be a Jew to be anti-Nazi,' I answered. 'All one has to be is a normal decent human being.' And so the subject was dropped.

A day or so later I was to appear at the Hall of the Daughters of the American Revolution in Washington, to recite the last speech from *The Great Dictator* over the radio. Beforehand I was called to meet President Roosevelt, at whose request we had sent the film to the White House. When I was ushered into his private study, he greeted me saying: 'Sit down, Charlie; your picture is giving us a lot of trouble in the Argentine.' This was his only comment about it. A friend of mine later summed it up by saying: 'You were received at the White House, but not embraced.'

I sat with the President for forty minutes, during which he served me several dry martinis which I tossed down quickly from shyness. When it was time to leave, I literally reeled out of the White House – then suddenly remembered that at ten o'clock I was to speak over the radio. It was to be a national hook-up, which meant speaking to over sixty million people. After taking several cold showers and drinking strong black coffee, I had more or less pulled myself together.

The States had not entered the war yet, so there were plenty of Nazis in the hall that night. No sooner had I begun my speech than they began to cough. It was too loud to be natural. It made me nervous so that my mouth became dry and my tongue began sticking to the roof of my palate and I could not articulate. The speech was six minutes long. In the middle of it I stopped and said that I could not continue unless I had a drink of water. Of course, there was not a drop in the house; and here I was keeping sixty million listeners waiting. After an interminable two minutes I was handed water in a small paper envelope. Thus I was able to finish the speech.

# twenty-six

IT was inevitable that Paulette and I should separate. We both knew it long before *The Dictator* was started, and now that it was completed we were confronted with making a decision. Paulette left word that she was going back to California to work in another picture for Paramount, so I stayed on for a while and played around New York. Frank, my butler, telephoned that when she returned to the Beverly Hills house she did not stay but packed up her things and left. When I returned home to Beverly Hills she had gone to Mexico to get a divorce. It was a very sad house. The wrench naturally hurt, for it was hard cleaving eight years' association from one's life.

Although *The Great Dictator* was extremely popular with the American public, it no doubt created underground antagonism. The first inkling of this came from the Press on my return to Beverly Hills, an ominous gathering of men, over twenty of them, who sat in silence in our glassed-in porch. I offered tham a drink and they refused – this was unusual for members of the Press.

'What's on your mind, Charlie?' said one, who evidently spoke for all of them.

'A little publicity for *The Dictator*,' I said jokingly.

I told them of my interview with the President and remarked that my film was giving the American Embassy trouble in the Argentine, believing it a good story, but they still remained silent. Then after a pause, I said humorously: 'That didn't seem to go over so well, did it?'

'No, it didn't,' said the spokesman. 'Your public relations are not very good: you left here ignoring the Press, and we don't like it.'

Although I was never too popular with the local Press, his remark rather amazed me. As a matter of fact, I had left Hollywood without seeing them because I believed that those who were not too friendly might tear *The Great Dictator* to bits before it had a chance to be seen in New York. And I could not afford to take chances with a $2,000,000 investment. I told them that an anti-Nazi picture had powerful enemies, even in America, and that to give the picture a chance I had decided to have it previewed at the last moment, before its presentation to the audience.

But nothing I said affected their antagonistic attitude. The climate began to change and many snide items began to appear in the Press; mild attacks at first, stories about my stinginess, then ugly rumours about Paulette and me. But in spite of the adverse publicity *The Great Dictator* continued breaking records both in England and America.

\*

Although America was not yet at war, Roosevelt was waging a cold one with Hitler. This made it very difficult for the President, for the Nazis had made inroads into American institutions and organizations; whether these organizations were aware of it or not, they were being used as tools of the Nazis.

Then came the sudden and dramatic news that Japan had attacked Pearl Harbor. The severity of it stunned America. But she immediately girded herself for war, and before long many divisions of American soldiers were overseas. At this juncture the Russians were holding off Hitler's hordes outside Moscow, and were calling for an immediate second front. Roosevelt recommended it; and although the Nazi sympathizers had now gone underground, their poison was still in the air. Every device was used to divide us from our Russian allies. Vicious propaganda was rife at that time, saying: 'Let them both bleed white, then we'll come in at the kill' – every kind of subterfuge was used to prevent a second front. Anxious days followed. Each day we heard of Russia's appalling casualties. Days went by into weeks and weeks into many months and the Nazis were still outside Moscow.

At this moment I believe my troubles began. I received a telephone call from the head of the American Committee for

Russian war relief in San Francisco, asking if I would take the place of Mr Joseph E. Davies, the American Ambassador to Russia, who was to speak, but at the last moment had been attacked with laryngitis. Although I had only a few hours' notice, I accepted. The meeting was scheduled for the following day, so I caught the evening train which arrived in San Francisco at eight in the morning.

The committee had a social itinerary mapped out for me – a lunch here and a dinner there – which gave me little time to think of a speech, and I was to be the principal speaker. However, at dinner I drank a couple of glasses of champagne and that helped matters.

The hall held ten thousand and was packed. On the stage were American admirals and generals, and Mayor Rossi of San Francisco. The speeches were restrained and equivocating. Said the Mayor: 'We must live with the fact that the Russians are our allies.' He was cautious not to overstate the Russian emergency, or overpraise their valour, or mention the fact that they were fighting and dying to hold back nearly two hundred divisions of Nazis. Our allies were strange bed-fellows was the attitude I felt that evening.

The head of the committee had prevailed on me to speak for an hour if possible. This terrified me. At the most, four minutes was my limit. But after listening to such weak palaver my indignation was aroused. I made four topic notes on the back of my dinner place-card. Pacing up and down backstage in a state of nerves and fear, I waited to go on. Then I heard my introduction.

I was wearing a black tie and dinner jacket. There was applause which gave me a little time to collect myself. When it subsided I said one word: 'Comrades!' and the house went up in a roar of laughter. When it subsided, I said emphatically: 'And I mean comrades.' There was renewed laughter, then applause. I continued: 'I assume there are many Russians here tonight, and the way your countrymen are fighting and dying at this very moment, it is an honour and a privilege to call you comrades.' Through the applause many stood up.

Now I became inflamed, thinking of the expression 'Let them both bleed white.' I was going to express my indignation about it – but an inner prompting stopped me, and instead I said: 'I am not a Communist, I am a human being, and I think I know the reactions of human beings. The Communists are no different from anyone else; whether they lose an arm or a leg, they suffer as all of us do, and die as all of us die. And the Communist mother is the same as any other mother. When she receives the tragic news that her sons will not return, she weeps as other mothers weep. I don't have to be a Communist to know that. I have only to be a human being to know that. And at this moment Russian mothers are doing a lot of weeping and their sons a lot of dying. . . .'

I spoke for forty minutes, now knowing what was coming next. I made them laugh and applaud with anecdotes about Roosevelt and about my war-bond speech in the First World War – I could do no wrong.

I continued: 'And now this war – I am here on behalf of Russian war relief.' I paused and repeated: 'Russian war relief. Money will help, but they need more than money. I am told that the Allies have two million soldiers languishing in the North of Ireland, while the Russians alone are facing about two hundred divisions of Nazis.' There was intense silence. 'The Russians,' I said emphatically, 'are our allies, they are not only fighting for their way of life, but for our way of life and if I know Americans they like to do their *own* fighting. Stalin wants it, Roosevelt has called for it – so let's all call for it – let's open a second front now!'

There was a wild uproar that lasted for seven minutes. That thought had been in the heart and mind of the audience. They would not let me go any further, they kept stamping and applauding. And as they stamped and yelled and threw their hats in the air, I began to wonder if I had said too much and had gone too far. Then I grew furious with myself for having such pusillanimous thoughts in the face of those thousands who were fighting and dying. When at last the audience was quiet, I said: 'As you feel this way about it, will each and every one please send a telegram to the President? Let's hope that by tomorrow he will receive ten thousand requests for a second front!'

After the meeting I felt the atmosphere charge with tension and uneasiness. Dudley Field Malone, John Garfield and myself went somewhere for supper. 'You have a lot of courage,' said Garfield, referring to my speech. His remark was disturbing, for I did not wish to be valorous or caught up in a political *cause célèbre*. I had only spoken what I sincerely felt and thought was right. Nevertheless, after John's remark I began to feel a depressing pall over the rest of the evening. But whatever menacing clouds I expected as a result of that speech evaporated, and back in Beverly Hills life went on as usual.

A few weeks later I had another request to speak by telephone at a mass meeting in Madison Square. As it was for the same cause I accepted – why not? It was sponsored by the most respectable of people and organizations. I spoke for fourteen minutes, which speech the Council of the Congress of Industrial Organizations thought fit to publish. I was not alone in this effort, as the following booklet issued by the C.I.O. will disclose:

### THE SPEECH
#### 'ON THE BATTLEFIELDS OF RUSSIA DEMOCRACY WILL LIVE OR DIE'

The great crowd, previously warned not to interrupt with applause, hushed and strained for every word.

Thus they listened for fourteen minutes to Charles Chaplin, the great people's artist of America, as he spoke to them by telephone from Hollywood.

In the early evening of 22 July 1942, sixty thousand trade unionists, members of civic, fraternal, veteran, community and church organizations and others gathered at Madison Square Park in New York to rally in support of President Franklin D. Roosevelt for the immediate opening of a second front to hasten the final victory over Hitler and the Axis.

The sponsors of the great demonstration were the 250 unions affiliated with the Greater New York Industrial Union Council, C.I.O. Wendell L. Willkie, Philip Murray, Sidney Hillman and many other prominent Americans sent enthusiastic messages to the rally.

Bright skies favoured the occasion. The flags of the Allied Nations flanked Old Glory on the speakers' platform and placards with slogans of support for the President and slogans for opening the second front dotted the sea of people that choked the streets around the park.

Lucy Monroe led the singing of *The Star-Spangled Banner* to open the meeting and Jane Froman, Arlene Francis and several other popular stars of the American Theatre Wing entertained. United States

Senators James M. Mead and Claude Pepper, Mayor F. H. La Guardia, Lieutenant Governor Charles Poletti, Representative Vito Marcantonio, Michael Quill and Joseph Curran, president of the New York C.I.O. Council, were the main speakers.

Said Senator Mead: 'We shall win this war only when we have enlisted the vast masses of people in Asia, in conquered Europe, in Africa, wholeheartedly and enthusiastically in the struggle for freedom.' And Senator Pepper: 'He who hampers our efforts, who cries for restraint, is an enemy of the Republic.' And Joseph Curran: 'We have the men. We have the materials. We know the one way to win – and that is to open a second front now.'

The massed crowd cheered with united voice every mention of the President, of the second front and of our heroic allies, the courageous fighters and people of the Soviet Union, Britain and China. Then came the address of Charles Chaplin via long-distance telephone.

### TO SUPPORT THE PRESIDENT'S RALLY
### FOR A SECOND FRONT NOW!
#### *Madison Square Park, July 22 1942*

'On the battlefields of Russia democracy will live or die. The fate of the Allied nations is in the hands of the Communists. If Russia is defeated the Asiatic continent – the largest and richest of this globe – would be under the domination of the Nazis. With practically the whole Orient in the hands of the Japanese the Nazis would then have access to nearly all the vital war materials of the world. What chance would we have then of defeating Hitler?

'With the difficulty of transportation, the problem of our communication lines thousands of miles away, the problem of steel, oil and rubber – and Hitler's strategy of divide and conquer – we would be in a desperate position if Russia should be defeated.

'Some people say it would prolong the war ten or twenty years. In my estimation this is putting it optimistically. Under such conditions and against such a formidable enemy the future would be very uncertain.

#### WHAT ARE WE WAITING FOR?

'Russians are in desperate need of help. They are pleading for a second front. Among the Allied nations there is a difference of opinion as to whether a second front is possible now. We hear that the Allies haven't sufficient supplies to support a second front. Then again we hear they have. We also hear that they don't want to risk a second front at this time in case of possible defeat. That they don't want to take a chance until they are sure and ready.

'But can we afford to wait until we are sure and ready? Can we afford to play safe? There is no safe strategy in war. At this moment the Germans are 35 miles from the Caucasus. If the Caucasus is lost 95 per cent of the Russian oil is lost. When tens of thousands are dying and millions are about to die we must speak honestly what's in our minds. The people are asking themselves questions. We hear of great expeditionary forces landing in Ireland, 95 per cent of our convoys successfully arriving in Europe, two million Englishmen fully equipped, raring to go. What are we waiting for when the situation is so desperate in Russia?

### WE CAN TAKE IT

'Note, official Washington and official London, these are not questions to create dissensions. We ask them in order to dispel confusion and to engender confidence and unity for eventual victory. And whatever the answer is we can take it.

'Russia is fighting with her back against the wall. That wall is the Allies' strongest defence. We defended Libya and lost. We defended Crete and lost. We defended the Philippines and other islands in the Pacific and lost. But we cannot afford to lose Russia, for that is the aggressive front line of democracy. When our world – our life – our civilization are crumbling about our feet, we've got to take a chance.

'If the Russians lose the Caucasus it will be the greatest disaster of the Allied cause. Then watch out for the appeasers, for they'll come out of their holes. They will want to make peace with a victorious Hitler. They will say: "It's useless to sacrifice any more American lives – we can make 'a good deal' with Hitler."

### BEWARE OF THE NAZI SNARE

'Watch out for this Nazi snare. These Nazi wolves will change into sheep's clothing. They will make peace very attractive to us and then before we are aware of it we will have succumbed to the Nazi ideology. Then we shall be enslaved. They will take away our liberty and control our minds. The world will be ruled by the Gestapo. They will rule us from the air. Yes, that's the power of the future.

'With the power of the skies in Nazi hands all opposition to the Nazi order will be blasted out of existence. Human progress will be lost. There will be no minority rights, no workers' rights, no citizens' rights. All that will be blasted too. Once we listen to the appeasers and make peace with a victorious Hitler his brutal order will control the earth.

### WE CAN TAKE A CHANCE

'Watch out for the appeasers who always crop up after a disaster.

'If we are on the watch and if we keep up our morale we have nothing to fear. Remember, morale saved England. And if we keep our morale, victory is assured.

'Hitler has taken many chances. His biggest one is the Russian campaign. God help him if he's not able to break through the Caucasus this summer. God help him if he has to go through another winter around Moscow. His chance is a precarious one, but he's taken it. If Hitler can take chances, can't we? Give us action. Give us more bombs over Berlin. Give us those Glenn Martin seaplanes to help our transport problem. Above all, give us a second front now.

### VICTORY IN THE SPRING

'Let us aim for victory in the spring. You in the factories, you in the fields, you in uniforms, you citizens of the world, let us work and fight towards that end. You, official Washington, and you, official London, let us make this our aim – victory in the spring.

'If we hold this thought, work with this thought, live with this thought, it will generate a spirit that will increase our energy and quicken our drive.

'Let us strive for the impossible. Remember the great achievements throughout history have been the conquest of what seemed the impossible.'

\*

For the time being my days were halcyon. But it was the calm before the storm. The circumstances that led up to this weird story started innocently enough. It was Sunday and after a game of tennis Tim Durant told me that he had a date with a young woman named Joan Barry, a friend of Paul Getty; she had just returned from Mexico City with a letter of introduction from a friend, A. C. Blumenthal. Tim said he was dining with her and another girl, and asked if I would like to come along as Miss Barry had expressed a desire to meet me. We met at Perino's restaurant. The lady in question was pleasant and cheerful enough and the four of us spent an innocuous evening together and I never thought of seeing her again.

But the following Sunday, which was open house for tennis, Tim brought her along. On Sunday evenings I always let the personnel go off and dined out, so I invited Tim and Miss Barry to dine at Romanoff's and after dinner I drove them home. The following morning, however, she called up and wanted to know if I would take her to lunch. I told her I was attending an auction in Santa Barbara, ninety miles away, and that if she had nothing else to do she could come along and we would lunch there and go to the auction later. After buying one or two things I drove her back to Los Angeles.

Miss Barry was a big handsome woman of twenty-two, well built, with upper regional domes immensely expansive and made alluring by an extremely low décolleté summer dress, which, on the drive home, evoked my libidinous curiosity. It was then she told me that she had quarrelled with Paul Getty and that she was returning to New York the following night, but that if I wanted her to stay she would do so and give up everything. I reared away in suspicion, for there was something too sudden, too odd, about the proposal. I told her quite frankly not to remain on my account, and with that I dropped her off outside her apartment and bade her good-bye.

To my surprise she phoned up a day or so later to say she was staying over in any case, and would I see her that evening. Persistence is the road to accomplishment. Thus she achieved her object and I began to see her often. The days that followed were not unpleasant, but there was something queer and not quite normal about them. Without telephoning she would suddenly show up late at night at my house. This was somewhat disturbing. Then for a week I would not hear from her. Although I would not admit it, I was beginning to feel uneasy. However, when she did show up she was disarmingly pleasant, so my doubts and apprehensions were allayed.

One day I lunched with Sir Cedric Hardwicke and Sinclair Lewis, who, during conversation, commented on the play *Shadow and Substance*, which Cedric had starred in. Lewis called the character of Bridget a modern Joan of Arc, and thought the play would make an excellent film. I became interested and told Cedric I would like to read it. He sent me a copy.

A night or so later Joan Barry came to dinner, and I talked about the play. She said she had seen it and would like to play the girl. I did not take her seriously, but that evening she read the part to me, and to my astonishment gave an excellent reading, even to the Irish accent. I was so enthused that I took a silent test of her to see if she were photogenic, and it turned out satisfactorily.

Now all my qualms about her oddities vanished. In fact, I thought I had made a discovery. I sent her to Max Reinhardt's school of acting as she needed technical training, and since she was busy there, I seldom saw her. I had not yet bought the rights of the play, so I got in touch with Cedric, and through his kind help the film rights were purchased for $25,000. I then put Barry under contract at a salary of $250 a week.

There are mystics who believe that our existence is a half-dream and that it is difficult to know where the dream ends and reality begins. Thus it was with me. For months I was absorbed in writing the script. Then strange and eerie things began to happen. Barry began driving up in her Cadillac at all hours of the night, very drunk, and I would have to awaken my chauffeur to drive her home. One time she smashed up her car in the driveway and had to leave it there. As her name was now associated with the Chaplin Studios, I became worried that if she were picked up by the police for drunken driving, it would create a scandal. Finally she got so obstreperous that when she called in the small hours I would neither answer the phone nor open the door to her. Then she began smashing in the windows. Overnight, my existence became a nightmare.

Then I discovered that she had been absent from the Reinhardt school for several weeks. When I confronted her about it, she suddenly announced that she did not want to be an actress, and that if I would pay her and her mother's fare back to New York and give her $5,000, she would tear up the contract. At this juncture I happily agreed to her demands, paid their fare and the $5,000, and was glad to be rid of her.

Although the Barry enterprise had caved in, I was not sorry that I had bought _Shadow and Substance_, for I had almost completed the script and thought it a very good one.

Since the San Francisco meeting months had elapsed and the Russians were still calling for a second front. Now another request came from New York, asking me to speak at Carnegie Hall. I debated with myself whether I should go or not, and concluded that I had started the ball rolling and that was enough. But a day later when Jack Warner was playing on my tennis court, I spoke about it and he shook his head cryptically. 'Don't go,' he said.

'Why not?' I asked.

He would not say, but added: 'Let me tip you off, don't go.' This had the opposite effect. It was a challenge. At that moment it needed very little eloquence to ignite the sympathy of all America for a second front, for Russia had just won the battle of Stalingrad. So I went, taking Tim Durant with me.

At the Carnegie Hall meeting, Pearl Buck, Rockwell Kent, Orson Welles and many other illustrious people were present. Orson Welles was to speak on that occasion, but as the opposition storm grew, he charted his craft very close to shore, I thought. He spoke before me, stating that he saw no reason why he should not speak, since it was for Russian war relief and the Russians were our allies. His speech was a meal without salt. This made me all the more determined to speak my mind. In my opening words I referred to a columnist who had accused me of wanting to run the war, and I said: 'From the raging fits he is having I should say he is jealous, and wants to run the war himself. The trouble is we disagree on strategy – he doesn't believe in a second front at this moment, but I do!'

'The meeting was a love feast between Charlie and the audience,' wrote the *Daily Worker*. But my emotions were mixed; although gratified, I was apprehensive.

After leaving Carnegie Hall, Tim and I had supper with Constance Collier, who had been present at the meeting. She was very moved by it – and Constance was anything but a leftist. When we reached the Waldorf-Astoria there were several telephone messages from Joan Barry. My flesh began to creep. I tore them up immediately, but the telephone rang again. I wanted to instruct the operator not to put any more calls through, but Tim said: 'You'd better not, you'd better answer or she'll be up here and create a scene.'

The next time the phone rang I answered. She seemed quite normal and pleasant and said she just wanted to come up and say hello. So I acquiesced and told Tim not to leave me alone with her. That evening she told me that since her arrival in New York she had been living at the Pierre Hotel, owned by Paul Getty. I lied and told her that we were staying for one or two days and that I would try and fit in a lunch somewhere. She stayed half an hour and asked if I would see her home to the

Pierre Hotel. When she insisted that I see her to the elevator, I became suspicious. However, I left her at the entrance and that was the first and last time I saw her in New York.

As a result of my second front speeches my social life in New York gradually receded. No more was I invited to spend weekends in opulent country houses. After the Carnegie Hall meeting Clifton Fadiman, writer and essayist, who was working for Columbia Broadcasting System, called at the hotel to ask me if I would care to broadcast internationally. They would give me seven minutes to say what I liked. I was tempted to accept until he mentioned that it would be on the Kate Smith programme. Then I refused on the grounds that my convictions about the war effort would end in an advertisement for Jello. I meant no offence to Fadiman. He is a gentle soul, gifted and cultured, and at the mention of Jello he actually blushed. I was immediately sorry and could have swallowed my words.

After that, a considerable number of letters came with offers of all kinds. One from the prominent 'America Firster', Gerald K. Smith, who wanted to debate with me on that subject. Other offers were to lecture, other to speak on behalf of the second front.

Now I felt I was caught up in a political avalanche. I began to question my motives: how much was I stimulated by the actor in me and the reaction of a live audience? Would I have entered this quixotic adventure if I had not made an anti-Nazi film? Was it a sublimation of all my irritations and reactions against the talking pictures? I suppose all these elements were involved, but the strongest one was my hate and contempt for the Nazi system.

# *twenty-seven*

BACK in Beverly Hills, while I was working on *Shadow and Substance* again, Orson Welles came to the house with a proposition, explaining that he thought of doing a series of documentaries, stories of real life, one to be on the celebrated French murderer, Bluebeard Landru, which he thought would be a wonderful dramatic part for me.

I was interested, as it would be a change from comedy, and a change from writing, acting and directing myself as I had done for years. So I asked to see the script.

'Oh, it isn't written yet,' he said, 'but all that's necessary is to take the records of the Landru trial and you'll have it.' He added: 'I thought you might like to help with the writing of it.'

I was disappointed. 'If I have to help in writing the script, I'm not interested,' I said, and the matter ended there.

But a day or so later it struck me that the idea of Landru would make a wonderful comedy. So I telephoned Welles. 'Look, your proposed documentary about Landru has given me an idea for a comedy. It has nothing to do with Landru, but to clear everything I am willing to pay you five thousand dollars, only because your proposition made me think of it.'

He hemmed and hawed.

'Listen, Landru is not an original story with you or anyone else,' I said; 'it is in the public domain.'

He thought a moment, then told me to get in touch with his manager. Thus a deal was negotiated: Welles to get $5,000 and I to be clear of all obligations. Welles accepted but asked for one provision: that after seeing the picture he could have the privilege of screen credit, to read: 'Idea suggested by Orson Welles.' I thought little of the request because of my enthusiasm. Had I foreseen the kudos he eventually tried to make out of it, I would have insisted on no screen credit at all.

Now I put aside *Shadow and Substance* and began writing *Monsieur Verdoux*. I had been working three months on it when Joan Barry blew into Beverly Hills, my butler informing me that she had telephoned. I said that under no circumstances would I see her.

The events that followed were not only sordid but sinister. Because I would not see her, she broke into the house, smashed windows, threatened my life and demanded money. Eventually I was compelled to call the police, something I should have done long before, in spite of it being a gala opportunity for the Press. But the police were most cooperative. They said they would withhold the charges of vagrancy against her if I were willing to pay her fare back to New York. So again I paid her fare, and the police warned her that if she were seen in the vicinity of Beverly Hills again she would be charged with vagrancy.

*

It seems a pity that after this sordid episode the happiest event of my life should follow contiguously, one might say. But shadows disappear into night and out of the dawn the sun rises.

One day, a few months later, Miss Mina Wallace, a Hollywood film agent, telephoned to say that she had a client just out from New York who, she thought, might fit the part of Bridget, the principal lead in *Shadow and Substance*. Having had trouble with *Monsieur Verdoux* because it was a difficult story to motivate, I took Miss Wallace's message as a lucky omen for reconsidering the filming of *Shadow and Substance*, and for temporarily putting aside *Monsieur Verdoux*. So I telephoned to find out more particulars. Miss Wallace said that her client was Oona O'Neill, daughter of the famous playwright Eugene O'Neill. I had never met Eugene O'Neill, but from the solemnity of his plays I had rather a sepia impression of what the daughter would be like. So I asked Miss Wallace laconically: 'Can she act?'

'She's had a little theatrical experience in summer stock in the East. You'd better take a film test of her and find out for yourself,' she said. 'Or better still, if you don't wish to commit yourself, come to my house for dinner and I'll have her there.'

I arrived early and on entering the sitting-room discovered a young lady seated alone by the fire. While waiting for Miss Wallace, I introduced myself, saying I presumed she was Miss O'Neill. She smiled. Contrary to my preconceived impression, I became aware of a luminous beauty, with a sequestered charm and a gentleness that was most appealing. While we waited for our hostess, we sat and talked.

Eventually Miss Wallace came in and we were formally introduced. There were four of us for dinner – Miss Wallace, Miss O'Neill, Tim Durant and myself. Although we did not talk business, we skirted around it. I mentioned that the girl in *Shadow and Substance* was very young, and Miss Wallace dropped the remark that Miss O'Neill was a little over seventeen. My heart sank. Although the part called for someone young, the character was extremely complex and would require an older and more experienced actress. So I reluctantly put her out of my mind.

But a few days later Miss Wallace telephoned to know if I was doing anything about Miss O'Neill, as the Fox film company was interested. It was then and there that I signed her up. This was the beginning of what was destined to be over twenty years of complete happiness – and I hope many more.

As I got to know Oona I was constantly surprised by her sense of humour and tolerance; she could always see the other person's point of view. This and multitudinous other reasons were why I fell in love with her. She had by now just turned eighteen; but I was confident that she was not subject to the caprices of that age. Oona was the exception to the rule – though at first I was afraid of the discrepancy in our ages. But Oona was resolute as though she had come upon a truth. So we decided to marry after completing the filming of *Shadow and Substance*.

I had completed the first draft of the script and was now preparing to go into production. If I could get on film that rare quality of charm Oona had, *Shadow and Substance* would be a success.

At this juncture, Barry again blew into town, and blithely announced to the butler over the telephone that she was destitute and three months pregnant, but made no accusation or hint as to who was responsible. It was certainly no concern of mine, so I told the butler if she started any skylarking around the house, scandal or no scandal, I would call the police. But the next day she showed up bright and cheerful and walked around the house and garden several times. Obviously she was following a planned procedure. It was disclosed later that she had gone to one of the sob sisters of the Press, who advised her to return to the house and get herself arrested. I spoke to her personally, warning her that if she did not leave the premises I would have to call the police. But she only laughed. Having come to the limit of enduring this blackmailing harassment, I told the butler to telephone the police.

A few hours later the newspapers were black with headlines. I was pilloried, excoriated and vilified: Chaplin, the father of her unborn child, had had her arrested, had left her destitute. A week later a paternity suit was brought against me. As a result of these accusations I called up Lloyd Wright, my lawyer, and told him that I had had nothing to do with the Barry woman in two years.

Knowing my intentions of going into production with *Shadow and Substance*, he discreetly suggested that I should put if off for the time being and that Oona should return to New York. But we would not consider this advice. Nor would we be governed by the lies of the Barry woman nor the headlines of the Press. As Oona and I had already talked of getting married, we decided to do so then and there. My friend Harry Crocker made all the preliminary arrangements. Now he was working for Hearst and promised to take only a few pictures of the wedding, explaining that it would be better to let Hearst have the exclusive story and Louella Parsons, a friend, write it up than subject ourselves to the belligerence of other newspapers.

We were married at Carpinteria, a quiet little village fifteen miles outside Santa Barbara. But before we could obtain the licence, we had to register at the Santa Barbara town hall. It was eight o'clock in the morning and little life was stirring in the town at that hour. The register clerk, if one of the couples happens to be celebrated, usually notifies the newspapers by pressing a secret button under the desk. So in order to avoid a photo festival Harry arranged that I should wait outside the office until Oona had registered. After taking down the usual details, her name and age, the clerk said: 'Now where's the young man?'

When I appeared he took it big. 'Well, this is a surprise!' And Harry saw his hand disappear under the counter. But we hurried him up, and after stalling as long as he could he reluctantly gave us the licence. Just as we left the building and were entering our car the Press drove into the courtyard. From then on it was a race for life, driving in the early morning through the deserted streets of Santa Barbara, skidding and screeching then turning suddenly into one by-street and up another. In this way we evaded them and arrived in Carpinteria, where Oona and I were quietly married.

We leased a house for two months in Santa Barbara. And in spite of the paroxysms of the Press, we spent a peaceful existence there, for they did not know where we were – although every time the door-bell rang we would jump.

In the evening we would go for quiet walks in the country, careful not to be seen or recognized. Occasionally I would sink into a deep depression, feeling that I had the acrimony and the hate of a whole nation upon me and that my film career was lost. At such times Oona would lift me out of this mood by reading *Trilby* to me, which is very Victorian and laughable, especially when the author goes on for pages of explanations and excuses for Trilby's continual generosity in giving away her virtue. This Oona would read curled up in an armchair before a log fire. In spite of an occasional depression those two months in Santa Barbara were poignantly romantic, motivated by bliss, anxiety and despair.

*

When we returned to Los Angeles, disturbing news came from my friend Justice Murphy of the United State Supreme Court, who informed me that at a dinner of influential politicians one of them had remarked that they were out 'to get Chaplin'. 'If you get into trouble,' wrote Justice Murphy, 'you will do better to get a small, unimportant lawyer and not an expensive one.'

It was some time, however, before the Federal Government got into action. They were supported by a unanimous Press, in whose eyes I was the blackest of villains.

In the meantime we were preparing for the paternity suit, which was a civil case and had nothing to do with the Federal Government. For the paternity suit Lloyd Wright suggested a blood-test which, if in my favour, would be absolute proof of my not being the father of the Barry child. Later he came with the news that he had reached an agreement with her lawyer. The terms were that if we gave Joan Barry $25,000 she and her child would submit to a blood-test, and if the test proved that I could not be the father, she would drop the paternity suit. I leaped at the offer. But it was a fourteen-to-one chance against me because so many people have the same blood type. He explained that if in the blood type of the child there was a type that was neither the mother's nor the accused father's, then that blood type must come from the blood of a third person.

After the Barry child was born, the Federal Government started a grand jury investigation, questioning Barry with the intention of indicting me – on what grounds I could not possibly imagine. Friends advised me to call up Giesler, the well-known criminal lawyer, and against Justice Murphy's advice I did so. This was a mistake, for it looked as though I were in serious trouble. Lloyd Wright had arranged a meeting with Giesler to discuss on what grounds the grand jury could bring an indictment. Both lawyers had heard that the Government wanted to prove the violation of the Mann Act.

Every once in a while the Federal Government used this bit of legal blackmail to discredit a political opponent. The original intention of the Mann Act was to prohibit the transporting of women from one state to another for prostitution. After the abolition of the red-light district there was little legitimate use for it, but it is still used to victimize citizens. Should a man accompany his divorced wife over the border to another state, and should he have intercourse with her, he has committed an offence against the Mann Act and is liable to five years in prison. It was this bogus piece of legal opportunism upon which the United States Government brought an indictment against me.

Besides this incredible charge, the Government was concocting another, which was based on an obsolete legal technicality so fantastic that eventually they dropped it. Wright and Giesler agreed that both charges were absurd and saw no difficulty in winning the case if I were indicted.

And now the grand jury investigation was on. I felt confident that the whole thing would collapse: after all, the Barry woman had, I understood, travelled to and from New York with her mother. A few days later, however, Giesler called me up. 'Charlie, you've been indicted on all counts,' he said. 'We will get the bill of particulars later. I will let you know the dates of the preliminary hearing.'

The following weeks were like a Kafka story. I found myself engrossed in the all-absorbing enterprise of fighting for my liberty. If convicted on all counts, I would be facing twenty years' imprisonment.

After the preliminary hearing in court, photographers and Press had a field day. They barged into the Federal Marshal's office over my protestations and photographed me while I was being fingerprinted.

'Have they a right to do this?' I asked.

'No,' said the Marshal, 'but you can't control these fellows.' This was an official of the Federal Government talking.

Now the Barry child was old enough to take a blood-test. A clinic was chosen by mutual agreement of her lawyer and mine, and Barry, her child and I submitted to the test.

Later my lawyer called up, his voice vibrant. 'Charlie, you are exonerated! The blood-test proves that you cannot be the father!'

'This,' I said emotionally, 'is retribution!'

The news created a momentary sensation in the Press. Said one newspaper: 'Charles Chaplin exonerated.' Said another: 'Blood-test definitely proves Chaplin not to be father!'

Although the result of the blood-test embarrassed the Federal Government it continued to pursue the case. As it drew near I was obliged to spend long dreary evenings at Giesler's house, going over every depressing detail of how and when I had met Joan Barry. An important letter came from a Catholic priest living in San Francisco, stating that he had information that Barry was being used by a fascist organization, and that he would be willing to come from San Francisco to Los Angeles to give evidence to that effect. But Giesler dismissed the matter as irrelevant.

We also had plenty of damaging evidence concerning Barry's character and her past. On these angles we had been working for several weeks, when one night, to my surprise, Giesler suddenly announced that attacking her character was old stuff, and although successful in the Errol Flynn trial, it would not be necessary here. 'We can win this case easily without using all this crap,' he said. It might be crap to Giesler, but the evidence we had of her background was very important to me.

I also had letters from Barry apologizing for all the trouble she had caused me and thanking me for all my kindness and generosity. These letters I wanted in evidence because they would have refuted the vicious stories of the Press. For that reason I was happy that the scandal had come to a head, for now the Press would have to print the truth and I would be exonerated at least in the eyes of the American public – so I thought.

At this point I must mention a word about Edgar Hoover and his F.B.I. organization, because, this being a Federal case, the F.B.I. was very much involved in trying to get evidence for the prosecuting attorney. I had met Hoover at dinner many years ago. After one has overcome a rather brutal face and broken nose, one finds him quite agreeable. On that occasion he spoke to me enthusiastically about attracting a fine type of man into his service, including law students.

And now a few nights after my indictment Edgar Hoover was in Chasen's Restaurant, sitting three tables away from Oona and me with his F.B.I. men. At the same table was Tippy Gray, whom I had seen sporadically about Hollywood since 1918. He would appear at Hollywood parties, a negative, easy-going type with a perpetual vacuous grin that rather irritated me. I took it for granted that he was a playboy or a small-bit man in films. Now I wondered what he was doing at Hoover's table. As Oona and I got up to leave, I turned just as Tippy Gray turned, and for a second our glances met. He grinned non-committally. Then I suddenly understood the invaluable use of that grin.

At last the day of the trial came. Giesler told me to meet him outside the Federal building punctually at ten minutes to ten so that we could walk into court together.

The courtroom was on the second floor. When we entered it our appearance made little stir – in fact members of the Press now ignored me. They would get plenty of material from the trial itself, I supposed. Giesler parked me in a chair, then circulated about the courtroom talking to several people. It seemed everyone's party but mine.

I looked at the Federal Attorney. He was reading papers, making entries, talking and laughing confidently with several men. Tippy Gray was there, and every once in a while he would cast a furtive glance at me, and grin non-committally.

Giesler had left paper and pencil on the table to make notes during the trial, so in order not to just sit and stare I began drawing. Immediately Giesler hurried over. 'Don't doodle!' he whispered, snatching the paper from me and tearing it up. 'If the Press get hold of it, they'll have it analysed and draw all sorts of conclusions from it.' I had drawn a little sketch of a river and a rustic bridge; something I used to draw as a child.

Eventually the tension in the courtroom tightened and everyone was in his place. The clerk then banged three times with his gavel and we were off. There were four counts against me: two for the Mann Act and two for some obsolete law that no one had ever heard of since the Civil War, to the effect that I had interfered with the rights of a citizen. First Giesler tried to have the whole indictment dismissed. But that was mere formality; there was as much chance of achieving that as of dismissing an audience from a circus after it had paid admission.

It took two days to select a jury; there was a panel of twenty-four to choose from, each side having the right to object to six of them in order to select a jury of twelve. Members of the jury are interrogated and under terrific scrutiny from both sides. The procedure is that the judge and the attorneys question a juror as to his qualifications for judging the case without bias, with such questions as: has he read the papers, has he been influenced by them or acquired any prejudice as a result of reading them, and does he know any person connected with the case? This was a cynical procedure, I thought, since ninety per cent of the Press had been piling up antagonism against me for fourteen months. The questioning of a potential juror takes about half an hour, in which time both prosecution and defence attorneys send their investigators scurrying to get information about him. As each potential juror was called, Giesler made notes and slipped them to his investigators, who immediately disappeared. Ten minutes later the investigator would return and slip Giesler a note with the information: 'John Dokes, clerk in haberdashery store, wife, two children, never goes to movies.' 'We'll keep him for a while,' whispered Giesler. And so the selecting went on, each side dismissing or accepting a juryman, the Federal Attorney conferring in whispers with his investigators; every once in a while Tippy Gray would look over at me with his usual smile.

After eight of the jury had been chosen, a woman entered the jury-box. Immediately Giesler said: 'I don't like her.' He kept repeating: 'I don't like her – there's something about her I don't like.' As she was still being questioned Giesler's investigator handed him a note. 'Just as I thought,' he whispered after reading it; 'she has been a reporter on the Los Angeles *Times!* We must get rid of her! Besides, the other side accepted her too quickly.' I tried to study her face, but I could not see very well, so I reached for my glasses. Giesler quickly grabbed my arm. 'Don't put on your glasses,' he whispered. I got the impression that she was immersed in herself, but without my glasses it was all indistinct. 'Unfortunately,' said Giesler, 'we have only two objections left, so we had better hold her for the time being.' But as the selecting went on he had to use up our last two objections on two who were obviously prejudiced against me, and he was forced to accept the lady reporter.

Listening to the legal abracadabra of both attorneys, it seemed to me a game they were playing and that I had little to do with it. And in spite of the absurdity of the charges there lurked in the back of my mind the possibility that I might be railroaded – but I could never quite believe it. And occasionally I had a thought about the future of my career, but now that was chaotic, remote. I put it out of my mind – I could think of only one thing at a time.

As with all trouble, one cannot be consistently serious about it. I remember at one time the court was having a recess to discuss a legal point. The jury had left, the attorneys and judge had retired to an ante-chamber, while the audience, a photographer and I were left in the courtroom. He was waiting to catch me in an off-beat pose. As I put on my glasses to read, he snatched up his camera and I snatched off my glasses. This got a laugh from those left in the courtroom. When he put down his camera, I put on my glasses again. It was a game of cat and mouse, played good-naturedly, he snatching up his camera and I snatching off my glasses – and the audience enjoyed it. When the court reassembled, of course, I took them off and assumed my serious demeanour.

The trial went on for several days. Because it was a Federal case, Mr Paul Getty, Joan Barry's friend, was forced to appear as a witness, as well as two young Germans and others. Paul Getty had to admit to his friendship with Joan Barry in the past and that he had also given her money. But what was important were those letters she had written to me, apologizing for all the trouble she had caused and thanking me for my kindness and generosity. Although Giesler tried to put these letters in as evidence, the court objected. But I did not think Giesler was insistent enough.

Evidence came out in the trial that on one of the nights before she broke into my house, she actually slept all night in the apartment of a young German, who on the witness stand was forced to admit it.

Being the centre of all these sordid facts was like being put into public stocks. But the moment I left the courtroom all was forgotten and after a quiet dinner with Oona I would fall into bed exhausted.

Besides the tension and worry of the trial, there was the boring routine of getting up at seven in the morning, then having to leave immediately after breakfast because it was an hour's drive through Los Angeles traffic, and to be strictly on time, ten minutes before the court opened.

At last the trial came to an end. Each attorney agreed to two and a half hours in summing up. I had not the faintest idea what they could talk about for all that time. To me it was all clear, cut and dried: the government case had collapsed. And of course the possibility of facing twenty years if I were found guilty on all counts never entered my mind. The judge's summing-up I thought could have been less vague. I tried to see what impression it was making on the lady of the *Times*, but her face was averted. When the jury was sent out to deliberate she filed out of court, looking neither right nor left.

As we left the courtroom Giesler whispered discreetly: 'Today we can't leave the building until a verdict is given, but,' he added optimistically, 'we can sit outside on the balustrade and get a little sun.' This subtle information gave me a feeling of a sinister omnipresence quietly tightening its grip around me, reminding me that for the moment I was the property of the law.

It was now half past one and I surmised that a verdict should be reached within twenty minutes at the most. So I thought I would wait before telephoning Oona. But an hour elapsed! I telephoned her that the jury were still out and that as soon as I heard the verdict I would let her know.

Another hour passed and still no verdict! What was causing the delay? It should not have taken them more than ten minutes – they could only arrive at a not-guilty verdict. In the meantime Giesler and I sat outside on the stone balustrade, neither one of us commenting on what was causing the delay, until Giesler was compelled to look at his watch. 'Four o'clock,' he said casually. 'I wonder what's holding them up?' This brought us to a calm open discussion as to what possible points in the case could have delayed them. . . .

At a quarter to five the bell rang to announce that the jury had reached a verdict. My heart gave a leap, and as we entered the building Giesler hastily whispered: 'Whatever the verdict is, don't show any emotion.' Passing us, racing up the stairs to the courtroom, breathless and excited, was the prosecuting attorney with his assistants cheerfully racing up after him. Tippy Gray was the last, and as he passed us he glanced grinningly over his shoulder.

The courtroom filled quickly and was packed with tension. For some reason I was calmly composed although my heart was thumping in my throat.

The clerk of the court hammered three taps, which signalled the judge's entrance, and we all stood up. When everyone was settled again, the jury entered, and the foreman handed a document to the clerk of the court. Giesler sat with his head down, staring at his feet, muttering nervously under his breath: 'If it's guilty, it will be the worst miscarriage of justice I have ever

423

known!' and kept repeating. 'This will be the worst miscarriage of justice I have ever known!'

The clerk of the court now read the document, then tapped with the gavel three times. In the intense silence he announced:

'Charles Chaplin, Case 337068 Criminal . . . On the first count –' (there was a long pause) 'not guilty!'

A sudden scream came from the audience, then a sudden silence as they waited for the clerk to continue. 'On the second count . . . not guilty!'

The audience broke into a pandemonium. I never knew I had so many friends – some broke through the partition rail and hugged and kissed me. I caught a glimpse of Tippy Gray. The grin had left his face and he wore a blank expression.

Then the judge addressed a few words to me: 'Mr Chaplin, your presence will no longer be required in the court; you are now free.' Then he offered me his hand from the bench and congratulated me, so did the prosecuting attorney. Then Giesler whispered: 'Now go over and shake hands with the jury.'

As I approached them, the lady whom Giesler had mistrusted stood up and extended her hand, and for the first time I got a close look at her face. It was beautiful, glowing with intelligence and understanding. As we shook hands she said, smilingly: 'It's all right, Charlie. It's still a free country.'

I could not trust myself to speak; her words had shattered me. I could only nod and smile as she continued: 'I could see you from the window of the jury-room pacing up and down, and I so wanted to tell you not to worry. But for one person we would have come to a decision in ten minutes.'

It was difficult not to weep at her words, but I just grinned and thanked her, then turned to thank the rest. All of them shook hands heartily but one woman, who held a look of hate. I was about to move away when the foreman's voice said: 'Come on, old girl, loosen up and shake hands!' Reluctantly she did so and I thanked her coldly.

Oona, who was four months pregnant, was sitting at home on the lawn. She was alone and when she heard the news over the radio she fainted.

We dined quietly at home that evening, just Oona and I. We

424

wanted no newspapers, no telephone calls. I did not want to see or speak to anyone. I felt empty, hurt and denuded of character. Even the presence of the household staff was embarrassing.

After dinner Oona made a stiff gin and tonic and we sat together by the fire and I told her the reason for the delayed verdict and about the lady saying that it was still a free country. After so many weeks of tension there was an anti-climax. That night I reeled off to bed with the happy thought of not having to get up early in the morning to attend court.

A day or so later, Lion Feuchtwanger said humorously: 'You are the one artist of the theatre who will go down in American history as having aroused the political antagonism of a whole nation.'

*

And now the paternity case which I thought had been disposed of by the blood-test loomed up again. By adroit finagling another lawyer, influential in local politics, was able to reopen the case; by his tricky device of transferring the guardianship of the child from the mother to the court, the mother's agreement was not violated and she was able to keep the $25,000. So now the court as guardian was able to sue me for the support of the child.

In the first trial the jury disagreed, much to the disappointment of my lawyer, who thought the case was won. But in the second trial, in spite of the blood-test, which has since been accepted as positive proof by Californian State law in a paternity case, a verdict was returned against me.

*

One thing Oona and I wanted was to get away from California. In the year we had been married we had both been put through a meat-grinder and we needed a rest. So we took our little black kitten and embarked on the train for New York; from there we went to Nyack, where we rented a house. It was away from everything, surrounded by stony, unproductive terrain; nevertheless, it had its own particular charm. It was an attractive, small house, built in 1780, and with the rent of it went a most sympathetic house-keeper who was also a wonderful cook.

With the house we inherited a sweet old black retriever who

425

attached himself to us like a lady's companion. He appeared regularly on the porch at breakfast-time and after a gentlemanly wag of his tail would lie down quietly and efface himself while we had breakfast. When our little black kitten first saw him she hissed and spat at him. But he simply lay down with his chin on the ground to show his willingness to coexist.

Those days in Nyack were idyllic, although lonely. We saw no one, and no one called. It was just as well, for I was not yet over the embarrassment of the trial.

Although the ordeal had crippled my creativeness, nevertheless I had almost completed *Monsieur Verdoux*. Now my desire to finish it was returning.

We had intended to stay at least six months in the East, and Oona was going to have her baby there. But I could not work in Nyack, so after five weeks we returned to California.

Soon after we married Oona had confessed she had no desire to become an actress either on the screen or the stage. This news pleased me, for at last I had a wife and not a career girl. It was then that I abandoned *Shadow and Substance* and went back to work on *Monsieur Verdoux* – until I was so rudely interrupted by the Government. I have often thought that the films lost an excellent comedienne, for Oona has a great sense of humour.

I remember, just before the trial, Oona and I went into a jeweller's shop in Beverly Hills to get her vanity case mended. While waiting we began looking over some bracelets. An exceptionally fine one set in diamonds and rubies we liked, but Oona thought the price was too high, so I told the jeweller we would think about it and we left the shop. As we got back into the car I said nervously: 'Hurry up. Drive on quickly!' Then I put my hand in my pocket and cautiously pulled out the bracelet which she had admired. 'I took it while he was showing you the other bracelets,' I said.

Oona turned white. 'Oh, you shouldn't have done it!' She drove on, then turned up a side-street, pulled over to the kerb and stopped the car. 'Let's think it over!' she said and repeated: 'You shouldn't have done it!'

'Well, I can't put it back now,' I said. But I could not keep the pretence up any longer, I burst out laughing and told her the joke: that while she was looking at the other things I had taken the jeweller aside and bought the bracelet.

'And you – thinking I'd stolen it – willing to be an accessory to the crime!' I said laughingly.

'Well, I didn't want to see you get into any more trouble,' she said.

# twenty-eight

DURING the trial we had been surrounded by many dear friends – all of them loyal and sympathetic. Salka Viertel, the Clifford Odets, the Hanns Eislers, the Feuchtwangers and many others.

Salka Viertel, the Polish actress, gave interesting supper parties at her house in Santa Monica. Salka attracted those of the arts and letters: Thomas Mann, Bertolt Brecht, Schoenberg, Hanns Eisler, Lion Feuchtwanger, Stephen Spender, Cyril Connolly and a host of others. Salka established 'une maison Coppet' wherever she resided.

At the Hanns Eislers' we used to meet Bertolt Brecht, who looked decidedly vigorous with his cropped head, and, as I remember, was always smoking a cigar. Months later I showed him the script of *Monsieur Verdoux*, which he thumbed through. His only comment: 'Oh, you write a script Chinese fashion.'

I asked Lion Feuchtwanger what he thought of the political situation in the States. Said he whimsically: 'There might be something significant in the fact that when I completed building my new house in Berlin, Hitler came to power and I moved out. When I had completed furnishing my flat in Paris, the Nazis marched in and again I moved out. And now in America I have just bought a house in Santa Monica.' He shrugged and smiled significantly.

Occasionally we saw the Aldous Huxleys. At that time he was very much lulled in the cradle of mysticism. Frankly I liked him better as the cynical young man of the twenties.

One day, our friend Frank Taylor telephoned to say that Dylan Thomas, the Welsh poet, would like to meet us. We said we would be delighted. 'Well,' said Frank hesitantly, 'I'll bring him round if he's sober.' Later that evening when the bell rang I opened the door and Dylan Thomas fell in. If this was being sober, what would he be like when he was drunk? A day or so later he came to dinner and made better sense. He read to us one of his poems, rendered in a deep resonant voice. I do not remember the imagery, but the word 'cellophane' flashed like reflected sunshine from his magical verse.

Among our friends was Theodore Dreiser, whom I greatly admired. He and his charming wife Helen would occasionally dine at our house. Although there was a burning indignation within him, Dreiser was a gentle, kindly soul. When he died, John Lawson, the playwright, who read the eulogy at the burial service, asked me if I would be one of the principal pall-bearers and read a poem at the service written by Dreiser, which I did.

Although I had gone through periodic qualms about my career, I never faltered in my belief that a good comedy would solve all my troubles. With this resolute feeling I completed *Monsieur Verdoux*. It was two years' work because it was difficult to motivate, but the actual shooting of it only took twelve weeks – a record time for me. Then I posted my script to the Breen Office for censorship. It was not long before I received a letter from them banning it in its entirety.

The Breen Office is a branch of the Legion of Decency, a self-imposed censorship by the Motion Picture Association. I agree that censorship is necessary, but it is difficult to apply. The only suggestion I offer is that its rules be malleable and not dogmatic, and not judged on the basis of subject matter, but on good taste, intelligence and sensitive treatment.

From a moral point of view I believe that physical violence and false philosophy are as harmful as a lurid sex scene. Bernard Shaw said that punching a villain on the jaw is too easy a way of solving life's problems.

Before discussing the censorship of *Monsieur Verdoux* it is necessary to give a brief synopsis of the story. Verdoux is a bluebeard, an insignificant bank clerk, who, having lost his job during the Depression, evolves a scheme of marrying old spinsters and murdering them for their money. His legitimate wife is an invalid who lives in the country with her little son, but she is ignorant of her husgand's criminal enterprise. After the murder of a victim, he goes home as would a bourgeois husband after a hard day's work. He is a paradox of virtue and vice: a man who, as he trims his rose garden, avoids stepping on a caterpillar, while at the end of the garden one of his victims is being consumed in an incinerator. The story contains diabolic humour, bitter satire and social criticism.

The censors sent me quite a lengthy letter explaining why they banned the picture in its entirety. The following part of their letter I quote:

> ... We pass over those elements which seem to be anti-social in their concept and significance. There are the sections of the story in which Verdoux indicts the 'System' and impugns the present-day social structure. Rather, we direct your attention to what is even more critical, and properly a matter of adjudication under the Code. ...
>
> Verdoux's claim is, derivatively, that it is ridiculous to be shocked by the extent of his atrocities, that they are a mere 'comedy of murders' in comparison with the legalized mass murders of war, which are embellished with gold braid by the 'System'. Without at all entering into any dialectics on the question of whether wars are mass murders or justifiable killings, the fact still remains that Verdoux, during the course of his speeches, makes a serious attempt to evaluate the moral quality of his crimes.
>
> The second basic reason for the unacceptability of this story, we can state more briefly. It lies in the fact that this is very largely a story of a type of confidence man who induces a number of women to turn over their finances to him by beguiling them into a series of mock marriages. This phase of the story has about it a distasteful flavour of illicit sex, which in our judgement is not good.

At this juncture they went into a long list of detailed objections. To give an example of some of them, I am first inserting a couples of pages from my script, concerning Lydia, one of Verdoux's illegal wives, an old woman whom he is about to murder that night.

*Lydia enters a dimly lit hall then turns off light and exits into her bedroom, from where a light switches on and streaks across the darkened hallway. Now Verdoux enters slowly. At the end of the hall is a large window through which a full moon is shining. Enraptured he moves slowly towards it.*

VERDOUX [*sotto voce*]: How beautiful ... this pale, Endymion hour ...
LYDIA'S VOICE [*from bedroom*]: What are you talking about?

VERDOUX [*trance-like*]: Endymion, my dear . . . a beautiful youth possessed by the moon.

LYDIA'S VOICE: Well, forget about him and come to bed.

VERDOUX: Yes, my dear . . . Our feet were soft in flowers.

*He exits into Lydia's bedroom, leaving hall empty in semi-darkness except for the light of the moon.*

VERDOUX'S VOICE [*from Lydia's bedroom*]: Look at that moon. I've never seen it so bright! . . . Indecent moon.

LYDIA'S VOICE: Indecent moon! What a fool you are . . . ha! ha! ha! Indecent moon!

*The music races up to a terrifying high crescendo, then the scene fades into morning. It is the same hallway, but now the sun is streaming through it. Verdoux enters from Lydia's bedroom humming.*

The censors' objections to the above scene were as follows: 'Please rephrase Lydia's line, "Well, forget about him and come to bed" to read, "and go to bed." We presume that this whole action will be played in such a way as to avoid any feeling that Verdoux and Lydia are about to indulge in marital privileges. Also change the repeated phrase "indecent moon", also the business of Verdoux appearing from his wife's bedroom humming the following morning.'

Their next objection was to the dialogue of a girl whom Verdoux meets late at night. They stated that the characterization of the girl was clearly that of a prostitute, and was therefore unacceptable.

Naturally, the girl in my story is a harlot and it would be infantile to think that she comes to Verdoux's apartment just to see his etchings. But in this case he picks her up for the purpose of trying a lethal poison on her which leaves no trace of evidence, but will kill her within an hour after she leaves his apartment. The scene is anything but lewd or titillating. My script read as follows:

*We fade into Verdoux's Paris apartment over a furniture store. After they enter he discovers that the girl has a little stray kitten concealed in her raincoat.*

VERDOUX: You like cats, eh?

GIRL: Not particularly, but it was all wet and cold. I don't suppose you have a little milk you could give it?

431

VERDOUX: On the contrary, I have. You see, the prospects are not as gloomy as you think.

GIRL: Do I sound that pessimistic?

VERDOUX: You do, but I don't think you are.

GIRL: Why?

VERDOUX: To be out on a night like this, you must be an optimist.

GIRL: I'm anything but that.

VERDOUX: Up against it, eh?

GIRL [*sarcastically*]: Your faculties of observation are remarkable.

VERDOUX: How long have you been at this game?

GIRL: Oh . . . three months.

VERDOUX: I don't believe you.

GIRL: Why?

VERDOUX: An attractive girl like you would have done better.

GIRL [*superciliously*]: Thanks.

VERDOUX: Now tell me the truth. You're just out of a hospital or a jail . . . which is it?

GIRL [*good-naturedly but challengingly*]: What do you want to know for?

VERDOUX: Because I want to help you.

GIRL: A philanthropist, eh?

VERDOUX [*courteously*]: Precisely . . . and I ask nothing in return.

GIRL [*studying him*]: What is this . . . the Salvation Army?

VERDOUX: Very well. If that's the way you feel, you're at liberty to go on your way.

GIRL [*laconically*]: I'm just out of jail.

VERDOUX: What were you in for?

GIRL [*shrugs*]: What's the difference? Petty larceny, they called it . . . pawning a rented typewriter.

VERDOUX: Dear, dear . . . couldn't you do better than that? What did you get?

GIRL: Three months.

VERDOUX: So this is your first day out of jail.

GIRL: Yes.

VERDOUX: Are you hungry?

*She nods and smiles wistfully.*

VERDOUX: Then while I tend to the culinary operations, you can help to bring in a few things from the kitchen. Come.

*They exit into the kitchen. He starts preparing scrambled eggs and helps her to put supper things on a tray which she carries into the sitting-room. The moment she exits he looks cautiously after her, then quickly opens a cabinet and takes out poison which he pours into a bottle of red wine,*

432

*then corks it, placing it on a tray with two glasses, then exits into living-room.*

VERDOUX: I don't know whether this will appeal to your appetite or not . . . scrambled eggs, toast and a little red wine.

GIRL: Wonderful!

*She puts down a book she has been reading and yawns.*

VERDOUX: I see you're tired, so immediately after supper I'll take you to your hotel.

*He uncorks bottle.*

GIRL [*studying him*]: You're very kind. I don't understand why you're doing all this for me.

VERDOUX: Why not? [*pouring the poisoned wine into her glass*]: Is a little kindness such a rare thing?

GIRL: I was beginning to think it was.

*He is about to pour the same wine into his own glass, but makes an excuse.*

VERDOUX: Oh, the toast!

*He disappears with the bottle into the kitchen, where he quickly changes it for another bottle, gathers up toast, and starts towards sitting-room again. In the sitting-room he enters and puts toast on table ('Voilà!') and from the changed bottle he pours himself a glass of wine.*

GIRL [*baffled*]: You're funny.

VERDOUX: Am I? Why?

GIRL: I don't know.

VERDOUX: However, you're hungry, so please go ahead.

*As she starts to eat he sees the book on the table.*

VERDOUX: What is that you're reading?

GIRL: Schopenhauer.

VERDOUX: Do you like him?

GIRL: So-so.

VERDOUX: Have you read his treatise on suicide?

GIRL: Wouldn't interest me.

VERDOUX [*hypnotically*]: Not if the end could be simple? Say, for instance, you went to sleep, and without any thought of death there was a sudden stoppage . . . wouldn't you prefer it to this drab existence?

GIRL: I wonder . . .

VERDOUX: It's the approach of death that terrifies.

GIRL [*meditating*]: I suppose if the unborn knew of the approach of life, they'd be just as terrified.

433

*Verdoux smiles approvingly and drinks his wine. She picks up her poisoned wine and is about to drink it, but pauses.*

GIRL [*considering*]: Yet life is wonderful.

VERDOUX: What's wonderful about it?

GIRL: Everything . . . a spring morning, a summer's night . . . music, art, love . . .

VERDOUX [*contemptuously*]: Love!

GIRL [*mildly challenging*]: There is such a thing.

VERDOUX: How do you know?

GIRL: I was in love once.

VERDOUX: You mean you were physically attracted by someone.

GIRL [*quizzingly*]: You don't like women, do you?

VERDOUX: On the contrary, I love women . . . but I don't admire them.

GIRL: Why?

VERDOUX: Women are of the earth . . . realistic, dominated by physical facts.

GIRL [*incredulously*]: What nonsense!

VERDOUX: Once a woman betrays a man, she despises him. In spite of his goodness and position, she will give him up for someone inferior . . . if that someone is more physically attractive.

GIRL: How little you know about women.

VERDOUX: You'd be surprised.

GIRL: That isn't love.

VERDOUX: What is love?

GIRL: Giving . . . sacrificing . . . the same thing a mother feels for her child.

VERDOUX [*smiling*]: Did you love that way?

GIRL: Yes.

VERDOUX: Whom?

GIRL: My husband.

VERDOUX [*surprised*]: You're married?

GIRL: I was . . . He died while I was in jail.

VERDOUX: I see . . . Tell me about him.

GIRL: That's a long story . . . [*a pause*]. He was wounded in the Spanish Civil War . . . a hopeless invalid.

VERDOUX [*leans forward*]: An invalid?

GIRL [*nods*]: That's why I loved him. He needed me . . . depended on me. He was like a child. But he was more than a child to me. He was a religion . . . my very breath . . . I'd have killed for him.

*She swallows her tears and is about to drink the poisoned wine.*

VERDOUX: Just a moment . . . I believe there is a little cork in that wine Let me get you another glass.

*He takes her wine and puts it on the sideboard, then takes a clean glass and from his bottle fills it with pure wine. For a moment they drink in silence. Verdoux then gets up from chair.*

VERDOUX: It's very late, and you're tired . . . Here . . . [*giving her money*] this will tide you over for a day or so . . . Good luck.

*She looks at the money.*

GIRL: Oh, this is too much . . . I didn't expect . . . [*buries her face in her hands and weeps*]. Silly . . . carrying on this way. I was beginning to lose faith in everything. Then this happens and you want to believe all over again.

VERDOUX: Don't believe too much. This is an evil world.

GIRL [*shakes her head*]: That isn't true. It's a blundering world, and a very sad one . . . yet a little kindness can make it beautiful.

VERDOUX: You'd better go before your philosophy corrupts me.

*Girl walks to the door, turns and smiles at him as she exits, saying 'Goodnight'.*

I quote a few of the censors' objections to the above scene:

'The dialogue between Verdoux and the girl, "To be out on a night like this, you must be an optimist" as well as the dialogue, "How long have you been at this game?" and, "An attractive girl like you would have done better", should be changed.

'We would like to state that the reference to the Salvation Army is likely, in our opinion, to give offence to that group.'

Towards the end of my script, Verdoux, after many adventures, meets the girl again. He is down and out, but she is quite prosperous. The censors objected to her prosperity. The scene is as follows:

*Fade into exterior of café. Verdoux is sitting at a table reading a newspaper about the war being imminent in Europe. He pays his bill and leaves. As he crosses the road he is almost run down by a smart limousine which swerves to the kerb. The chauffeur stops and toots his horn, and from the limousine window a gloved hand beckons to him, and to his surprise he sees at the window of the limousine the girl he once befriended smiling at him. She is elegantly dressed.*

GIRL: How do you do, Mr Philanthropist.

*Verdoux is puzzled.*

GIRL [*continuing*]: Don't you remember me? You took me to your apartment . . . one rainy night.

VERDOUX [*surprised*]: Really?

435

GIRL: And after feeding me and giving me money, you sent me on my way like a good little girl.

VERDOUX [*humorously*]: I must have been a fool.

GIRL [*sincerely*]: No, you were very kind – where are you going?

VERDOUX: Nowhere.

GIRL: Get in.

*Verdoux steps into car.*

*Interior of limousine.*

GIRL [*to chauffeur*]: To the Café LaFarge . . . I still think you don't remember me . . . but why should you?

VERDOUX [*looking at her admiringly*]: There is every apparent reason why I should.

GIRL [*smiles*]: Don't you remember? The night we met . . . I was just out of jail.

*Verdoux puts finger to lips.*

VERDOUX: Shhh! [*He points to chauffeur, then feels glass.*] It's all right . . . the window's up. [*He looks at her bewildered.*] But you . . . all this . . . [*indicating car*]. What's happened?

GIRL: The old story . . . from rags to riches. After I saw you, my luck changed. I met someone very rich – a munitions manufacturer.

VERDOUX: That's the business I should have been in. What sort of chap is he?

GIRL: Very kind and generous, but in business he's quite ruthless.

VERDOUX: Business is a ruthless business, my dear . . . Do you love him?

GIRL: No, but that's what keeps him interested.

The censors' objections to the above scenes were as follows: 'Please change the underlined dialogue: "You sent me on my way like a good little girl", and the rejoinder, "I must have been a fool"; this to get away from the present suggestive flavour of the dialogue; and please inject into the dialogue some reference to the munitions manufacturer as the girl's fiancé; this, to avoid the suggestion that the girl is now a kept woman.'

Other objections were to other scenes and sundry bits of business. I quote:

There will be no vulgar emphasis on the 'outlandish curves, both in front and behind', of the middle-aged woman.

There must be nothing offensive in the costumes or dance routines of the show girls. Specifically, there must be no showing of the bare leg above the garter.

436

The joke about 'scraping her bottom' is unacceptable.

There should be no showing of, or suggestion of, toilets in the bathroom.

Please change the word 'voluptuous' in Verdoux's speech.

The letter concluded by stating that they would be only too happy to place themselves at my disposal to discuss the matter and that it might be possible to bring the story within the requirements of the Production Code without seriously impairing its entertainment value. So I presented myself at the Breen Office and was ushered into the presence of Mr Breen. A moment later one of Mr Breen's assistants, a tall, dour young man, appeared. His tone was anything but friendly.

'What have you against the Catholic Church?' he said.

'Why do you ask?' I replied.

'Here,' he said, slamming a copy of my script on the table and turning its pages. 'The scene in the condemned cell where the criminal Verdoux says to the priest: "What can I do for you, my good man?" '

'Well, isn't he a good man?'

'That's facetious,' he said, waving a disparaging hand.

'I find nothing facetious in calling a man "good",' I answered.

As we went on discussing, I found myself enacting a sort of Shavian dialogue with him.

'You don't call a priest "a good man", you call him "Father".'

'Very well, we'll call him "Father",' I said.

'And this line,' said he, pointing on another page. 'You have the priest say: "I've come to ask you to make your peace with God." And Verdoux replies: "I am at peace with God, my conflict is with man." You know that's persiflage.'

'You have a right to your opinion,' I continued. 'I also have a right to mine.'

'And this,' he interrupted, reading from the script. 'The priest says: "Have you no remorse for your sins?" And Verdoux answers: "Who knows what sin is, born as it was from Heaven, from God's fallen angel, who knows what mysterious destiny it serves?" '

'I believe that sin is just as great a mystery as virtue,' I answered.

'That's a lot of pseudo-philosophizing,' he said contemptuously. 'Then you have Verdoux look at the priest and say:

437

"What would you be doing without sin?" '

'I admit that line is a little controversial, but after all it is supposed to be ironically humorous and will not be addressed to the priest in a disrespectful way.'

'But you have Verdoux continually scoring off the priest.'

'What do you want the priest to play, a comedy part?'

'Of course not, but why don't you give him some worth-while answer?'

'Look,' I said, 'the criminal is going to his death and attempts to go with bravado. The priest is dignified throughout and his lines are appropriate. However, I'll think up something for the priest to answer.'

'And this line,' he continued: ' "May the Lord have mercy on your soul." And Verdoux says: "Why not? After all it belongs to Him." '

'What's wrong with that?' I asked.

He repeated laconically: ' "Why not!" You don't talk to a priest like that.'

'That line is said introspectively. You must wait until you see the film,' I said.

'You impugn society and the whole state,' he said.

'Well, after all, the state and society are not Simon pure, and criticism of them is not inadmissible, surely?'

With one or two other minor changes the script was eventually passed. And in all justice to Mr Breen a lot of his criticism was constructive. Said he wistfully: 'Don't make the girl another prostitute. Almost every script in Hollywood has a prostitute.'

I must confess I felt embarrassed. However, I promised not to stress the fact.

When the film was finished, it was shown to about twenty or thirty members of the Legion of Decency, representatives of the censors and religious groups of various denominations. I have never felt so lonely as I did on that occasion. However, when the picture was over and the lights went up, Breen turned to the rest. 'I think it's all right . . . let it go!' he said abruptly.

There was silence; then someone said: 'Well, it's okay by me, there's no cleavage.' The others were glum.

Breen with a wry face, addressing the others, made a sweeping gesture. 'It's okay – we can let it go, eh?'

There was little response; some nodded reluctantly. Breen quickly swept aside any objections they might have had, and, patting me on the back, said: 'All right, Charlie, go ahead and roll them' – meaning, 'Print your positive film'.

I was a little bewildered by their acceptance of the picture, considering that in the beginning they had wanted it completely banned. I was suspicious of this sweeping approval. Would they use other means?

*

While re-editing *Verdoux*, I received a telephone message from a United States marshal, saying that he had a summons for me to appear in Washington before the Committee on Un-American Activities. There were nineteen of us summoned.

Senator Pepper of Florida was in Los Angeles at the time, and it was suggested that we meet with the Senator for advice. I did not go, because my situation was different: I was not an American citizen. At that meeting everyone agreed to stand on their Constitutional rights if called to Washington. (Those who stood on them went to jail for a year for contempt of court.)

The summons stated that I would be notified within ten days of my actual appearance in Washington; but, soon after, a telegram arrived stating that my appearance had been postponed for another ten days.

After the third postponement I sent them a telegram stating that I had a large organization suspended, causing me considerable expense, and that since their committee had recently been in Hollywood interrogating my friend Hanns Eisler, they could have interrogated me at the same time and saved the public money. 'However,' I concluded, 'for your convenience I will tell you what I think you want to know. I am not a Communist, neither have I ever joined any political party or organization in my life. I am what you call "a peace-monger.". I hope this will not offend you. So please state definitely when I am to be called to Washington. Yours truly, Charles Chaplin.'

I received a surprisingly courteous reply to the effect that my appearance would not be necessary, and that I could consider the matter closed.

439

# *twenty-nine*

DURING all my personal problems, I had not given much attention to the business of United Artists. Now my lawyer warned me that the company was $1,000,000 in the red. In its prosperous days it had grossed between $40,000,000 and $50,000,000 a year, yet I do not remember receiving more than two dividends from it. During the peak of this prosperity, United Artists had acquired twenty-five per cent equity in four hundred English theatres without paying a penny for them. I am not sure how we acquired them. I believe they were given to us in exchange for guaranteeing them film products. Other American film companies acquired large amounts of stock in British cinemas the same way. At one time our equity in the Rank organization was worth $10,000,000.

But one by one the United Artists stockholders sold their shares back to the company, and in paying for them the company till was almost depleted. In this way I suddenly found myself a half-owner in a United Artists that was $1,000,000 in debt, with Mary Pickford as my partner. She wrote expressing alarm at the fact that all the banks had refused to give us further credit. I was not too concerned, because we had been in debt before and a successful picture had always pulled us out. Besides, I had just completed *Monsieur Verdoux*, which I expected to be a tremendous box-office success. My representative, Arthur Kelly, prognosticated a gross of at least $12,000,000. If this were true, it would pay off the company's debt and give it $1,000,000 profit besides.

In Hollywood I had a private showing for my friends. At the conclusion Thomas Mann, Lion Feuchtwanger and several others stood up and applauded for over a minute.

With confidence I embarked for New York. But on my arrival I was immediately attacked by the *Daily News*:

Chaplin's in town for the opening of his picture. After his exploits as a 'fellow traveller', I dare him to show his face at a Press conference, for I shall be there to ask him one or two embarrassing questions.

The publicity staff of United Artists deliberated whether it was advisable for me to meet the American Press. I was indignant, because I had already met the foreign Press the morning before, and they had given me a warm, enthusiastic welcome. Besides, I am not one to be brow-beaten.

The following morning we reserved a large room in the hotel and I met the American Press. After cocktails were served I made my appearance, but I could smell mischief. I spoke from a rostrum at the back of a small table, and with as much charm as I could pin on, I said:

'How do you do, ladies and gentlemen. I am here to impart any facts that might interest you in connexion with my picture and my future plans.'

They remained silent. 'Don't all speak at once,' I said, smiling.

Eventually a woman reporter sitting near the front said: 'Are you a Communist?'

'No,' I answered definitely. 'The next question please.'

Then a voice began mumbling. I thought it might be my friend from the *Daily News*, but he was conspicuous by his absence. Instead the speaker was a begrimed-looking object with his overcoat on, bent closely over a manuscript from which he was reading.

'Pardon me,' I said. 'You'll have to read that again, I don't understand a word you're saying.'

He started: 'We of the Catholic War Veterans . . .'

I interrupted: 'I'm not here to answer any Catholic War Veterans; this is a meeting of the Press.'

'Why haven't you become a citizen?' said another voice.

'I see no reason to change my nationality. I consider myself a citizen of the world,' I answered.

There was quite a stir. Two or three people wanted to talk at once. One voice dominated, however: 'But you earn your money in America.'

'Well,' I said smilingly, 'if you're putting it on a mercenary basis, we'll have the record straight. My business is an international one; seventy per cent of all my income is earned abroad, and the United States enjoys one hundred per cent taxation on it, so you see I am a very good paying guest.'

Again the Catholic Legion piped up: 'Whether you earn your money here or not, we who landed on those beaches in France resent your not being a citizen of this country.'

'You're not the only guy who landed on those beaches,' I said. 'My two sons were also there in Patton's army, right up in the front line, and they're not beefing or exploiting the fact as you're doing.'

'Do you know Hanns Eisler?' said another reporter.

'Yes, he's a very dear friend of mine, and a great musician.'

'Do you know that he's a Communist?'

'I don't care what he is; my friendship is not based on politics.'

'You seem to like the Communists, though,' said another.

'Nobody is going to tell me whom to like or dislike. We haven't come to that yet.'

Then a voice out of the belligerence said: 'How does it feel to be an artist who has enriched the world with so much happiness and understanding of the little people, and to be derided and held up to hate and scorn by the so-called representatives of the American Press?'

I was so deaf to any expression of sympathy that I answered abruptly: 'I'm sorry, I didn't follow you, you'll have to repeat that question again.'

My publicity man nudged me and whispered: 'This fellow's for you, he said a very fine thing.' It was Jim Agee, the American poet and novelist, at that time working as a special feature writer and critic for *Time* magazine. I was thrown off my guard and confused.

'I'm sorry,' I said, 'I didn't hear you – Would you kindly repeat that again?'

'I don't know if I can,' he said, slightly embarrassed, then he repeated approximately the same words.

I could think of no answer, so I shook my head and said: 'No comment . . . but thank you.'

I was no good after that. His kind words had left me without any more fight. 'I'm sorry, ladies and gentlemen,' I said, 'I thought this conference was to be an interview about my film; instead it has turned into a political brawl, so I have nothing further to say.'

After the interview I was inwardly sick at heart, for I knew that a virulent hostility was against me.

Still I could not quite believe it. I had had wonderful mail congratulating me on *The Great Dictator*, which had grossed more money than any picture I had ever made, and before that picture I had gone through plenty of adverse publicity. Besides, I had great confidence in the success of *Monsieur Verdoux*, and the staff of United Artists felt the same.

Mary Pickford telephoned to say that she would like to go with Oona and me to the opening, so we invited here to dine with us at the '21' restaurant. Mary was quite late for dinner. She said she had been detained at a cocktail party and had had difficulty in tearing herself away.

When we arrived at the theatre crowds were milling outside. As we pressed our way through into the lobby, we discovered a man broadcasting over the radio: 'And now Charlie Chaplin and his wife have arrived. Ah, and with them as their guest that wonderful little actress of the silent days who is still America's sweetheart, Miss Mary Pickford. Mary, won't you say a few words about this wonderful opening?'

The lobby was packed, and Mary propelled her way over to the microphone, still holding on to my hand.

'And now, ladies and gentlemen, here is Miss Mary Pickford.'

In the midst of the shoving and pushing, said Mary: 'Two thousand years ago Christ was born, and tonight . . .' She got no further, for, still holding on to my hand, she was yanked away from the mike by a sudden push from the crowd – I have often wondered since what was coming next.

There was an uneasy atmosphere in the theatre that night, a feeling that the audience had come to prove something. The moment the film started, instead of the eager anticipation and the happy stir of the past that had greeted my films, there was nervous applause scattered with a few hisses. I loathe to admit it but those few hisses hurt more than all the antagonism of the Press.

As the picture progressed I began to get worried. The laughter was there, but divided. It was not the laughter of old, of *The Gold Rush*, of *City Lights*, or *Shoulder Arms*. It was challenging laughter against the hissing faction in the theatre. My heart began to sink. I could not sit in my seat any longer. I whispered to

Oona: 'I'm going out in the lobby, I can't take it.' She squeezed my hand. My crumpled programme, which I had twisted beyond repair, smarted the palms of my hands, so I discarded it under my seat. I crept up the aisle and walked about the lobby. I was torn between listening for laughs and getting away from it all. Then I crept up into the circle to see what it was like there. One man was laughing more than the rest, undoubtedly a friend, but it was convulsive and nervous laughter, as though he wanted to prove something. It was the same thing in the gallery and the circle.

For two hours I paced around in the lobby, in the street, around the theatre, then back to look at the film. It seemed to go on interminably. At last it was over. Earl Wilson, the columnist, a very decent chap, was one of the first I met in the lobby. 'I liked it,' he said, emphasizing the 'I'. Then up came Arthur Kelly, my representative. 'Of course, it's not going to gross any twelve million,' he said. 'Well, I'll settle for half,' I said jokingly.

We gave a supper party afterwards for about a hundred and fifty people – a few were old friends. That evening there were many cross-currents, and despite the champagne it was depressing. Oona stole home to bed, but I stayed half an hour longer.

Bayard Swope, a man whom I liked and thought astute, was arguing with my friend Don Stewart about the film. Swope hated it. That night only a few complimented me. Don Stewart, a little drunk like myself, said: 'Charlie, they're all a lot of bastards trying to make politics out of your picture, but it's great and the audience loved it.'

By this time I did not care what anyone thought, I had no more resistance. Don Stewart saw me back to the hotel. Oona was already asleep when we arrived.

'What floor is this?' Don asked.

'The seventeenth.'

'Jesus! Do you realize what room this is? The one where the boy stepped out on the ledge and stood for twelve hours before plunging off and killing himself!'

This news was a fitting climax to the evening. However, I believe *Monsieur Verdoux* is the cleverest and most brilliant film I have yet made.

To my surprise *Monsieur Verdoux* had a run of six weeks in New York and did very good business. But it suddenly fell off.

When I asked Grad Seers of United Artists about it he said: 'Any picture you make will always do big business the first three or four weeks, because you have the following of your old fans. But after that comes the general public, and frankly the Press have been continually hammering at you for more than ten years and it's bound to have penetration; that's why the business fell off.'

'But surely the general public has a sense of humour?' I said.

'Here!' He showed me the *Daily News* and the Hearst papers. 'And that goes all over the country.'

One had a picture of the New Jersey Catholic Legion picketing outside the theatre showing *Monsieur Verdoux* in that state. They were carrying signs that read:

> 'Chaplin's a fellow traveller.'
> 'Kick the alien out of the country.'
> 'Chaplin's been a paying guest too long.'
> 'Chaplin, the ingrate and communist sympathizer.'
> 'Send Chaplin to Russia . . .'

When a world of disappointment and trouble descends on one, if one doesn't turn to despair one resorts to either philosophy or humour. And when Grad showed me the picture of the picketers, with not a customer outside the theatre, I said jokingly: 'Evidently taken at five o'clock in the morning.' However, where *Monsieur Verdoux* played without interference, it did more than ordinary good business.

The picture was booked by all the big circuits round the country. But after receiving threatening letters from the American Legion and other pressure groups they cancelled the showings. The Legion had an effective way of frightening the exhibitors by threatening to boycott a theatre for a year if they showed a Chaplin picture or other films of which they disapproved. In Denver the film opened one night to big business and closed the following night due to this threatening procedure.

Our New York sojourn was the unhappiest we have ever spent there. Each day we would receive news of cancellations of the film. Besides this, I was embroiled in a plagiarism suit over *The Great Dictator*; and at the height of the intense hate and antagonism of both the Press and the public, and while four senators were denouncing me on the floor of the Senate, the case was tried with a jury, in spite of my wanting to postpone it.

Before going further, I want to set the record straight by saying that I have always solely conceived and written my own scripts. The case had hardly started when the judge announced that his father was dying, and could we come to a settlement so that he could get away and be with him? The opposing side saw the technical advantage and readily jumped at the opportunity for a settlement. Under normal circumstances I would have insisted on continuing the case. But because of my unpopularity in the States at that moment and being under such court pressure, I was terrified, not knowing what to expect next, so we came to a settlement.

All hopes of a $12,000,000 gross for *Verdoux* had vanished. It would hardly pay its own cost, so now the United Artists company was in a desperate crisis. To economize, Mary insisted on firing my representative, Arthur Kelly, and was indignant when I reminded her that I was also half-owner of the company. 'If my representatives go, Mary, then so must yours,' I said. This brought about an impasse which terminated in my saying: 'It's up to one of us to buy or sell, name your own price.' But Mary would not name a price; neither would I.

Eventually, a firm of lawyers representing an Eastern circuit of theatres came to the rescue. They wanted control of the company and were willing to pay us $12,000,000 – $7,000,000 in cash and $5,000,000 in stock. This was a godsend.

'Look,' I said to Mary, 'give me five million in cash now and I'll get out and you can have the rest.' She agreed and so did the company.

After weeks of negotiating, documents were drawn up to that effect. Eventually my lawyer called up and said: 'Charlie, in ten minutes you will be worth five million.'

But ten minutes later he telephoned: 'Charlie, the deal's off. Mary had the pen in her hand and was about to sign, then suddenly said: "No! Why should he get the five million dollars now, and I have to wait two years for mine?" We argued that she was getting seven million dollars – two million dollars more than you. But her excuse was that it would create problems with her income tax.' That had been our golden opportunity; later we were forced to sell for a considerable amount less.

*

446

We returned to California and I completely recovered from the ordeal of *Monsieur Verdoux*, so I began ruminating ideas again. For I was optimistic and still not convinced that I had completely lost the affection of the American people, that they could be so politically conscious or so humourless as to boycott anyone that could amuse them. I had an idea and under its compulsion I did not give a damn what the outcome would be; the film had to be made.

The world, no matter what modern veneer it may assume, always loves a love story. As Hazlitt says, sentiment is more appealing than intellect and is also the greater contribution to a work of art. And my idea was a love story; besides, it was something completely opposite to the cynical pessimism of *Monsieur Verdoux*. But, what was more important, the idea stimulated me.

*Limelight* required eighteen months' preparation. There were twelve minutes of ballet music to compose, which presented an almost insuperable task because I had to imagine the action of the ballet. In the past I had composed music only when my film was completed and I could see its action. Nevertheless, by imagining the dancing I composed all the music. But when it was completed I wondered whether it was suitable for ballet, for the choreography would more or less have to be invented by the dancers themselves.

Being a great admirer of André Eglevsky, I thought of him in the ballet. He was in New York, so I phoned him and asked him if he would be willing to do his 'Bluebird' dance to different music and if he could suggest a ballerina to dance with him. He said he would have to hear the music first. The 'Bluebird' dance is to the music of Tchaikovsky and lasts forty-five seconds. I had therefore composed something for that length of time.

We had been months arranging the twelve minutes of ballet music and had recorded it with a fifty-piece orchestra and I was anxious to get their reaction. Eventually Melissa Hayden, the ballerina, and André Eglevsky flew out to Hollywood to hear it. I was extremely nervous and self-conscious as they sat and listened, but, thank God, both approved and said it was balletique. It was one of the thrilling moments of my film career to see them dance to it. Their interpretation was most flattering and gave the music a classic significance.

447

In casting the girl's part I wanted the impossible: beauty, talent, and a great emotional range. After months of searching and testing with disappointing results I eventually had the good fortune to sign up Claire Bloom, who was recommended by my friend Arthur Laurents.

Something in our nature makes us forget hate and unpleasant things. The trial and all the acrimony that went with it evaporated like the snows. In the interim Oona had had four children: Geraldine, Michael, Josie and Vicki. Life in Beverly Hills was now pleasant. We had also established a happy ménage and everything worked well. We had open house on Sunday and saw many of our friends, among them Jim Agee, who had come to Hollywood to write a script for John Huston.

Will Durant, author and philosopher, was also in Hollywood lecturing at U.C.L.A. He was an old friend and occasionally dined at our house. They were amusing evenings. Will, an enthusiast, who needed no stimulant to intoxicate himself but life itself, once asked me: 'What is your conception of beauty?' I said I thought it was an omnipresence of death and loveliness, a smiling sadness that we discern in nature and all things, a mystic communion that the poet feels – an expression of it can be a dustbin with a shaft of sunlight across it, or it can be a rose in the gutter. El Greco saw it in our Saviour on the Cross.

We met Will again at a dinner at Douglas Fairbanks Jr's house. Clemence Dane and Clare Boothe Luce were there. I first met Clare many years before in New York at W. R. Hearst's fancy dress ball. She was ravishingly beautiful that night in an eighteenth-century costume and a white wig, and was quite charming until I heard her wrangling with my friend George Moore, a cultured and sensitive man. In the midst of her coterie of admirers, she was dressing him down quite audibly: 'You seem to be a bit of a mystery: how do you make your money?'

This was rather cruel, especially in the presence of others. But George was sweet and answered laughingly: 'I sell coal, play a little polo with my friend Hitchcock, and here' (I happened to be passing), 'my friend Charlie Chaplin knows me.' My impression of her changed from that moment. And I was not surprised to hear that later she had become a Congresswoman – and had bestowed on American politics that profound philosophical aphorism: 'globe-baloney'.

That night I listened to Clare Luce's oracular preachments; of course the subject turned to religion (she had recently joined the Catholic Church), and in the mêlée of discussion I said: 'One is not required to wear the imprint of Christianity on one's forehead; it is manifest in both saint and sinner alike; the spirit of the Holy Ghost is in everything.' That night we parted with a slight feeling of estrangement.

*

When *Limelight* was finished I had fewer qualms about its success than any other picture I had ever made. We had a private showing for our friends and everyone was enthusiastic. So we began thinking about leaving for Europe, for Oona was anxious to send the children to school there, away from the influence of Hollywood.

I had made an application for a re-entry permit three months previously but had received no reply. Nevertheless, I went about arranging my business affairs in preparation for leaving. My taxes had been filed and they had all been cleared. But when the Internal Revenue Service heard that I was leaving for Europe, they discovered I owed them more money. And now they concocted a sum that went into six figures, demanding I put up $2,000,000, which was ten times more than they were claiming. My instinct told me to put up nothing and to insist on the case coming to court immediately. This brought about a quick settlement for a very nominal sum. Now that they had no further claim, I again applied for a re-entry permit and waited for weeks, but without answer. So I sent a letter to Washington, notifying them that if they did not wish to give me a re-entry permit I intended leaving in any case.

A week later I received a telephone call from the Immigration Department saying that they would like to ask me a few more questions. Could they come to the house?

'By all means,' I answered.

Three men and a woman arrived, the woman carrying a shorthand typewriter. The others carried small square brief-cases – obviously containing tape-recording machines. The head interrogator was a tall lean man of about forty, handsome and astute. I was aware that they were four to one and I should have had my lawyer present, but I had nothing to hide.

I led them into the sun-porch and the woman brought out her shorthand typewriter and placed it on a small table. The others sat on a settee, their tape-recording cases before them. The interrogator brought out a dossier a foot high, which he placed neatly on the table beside him. I sat opposite him. Then he began looking over his dossier page by page.

'Is Charles Chaplin your real name?'

'Yes.'

'Some people say your name is – ' (here he mentioned a very foreign name) 'and that you are from Galicia.'

'No. My name is Charles Chaplin, the same as my father, and I was born in London, England.'

'You say you've never been a Communist?'

'Never. I have never joined a political organization in my life.'

'You made a speech in which you said "comrades" – what did you mean by that?'

'Exactly that. Look it up in the dictionary. The Communists have no priority on that word.'

He continued this line of questioning, then suddenly asked: 'Have you ever committed adultery?'

'Listen,' I answered, 'if you're looking for a technicality to keep me out of the country, tell me and I'll arrange my affairs accordingly, because I don't wish to stay *persona non grata* anywhere.'

'Oh no,' he said, 'this is a question on every re-entry permit.'

'What is the definition of "adultery"?' I asked.

We both looked it up in the dictionary. 'Let's say "fornication with another man's wife",' he said.

I deliberated a moment. 'Not to my knowledge,' I said.

'If this country were invaded, would you fight for it?'

'Of course. I love this country – this is my home, I've lived here for forty years,' I answered.

'But you have never become a citizen.'

'There's no law against that. However, I pay my taxes here.'

'But why do you follow the Party line?'

'If you'll tell me what the Party line is, I'll tell you whether I follow it or not.'

A pause followed and I broke in: 'Do you know how I got into all this trouble?'

He shook his head.

'By obliging your Government.'

He raised his brow in surprise.

'Your Ambassador to Russia, Mr Joseph Davies, was to speak in San Francisco on behalf of Russian war relief, but at the last moment was taken with an attack of laryngitis; and a high representative of your Government asked me if I would oblige and speak in his place and I've had my knuckles rapped ever since.'

I was interrogated for three hours. A week later they telephoned again and asked if I would go down to the Immigration Office. My lawyer insisted on going with me, 'in case they want to ask any further questions,' he said.

When we arrived I could not have been greeted more cordially. The head of the Immigration Department, a kindly middle-aged man, spoke almost consolingly: 'I'm sorry we've delayed you, Mr Chaplin. But now that we have established a branch of the Immigration Department in Los Angeles, we shall act more quickly without having applications going to and from Washington. There is just another question, Mr Chaplin – how long will you be away?'

'Not more than six months,' I answered. 'We're just going on a holiday.'

'Otherwise, if you're away longer, you must ask for an extension.' He placed a document on the table, then left the room. Quickly my lawyer looked at it. 'That's it!' said he. 'That's the permit!'

The man returned with a pen. 'Will you sign here, Mr Chaplin? And of course you will have to get your sailing papers.'

After I had signed it, he patted me affectionately on the back. 'Here is your permit. I hope you have a very nice holiday, Charlie – and hurry back home!'

It was Saturday, and we were leaving on Sunday morning by train for New York. I wanted Oona to have access to my safe-deposit box in case anything should happen to me, as it contained most of my fortune. But Oona kept putting off signing the papers at the bank. And now it was our last day in Los Angeles, and the banks would be closed in ten minutes. 'We have just ten minutes

to go, so let's hurry,' I said. About such matters Oona is a pro-
crastinator. 'Why can't we wait until we get back from our
holiday?' she said. But I insisted. And a good thing I did, because
otherwise we might have spent the rest of our lives in litigation
trying to get our fortune out of the country.

It was a poignant day when we left for New York. While Oona
was making final household arrangements I stood outside on the
lawn viewing the house with ambivalent feelings. So much had
happened to me in that house, so much happiness, so much
anguish. Now the garden and the house looked so peaceful and
friendly that I felt wistful about leaving it.

After bidding good-bye to Helen, the maid, and Henry, the
butler, I brushed by into the kitchen and said good-bye to Anna,
the cook. I am exceedingly shy on these occasions, and Anna, a
rotund, heavy woman, was slightly deaf. 'Good-bye,' I said again
and touched her on the arm. Oona was the last to leave; later
she told me that she had found the cook and the maid in tears.
Jerry Epstein, my assistant director, was at the station to see us
off.

The journey across the country was relaxing. We spent a week
in New York before sailing. Just as I was preparing to enjoy myself, my lawyer, Charles Schwartz, called up to say that an ex-
employee of United Artists was suing the company for so many
millions. 'It's nothing but a nuisance action, Charlie; all the same
I want you to keep from being served a summons, as it could
mean your being called back from your vacation.' So for the last
four days I was confined to my room and denied the enjoyment of
seeing New York with Oona and the children. However, I
intended to show up for the Press preview of *Limelight* – summons or no summons.

Crocker, now my publicity man, had arranged a lunch with the
editorial staff of *Time* and *Life* magazines, an occasion of having
to jump through the proverbial hoop for publicity. Their offices
with their barren white plaster walls were a fit setting for the
frigid atmosphere of that lunch, as I sat labouring to be friendly
and amusing facing a row of solemn, cropped-headed space-men
– the *Time* staff. And the food was just as frigid as the atmosphere,
consisting of tasteless chicken with sallow, starchy gravy. But as
far as gaining good publicity for *Limelight*, neither my presence,

my attempts to be engaging, nor the food, did me any good; their magazine ruthlessly panned the picture.

Although at the Press preview unfriendliness was undoubtedly in the theatre, later I was agreeably surprised by the reviews in some of the important newspapers.

# *thirty*

I BOARDED the *Queen Elizabeth* at five in the morning, a romantic hour but for the sordid reason of having to avoid a process-server. My lawyer's instructions were to steal aboard, lock myself in my suite and not to appear on deck until the pilot disembarked. Being groomed for the last ten years to expect the worst, I obeyed.

I had been looking forward to standing on the top deck with my family, enjoying that stirring moment of a ship's severance as it glides off and away into another life. Instead I was ignominiously locked in my cabin, peering through the porthole.

'It's me,' said Oona, rapping on the door.

I opened it.

'Jim Agee has just arrived to see us off. He is standing on the dock. I shouted that you were hiding from process-servers and that you'd wave to him from the porthole. There he is now at the end of the pier,' she said.

I saw Jim a little apart from a group of people, standing in fierce sunlight scanning the boat. Quickly I took my fedora hat and put my arm through the porthole and waved, while Oona looked out of the second porthole. 'No, he hasn't seen you yet,' she said.

And Jim never did see me; and that was the last I ever saw of Jim, standing alone as though apart from the world, peering and searching. Two years later he died of a heart-attack.

At last we were on our way and, before the pilot left, I unlocked the door and came out on deck a free man. There it was – the towering skyline of New York, aloof and magnanimous, racing away from me in sunlight, becoming ethereally more beautiful every moment . . . and as that vast continent disappeared into the mist it gave me a peculiar feeling.

Although excited with the anticipation of visiting England with my family, I was pleasantly relaxed. The wide expanse of the Atlantic is cleansing. I felt like another person. No longer was I a myth of the film world, or a target of acrimony, but a married man with a wife and family on a holiday. The children were on the top deck engrossed in play while Oona and I sat in a couple of deck-chairs. And in this mood I had a realization of perfect happiness – something very near to sadness.

We talked affectionately of friends we were leaving behind. We even talked of the friendliness of the Immigration Department. How easily one succumbs to a small courtesy – enmity is difficult to nourish.

Oona and I intended taking a long vacation and devoting ourselves to pleasure, and with the launching of *Limelight* our vacation would not be aimless. The knowledge of combining business with pleasure was exceedingly pleasant.

Lunch the next day could not have been gayer. Our guests were the Artur Rubinsteins and Adolph Green. But in the middle of it Harry Crocker was handed a cablegram. He was about to put it in his pocket, but the messenger said: 'They're waiting for an answer over the wireless.' A cloud came over Harry's face as he read it; then he excused himself and left the table.

Later he called me into his cabin and read the cable. It stated that I was to be barred from the United States, and that before I could re-enter the country I would have to go before an Immigration Board of Enquiry to answer charges of a political nature and of moral turpitude. The United Press wanted to know if I had any comments to make.

Every nerve in me tensed. Whether I re-entered that unhappy country or not was of little consequence to me. I would like to have told them that the sooner I was rid of that hate-beleaguered atmosphere the better, that I was fed up with America's insults and moral pomposity, and that the whole subject was damned boring. But everything I possessed was in the States and I was terrified they might find a way of confiscating it. Now I could expect any unscrupulous action from them. So instead I came out with a pompous statement to the effect that I would return and answer their charges, and that my re-entry permit was not a 'scrap of paper', but a document given to me in good faith by the United States Government – blah, blah, blah.

There was no further rest on the boat. Press radiograms from all parts of the world wanted statements. At Cherbourg, our first stop before Southampton, a hundred or more European newsmen embarked wanting interviews. We arranged to give them an hour in the buffet room after lunch. Although they were sympathetic, the ordeal was dreary and exhausting.

\*

The journey from Southampton to London was one of uneasy suspense; for more important than being barred from the U.S. was my anxiety to know what Oona's and the children's reaction would be to their first view of the English countryside. For years I had been extolling the wondrous beauty of the south-western part of England, Devonshire and Cornwall, and now we were passing through dreary clusters of red brick buildings and lanes of uniform houses climbing over hills. Said Oona: 'They all look alike.'

'Give us a chance,' I said. 'We're only just outside Southampton.' And as we travelled along, of course the countryside grew more beautiful.

When we arrived in London at Waterloo Station, the faithful crowd was still there, and was just as loyal and enthusiastic as ever. They waved and cheered as we left the station. 'Give it to 'em, Charlie,' said one. It was indeed heart-warming.

When at last Oona and I had a moment to ourselves, we stood at the window of our suite on the fifth floor of the Savoy Hotel. I pointed to the new Waterloo Bridge; although beautiful, it meant little to me now, only that its road led over to my boyhood. We stood silent, drinking in the most stirring view of a city in all this world. I have admired the romantic elegance of the Place de la Concorde in Paris, have felt the mystic message from a thousand glittering windows at sunset in New York, but to me the view of the London Thames from our hotel window transcends them all for utilitarian grandeur – something deeply human.

I glanced at Oona as she stood taking in the view, her face tense with excitement which made her look younger than her twenty-seven years. Since our marriage she had been through many an ordeal with me; and as she gazed upon London, the sunlight playing about her dark hair, I saw for the first time one or two silver threads. I made no comment, but at that moment I felt slavishly dedicated to her as she said quietly: 'I like London.'

Twenty years had elapsed since I had been here last. From my view the river bends and the contours of its banks have ugly, modern shapes that marred the skyline. Half of my boyhood had gone in the charred embers of its sooty, vacant lots.

As Oona and I wandered through Leicester Square and Piccadilly, now adulterated by American gimcracks, lunch counters, hot-dog stands and milk bars, we saw hatless youths and blue-jeaned girls ambling about. I remember when one dressed the part for the West End, and strolled with yellow gloves and a walking-stick. But that world has gone, and another takes its place, eyes see differently, emotions react to other themes. Men weep at jazz, and violence has become sexual. Time marches on.

We taxied over to Kennington to look at 3 Pownall Terrace, but the house was empty, ready to be demolished. We paused before 287 Kennington Road where Sydney and I had lived with my father. We passed through Belgravia and saw in the rooms of those once magnificent private houses neon lights and clerks working at desks; other houses were replaced by oblong shapes, glass tanks and cement match-boxes towering upwards – all in the name of progress.

We had many problems: first, getting our money out of the States. This meant Oona would have to fly back to California and take everything from our safe-deposit box. She was away ten days. When she returned, she told me in detail what had happened. At the bank the clerk studied her signature, looked at her, then left and had quite a conference with the bank manager. Oona had a moment of uneasiness until they opened our deposit box.

She said that after completing the business at the bank she went to the house in Beverly Hills. Everything was just as we had left it and the flowers and the grounds looked lovely. She stood alone a moment in the living-room and was quite emotional. Then later she saw Henry, our Swiss butler, who told her that since we went away the F.B.I. men had called twice and interrogated him, wanting to know what kind of a man I was, if he knew of any wild parties with nude girls that had gone on in the house, etc. When he told them that I lived quietly with my wife and family, they began to bully him and asked what nationality he was and how long he had been in the country, and demanded to see his passport.

Oona said that when she heard all this, whatever attachment she had for the house was severed then and there. Even the tears of Helen, our maid, who wept when Oona left, had little effect but to hasten her departure.

Friends have asked how I came to engender this American antagonism. My prodigious sin was, and still is, being a non-conformist. Although I am not a Communist I refused to fall in line by hating them. This, of course, has offended many, including the American Legion. I am not opposed to that organization in its true constructive sense; such measures as the G.I. Bill of Rights and other benefits for ex-soldiers and the needy children of veterans are excellent and humanitarian. But when the legionnaires go beyond their legitimate rights, and under the guise of patriotism use their power to encroach upon others, then they commit an offence against the fundamental structure of the American Government. Such super-patriots could be the cells to turn America into a fascist state.

Secondly, I was opposed to the Committee on Un-American Activities – a dishonest phrase to begin with, elastic enough to wrap around the throat and strangle the voice of any American citizen whose honest opinion is a minority one.

Thirdly, I have never attempted to become an American citizen. Yet scores of Americans earning their living in England have never attempted to become British subjects; for example, an American executive of M.G.M. earning in dollars a four-figure salary a week has lived and worked in England for over thirty-five years without becoming a British subject, and the English have never bothered about it.

This explanation is not an apology. When I began this book I asked myself the reason for writing it. There are many reasons but apology is not one of them. In summing up my situation, I would say that in an atmosphere of powerful cliques and invisible governments I engendered a nation's antagonism and unfortunately lost the affection of the American public.

*

*Limelight* was booked to open at the Odeon in Leicester Square.

I was uneasy as to what the reception would be, as it was not the usual Chaplin comedy. Before the première we had a preview for the Press. Time had sufficiently removed me from the film to view it objectively, and I must say I was moved by it. This was not being narcissistic, for I can enjoy certain sequences in my films and loathe others. However, I never wept as some snide reporter said I did – and even if I had, so what? If the author does not feel emotional about his work he can hardly expect the public to. Frankly I enjoy my comedies even more than the audience.

The première of *Limelight* was for charity, and Princess Margaret attended. The next day it opened to the general public. Although the reviews were lukewarm it broke world records, and in spite of the fact that it was boycotted in America it grossed more money than any picture I have ever made.

Before leaving London for Paris, Oona and I were the guests of Lord Strabolgi at a dinner in the House of Lords. I sat next to Herbert Morrison and was surprised to hear that as a socialist he supported the policy of atomic defence. I told him that no matter how much we increased our atomic piles, England would always be a vulnerable target; she was a small island, and retaliation would be little consolation after we had been reduced to ashes. I am convinced that the soundest strategy for England's defence is absolute neutrality, for in an atomic era I doubt that absolute neutrality would be violated. But my views were by no means in accord with Morrison's.

I am surprised how many intelligent people talk in favour of atomic weapons. At another house I met Lord Salisbury, who was of the same opinion as Morrison, and in expressing my abhorrence of nuclear defence I felt that I did not stand in good stead with his Lordship.

At this juncture, I think it appropriate to sum up the state of the world as I see it today. The accumulating complexities of modern life, the kinetic invasion of the twentieth century finds the individual hemmed in by gigantic institutions that threaten from all sides, politically, scientifically and economically. We are becoming the victims of soul-conditioning, of sanctions and permits.

This matrix into which we have allowed ourselves to be cast is due to a lack of cultural insight. We have gone blindly into ugliness and congestion and have lost our appreciation of the aesthetic. Our living sense has been blunted by profit, power and monopoly. We have permitted these forces to envelop us with an utter disregard of the ominous consequences.

Science, without thoughtful direction or sense of responsibility, has delivered up to politicians and the *militaire* weapons of such destruction that they hold in their hands the destiny of every living thing on this earth.

This plethora of power given into the hands of men whose moral responsibility and intellectual competence are to say the least not infallible, and in many cases questionable, could end in a war of extermination of all life on earth. Yet we go blindly on.

As Dr Robert Oppenheimer once told me: 'Man is driven by a compulsion to know.' Well and good – but in many cases with a disregard of the consequences. With this the Doctor agreed. Some scientists are like religious fanatics. They rush ahead, believing that what they discover is always for good and that their credo to know is a moral one.

Man is an animal with primary instincts of survival. Consequently, his ingenuity has developed first and his soul afterwards. Thus the progress of science is far ahead of man's ethical behaviour.

Altruism is slow along the path of human progress. It ambles and stumbles along after science. And only by force of circumstances is it allowed to function. Poverty was not reduced by altruism or the philanthropy of governments, but by the forces of dialectic materialism.

Carlyle said that the salvation of the world will be brought about by people thinking. But in order to bring this about, man must be forced into serious circumstances.

Thus, in splitting the atom, he is driven into a corner and made to think. He has the choice to destroy himself or to behave himself; the momentum of science is forcing him to make this decision. And under these circumstances, I believe that eventually his altruism will survive and his good-will towards mankind will triumph.

*

After leaving America life was on another level. In Paris and Rome we were received like conquering heroes: invited by President Vincent Auriol to lunch at the Élysée and invited to lunch at the British Embassy. Then the French Government elevated me to the rank of Officer of the Legion of Honour, and on that same day the Société des Auteurs et Compositeurs Dramatiques made me an honorary member. A letter referring to that occasion which I received from Mr Roger Ferdinand, the President, was most affecting. It is here translated.

Dear Mr Chaplin,

Should certain people be surprised at the publicity given to your presence here, they would be ill acquainted with the reasons for which we love and admire you; they would also be very bad judges of human values, and would not have taken the trouble to count the blessings that you have heaped upon us during the last forty years, nor have appreciated your teaching, or the quality of the joys and emotions that you have lavished upon us, at their true worth; to say the least they would be thoroughly ungrateful.

You are among the greatest personalities of the world and your claim to fame is equal to that of those who can be placed among the most illustrious.

There is your genius, for a start. This much abused word, genius, takes on its real sense when applied to a man who is not only a marvellous comedian, but also an author, composer, producer, and, best of all, a man of warmth and magnanimity. For you are all of these, and moreover with a simplicity which increases your stature and makes a warm, spontaneous appeal, without calculation or effort, to the hearts of men today, which are as tormented as your own. But genius is not sufficient to merit esteem; neither is it sufficient to engender love. And yet love is the only word for the sentiment you inspire.

When we saw *Limelight* we laughed, often heartily, and we wept, with real tears – yours, for you gave us the precious gift of tears.

In truth, real fame is never usurped; it only has a sense, a value and duration when it is turned to a good cause. And your victory is in the fact that you have human generosity and spontaneity that are not inhibited by rules or cleverness but stem from your own sufferings, your joys, hopes and disappointments; all that is understood by those who suffer beyond their strength and ask for pity, and who constantly hope to be comforted, to be made to forget for a moment, by that laughter which does not pretend to cure, but only to console.

One could imagine, even if we did not know it, the price that you have paid for this marvellous gift of being able to make us laugh and then suddenly cry. One can guess or, better still, perceive what sufferings you have yourself undergone to be able to portray in detail all those little things that touch us so deeply, and which you have taken from moments of your own life.

For you have a good memory. You are faithful to the memories of your childhood. You have forgotten nothing of its sadness, its bereavements; you have wanted to spare others the harm you suffered, or at least you have wanted to give everybody reason for hope. You have never betrayed your sad youth, and fame has never had the power to separate you from the past – for, alas, these things can happen.

This fidelity to your earliest memories is perhaps your greatest merit and the most important of your assets, and also the real reason why the crowds adore you. They respond to the subtleties of your acting. It seems as if you are always in direct touch with the hearts of others. And indeed nothing is more harmonious than this cooperation of author, the actor and director, who place their combined talents at the service of all that is humane and good.

This is why your work is always generous. It is not handicapped by theories – scarcely even by technique; it is forever a confession, a confidence, a prayer. And each person is your accomplice because he thinks and feels as you do.

You have, by your talent alone, subdued the critics because you have succeeded in captivating them. This is a difficult task. They will never admit that you respond equally to the charm of old-fashioned melodrama and to the devilish zest of Feydeau. And yet you do, while also possessing a certain grace that makes us think of Musset – although you imitate no one and resemble no one. That is also the secret of your glory.

Today our Society of Authors and Dramatists has the honour and joy of welcoming you. We are thus adding, for a few moments, to the weight of the engagements you so valiantly undertake. We are most anxious to receive you into our midst and to tell you how much we admire and love you, and also to say that you are really one of us. For in your films the story is written by Mr Chaplin. So is the music by him, and the direction. And the comedian is an additional, and also first-class, contribution.

You have here the authors of France, authors of plays and of films, composers, producers – all of them like you, in their own way, familiar with the pride and the self-sacrifice of hard work which you know so well, having one ambition, to move and amuse the crowds, to show them the joys and sorrows of life, to portray the fear of lost love, pity for undeserved tribulations, and a desire to mend what is marred in a spirit of peace, hope and fraternity.

Thank you, Mr Chaplin.

(Signed) Roger Ferdinand.

462

The première of *Limelight* was attended by a most distinguished audience, including French cabinet ministers and foreign ambassadors. The American Ambassador, however, did not come.

At the Comédie Française we were the guests of honour at a special performance of Molière's *Don Juan*, which was enacted by the greatest representative artists of France. That night the fountains of the Palais Royale were lit up and flowing and Oona and I were met by students of the Comédie Française, dressed in eighteenth-century liveries and holding lighted candelabras, who escorted us to the Grand Circle filled with the most beautiful women in all Europe.

In Rome our reception was the same, I was honoured and decorated and received by the President and the Ministers. On that occasion an amusing incident happened at the preview of *Limelight*. The Minister of Fine Arts suggested that I enter by the stage door in order to avoid the crowds. I thought the Minister's suggestion rather peculiar and told him that if the people were patient enough to stand outside the theatre wanting to see me, I could at least be gracious enough to enter the front way and show myself. I thought the Minister wore a curious expression as he mildly reiterated that it would save me a great deal of trouble going in the back way. But I insisted, so he pressed no further.

That night was the usual glittering preview. When we drove up in a limousine, the crowds were roped off on the far side of the street – too far, I thought. With all my graciousness and charm I stepped out and around the limousine into the middle of the road, and, before a flood of arc-lights, with a big smile threw up my arms de Gaulle fashion. Instantly a barrage of cabbages and tomatoes flew by me. I was not too sure what they were or what had happened until I heard my Italian friend, the interpreter, moaning at the back of me: 'To think this should happen in my country.' However, nothing hit me and we hurried into the theatre. Then the humour of the situation struck me and I could not stop laughing. Even my Italian friend had to laugh with me.

Later we learned that the offenders were young neo-fascists. I must say there was no vehemence in their throwing; it was more of a demonstration. Four of them were immediately arrested and the police wanted to know if I wished to bring any charge against them. 'Of course not,' I said; 'they are only young boys' – they were youths of fourteen and sixteen – and so the matter was dropped.

Before leaving Paris for Rome, Louis Aragon, poet and editor of *Les Lettres Françaises*, had telephoned so say that Jean-Paul Sartre and Picasso would like to meet me, so I invited them to dinner. They suggested somewhere quiet, so we dined in my rooms at the hotel. When Harry Crocker, my publicity man, heard about it, he almost had a conniption fit. 'This will undo all the good we have done since we left the States.'

'But, Harry, this is Europe, not the States, and these gentlemen happen to be three of the world's great figures,' I said. I had been careful not to confide to Harry or anyone that I had no intention of returning to America because I still had property there which I had not yet disposed of. Harry had me almost believing that a meeting with Aragon, Picasso and Sartre was a conspiracy to overthrow Western democracy. Nevertheless, his concern did not deter him from staying behind to have them sign his autograph book. Harry was not invited to dinner. I told him we expected Stalin to arrive later and did not want any publicity about it.

I was not too sure about the evening. Only Aragon could speak English, and conversation through an interpreter is like shooting at a distant target and waiting for the result of your aim.

Aragon is handsome with well-defined features. Picasso has a quizzical, humorous look, and could pass for an acrobat or a clown more readily than a painter. Sartre has a round face and, although his features do not bear analysis, they have a subtle beauty and sensitiveness. Sartre revealed little of what went on in his mind. That evening, after the party had broken up, Picasso took us to the Left Bank studio which he still uses. As we climbed the stairs we saw a sign on the door of the apartment below him: 'This is not Picasso's studio – another flight up, please.'

We came upon the most deplorable, barnlike garret, that even Chatterton would have been loth to die in. Hanging from a nail in one rafter was a stark electric bulb, which enabled us to see a rickety old iron bed and a broken-down stove. Resting against the wall was a pile of old dusty canvases. He picked up one – a Cézanne, and a most beautiful one. He picked up another and another. We must have looked at fifty masterpieces. I was tempted to offer him a round sum for the lot – just to get rid of the litter. In that Gorki's 'lower depth' was a gold mine.

# *thirty-one*

AFTER the Paris and Rome openings we returned to London where we stayed several weeks. I had yet to find a home for my family. A friend suggested Switzerland. Of course I should like to have settled in London, but we were doubtful if the climate would be suitable for the children; and, at that time, we were frankly concerned about blocked currency.

So with a tinge of melancholy we picked up our belongings and with the four children arrived in Switzerland. We settled temporarily at the Beau Rivage Hotel, Lausanne, facing the lake. It was autumn and rather drear, but the mountains were beautiful.

We were four months searching for a suitable house. Oona, expecting her fifth child, said emphatically that after the hospital she did not wish to return to a hotel. It was this emergency that made me hustle and look around, and eventually settle at the Manoir de Ban in the village of Corsier, a little above Vevey. To our amazement we discovered that it had thirty-seven acres, with an orchard which among other things produces large black cherries, delicious green plums, apples and pears; and a vegetable garden that grows strawberries and wonderful asparagus and corn, to which, in season, no matter where we are, we make a special pilgrimage. In front of the terrace is a five-acre lawn with magnificent tall trees which frame the mountains and the lake in the distance.

I acquired a very competent staff: Miss Rachel Ford, who established our household and then became my business manager, and Mme Burnier, my Swiss-English secretary, who retyped this book many times.

We were a little awed at the pretentiousness of the place and wondered whether it would be commensurate with our income,

465

but when the owner told us what it could be run for, we discovered it was within the bounds of our budget. Thus we came to live in the village of Corsier, which has a population of 1,350.

It took at least a year before we could get oriented. For a while the children went to the village school of Corsier. It was quite a problem for them to be suddenly taught everything in French, and we had qualms as to the psychological effect it might have on them. But it was not long before they spoke French fluently, and it was quite moving to see how well they adapted themselves to the Swiss way of life. Even Kay Kay and Pinnie, the children's nurses, began struggling with French.

And now we began to divest ourselves of every tie in the United States. This took a considerable time. I went to the American Consul and handed in my re-entry permit, telling him that I had given up my residence in the United States.

'You're not going back, Charlie?'

'No,' I said, almost apologetically. 'I'm a little too old to take any more of that nonsense.'

He made no comment, but said: 'Well, you can always get back on an ordinary visa if you want to return.'

I smiled and shook my head. 'I've decided to settle in Switzerland.' We shook hands and that was that.

Now Oona decided to give up her American citizenship. So while visiting London she notified the American Embassy. They said, however, it would take at least three-quarters of an hour to go through the formalities. 'What nonsense!' I told Oona. 'It seems ridiculous that it should take so long. I'll go with you.'

When we arrived at the Embassy, all the insults and slanders of the past inflated within me like a balloon ready to burst. In a loud voice I demanded the office of the Immigration Department. Oona was embarrassed. One of the office doors opened and a man appeared and said: 'Hello, Charlie, won't you come in the office with your wife?'

He must have read my mind, for his opening remark was: 'An American giving up his citizenship should know what he is doing and be in his right mind. That's why we have this procedure of questioning: it's for the protection of the citizen.'

Naturally, this made sense to me.

He was a man in his late fifties. 'I saw you in Denver in 1911 at the old Empress Theatre,' he said, looking at me reproachfully.

Of course I melted and we spoke about the good old days.

When the ordeal was finished, the last paper signed, and we had said our cheery good-bye, I was slightly sad at my lack of feeling in the matter.

\*

In London we occasionally see friends, among whom are Sydney Bernstein, Ivor Montagu, Sir Edward Beddington-Behrens, Donald Ogden Stewart, Ella Winter, Graham Greene, J. B. Priestley, Max Reinhardt and Douglas Fairbanks Jr. Although some we rarely see, the thought of them is comforting, like the pleasure of knowing there is a mooring somewhere, if occasionally we want to sail into port.

On one of our visits to London we received a message that Khrushchev and Bulganin would like to meet us at a reception given by the Soviet Embassy at Claridge's Hotel. When we arrived, the lobby was packed with smiling and excited crowds. With the help of a member of the Russian Embassy we began ploughing through them. Suddenly coming from the opposite direction we saw Khrushchev and Bulganin; they too were ploughing, and from their expression they had given up in disgust and were retreating.

One could see that Khrushchev even in distress is not without humour. As he pressed forward to an exit, our escort called after him: 'Khrushchev!' But he waved him away, he was fed up. 'Khrushchev, Charlie Chaplin!' our man shouted. Both Bulganin and Khrushchev stopped and turned and their faces lit up. I was indeed flattered. In the surging and eddying of the crowd we were introduced. Through an interpreter Khrushchev said something about how much the Russian people appreciated my films, then we were offered some vodka. I thought the pepper-box had spilled into it, but Oona loved it.

We managed to make a small circle so that we could be photographed together. Because of the din I could not say anything. 'Let's go into the next room,' said Khrushchev. The crowd saw our intentions and a battle royal ensued. With the aid of four men we were catapulted into a private room. Once alone, Khrushchev and all of us sighed: 'Phew!' Now I had a chance to collect my wits and talk. Khrushchev had just made a wonderful speech of goodwill on his arrival in London. It had come like a ray of sunshine, and I told him so, saying that it had given hope for peace to millions throughout the world.

We were interrupted by an American reporter: 'I understand, Mr Khrushchev, your son was out on the town, last night, enjoying himself.'

Khrushchev's smile was one of nettled amusement. 'My son is a serious young man, studying hard to be an engineer – but he occasionally enjoys himself, I hope.'

A few minutes later a message came to say that Mr Harold Stassen was outside and would like to see Mr Khrushchev. He turned to me jokingly: 'Do you mind – he's an American?'

I laughed: 'I don't mind.' Later Mr and Mrs Stassen and Mr and Mrs Gromyko were shot through the door. Khrushchev then excused himself, saying he would only be a few minutes, and went to a far corner of the room to talk with Stassen and Gromyko.

To make conversation I asked Mrs Gromyko if she was returning to Russia. She said she was going back to the United States. I remarked that she and her husband had been there a long time. She laughed, a little embarrassed. 'I don't mind it,' she said; 'I like it there.'

I said: 'I don't think the real America is in New York or on the Pacific Coast; personally, I like the Middle West much better, places like North and South Dakota, Minneapolis and Saint Paul. There, I think, are the true Americans.'

Mrs Stassen suddenly exclaimed: 'Oh, I'm so glad you said that! Minnesota is where my husband and I come from.' She laughed nervously and repeated: 'I'm so glad you said that.' I think she had an idea I was going to heap a tirade on the United States, and that the slings and arrows I had received from that country had left me bitter. But it was not so – and, even if it had been, I am not one to vent my spleen on a very charming lady like Mrs Stassen.

I could see that Khrushchev and the rest were in for a long session, so Oona and I got up. When Khrushchev saw the stir he left Stassen and came over to say goodbye. As we shook hands I caught a glimpse of Stassen; he had backed up to the wall and was looking straight ahead in a non-committal way. I bade everyone good-bye, ignoring Stassen – which under the circumstances I felt was the diplomatic thing to do – but from the brief glance I had of him I liked him.

The next evening Oona and I dined alone in the Grill at the Savoy. In the middle of our dessert Sir Winston Churchill and Lady Churchill came in and stood before our table. I had not seen Sir Winston or heard from him since 1931. But after the opening of *Limelight* in London, I had received a message from United Artists, our distributors, asking permission to show Sir Winston the film at his house. Of course I had been only too pleased. A few days later he sent a charming letter of thanks, telling me how much he had enjoyed it.

And now Sir Winston stood before our table, confronting us. 'Well!' he said.

There seemed to be a disapproving note in the 'Well!'

I quickly stood up, all smiling, and introduced Oona, who at that moment was about to retire.

After Oona had left I asked if I could join them for coffee, and went across to their table. Lady Churchill said she had read in the papers about my meeting with Khrushchev.

'I always got along well with Khrushchev,' said Sir Winston.

But all the time I could see that Sir Winston was nursing a grievance. Of course, much had happened since 1931. He had saved England with his indomitable courage and inspiring rhetoric; but I thought his 'iron curtain' Fulton speech had achieved nothing but an intensification of the cold war.

The conversation turned to my film *Limelight*. Eventually he said: 'I sent you a letter two years ago complimenting you on your film. Did you get it?'

'Oh yes,' I said enthusiastically.

'Then why didn't you answer it?'

'I didn't think it called for an answer,' I said apologetically.

But he was not to be cozened. 'Hmmm,' he said disgruntledly, 'I thought it was some form of rebuke.'

'Oh no, of course not,' I answered.

'However,' he added, by way of dismissing me, 'I always enjoy your pictures.'

I was charmed with the great man's modesty in remembering that unanswered letter of two years ago. But I have never seen eye to eye with his politics. 'I am not here to preside over the dissolution of the British Empire,' said Churchill. This may be rhetoric, but it is a fatuous statement in the face of modern facts.

This dissolution is not the result of politics, revolutionary armies, Communist propaganda, rabble-rousing or soap boxing. It is the soap wrappings that are the conspirators: those international advertisers – radio, television and motion pictures – the automobile and tractor, the innovation in science, the acceleration of speed and communication. These are the revolutionaries that are responsible for the dissolution of empires.

*

Soon after returning to Switzerland, I received a letter from Nehru enclosing a note of introduction from Lady Mountbatten. She was sure Nehru and I had a great deal in common with each other. He was passing Corsier and perhaps we could meet. As he was holding his annual meeting of ambassadors in Lucerne, he wrote that he would be delighted if I could come and spend the night there; the following day he would drop me off at the Manoir de Ban. So I went to Lucerne.

I was surprised to find a small man like myself. His daughter, Mrs Gandhi, was also present – a charming quiet lady. Nehru impressed me as a man of moods, austere and sensitive, with an exceedingly alert and appraising mind. He was diffident at first, until we left Lucerne together and drove to the Manoir de Ban where I had invited him for lunch, his daughter trailing in another car as she was going on to Geneva. On the way we had an interesting talk. He spoke highly of Lord Mountbatten who, as Viceroy of India, had done an excellent job in terminating England's interests there.

I asked him in which ideological direction India was going. He said: 'In whatever direction, it is for the betterment of the Indian people,' and added that they had already inaugurated a five-year plan. He talked brilliantly throughout the journey, while his chauffeur must have been going at seventy miles an hour or more, speeding along precipitous, narrow roads, and coming suddenly upon sharp turns. Nehru was engrossed in explaining India's politics, but I must confess I missed half of what he was saying, so occupied was I with back-seat driving. As the brakes screeched and threw us forward, Nehru continued unperturbed. Thank heavens there was a respite when eventually the car stopped for a moment at a cross-roads, where his daughter was to leave us. It was then that he became a loving and solicitous father, embracing his daughter as he said to her tenderly: 'Take care of yourself' – words which would have been more appropriate coming from the daughter to the father.

*

During the Korean crisis, when the world held its breath over that extremely dangerous brink, the Chinese Embassy telephoned to ask if I would allow *City Lights* to be shown in Geneva before Chou En-lai, who was the pivotal centre around which the decision of peace or war was to be decided.

The following day the Prime Minister invited us to have dinner with him in Geneva. Before we left for Geneva the Prime Minister's secretary telephoned to say that His Excellency might be detained, as important business had suddenly arisen at the conference (an understatement), and that we were not to wait for him; he would join us later.

When we arrived, to our surprise Chou En-lai was waiting on the steps of his residence to greet us. Like the rest of the world I was anxious to know what had happened at the conference, so I asked him. He tapped me confidentially on the shoulder. 'It has all been amicably settled,' he said, 'five minutes ago.'

I had heard many interesting stories about how the Communists had been driven far into the interior of China in the thirties, and how, under the leadership of Mao Tse-tung, a scattered few became reorganized and began marching back to Peking, gathering military impetus as they went. That march back won them the support of six hundred million Chinese people.

Chou En-lai that night told us a touching story of Mao Tse-tung's triumphant entry into Peking. There were a million Chinese present to welcome him. A large platform, fifteen feet high, had been built at the end of the vast square, and as he mounted the steps from the back the top of his head appeared and a roar of welcome surged up from a million throats, increasing and increasing as the lone figure came fully into view.

And when Mao Tse-tung, the conqueror of China, saw that vast multitude, he stood for a moment, then suddenly covered his face with both hands and wept.

Chou En-lai had shared with him the hardships and heartbreaks of that famous march across China, yet as I looked at his vigorous, handsome face I was astonished to see how calm and youthful he looked.

I told him that the last time I had been in Shanghai was in 1936.

'Oh yes,' he said, thoughtfully, 'that was before we were on the march.'

'Well, you haven't far to go now,' I said jokingly.

At dinner we drank Chinese champagne (not bad), and like the Russians made many toasts. I toasted the future of China and said that although I was not a Communist I wholeheartedly joined in their hope and desire for a better life for the Chinese people, and for all people.

\*

In Vevey we have new friends, among them Mr Emile Rossier and Mr Michel Rossier and their families, all of them lovers of music. Through Emile I met Clara Haskil, the concert pianist. She lived in Vevey and whenever in town Clara and both the Rossier families would come to dinner, and afterwards Clara would play for us. Although past sixty, she was at the apogee of her career, having her greatest triumphs both in Europe and America. But in 1960 she slipped off the step of a train in Belgium and was taken to hospital where she died.

Often I play her records, the last she made before her death. Before I started the task of rewriting this manuscript for the sixth time, I put on Beethoven's Piano Concerto No. 3 with Clara at the piano and Markevitch conducting – which to me is as near an approximation of truth as any great work of art could be and which has been a source of encouragement for me to finish this book.

If we were not so preoccupied with our family, we could have quite a social life in Switzerland, for we live relatively near the Queen of Spain and the Count and the Countess Chevreau d'Antraigues, who have been most cordial to us, and there are a number of film stars and writers who live near. We often see

George and Benita Sanders and Noël Coward is also a neighbour. In the spring many of our American and English friends visit us. Truman Capote, who occasionally works in Switzerland, often drops by. During the Easter holidays, we take the children to the south of Ireland. This is something that the whole family looks forward to every year.

In summer we dine on the terrace in shorts and stay out till ten watching the twilight. Often on the spur of the moment we decide to go to London and Paris, sometimes to Venice or Rome – all within easy reach of a couple of hours.

In Paris we are often entertained by Paul-Louis Weiller, our very dear friend, who in August invites the whole family for one month to La Reine Jeanne, his beautiful estate on the Mediterranean, where the children get all the swimming and water-skiing they want.

Friends have asked me if I miss the United States – New York? In candour I do not. America has changed, so has New York. The gigantic scale of industrial institutions, of Press, television and commercial advertising has completely divorced me from the American way of life. I want the other side of the coin, a simpler personal sense of living – not the ostentatious avenues and towering buildings which are an ever-reminder of big business and its ponderous achievements.

It was more than a year before I could liquidate all my interests in the United States. They wanted to tax my European earnings on *Limelight* up to 1955, claiming that I was still an American resident in spite of having barred me from that country since 1952. I had no legal address since, as my American lawyer said, I would have little chance of getting back into the country to defend the case.

Having dissolved all my American companies and divested myself of every American interest, I was in a position to tell them to go sit on a tack. But not wishing to be under an obligation to another nation's protection, I settled for an amount considerably less than their claim and considerably more than I should have paid.

Cutting my last ties from the United States was sad. When Helen, our maid at the Beverly Hills house, heard that we were not returning, she wrote the following letter:

473

**Dear Mr and Mrs Chaplin,**

I have written you so many letters, but never mailed them. It seems just everything has gone wrong since you left – I myself have never suffered so much grief over anyone else except my own family. But everything is so unnecessary and unneeded and unjust and I just can't get over it. And then we received the sad news that we feared might come – to pack most everything – it just isn't possible – it just can't be – the things we packed have nearly been washed away with tears and I still have a headache from grief – I don't know how you folks stand it. *Please*, PLEASE, Mrs C, *don't let* Mr C sell the house if you can help it. Every room still bears its own personality even though there are mostly the rugs and draperies there – I am so positive minded about this house I would never let anyone else have it. If I only had the money myself, but that's silly and out of reason for me too. Cut off all the excess that's possible if you wish. But *please*, PLEASE keep the house. I know I should not say this but I can't help it – and I shall never give up the idea but that some day you will all return. Mrs C, enough of that for now – I have three letters to send you but I must get some larger envelopes. Give my regards to everyone, and excuse my pencil as even my pen has gone wrong.

Sincerely, Helen.

We also received a letter from Henry, our butler, who wrote as follows:

**Dear Mr and Mrs Chaplin,**

I have not written you for a long time as I have an awful time to express myself correctly with my Swiss—English. I had one happy story a few weeks ago, as I had a chance to see the picture *Limelight*. It was a private showing. Miss Runser invited me. There were about twenty people present. Mr and Mrs Sydney Chaplin, Miss Runser and Rolly were the only ones I knew. I took my seat way in the rear, to be alone with my thoughts. It was well worth it. I probably laughed the loudest but also had the most tears in my eyes. The best picture I've ever seen. It has never been shown in L.A. There are several records played over the radio, music from *Limelight*. Beautiful music. They electrify me when I hear them. Mr C the composer is never mentioned. I am happy to hear the children like Switzerland. Of course, for grown up people it takes more time to get used to any foreign country. I do say Switzerland is one of the better ones. The best schools on the globe. Also the oldest republic on the globe, since 1191. First of August is the 4th of July there. Independence Day. Not a holiday, but you will see the fires on all mountain tops. As a whole, one of the few conservative and prosperous countries. I left there in 1918 for South America. Have been back twice since. I also served two terms in the Swiss Army. Born in St Gallen, eastern part of Switzerland. I have one younger brother in Berne and one in St. Gallen.

The very best wishes to all of you.

Respectfully yours, Henry.

All those who worked for me in California were still on salary, but I could not afford to continue paying them now that I was domiciled in Switzerland. So I arranged for their severance pay, giving them each a bonus, which total amounted to eighty thousand dollars. Edna Purviance, besides receiving her bonus, remained in my employment up to the day she died.

During the casting of *Monsieur Verdoux*, I had thought of Edna for the important part of Madame Grosnay. I had not seen her for twenty years, for she never came to the studio because her weekly cheque was mailed to her by the office. She confessed afterwards that when she received a call from the studio she was more shocked than thrilled.

When Edna arrived, Rolly, the cameraman, came into my dressing-room. He, too, had not seen her in twenty years. 'She's here,' he said, his eyes glistening. 'Of course, she's not the same – but she looks great!' He told me that she was waiting on the lawn, outside her dressing-room.

I wanted no emotional reunion scene, so I assumed a matter-of-fact manner as if it had been only a few weeks since I last saw her. 'Well! Well! We've eventually got round to you,' I said cheerily.

In the sunlight I noticed that her lip trembled as she smiled, then I plunged into the reason why I had called her, and told her enthusiastically about the film. 'It sounds wonderful,' she said – Edna was always an enthusiast.

She read for the part and was not bad; but all the while her presence affected me with a depressing nostalgia, for she was associated with my early successes – those days when everything was the future!

Edna threw herself into the role, but it was fruitless – the part required European sophistication, which Edna never had – and after working with her three or four days I was forced to admit that she was unsuitable. Edna herself was more relieved than

475

disappointed. I did not see or hear from her again until she wrote to me in Switzerland to acknowledge her severance pay:

Dear Charlie,

For the first time I am able to write my thanks for your friendship down the years, and for all you have done for me. In early life we do not seem to have so many troubles and I know you have had your share. I trust your cup of happiness is full with a charming wife and family. . . .

[Here she described her illness and the terrific expense of doctors and nurses, but she finished as she always did with a joke:]

Just a story I heard. A chap was sealed in a rocket ship and shot upwards to see how high he could go – was told to keep track of the altitude. So he kept counting 25,000 – 30,000 – 100,000 – 500,000 . . . When he got this far he said 'Jesus Christ!' to himself, and a very silent soft voice answered back: 'Yessss –?'

Please, please, Charlie, let me hear something from you in the near future. And please come back, you belong here.

Sincerely your truest and best admirer,

Love, Edna.

Through all the years I had never written a letter to Edna; I always communicated with her through the studio. Her last letter was an acknowledgement of the news that she was still on the payroll:

November 13th, 1956.

Dear Charlie,

Here I am again with a heart full of thanks, and back in hospital (Cedars of Lebanon), taking cobalt X-ray treatment on my neck. There cannot be a hell hereafter! It all comes while one can wriggle even a little finger. However, it is the best known treatment for what ails me. Hope to be going home at the end of the week, then can be an outside patient (how wonderful!). Am thankful my innards are O.K., this is purely and simply local, so they say – all of which reminds me of the fellow standing on the corner of Seventh and Broadway tearing up little bits of paper, throwing them to the four winds. A cop comes along and asks him, what was the big idea. He answers: 'Just keeping elephants away.' The cop says: 'There aren't any elephants in this district.' The fellow answers: 'Well, it works, doesn't it?' This is my silly for the day, so forgive me.

Hope you and the family are well and enjoying everything you have worked for.

Love always, Edna.

476

Shortly after I received this letter she died. And so the world grows young. And youth takes over. And we who have lived a little longer become a little more estranged as we journey on our way.

So now I shall end this Odyssey of mine. I realize that time and circumstances have favoured me. I have been cosseted in the world's affections, loved and hated. Yes, the world has given me its best and little of its worst. Whatever were my ill vicissitudes, I believe that fortune and ill-fortune drift upon one haphazardly as clouds. Knowing this, I am never too shocked at the bad things that happen and am agreeably surprised at the good. I have no design for living, no philosophy – whether sage or fool, we must all struggle with life. I vacillate with inconsistencies; at times small things will annoy me and catastrophes will leave me indifferent.

Nevertheless, my life is more thrilling today than it ever was. I am in good health and still creative and have plans to produce more pictures – perhaps not with myself, but to write and direct them for members of my family – some of whom have quite an aptitude for the theatre. I am still very ambitious; I could never retire. There are many things I want to do; besides having a few unfinished cinema scripts, I should like to write a play and an opera – if time will allow.

Schopenhauer said happiness is a negative state – but I disagree. For the last twenty years I have known what happiness means. I have the good fortune to be married to a wonderful wife. I wish I could write more about this, but it involves love, and perfect love is the most beautiful of all frustrations because it is more than one can express. As I live with Oona, the depth and beauty of her character are a continual revelation to me. Even as she walks ahead of me along the narrow sidewalks of Vevey with simple dignity, her neat little figure straight, her dark hair smoothed back showing a few silver threads, a sudden wave of love and admiration comes over me for all that she is – and a lump comes into my throat.

With such happiness, I sometimes sit out on our terrace at sunset and look over a vast green lawn to the lake in the distance, and beyond the lake to the reassuring mountains, and in this mood think of nothing but enjoy their magnificent serenity.

# CHARLES CHAPLIN

## THE KEYSTONE FILMS

1914   Making a Living (1 reel)
Kid Auto Races at Venice (split reel)
Mabel's Strange Predicament (1 reel)
Between Showers (1 reel)
A Film Johnnie (1 reel)
Tango Tangles (1 reel)
His Favourite Pastime (1 reel)
Cruel, Cruel Love (1 reel)
The Star Boarder (1 reel)
Mabel at the Wheel (2 reels)
Twenty Minutes of Love (1 reel)
Caught in a Cabaret (2 reels)
Caught in the Rain (1 reel)
A Busy Day (split reel)
The Fatal Mallet (1 reel)
Her Friend the Bandit (1 reel)
The Knockout (2 reels)
Mabel's Busy Day (1 reel)
Mabel's Married Life (1 reel)
Laughing Gas (1 reel)
The Property Man (2 reels)
The Face on the Bar-room Floor (1 reel)
Recreation (split reel)
The Masquerader (1 reel)
His New Profession (1 reel)
The Rounders (1 reel)
The New Janitor (1 reel)
Those Love Pangs (1 reel)
Dough and Dynamite (2 reels)
Gentlemen of Nerve (1 reel)
His Musical Career (1 reel)
His Trysting Place (2 reels)
Tillie's Punctured Romance (6 reels)
Getting Acquainted (1 reel)
His Prehistoric Past (2 reels)

## THE ESSANAY FILMS

1915 His New Job (2 reels)
A Night Out (2 reels)
The Champion (2 reels)
In the Park (1 reel)
The Jitney Elopement (2 reels)
The Tramp (2 reels)
By the Sea (1 reel)
Work (2 reels)
A Woman (2 reels)
The Bank (2 reels)
Shanghaied (2 reels)
A Night in the Show (2 reels)
1916 Carmen (4 reels)
Police (2 reels)
1918 Triple Trouble (2 reels)

## THE MUTUAL FILMS

1916 The Floorwalker (2 reels)
The Fireman (2 reels)
The Vagabond (2 reels)
One a.m. (2 reels)
The Count (2 reels)
The Pawnshop (2 reels)
Behind the Screen (2 reels)
The Rink (2 reels)
1917 Easy Street (2 reels)
The Cure (2 reels)
The Immigrant (2 reels)
The Advenurer (2 reels)

## THE FIRST NATIONAL FILMS

1918 A Dog's Life (3 reels)
The Bond (split reel)
Shoulder Arms (3 reels)
1919 Sunnyside (3 reels)
A Day's Pleasure (2 reels)
1920 The Kid (6 reels)
The Idle Class (2 reels)
1922 Pay Day (2 reels)
1923 The Pilgrim (4 reels)

## UNITED ARTISTS FILMS
### (all full-length)

1923   A Woman of Paris
1925   The Gold Rush
1928   The Circus
1931   City Lights
1936   Modern Times
1940   The Great Dictator
1947   Monsieur Verdoux
1953   Limelight
1957   The King in New York

# Index

intellect and emotion in the theatre, C. on, 250 ff.

Irving, Sir Henry,
C. at funeral of, 91; and Nat Goodwin, 174; 'noble, sensitive', 258

Irving, Washington, C. and works of, 135

*Ivan the Terrible*: 'the acme of all historical pictures', 320

*Jack Jones* (music-hall song), C. and, 18

Jackson family (of the Eight Lancashire Lads), 43 ff., 349

*Jail Birds* (Karno sketch), 92

Japan, C. in, 362–71, 380

Jeffers, Robinson, 384

*Jim, the Romance of a Cockney* H. A. Saintsbury's melodrama), C.'s part in, 77–81

jobs, C.'s earliest, 60–64, 71–3

Johnson, Dr Hewlett, C.'s view of, 339

joke-book, C. uses a, 95

Jolson, Al, C. on 256

Joyce, Peggy Hopkins, 293–4

Karno, Fred, 73, 92, 116; as a comedian, 98; engages C. for Harry Weldon sketch, 98–101, 114; and *Mumming Birds*, 103, 114, 116; popularity of his shows in America, 121; C. on his houseboat, 133

Karno, Fred, Junr, 140

Kay Kay (C.'s children's nurse), 466

Kelly, Arthur (Hetty's brother), 137, 263

Kelly, Hetty, C. and, 103–7, 115–16, 259, 263

Kendal, Mr and Mrs, C. turns down a part with, 91

Kessel, Charles, 138–9

Kessel and Bauman (Amer. film producers), 138, 159

Keynes, John Maynard, 331

Keystone Film Company,
C. joins, 138 ff.; 'a wrench leaving', 161; *see also* Sennett, Mack. For list of films *see* p. 478

Khrushchev, Nikita, C.'s meeting with, 467–9

*Kid, The*, 230–35; C.'s disagreement with First National over, 237; trial showings of, 238, 242–3; 'proclaimed a classic', 249–50

Kinsey-Taylor, Dr, C. as pageboy to, 61

Kitchen, Fred (comedian), 92

Kitchener, Field Marshal Lord, C. and, 91

Klieg lights, 157

Knoblock, Edward, 260, 261, 268, 269, 272

knowledge, C.'s motives for 'passionately wanting', 134

Kono (C.'s Japanese secretary), 366 ff. *passim*

Korda, Sir Alexander, 386

Leemmle, Carl, 160, 316

Lambeth Workhouse, 25–7

Larkin, Jim, 280–81

Laski, Harold, 341

*Laughing Gas*, C. directs for Keystone, 157

Lawson, John, 429

Legion of Decency, and *Monsieur Verdoux*, 429, 438; *see also* Breen office.

Legion of Honour, C. as member of, 275, 353

Lehrman, Henry (Keystone film director), 144; 'thought I knew too much', 145; 'mutilated my funny business', 145, 148

Leno, Dan, 47, 132

'Lestock, the Dashing Eva', 56–7

Lewis, Sinclair, 408

Liberty Bond Drives (U.S.A.), C. and the, 213–17

life, C.'s views on, 199–200, 206, 210, 287, 290

Lillie, Beatrice, 303

*Limelight*, 257, 447, 449, 452–3, 458–9, 463

Lipton, Sir Thomas, 310–11

literature, C.'s interest in, 48, 244; *see also* entries for individual authors

Lloyd, Harold, 171

Lloyd, Marie, 47

Locke, William J., 200

Lockhart's tea rooms (London), C.'s memories of, 62

London, C.'s early life in, 13 ff.; revisits the old homes in, 259 ff.

*London Topical Times*, C.'s good notice in, 81

loneliness, C. and, 82, 137, 177, 287, 372, 375, 426; 'it is repellent', 180; 'much has been written about my loneliness', 266

Louis Ferdinand, grandson of the Kaiser, 373

Louise (C.'s father's mistress), 33–40, 87

love affairs, C.'s, 41, 103 ff., 134, 156, 352, 354–6, 361

Lucas, E. V., 268

Luce, Clare Boothe, 448–9

Ludwig, Emil, 351

*Lusitania*, s.s., sinking of the, 212

Lutyens, Sir Edwin, 268, 271–2

*Mabel's Strange Predicament* (C.'s early Keystone film), 148–9

McCarthy family (Kennington neighbours), 11, 66–8

McCormick, Anne O'Hare, 396

MacDonald, Malcolm, 337

MacDonald, Ramsay, 332, 338

Mack, Charlie, 198

McKay, Claude (Jamaican poet), 280

*Madison's Budget* (Amer. joke-book), 95

Maeterlinck, Madame, 260

*Male and Female* (De Mille film), 173

Malone, Dudley Field, 244, 246, 403

Manchester: 'cataleptic' on Sunday, 358–9

Mann, Thomas, 316, 384, 428, 440

Manoir de Ban (C.'s home in Switzerland), 465

Manon, Charlie, C.'s brother joins troupe, 92

Mao Tse-tung, 472

Marceline (French clown), 45–6; suicide, 46

*Marriage Circle, The* (Lubitsch film), 295

marriages, C.'s, 228, 300, 380

Mary, Queen, inspiration for her doll's house, 272

Masefield, John, 303

Maugham, W. Somerset, 200; C. on *Rain*, 127, 200; C. corrects his quotation of C.'s comments, 266–7; his output, 384

Maxwell, Elsa, 276

Mayer, Louis B., and Mildred Harris's contract, 229

Mead, Senator James M., 405

Meighan, Thomas, 202; and Edna Purviance, 204–5

Melba, Dame Nellie, 191

Menjou, Adolphe, 295

mergers of film-producing companies, 220–21

*Merry Major, The* (sketch), C. plays juvenile lead in, 97

'Method' school of acting, C. on the, 254–5

Metro-Goldwyn-Mayer Co., 229; and Hearst Productions, 314

Meyer, Walter (Einstein's assistant), 316

'million-dollar carpet', the (Alexandria Hotel, Los Angeles), 183–4

millionaires, C. on, 306

*Miracle, The* (Reinhardt's spectacle), 180

*Miss Priscilla's Cat* (C.'s comedy recitation, as a boy), 41

*Mr Perkins, M.P.* (Karno sketch), 122

Mizner, Wilson, 217

*Modern Times*, 209; original idea for, 377–8; 'a great success', 382

Molnár, Erik, and emotion in the theatre, 252

money, C. and,
'like an avalanche ... frightening', 174; 'it all seemed slightly mad', 188; 'it was legendary', 189; 'the delights of', 261

*Monsieur Verdoux*, 412–13, 426; censorship and, 429 ff.; sequences from script of, 430–36; opening of, 443–4

Montagu, Ivor, 319, 467

Monterey, Carlotta, 155

Moore, Alexander, 311

Moore, George, 448–9

Morgan, Anne (daughter of J. P. Morgan), 272–3, 275–6

Morris, Gouverneur, 200; on *The Kid*, 233–4

Mirros, William (Amer. theatre-owner), 121; C. at his 42nd Street theatre, 129

Morrison, Herbert, 459

Mosley, Sir Oswald, 350–51

Mountbatten, Lord, 470

*Mumming Birds* (Karno sketch), 92; C. in, 103, 116

Munnings, Sir Alfred, 331–2

Murray, Philip, 404

music,
'I had great ambitions', 125; as creator of C.'s moods and themes, 209; C. composes for his films, 325

musicians, C. on, 389–90

Mutual Film Corporation, C. joins, 177–9; his films for, 187, 479

Nast, Condé, 243

National Society for the Prevention of Cruelty to Children, C.'s plight reported to, 39

Nazism, C.'s hatred for, 398–9, 406–7, 411

Negri, Pola, C. and 274, 295–8

Nehru, Pandit Jawaharlal, 470–71

*New Janitor, The* (C.'s Keystone film), 154

New York, C. in, 119–24; 'this is where I belong!' 121; 177, 178, 191, 306, 327; 'stepping on air in', 243

Nichols, 'Pop' (Keystone film director): 'had but one gag', 149

*Night at the Club, A* (Karno sketch), C. plays the 'drunk' in, 139; Ellsworth says 'very funny', 147

*Night in an English Music Hall, A* (Karno sketch): 'tremendous success' in U.S.A., 129

Nijinsky, Vaslav, 191–3

Niles (California), C. at Essanay studios at, 161, 167–70

Noailles, Countess, 352

Normand, Mabel, 138, 141, 143, 145, 146; C. rebels against direction by, 149–51; 'we remained only good friends', 155

Norris. Kathleen, 200


Odets, Clifford, 428

Old Testament, C. on 'horrific cruelty' of the, 134

Olivier, Laurence, Shakespeare in 'white tie and tails', 254

*Olympic*, s.s., C.'s voyages in, 134, 260–61, 329

O'Neill, Eugene, 245

O'Neill, Oona ('a luminous beauty'), 413–14; C.'s marriage to, 415–16, 425–6, 452; gives up American citizenship, 466

opera's emotional effect on C., 136–7

Oppenheimer, Dr Robert, 460

orientation, importance of, in acting technique, 256

Orpen, Sir William, 277

*Our America* (Waldo Frank), 245

outside location: 'I loathe working on', 219

Oxford Music Hall (London), C. plays at the, 114–15

Reynolds, Dr Cecil, 247–9, 297–8
*Rhetoric* (Kellogg), C. and, 123
Ringling Brothers' Circus, 46
Ritz Hotel (London), 264; treacle pudding at the, 268
Roach, Hal, 171
Robbins, Jess (of Essanay Co.), 160
*Robin Hood* (Fairbanks' film), 198
Robinson, Carlisle ('Carl'), 231, 259
Rock, Charles (Eng. actor), 81
Rockefeller, John D., 306
Rocksavage, Lady, 273, 276
Rocksavage, Lord, 276
Roget's *Thesaurus*, Negro truck-driver introduces C. to, 244
'Roman Senator', the: *see* Elliott, Maxine
romance and adventure, C.'s longing for, 93, 102
Roosevelt, Franklin D., 214, 373, 399
Rossier, Emile, 472
Rossier, Michel, 472
Royal Aquarium (London), 14
Royal Command Performance, C. declines request to appear at, 349
Russell, Jimmy, 279
Russia, C. and, 271, 314, speeches in support of 'second front', 401 ff.


Sage, Russell, 304
Saintsbury, H. A.
    C.'s stage engagement with, 77–9; 'the best Sherlock Holmes', 81–2
Salt Lake City, C. in, 130, 237
San Francisco, C. in, 128–9, 161, 169
San Simeon, W. R. Hearst's ranch at, 307–9
Sanders, George and Benita, 473
Santa Barbara, C. and Oona at, 416
Santa Monica, 156; C.'s house at, 174; Marion Davies' beach-house at, 306, 311
Sartre, Jean-Paul, 464

Sassoon, Sir Philip, 268, 273–4, 315, 330, 346–7; his hospitality 'something out of the *Arabian Nights*', 276–7
Schenck, Joe, 291–2, 322–3, 326, 350, 375
Schoenberg, Arnold, 391–2, 428
schools and schooldays, 27–33, 40–42
Schopenhauer, Arthur, C. and writings of, 134–5
Schwartz, Charles, C.'s lawyer, 452
scientists, C. on 389
Scottie, Death Valley, 185–6
'scratch crowd' (vaudeville term), 116
sea, C.'s first sight of the, 24
sea-voyages, C.'s views on, 379
Second World War, C. and the, 386 ff.
Seers, Grad, 445
self-analysis, C.'s, 267
Sennett, Mack, 129, 138; engages C. for Keystone Co., 139, 141–5; 'enthusiasm his secret of success', 146; working with C., 147, 148–53, 154, 155, 157–9
sex,
    'I do not believe it is the most important element', 206; C.'s sex-life, 206–8; 'I can add nothing new', 354; H. G. Wells on, 354; *see also* love affairs
*Shadow and Substance*,
    C. considers as film project, 408–9; abandoned, 426
Shakespeare, William, 253; 'I hardly think' he wrote the works, 358–9
*Shamus O'Brien* (Irish melodrama), C.'s parents in, 17
Shaw, George Bernard, 93, 269, 331–2, 337
    Shaw, Mrs G. B., 332
    Sheridan, Clare, 285–₵
    Sheridan, Mark, (comedian), 46

Tate's Café (San Francisco), 169
Taylor, Frank, and Dylan Thomas 428
'tears as well as laughter' (in C.'s films), 155
Teddy boys, C.'s defence of, 93
Tellegen, Lou, 155
Terry, Dame Ellen, 257
Thalberg, Irving, 294
theatre, the,
  C.'s early interest in, 21, 41, 48, 93; his views on, 250 ff.
theatricialism, C. on, 252
thinking, C. on, 247
Thomas, Dylan, C. and 428–9
Thomas, Olive, 226, 243
Thorndike, Dame Sybil, 257
Three Stags, the (public house, Kennington Road), 58
time-saving: 'the basic virtue' in film making, 250
Tinney, Frank, 257
Tivoli Music Hall (London), C. appears at, 103
touring companies, C.'s loneliness in, 83–4
toy-making, C.'s job in, 65
tragedy and comedy, combination of, 40
'tramp character', the, 44, 145; origin of the costume, 145; 'growing more complex', 208; dilemma of talking films and, 360, 382
Tree, Sir Herbert Beerbohm, 194–7, 258
Tree, Iris, 196–7
tricky effects: 'I loathe them', 250
truth, C. on, 255, 286
Turpin, Ben, 165, 169
Twain, Mark, C. and works of, 142
Twelve Just Men (C. writes sketch), 97
Twenty Minutes of Love
  'I made it in an afternoon', 157; music sets mood for, 209

Un-American Activities, Committee on, 439, 458

United Artists,
  formation of, 221; and mergers, 292; alarm over The Great Dictator, 387; sale of, 446; list of C.'s films for, 480
Universal Company, 160

Valentino, Rudolph, 186–7, 312
Vanbrugh, Dame Irene, 89, 257
Vanderbilt, Cornelius, and German concentration camps, 316
Variety (Amer. stage periodical), 124, 304
vaudeville, English and American compared, 135
Venice, C. on, 352
Vienna, romance in, 352
Viertel, Salka, 428
violence in the theatre, C. on, 429

Wagner, Rob, 214–16 passim
Wainewright, J. G., 254
Wallace, Mina, 413–14
Waller, Lewis, 91
war-wounded, C. and the, 277, 386
Ward, Fanny, 204
Warfield, David, 256
Warner Brothers,
  and Hearst Productions, 314; first talking picture, 321
Watson's Beef Trust (Amer. burlesque show), 126
Weber, Lois, 226
Weiller, Commandant Paul-Louis, 276, 473
Weldon, Harry, 92; and C., in The Football Match, 98–101, 114
Welles, Orson, 410; and idea for Monsieur Verdoux, 412–13
Wells, H. G., 259, 268; C. and, 270–71, 277–8, 341–4 passim; on sex, 354; work output, 384
West, Rebecca, 271
Wharton, Edith, 200
Whimsical Walker, 121
Whispering Chorus, The (De Mille film), 173